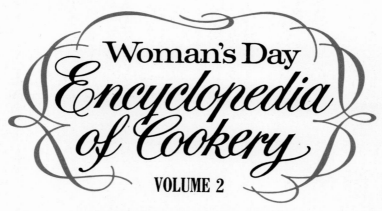

Woman's Day
Encyclopedia of Cookery
VOLUME 2

*in 12 volumes—over 2,000 pages—
with more than 1,500 illustrations in color,
1,000 entries and 8,500 recipes
1,200 menus, 50 specialty cook books
and a host of delightful features by distinguished food writers.*

Prepared and edited by the Editors of Woman's Day
Editor: EILEEN TIGHE
Managing Editor: EVELYN GRANT   *Food Editor:* GLENNA MCGINNIS
Art Consultant: HAROLD SITTERLE   *Photographic Editor:* BEN CALVO
Associates: OLIVIA RISBERG, CHARLOTTE SCRIPTURE,
CAROLYN STORM, JOHANNA BAFARO

SPECIAL PROJECT STAFF
Editor: NIKA STANDEN HAZELTON   *Art Director:* LEONARD A. ROMAGNA
Associates: L. GERALDINE MARSTELLER, HELEN FEINGOLD,
SUSAN J. KNOX, INEZ M. KRECH

FAWCETT PUBLICATIONS, INC.   NEW YORK

PRINTED AND BOUND BY
FAWCETT-HAYNES PRINTING CORPORATION
ROCKVILLE, MARYLAND

Table of Contents

VOLUME 2

BÉARNAISE TO CASSOULET

Definitions and 658 Recipes
How to buy, store, prepare, cook, and serve •
Nutritive Food Values • Caloric Values

To help you plan more varied meals
with the recipes in this volume

Foreword

To the best of our knowledge, no work of this magnitude ever has been undertaken by any author, editor, or publisher in America. The editors of Woman's Day, with a special staff of experts, present to you this Encyclopedia of Cookery, a comprehensive and colorful library on all culinary matters. The twelve-volume encyclopedia contains in its 2,000 pages over 8,500 recipes from all over the world, 1,500 food illustrations in color, 1,200 menus, 50 special cook books and over 1,000 food definitions. In addition, there are full details about all foods, their nutritive and caloric values, how to buy, serve, prepare, and cook them. There is a history of food and cooking, articles on nutrition, diet, entertaining, menu planning, herbs and spices. Every topic of culinary interest is covered. Five years of intensive work have gone into its preparation, backed by twenty-five years of food and cookery experience in the publication of Woman's Day.

We think you will find this Encyclopedia of Cookery the most complete and authoritative work ever published on the subject. It is a library for everyone who cares about good food and the fine art of preparing it.

The Editors

BÉARNAISE

BÉARNAISE—A classic French sauce, made with eggs, butter, wine, vinegar, shallots, pepper, and tarragon. It resembles hollandaise sauce in consistency. *Béarnaise* is used for steaks, boiled or fried fish, broiled chicken, egg dishes, and croquettes. Though it takes its name from the Béarn, a French province in the Pyrenees, some authorities say that the sauce did not originate in this region where oil, not butter, cookery is customary but was created near Paris, in a restaurant called Pavillion Henry IV. Henry IV was the French king once called *le grand Béarnais.* It was he who hoped that during his reign every Frenchman would have a chicken in the pot every Sunday.

TRUE BÉARNAISE SAUCE
1 teaspoon minced shallot or onion
1 small tarragon sprig, chopped
1 small chervil sprig, chopped
2 peppercorns
⅛ teaspoon salt
¼ cup tarragon vinegar
5 egg yolks
¾ cup butter, melted
    Dash of cayenne

Combine minced shallot, tarragon, chervil, peppercorns, salt, and vinegar. Cook over low heat until the vinegar has been reduced by two thirds. Cool to lukewarm. Remove peppercorns. Add egg yolks and stir briskly, preferably with a wire whisk. Place over very low heat and gradually add melted butter. Stir until sauce thickens. Season with cayenne. Makes about 1½ cups sauce.

BEAT—In cookery this term means to stir vigorously, using a spoon, a hand rotary egg beater, or an electric mixer at medium to fast speed. Beating not only mixes ingredients and makes them smooth but also, especially in the case of eggs, for example, makes them fluffy by incorporating air. In some baking, this air acts as a natural leavening.

BEATEN BISCUIT—This crackerlike Southern bread harks back to pre-Civil war plantation days when kitchen help was assured, for labor, not a leavener, softens the gluten of the flour in these biscuits. They are baked slowly, are of a pale gold color, and have a characteristically dry brittle texture.

It is reported that one Mississippi cook allowed 100 strokes to beat everyday biscuits, and from 150 to 200 when guests were expected. There were beaten-biscuit machines, consisting of a marble slab or a wooden box with a double roller and a handle to turn. The dough was put through the rollers many times, or until it blistered and became smooth. Beaten biscuits are part of America's food folklore.

BEATEN BISCUITS
3 cups sifted all-purpose flour
¾ teaspoon sugar
½ teaspoon salt
⅓ cup soft butter or other shortening
⅔ to ¾ cup milk

Sift flour, sugar, and salt. Cut in butter. Add just enough milk to make a stiff dough. Knead on floured board until dough becomes soft and pliable. Force dough through a food chopper several times, using coarse blade. Or beat steadily with a wooden mallet or potato masher for 30 minutes, or until dough blisters, keeping edges turned in. Roll to ½-inch thickness and cut with ½-inch biscuit cutter. Prick with fork. Bake in preheated moderate oven (350°F.) for about 30 minutes. Biscuits should be a delicate ivory color. Makes about 1½ dozen.

BÉCHAMEL—A creamy French white sauce, and so basic to French cooking that it is called a *sauce mère,* or mother sauce. Its American equivalent is white sauce. Béchamel is the basis for other sauces, and for innumerable dishes.

Béchamel used to be a more complicated sauce than it is today. In the days of King Louis XIV of France it was made of milk, veal, seasonings, and cream. In modern French cooking, Béchamel is made with milk, butter, and flour, in various degrees of thickness, like a white sauce. Later, it may be enriched with butter, cream, cheese, herbs, or other flavorings. Depending on these, it changes its name. For instance, a Béchamel with cream is a sauce *suprême,* one with cheese a sauce *Mornay.*

First cousin to Béchamel is *Velouté* sauce, which is made with chicken, veal, or fish broth, and to which wine, milk, or cream is sometimes added. *Velouté* can also be enriched at will.

Béchamel and sauces based on Béchamel are used with eggs, fish, chicken, veal, and vegetables, and as a base for cream soups, soufflés, croquettes, etc. Béchamel should always be made in a heavy-bottomed saucepan to prevent scorching and discoloring of the *roux,* the butter and flour cooked together in the first step of making the sauce.

BÉCHAMEL
2 tablespoons butter
2 tablespoons all-purpose flour
1 cup hot milk
    Salt
    White pepper
    Ground nutmeg (optional)

Melt butter in a saucepan over moderate heat. Do not let it brown. Add flour and stir until mixture is well blended. Gradually stir in hot milk. Cook over medium heat, stirring constantly, until mixture comes to a boil and thickens. Simmer, stirring frequently, over very low heat for 5 minutes. Season with salt and pepper to taste and with a pinch of nutmeg, if desired. Makes about 1 cup sauce.
Note: This recipe makes a medium thick sauce.

VARIATIONS OF BÉCHAMEL SAUCE
For that definite French touch, enrich Béchamel sauce and its variations with butter in this manner: Depending on taste, use from ½ to 3 tablespoons fresh butter. Remove finished sauce from heat. Stir in butter, ½ tablespoon at a time. Make sure butter has been absorbed by sauce before stirring in next amount. Serve immediately over food, or separately.

Mornay Sauce
Add ½ cup grated cheese to 1 cup hot sauce and stir over low heat until the cheese is melted. Season with mustard and/or Worcestershire to taste.

Velouté Sauce
Substitute hot chicken, beef, fish, or vegetable broth for the milk.

Cream Sauce
Add 2 to 3 tablespoons heavy cream to 1 cup finished sauce. This sauce is often flavored with a little onion. To do this, put an onion ring into the milk when heating it, and remove the onion before using the milk.

Mustard or Curry Sauce
For 1 cup sauce, combine 1 teaspoon dry mustard or ½ to 1 teaspoon curry powder with the flour used in the sauce. Mustard sauce is excellent for fish and broiled meats, while curry sauce is also fine for vegetables.

Herb Sauce
Add 1 teaspoon of any freshly chopped herb or ½ teaspoon dried herb to 1 cup hot sauce. Cook for a few minutes longer to let herbs release their flavor.

Sauce Aurore
Add from 2 to 4 tablespoons tomato purée or 1 tablespoon tomato paste to 1 cup hot sauce. Cook for a few minutes longer. The tomato may be increased to suit taste and color requirements.

The Rib Roast:

A magnificent cut of beef any way you roast it.
We show it rare, succulent, and carved to perfection.

BEEF
COOK BOOK

By far the most popular of all
American meats, American beef enjoys
the reputation of being
the world's finest

BEEF—Beef is the flesh of an adult animal of the *Bovidae* family of ruminants which has been killed for food. Practically all the beef we eat comes from steers (males castrated when very young), heifers (females that have never borne a calf), and cows (mature animals that have borne at least one calf). High-quality beef comes from animals that generally weigh from 900 to 1,300 pounds each, and range in age from one to three years.

Beef cattle are bred throughout the United States in a highly scientific manner, to adapt to local conditions, climates, and food preferences. The best-known breeds are Shorthorn and Hereford, originally from England, Aberdeen Angus, from Scotland, and the Brahman and Santa Gertrudis, bred especially to thrive in warm climates.

Early Use of Cattle

Long before written records were kept, man used cattle for food. The magnificent paintings of great horned bulls in the prehistoric Lascaux caves in southwestern France attest to the high rank they were given at that remote date. No one knows exactly when cattle were domesticated but it was surely in these prehistoric times. The Neolithic Swiss lake dwellings of some 3,000 years ago reveal evidence of domesticated cattle. Before this, man must have followed herds of cattle as our Plains Indians followed the buffalo. After the last glacier receded to the north, the ancestors of today's cattle family could be seen munching the new plant life that appeared on the recently reforested tundras of Europe. This wild species, belonging to the genus *Bos*, appeared both in Europe and Asia. Previously the cave artist left graphic evidence of his dependence upon the mammoth, bison, horse, reindeer, and elk; now the wild bull took his place in the cave gallery.

Since early times there is no question as to the dual role played by these animals. They were not only a source of food but an object of worship. Eating the flesh of animals offered to the gods, or the embodiment of the god himself, gave man divine strength. Was it for power or from hunger that Theagenes, the young adventurer of an early Greek romance, ate the Thracian bull? Whole bulls were roasted for the Grecian army. Although the more agrarian societies resisted eating their patient, hard-working companions, man is an eater of meat, and beef for most was too tasty to resist. The Sumerians as well as the early Minoans revered the mighty bull, yet had no compunctions about keeping a herd of cattle on hand for food. The Bible mentions cattle repeatedly: it tell us about the worship of the Golden Calf (Exodus 32:4) and the killing of the fatted calf for the return of the Prodigal Son (Luke 15:11-32).

Cattle raising was practiced all over Europe. Alexander the Great added to the stock in Greece by importing 2,000 Indian cattle. The Romans took their breeds north with them as they conquered. Our backyard barbecue may have its ancestry among ancient Saxon customs. They were early masters of the live-coal fire.

The word "steak" comes from two Old Norse words meaning "to roast on a spit" and "to be roasted." Norman invaders brought to the English language the Norman-French word for beef. It is interesting to note, however, that the Anglo-Saxon word ox was retained for the lesser parts of the animal: oxtail, ox head, ox muzzle. These presumably were left to the Saxon underlings by their Norman overlords.

By the Middle Ages, when a man's wealth was measured by what he possessed, a large herd of cattle became a considerable status symbol.

English Beef

England emerged as the European country most noted for her beef. But the French named the cut of beef over the loin from the French *sur,* meaning "over" or "above." "Surloin" became sirloin around 1600 and the English took over from there, producing three different versions of a story designed to establish the purely English origin of the name of the cut. The roles of Charles II, James I, and Henry VIII are interchangeable, and since it none the least diminishes the good story, Swift's version is submitted.

Miss Notable: But pray, why is it called Sirloin?

Lord Smart: Why, you must know that our King James I, who loved good eating, being invited to dinner by one of his nobles, and seeing a large loin of beef at his table, drew out his sword, and in a frolic knighted it.

When an Englishman spoke of meat, he meant beef. An article on health written in 1589 states that "Biefe of all flesh is most usuall among English men."

The English yeoman until the time of the Industrial Revolution was a freeman who earned his living from the land. He served his country voluntarily whenever and wherever he was needed. In 1669, after the Grand Duke of Tuscany inspected the yeomen of the King's Body Guard, he commented on the fact that these strong men were "great eaters of beef, of which a very large ration is given them daily and they might be called beef-eaters." To this day the yeomen warders serving under the Constable of the Tower of London are called Beef-eaters.

American Beef

It is a curious fact that no cattle are native to North America or South America. The buffalo, so common when the early settlers arrived on this continent, is the closest relative to the early wild cattle of Europe and Asia. Shiploads of cattle, along with other supplies from Europe, were brought into the original colonies. Cattle imported to the southwest by the Spanish developed into the Texas Longhorn. Although they are now almost extinct, they were once the standard stock for western ranches.

Not to be outdone, Americans contributed their share to the nomenclature of beef. In this case our share is the "porterhouse" steak. Around 1814 restaurants lined the New York waterfront catering to ships' crews and travelers. Since a meal and a glass of ale or porter was the fare, such places were referred to as "porterhouses." A certain Martin Morrison ran such a porterhouse that became noted for steaks. Caught short one evening for a favorite customer, Morrison was forced to slice a steak from what was to be his family's dinner roast. The customer was so pleased with this steak cut from the short loin that he ordered another, and thereafter always demanded such a cut. Others followed and the porterhouse steak was born.

In 1854 the editors of *Harper's Weekly* concluded, after a regional squabble as to what was America's favorite food, that steak was the most universally enjoyed meal. Modern breeds of beef have greatly improved this favorite meal. Two hundred years ago beef cattle still looked like the utility work animal of the past. Those large animals had muscular bodies, with long legs and strong heads and necks. Today's beef cattle are short-legged, compact-bodied animals with wide loins and quarters. Americans do not consume all this beef in steaks—there is the hamburger. This country holds the record for hamburger eating in general, and specifically by one Philip Yazdzik who consumed seventy-seven at one sitting in Chicago in 1955.

FRESH BEEF

Availability—Year-round retail prices of beef generally show a seasonal pattern since it is most plentiful between January and April.

Beef is also available canned in an enormous variety of products and can sizes.

Purchasing Guide—The inspection stamp (federal, state, or city) guarantees the wholesomeness and quality of the meat.

The grade or brand stamp is based on the conformation, finish, and quality of the meat. Good conformation refers to the build of the animal with a large proportion of meat to bone. Good finish refers to the quality, quantity, and distribution of fat and means that there is abundant marbling (intermingling of fat with lean) and an even layer of fat over the exterior surface. Good quality implies good marbling, fine-textured lean meat of light red to deep red color, with white smooth fat and red porous bones. The federal grades used, enclosed in a shield with the letters USDA, in order of descending quality, are: Prime, Choice, Good, Standard, Commercial, Utility, Cutter, and Canner. Prime is usually available only to hotels and restaurants. Choice grade is well-marbled meat, tender and juicy. Good grade has slightly less fat with meat of acceptable quality. Standard grade has a very thin covering of fat with lean, less tender meat. Commercial grade has meat from older cattle and since it is less tender, must be cooked by moist heat. Utility, Cutter, and Canner are cured, canned, or used in making sausage and other meat products. Many packers use their own brand names to designate the different grades.

Less tender cuts of meat may be tenderized mechanically by pounding, scoring, and grinding, or chemically by sprinkling a commercial tenderizer (papain) on the meat according to package directions. Let meat stand at room temperature to allow tenderizer to act. A recent development in chemical tenderizing is to inject the live animal with a vegetable enzyme (papayan) before butchering. This has the effect of tenderizing all meat tissues and of decreasing the cooking time.

An average-size family need not hesitate to buy the larger cuts of beef on sale. Take advantage of the bargains and tailor the cutting of the meat to suit the needs of your family. Buy a large pot roast. Use one third as a pot roast, cut another third into slices for Swiss steak, and cube the remainder for stew. A large rib roast can be roasted, some of it cut into rib steaks, the short ribs braised with vegetables, the bones saved for stock, and cooked meat scraps ground into a supper hash.

The following rule-of-thumb may be used for determining the amount to buy:

☐ ¼ to ⅓ pound per serving for boneless cuts (ground beef, boneless stew, boned roasts and steaks, flank and variety meats).

☐ ½ to ¾ pound per serving for cuts with some bone (rib roast, unboned steak, chops).

☐ ¾ to 1 pound per serving for bony and fatty cuts (short ribs, plate, brisket).

Storage—Remove or loosen wrapper; store unwrapped in meat container or loosely wrapped in coldest part of refrigerator. To keep cooked beef and gravy, cool quickly, cover tightly, and place in coldest part of the refrigerator.

☐ Refrigerator shelf:
Ground beef and stew meat, raw: 1 to 2 days
Variety meats and bone marrow, raw: 1 to 2 days
Steak, raw: 2 to 4 days
Roasts, raw: 3 to 6 days
Cold cuts and frankfurters, raw: 1 to 4 days

☐ Refrigerator frozen-food compartment, prepared for freezing:
Ground beef and variety meats: 2 to 4 days
Beef, raw: 1 week
Beef, cooked: 4 to 5 days

☐ Freezer, prepared for freezing: If beef cannot be used within the time suggested, wrap closely and seal tightly in moisture-vaporproof material and freeze quickly. Store at 0°F. or lower, a maximum of 3 to 4 months for ground beef and variety meats, and 6 to 8 months for other beef. Freeze cooked beef and gravy quickly and use within 2 to 3 months. Do not refreeze.

Nutritive Food Values—Beef is an excellent source of high-quality protein, and provides good amounts of iron and niacin. Three ounces of cooked, boneless, lean beef supplies the following percentages of the recommended daily allowances for a 25-year-old man: 30% protein, 27% iron, 10% riboflavin, 22% niacin, and 4% thiamine.

Three and a half ounces of raw beef, choice grade, give the following calories:

☐ Chuck (82% lean, 18% fat) = 257 calories
☐ Flank steak (100% lean) = 144 calories
☐ Hamburger (lean) = 179 calories
☐ Porterhouse steak (63% lean, 37% fat) = 390 calories
☐ Rib roast (64% lean, 36% fat) = 401 calories
☐ Round (89% lean, 11% fat) = 197 calories
☐ Rump (75% lean, 25% fat) = 303 calories
☐ Sirloin steak (73% lean, 27% fat) = 313 calories

Three and a half ounces of variety meat, raw, give the following calories:

☐ Brains = 125 calories
☐ Heart, lean = 108 calories
☐ Kidney = 130 calories
☐ Liver = 140 calories
☐ Tongue = 231 calories
Tongue, canned, or pickled = 267 calories
☐ Tripe, fresh = 100 calories
Tripe, pickled = 62 calories

Loss of vitamins increases with high cooking temperatures, long cooking times, and cooking in liquid; however, the liquid will contain a large percentage of the vitamins lost. Use this liquid in gravies, sauces, soups.

Basic Preparation

1. Use dry heat for the more tender cuts of beef. This method includes roasting, broiling, panbroiling, panfrying.
2. Use moist heat for the less tender cuts of beef. This method includes braising and cooking in liquid: pot roasting, stewing, and fricasseeing.

Using methods suggested for each, long cooking decreases the tenderness of tender cuts and increases the tenderness of less tender cuts. There is evidence that marinating does not appreciably affect tenderness.

Note: Meat continues to cook after it is removed from the oven or cooking utensil. Heat is conducted from the exterior to the interior, where the temperature increases. This occurs to a greater extent with higher cooking temperature, larger size, and lower interior temperature of meat.

☐ **To Freeze**

Raw beef and variety meats—Freeze as soon as possible after purchase. Wrap meat in one-meal portions in the style you are going to use in cooking. Wrap in moistureproof wrapping with a drugstore fold, excluding all air and separating pieces of meat, such as hamburgers, with sheets of freezer paper. Secure edges with freezer tape. Date and label package and rotate packages to keep meat fresh.

Cooked beef—Should be cooled as rapidly as possible and stored as above.

Beef for Roasting

Purchasing Guide—Among the most tender cuts are *rib oven roasts*. There are usually seven ribs in the section from which the butcher cuts these roasts. Also it is well to remember that roasts cut from this section are of different qualities. The choicest, that is, the most tender and the most expensive rib roasts, are called first ribs or sometimes the eleventh and twelfth ribs. Next are the center-rib roasts and finally larger rib roasts, called sixth and seventh ribs, usually priced below the other cuts. All rib roasts come in any of the following styles: 1. Standing 10 inch Rib Roast, measuring from backbone to end of ribs, with backbone and small bones still on, will weigh 6 to 8 pounds. 2. Standing 7-inch Rib Roast is the same as above roast but 3 inches of the short ribs, part of the backbone, and small bones have been cut off. It will weigh 5 to 7 pounds. 3. Rolled Rib Roast is like the standing 10-inch rib roast but *all* bones have been removed, the meat rolled and tied, with the boned short ribs sometimes wrapped around the roast. It also will weigh about 6 pounds.

Other cuts for roasting include: *tenderloin, Delmonico (Rib Eye)*, and if high-

RETAIL CUTS OF BEEF— WHERE THEY COME FROM

TENDER
1. Rib Section
Standing rib roast
Rib steak
Rib steak, Boneless
Delmonico (Rib Eye) steak
Delmonico (Rib Eye) roast
2. Loin Section
Short Loin
Club steak
T-bone steak
Porterhouse steak
Top loin steak
Filet mignon (tenderloin) steak
Pinbone sirloin steak
Flat-bone sirloin steak
Wedge-bone sirloin steak
Boneless sirloin steak

LESS TENDER
3. Chuck Section
Inside chuck roll
Chuck tender
Blade pot roast or steak
Boneless shoulder pot roast or steak
Chuck short ribs
Petite steaks*
Arm pot roast or steak
Boston cut
4. Round Section
Round steak
Top round steak*
Outside (bottom) round steak
Eye of round
Standing rump*
Rolled rump*
Heel of round
5. Shank Section
Shank cross cuts
Beef for stew
(also from other cuts)
6. Brisket Section
Fresh brisket
Corned brisket
7. Short Plate Section
Short ribs
Skirt steak fillets*
Rolled plate
Plate beef
8. Flank Section
Flank steak*
Flank steak fillets*
9. Tip (Knuckle) Section
Tip steak*
Sirloin tip*
Cube steak*

GROUND BEEF
Ground beef (flank, short plate, shank, brisket, rib, chuck, loin, round)
Beef patties

May be roasted, broiled, panbroiled, or panfried from high-quality beef.

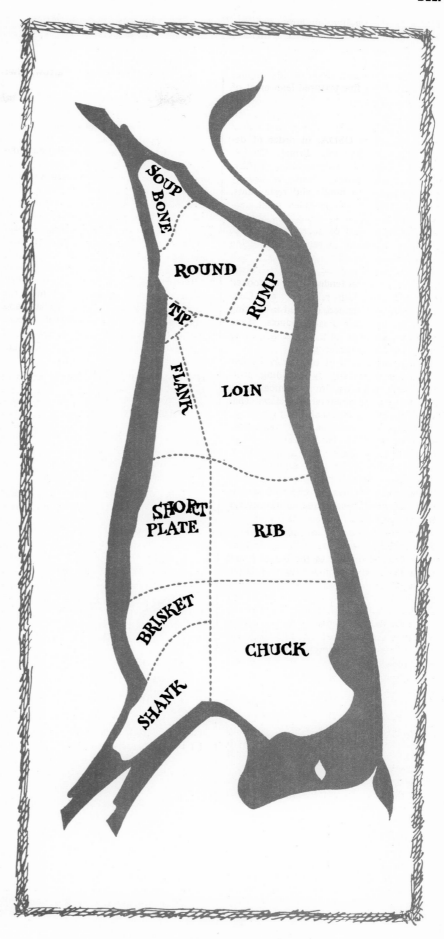

quality meat, the *standing rump, rolled rump,* and *sirloin tip.* See chart of Retail Cuts of Beef, page 179, and Timetable for Roasting Beef, below.

Basic Preparation

☐ **To Roast at 325°F.**—Place a standing rib roast, fat side up, in a shallow open pan. No rack is needed, for the rib bones will keep the meat off the bottom of the pan. A rolled rib roast and all other boneless cuts should be put on a rack. Insert a meat thermometer into center of roast. Do not add water or cover meat. Roast in preheated slow oven (325°F.) until thermometer registers degree of doneness desired. See Timetable for interior temperature and time. When done, remove roast to a platter or smaller pan and keep warm. Use drippings in pan for gravy or juice. However, beef may be roasted as *you* like it. So, if preferred, here are three other methods.

☐ **To Roast at 450°F., lowering to 325°F., if you wish beef with a crisp crust on the outside**—Place standing or rolled roast in pan as above. Season with salt and pepper and rub with flour. Insert meat thermometer. Put in preheated very hot oven (450°F.) for 20 minutes. Reduce heat to slow (325°F.), and continue roasting to desired doneness (140°F. for rare, 160°F. for medium, and 170°F. for well done). Caution: To keep meat fat from splattering over oven, place a loose tent of foil over the meat.

☐ **To Roast, covered with foil, at 425° F.**—Preheat oven to hot (425°F.). Wrap meat closely in foil, sealing tightly. Place on a rack. Insert meat thermometer through foil. Roast according to chart. Open foil to allow roast to brown for 45 minutes before removing from oven.

☐ **To Roast at 200°F. if you wish beef rare all the way through**—Prepare a standing or rolled beef roast as above. Roast in a very slow oven (200°F.) for 1 hour per pound. For successful low-temperature roasting, the oven must maintain an even 200°F.

☐ **To Make Pan Gravy**—For each cup of gravy desired, use 2 tablespoons drippings, 2 tablespoons flour, and 1 cup liquid. Lift roast from pan and pour off all fat except the amount needed. Leave any brown bits in the pan. Blend in flour completely. Place pan over moderately low heat; cook and stir until flour bubbles and begins to brown. Remove from heat, gradually stir in water or other liquid, combining thoroughly. Return pan to heat. Continue to cook over low heat and stir until gravy thickens and is cooked, 3 to 5 minutes. Season; strain if desired.

Note: If pan drippings are not brown, a liquid gravy coloring may be added to attain desired color.

The term *au jus* refers to any liquid drippings from the roast, without fat, plus the juices from carving the meat. Juices are heated and spooned over the meat when served.

☐ **To Roast Beef in an Electric Rotisserie**—Any of the cuts that can be roasted in an oven lend themselves to rotisserie roasting. Since rotisseries vary greatly from each other in size, strength of heating unit, etc., all of which affect the cooking times of the meat, consult manufacturer's directions to obtain accurate cooking times.

Beef for Steak

Purchasing Guide—Personal preference tempered by market prices may be one guide for the selection of a steak. However, it is well to keep in mind that there are many cuts of beef called steak, and that steaks may be called by different names in different parts of the United States. As shown on the Chart of Retail Cuts of Beef the most commonly known cuts are:

Rib section:
Rib steaks, with and without bone
Delmonico (rib eye) steaks

Loin section:
Club
T-bone
Porterhouse
Top loin
Filet Mignon (or tenderloin)

Sirloin:
Pinbone
Flat bone
Wedge bone
Boneless

With the cut determined, appetite may dictate the amount of steak to buy, and personal preference the thickness. If everyone agrees on a thick, juicy steak, cooked medium or rare, select a cut 1½ to 2 inches thick. If steak is liked well done, use one or more thinner steaks. All steaks vary somewhat in general shape, type and location of bone. The cooking, however, is the same.

Basic Preparation—There are three ways to cook steak: broiling, panbroiling, or panfrying.

☐ **To Broil**—A perfectly broiled steak has a beautifully browned exterior and a juicy interior cooked to the stage preferred. (See Timetable for Broiling Beef.) Broiling is cooking by direct heat and it can be done equally well with an electric unit, gas flame, or live coals. Some directions specify preheating the broiler before using. If so, preheat with the door closed, and allow 5 to 10 minutes.

TIMETABLE FOR ROASTING BEEF

CUT	APPROX. WEIGHT (POUNDS)	OVEN TEMPERATURE CONSTANT	INTERIOR TEMPERATURE WHEN REMOVED FROM OVEN	APPROX. COOKING TIME (MINUTES PER POUND)
Standing Rib*	6 to 8	300°F. to 325°F.	140°F. (rare)	23 to 25
			160°F. (medium)	27 to 30
			170°F. (well)	32 to 35
	4 to 6	300°F. to 325°F.	140°F. (rare)	26 to 32
			160°F. (medium)	34 to 38
			170°F. (well)	40 to 42
Rolled Rib	5 to 7	300°F. to 325°F.	140°F. (rare)	32
			160°F. (medium)	38
			170°F. (well)	48
Delmonico (rib eye)	4 to 6	350°F.	140°F. (rare)	18 to 20
			160°F. (medium)	20 to 22
			170°F. (well)	22 to 24
Tenderloin, whole	4 to 6	425°F.	140°F. (rare)	45 to 60 (total)
Tenderloin, half	2 to 3	425°F.	140°F. (rare)	45 to 50 (total)
Rolled Rump (high quality)	4 to 6	300°F. to 325°F.	150°F. to 170°F.	25 to 30
Sirloin Tip (high quality)	3½ to 4	300°F. to 325°F.	150°F. to 170°F.	35 to 40
Standing Rump (high quality)	5 to 7	300°F. to 325°F.	150°F. to 170°F.	25 to 30

Ribs which measure 6 to 7 inches from chine to tip of rib.

BEEF

181

To Broil in the Range—Rub steak with garlic, if desired. Put on a preheated rack placed so that the top of the meat is 3 inches below the heat. When half the broiling time has passed, pull out rack and season steak with salt and pepper. Turn with tongs or fork thrust into the fat. Then broil the other side for the allotted time. See the Timetable for Broiling Beef thick or thin, rare, medium, or well done. If you use a portable electric broiler, the manufacturer's directions should be followed.

To Broil over Charcoal—Have a large enough fire to start with to provide a good bed of coals, but don't start cooking until the flames die down and there is only a bed of glowing coals. Usually the grill is from 3 to 6 inches from the coals, depending on the thickness of the steaks and the degree of doneness desired. The thicker the steaks or the more well done you want them, the farther they should be placed from the coals. Also, they should be far enough from coals so that flames caused by dripping fat will not touch the meat. Choose top-quality steaks at least 1 inch thick. Trim off excess fat. Score the fat to prevent curling during cooking. Broil one side until well browned. Season and turn with tongs. Broil second side to the desired stage, or until well browned. Season and serve. It is not possible to give an exact time for broiling steaks by this method. Variations in heat from coals, thickness of steak, distance from coals, and many other factors must be taken into consideration. Therefore, it will be necessary to experiment a few times with individual equipment to have steaks done to perfection. Roughly, a 1-inch steak takes about 20 minutes for medium rare and a 2-inch steak takes about 40 minutes for medium rare. To broil steaks with barbecue sauce, sear steaks quickly on both sides. Then turn frequently and baste each time with the sauce until steaks are cooked to desired doneness.

☐ To Panbroil—Any steak suitable for broiling can also be panbroiled. This method is especially desirable for thinly cut steak. A heavy skillet or griddle is necessary for satisfactory panbroiling. The heat is transmitted to meat through the metal, not directly, as in broiling. Rub skillet with just enough fat to keep meat from sticking; heat skillet. Rub steak with cut garlic clove, if desired. Put in skillet; brown one side, turn, and brown other side. Reduce heat and cook for 2 to 10 minutes on each side, or until desired doneness is reached, turning steak to cook it evenly. Pour off fat if it accumulates. Season just before serving.

☐ To Panfry—In some areas, this is a popular method for cooking steak. It is suitable only for steak 1 inch or less thick. Meat cooked this way is almost always well done. Steaks can be fried plain or first dipped into seasoned flour or crumbs. Select a large, heavy skillet. Heat enough fat to cover bottom of pan. Pieces of beef fat can be cut off steaks and fried until the fat runs. Fat should be very hot. Drop steaks into the hot fat and brown quickly on both sides. Reduce heat and cook, uncovered, until done, turning occasionally.

☐ To Make Onion Gravy for Panfried Steak—Pour off all except 2 tablespoons fat for each cup of gravy desired. Stir in 2 tablespoons flour and brown slowly. Add ¼ to ½ cup sliced or chopped onion and brown lightly, stirring often. Gradually stir in 1 cup cold water, meat stock, or vegetable cooking water. Cook, stirring constantly, until thickened. Season.

Serving Steak—Always serve broiled meat on a warm platter.

If the steak is to be carved at the table, it is more practical to use very little garnish. A bit of parsley, watercress, or green celery leaves will do. If a vegetable, such as broiled mushrooms or tomatoes, is served, it can be used as a garnish. For the sake of the carver, put the vegetable on only one side of the meat. A lump of plain butter, or softened butter combined with herbs and other seasonings, on top of steak adds to its appearance and flavor. Gravies and sauces can be served on the side.

The Less Tender Cuts

Purchasing Guide—All beef can be cooked so that the meat is tender and juicy. But many delicious dishes are overlooked because of unfamiliarity with the cut and the way in which it should be cooked. Actually, there is only one basic method for cooking the less tender cuts: moist heat.

In general, these are cuts suitable for cooking in moist heat, although the

TIMETABLE FOR BROILING BEEF

This timetable is based on broiling at a moderate temperature of 350°F. in a preheated broiler. Rare steaks are broiled to an internal temperature of 140°F., medium to 160°F., and well done to 170°F.

CUT	WEIGHT (POUNDS)	Rare	Medium	Well Done
Chuck steak (high quality)				
1 inch	1½ to 2½	24	30	36
1½ inches	2 to 4	40	45	50
Club steak				
1 inch	1 to 1½	15	20	25
1½ inches	1½ to 2	25	30	35
2 inches	2 to 2½	35	45	55
Delmonico steak (rib eye)				
1 inch	8 ounces	15	20	25
1½ inches	12 ounces	25	30	35
2 inches	16 ounces	35	45	55
Filet Mignon (Tenderloin)	4 to 8 ounces	10 to 15	15 to 20	20 to 25
Ground Beef Patties				
1 inch thick	4 ounces	15	25	35
Porterhouse steak				
1 inch	1¼ to 2	20	25	30
1½ inches	2 to 3	30	35	40
2 inches	2½ to 3½	40	45	50
Rib steak				
1 inch	1 to 1½	15	20	25
1½ inches	1½ to 2	25	30	35
2 inches	2 to 2½	35	45	55
Sirloin steak (top loin)				
1 inch	1½ to 3	20	25	30
1½ inches	2¼ to 4	30	35	40
2 inches	3 to 5	40	45	50
T-bone steak				
1 inch	1¼ to 2	10	12	15
1½ inches	2 to 3	18	20	25
2 inches	2½ to 3½	32	36	40

To broil frozen steaks—Place under broiler 4 inches away from heat. Thicker steaks will need ¼ to ½ more broiling time than required on chart.

ENCYCLOPEDIA OF COOKERY

names and ways of cutting vary somewhat according to locality.

From the chuck section:
Inside chuck roll
Chuck tender
Blade pot roast or steak
Boneless shoulder pot roast or steak
Chuck short ribs
Petite steaks*
Arm pot roast or steak
Boston cut

From the round section:
Round steak
Top round steak*
Outside (bottom) round steak
Eye of round
Standing rump*
Rolled rump*
Heel of round

From the foreshank:
Shank cross cuts
Beef for stew (may also come from other cuts)

From the brisket section:
Fresh brisket
Corned brisket (see also cured beef)

From the short plate section:
Short ribs
Skirt steak fillets*
Rolled plate
Plate beef

From the flank steak section:
Flank steak*
Flank steak fillets*

From the tip (knuckle) section:
Tip steak*
Sirloin tip*
Cube steak*

*Cuts may be broiled or roasted
if beef is of high quality.*

Basic Preparation

☐ **To Braise**—Meat is browned slowly, seasoned, and a little liquid such as water, broth, or vegetable juice is added; the heat is lowered to the point where the *meat barely simmers,* the pan is covered tightly, and cooking continues until meat is completely tender. The meat cooks by steam.

☐ **To Cook in Liquid**—The procedure is almost exactly as above, but a large quantity of liquid is added, usually enough to cover the meat. Recipes, however, are usually required because of the differences in flavors, other foods to be added, the size, shape, and thickness of meat, and a few changes in procedure, such as flouring the meat. The cut of meat is also usually specified, although this may be interchangeable within a group and according to size and taste.

Ground Beef

As Americans we eat more ground beef, hamburger to most of us, than any other cut of meat. It's cooked plain in patties, with all kinds of toppings and fillings, served with, on, and in all the pastas from noodles and spaghetti to ravioli,

made into tiny or man-sized meatballs, baked in casseroles and meat loaves, dropped into soups.

It is called simply "ground beef," sometimes "hamburger" in recipes. Occasionally the specific cut of beef is given, such as ground chuck or ground round.

Regular ground beef should not contain more than 25 per cent fat. Lean ground beef should contain not more than 12 per cent fat.

It can be cooked as hamburgers from the frozen state, but it must be completely thawed before shaping into loaves, balls, etc.

Beef: Variety Meats

Beef variety meats include brain, heart, kidneys, liver, marrow bones, oxtail, tongue, and tripe. They have high nutritive values, are thrifty, and, properly prepared, they make welcome additions to the family diet.

Beef brains weigh about 13 to 14 ounces. They are tender and have a delicate flavor. Wash well and remove outer membranes before cooking. Simmer for 10 minutes in 1 quart water with 1 teaspoon salt and 2 tablespoons vinegar added. Drain and use according to recipe directions.

Beef hearts weigh about 3 to 4 pounds. They are tough but flavorful, and must be cooked by slow, moist heat. The large veins and arteries should be removed before cooking.

Beef kidneys weigh about 1 pound. They are large, oval, and shaped with many lobes. They are not tender and, unless properly prepared, they have a strong taste. Before cooking, all the fat, gristle, and membrane should be removed. To remove all the strong flavor and obtain a very palatable meat, it is *essential* that they be soaked in plain cold water or in cold water with lemon juice (1 quart water to ¼ cup lemon juice) for 30 to 40 minutes, changing the water once during soaking. After draining, cook according to recipe directions.

Beef liver is sold sliced either as beef liver or baby-beef liver. A whole liver weighs from 10 to 15 pounds. Beef liver is usually sold frozen, but this does not affect the taste.

Beef marrow bones are the long bones of the animal, the leg bone, for example. They contain a soft, flavorful fat substance called marrow. Marrow is used to make balls for soup, to add flavor to many dishes, to garnish meat, and to cook and eat as a tidbit. Since it is delicate and rich, it needs no sauces. To extract the marrow, ask the butcher to cut the bone into 1½-inch lengths. Allow the marrow from three to five 1½-inch bones for each serving when the marrow is eaten for its own sake. As a garnish, allow one piece for each serving.

Oxtails weigh from 1½ to 2 pounds, with plenty of rich, tasty meat. They require long, slow cooking: braising or cooking in plenty of liquid.

Beef tongue usually weighs 3 to 4 pounds. It is sold fresh, pickled, corned, or smoked. Tongues are tough and should be cooked over low heat for several hours. Soak a fresh tongue in cold water to cover with 2 tablespoons vinegar added. Soak for several hours. Drain and cook. Pickled, corned, or smoked tongue should be covered with boiling water and cooked for 1 hour. Drain, add fresh boiling water, and continue cooking until tender. When tender, the gristle and the bone at the thick end should be removed. Split the skin the length of the tongue and remove. Cut the meat into thin slices crosswise.

Beef tripe comes from the first and second stomachs of the beef. It is sold fresh, pickled, canned, or precooked. Tripe requires plenty of cooking to become tender. There are four types of tripe: the fat part of the belly is usually sold precooked, and three types of honeycomb tripe which come from the second stomach (partially honeycombed, dark, and light). Fresh tripe should be trimmed, washed, soaked overnight, and blanched in salted water for 30 minutes. It should be cooked slowly over low heat for 12 hours. Most tripe sold today is precooked and only requires 1 to 2 hours cooking.

CURED BEEF

Cured beef and beef products include the following:

Beef-bacon slices: available packaged as bacon; cook as bacon.

Corned beef: available in whole or half brisket. Allow ½ pound per serving. Also in cans or jars and sliced in packages.

Dried chipped beef: available in packages or jars. Allow 1 to 2 ounces per serving. Use right from package or cover with boiling water, let stand for 1 minute, and drain.

Dried sliced beef: available in a film package.

Storage—Cover packaged, cured beef tightly and store in coldest part of refrigerator.

☐ Refrigerator shelf: Use within 1 week
☐ Refrigerator frozen-food compartment, prepared for freezing: Store only 2 weeks
☐ Freezer, prepared for freezing: Must be used within 2 months

Do not freeze unless absolutely necessary. Freezing is not recommended for cured or precooked meat such as cold cuts or frankfurters. The salt in these foods prevents the proper freezing of the fats and they become rancid.

- ☐ Meats in jars on kitchen shelf: Must be used within 6 weeks
- ☐ Meats in jars on refrigerator shelf, opened but covered: Must be used in 3 to 5 days

Caloric Values—Three and a half ounces give the following calories.

- ☐ Beef, corned, boneless, uncooked, medium fat = 293 calories
- ☐ Beef, corned, boneless, cooked, medium fat = 372 calories
- ☐ Beef, canned corned, boneless, medium fat = 216
- ☐ Beef, dried, chipped = 203 calories
- ☐ Beef, dried, uncooked = 203 calories
- ☐ Canned corned-beef hash, with potato = 181 calories

FREEZE-DRIED BEEF

Commercial freeze-drying is the process whereby a food item is frozen and then dried by sublimation (the process of changing a solid to vapor, and again to solid). The food loses 50 to 75% of its weight, 98% of its water, becoming lightweight, porous, and brittle in form. Sealed in an airtight container, it may be stored for 1 year at room temperature. Normal weight and texture are restored by covering it with water to reconstitute the food. The item may then be cooked as usual or, if it was precooked, it may be soaked in hot water and served. This process has been successfully applied to many foods. Available freeze-dried beef items include: beefsteak, beef and potato hash, chili con carne, vegetable and beef dinner, beef noodle soup, and old-fashioned beef soup. These foods are available mainly in specialty food stores and in stores carrying camping supplies. The soups are available in some local food stores.

ROASTED BEEF TENDERLOIN

The most tender of all beef cuts. Buy a tenderloin weighing 4 to 6 pounds; have it trimmed and larded. Put on a rack in a shallow roasting pan, brush with oil, and roast in preheated very hot oven (450°F.) for 30 to 40 minutes for rare, and 45 to 60 minutes for medium. Makes 6 to 8 servings.

ROAST BEEF ON A SPIT

Bone, roll, and tie a tender cut of beef. Put spit lengthwise through center of roast and lock with prongs. Insert meat thermometer. Slip the spit into rotisserie and roast, using medium heat over glow-ing coals. Brush with basting liquids. Various liquids, such as broth or barbecue sauce, can be used for basting liquid. A 5- to 6-pound roast will take about 1¼ hours for rare, and 1½ to 2 hours for medium to well done. Makes about 10 to 12 servings.

BEEF BIRDS IN WINE

½ cup chopped cooked mushrooms or sausage meat
1 onion, chopped
4 large thin slices of roast beef
2 tablespoons fat
2 tablespoons all-purpose flour
⅓ cup each of red wine, water, and meat stock
Salt and pepper to taste
½ bay leaf
Pinch of thyme
2 cups (one 1-pound can) sliced carrots, drained
Chopped parsley

Mix mushrooms and onion. Put a spoonful on each slice of roast beef. Roll like sausages and fasten with toothpicks. Brown rolls on all sides in hot fat. Remove rolls from pan and keep warm. Stir flour into pan drippings. Gradually stir in red wine, water, and meat stock. Add seasonings. Cook over low heat, stirring constantly, until sauce is thickened. Add meat rolls and simmer, covered, for 1 hour, adding more liquid if necessary. Add carrots and reheat slightly. Garnish with chopped parsley. Makes 4 servings.

DEVILED ROAST BEEF SLICES

4 slices of roast beef (¼ to ½ inch thick)
Prepared mustard
Fine dry bread crumbs
Beef drippings
1 cup beef gravy
½ teaspoon dry mustard
Dash of hot pepper sauce
1 tablespoon Worcestershire
Garlic salt and pepper to taste

Spread slices of roast beef with prepared mustard. Dip into crumbs. Fry in drippings until browned. Add remaining ingredients to drippings, heat and serve with the meat. Makes 4 servings.

LONDON BROIL

Salt both sides of a flank steak well and smear both sides generously with French dressing. Let steak marinate in the refrigerator for several hours. Broil under high heat 2 inches from heat, allowing 5 to 7 minutes for each side. Carve on a board containing a gravy well, or on a tray or deep platter. Slice very thin, against the grain. Mushrooms and onions are an excellent accompaniment and blend deliciously with the steak juices, which can be thickened if desired. Makes 4 to 6 servings if a whole steak is used.

FLANK STEAK TERIYAKI BARBECUE

¾ cup cooking oil
¼ cup each of soy sauce and honey
2 tablespoons each of cider vinegar and finely chopped green onions

1 large garlic clove, minced or mashed
1½ teaspoons ground ginger
1 flank steak, about 2 pounds (not scored)

Combine oil, soy sauce, honey, vinegar, onion, garlic, and ginger. Pour over steak and allow to marinate for 4 hours or more; turn occasionally. Barbecue steak over hot coals heated to turn gray, turning once, until done to your preference (about 5 minutes each side for medium rare). Baste occasionally with marinade. Carve into thin slices, cutting on the diagonal from top to bottom of steak (as for London Broil). Makes 4 servings.
Note: You can oven-broil this steak, if preferred.

DEVILED FLANK STEAK

1½ pounds flank steak
All-purpose flour
1 onion, minced
3 tablespoons fat
2 teaspoons salt
¼ teaspoon pepper
¼ teaspoon paprika
1 teaspoon prepared mustard
1 teaspoon vinegar
½ cup tomato sauce
1½ cups hot water

Cut steak into strips across the grain. Roll in flour; brown meat and onion in hot fat. Stir in 2 tablespoons flour and seasonings. Add remaining ingredients; cover and simmer for 1 hour, or until meat is tender. Good with rice, noodles, or mashed potato. Makes 4 servings.

OVEN BEEF STROGANOFF

2½ pounds boneless sirloin of beef, cut into strips (1 x ⅛ inches)
2 tablespoons butter
1 onion, minced
2 tablespoons all-purpose flour
2 beef bouillon cubes
2 cups hot water
Dash of hot pepper sauce
¾ teaspoon salt
¼ teaspoon pepper
1 tablespoon each of prepared mustard, Worcestershire, and ketchup
½ cup dairy sour cream

Cook meat in 1 tablespoon butter until it loses its red color. Add onion; cook for 5 minutes. Put into casserole. Melt remaining butter in saucepan; blend in flour. Add bouillon cubes, hot water, hot pepper sauce, salt, pepper, mustard, Worcestershire, and ketchup. Cook until thickened. Beat in dairy sour cream; pour mixture over meat. Cool, cover, and refrigerate. The day of the dinner, bake beef in preheated moderate oven (350°F.) for 45 minutes. Makes 4 to 6 servings.

PRESSED BEEF

1 flank steak (about 2 pounds)
6 cups boiling water
2 teaspoons salt
¼ cup cider vinegar
½ teaspoon peppercorns
1 small bay leaf
White horseradish

Place flank steak in a kettle with boiling water. Add remaining ingredients except horseradish. Simmer over low heat for 3 hours, or until meat is very tender. Drain and reserve liquid. Grind beef very fine and pack into a loaf pan (9 x 5 x 3 inches). Strain reserved liquid. Simmer, uncovered, until liquid is reduced to 1 cup. Pour over meat. Cover with wax paper. Press with a heavy weight. Chill overnight. Turn out and slice thin. Serve with prepared white horseradish. Makes 6 servings.

ROLLED STUFFED FLANK STEAK

- 2 onions, chopped
- ¾ teaspoon salt
- ⅛ teaspoon pepper
- 1 teaspoon crumbled dried sage or thyme
- 2 tablespoons cooking oil or other fat
- 1½ cups fine bread crumbs
  Few celery leaves or parsley sprig, minced
- 1 flank steak (2 to 3 pounds)

Sauté the onions with seasonings in hot fat for 2 to 3 minutes. Add bread crumbs and celery leaves. Mix thoroughly. Pound flank steak with a mallet or wooden potato masher. Spread stuffing on meat. Roll meat lengthwise and tie securely in 4 or 5 places. Place it on a rack in a baking pan. Roast in preheated moderate oven (300°F.) for 2½ hours. Serve on hot platter. Remove strings and carve diagonally across the grain of the meat. Glazed carrot slices make a good vegetable garnish for this dish. Makes 6 generous servings.

SWISS CUBE STEAKS

- 1½ pounds cube steaks
- 2 tablespoons all-purpose flour
- ½ teaspoon salt
- ⅛ teaspoon pepper
- 2 tablespoons fat
- 1 can (8 ounces) tomato sauce
- 1 cup water
- 1 teaspoon Worcestershire
- 1 celery stalk, sliced
- 1 onion, chopped
- 1 garlic clove, minced

Shake steaks in a plastic bag with flour, salt, and pepper until steaks are well coated. Brown on both sides in hot fat. Add remaining ingredients, cover, and simmer for 1 hour, or until meat is tender. Makes 4 servings.

POT ROAST OF BEEF

- 5 to 6 pounds rolled boneless or bone-in beef chuck
  All-purpose flour
  Fat from chuck
- 1 cup water
  Salt and pepper

Dust meat lightly with flour. Brown slowly on all sides in hot fat in Dutch

Steak Tartare

Skillet Pot Roast with Vegetables

Roast Beef on a Spit

oven or heavy kettle with tight-fitting cover. Slip a rack under meat. Add water and season meat. Cover tightly and cook over very low heat for 3 hours, or until meat is very tender; add a little more water if necessary and turn meat halfway through cooking time. Remove meat and, if desired, thicken liquid with a flour-and-water paste for gravy. Makes 10 to 12 servings.

Oven Pot Roast of Beef

Follow Pot Roast of Beef recipe, page 184, including browning on top of range, but bake meat, covered, in preheated moderate oven (350°F.) for same length of time. If handles and cover of browning pan are not ovenproof, transfer meat to casserole after browning.

Yankee Pot Roast

Follow either Pot Roast of Beef recipe, above. One hour before roast is done, add 2 cups diced carrots, 2 cups sliced celery, 2 cups diced yellow turnip, and 1 cup chopped onion. Serve vegetables and unthickened liquid as sauce on sliced meat.

Pot Roast of Beef, Burgundy

Follow Pot Roast of Beef recipe (page 184), substituting 1 cup Burgundy for the water and adding 1 minced garlic clove and 1 crumbled bay leaf.

Barbecued Pot Roast

Follow Pot Roast of Beef recipe (page 184), substituting 1 cup bottled barbecue sauce for the water.

SKILLET POT ROAST WITH VEGETABLES

3 to 4 pounds beef for pot roast
2 tablespoons fat
  Salt and pepper
  Onion salt
½ cup water
  Small new unpeeled potatoes
  Carrots
¾ pound whole green beans
  Summer squash or zucchini
  Small white onions

In 12-inch skillet brown meat on all sides in hot fat. Sprinkle with salt, pepper, and onion salt. Add water, cover tightly, and simmer for about 2½ hours, adding more water if necessary. Add potatoes and carrots, 2 of each per serving. Cook for 30 minutes. Add green beans, squash, and small onions. For each serving, allow 1 small squash and 2 onions. Cover; simmer for about 30 minutes. Makes 4 servings. Some meat will be left over for another meal.

BEEF À LA MODE

½ pound salt pork
5 pounds boneless beef chuck, rolled
3 cups water
2 cleaned calves' feet
3 tablespoons dry red wine

2 teaspoons salt
4 whole cloves
½ teaspoon leaf thyme
8 small white onions
8 small carrots
3 celery stalks, cut into 2-inch pieces
½ pound whole green beans
6 parsley sprigs
  All-purpose flour

Cut pork into ½-inch cubes. Fry in heavy kettle or Dutch oven until golden and crisp. Remove pork and reserve. Brown roast on all sides in fat or, if possible, have meat well larded with salt pork and brown slowly without adding fat. Pour off fat. Add water, calves' feet, wine, salt, cloves, and thyme. Bring to boil and boil for 10 minutes. Skim; simmer, covered, for 3½ to 4 hours. One hour before meat is done, add vegetables. Finish cooking. Add salt pork. To serve: Remove meat to serving dish or platter with vegetables; discard feet. Garnish with parsley. Strain liquid, thicken with a little flour mixed with cold water and pour over meat and vegetables. If preferred, do not thicken liquid; or remove part of it and chill in the refrigerator. It will jell and can be sliced thin and served with leftover cold meat and salad greens. Makes 8 servings.

SAUERBRATEN

4 pounds beef for pot roast
2 teaspoons salt
1 teaspoon ground ginger
2 cups cider vinegar
2½ cups water
2 medium onions, sliced
2 tablespoons mixed whole pickling spice
2 bay leaves
1 teaspoon peppercorns
8 whole cloves
⅓ cup sugar
2 tablespoons fat
  Flour or gingersnaps

Rub meat with salt and ginger; put in large bowl. Combine remaining ingredients except fat and flour; bring to boil and pour over meat. Cool. Cover and put in refrigerator for 3 days. Turn meat once each day. Remove meat from pickling liquid; reserve liquid. Dry meat with paper towel. Brown meat on all sides in fat in heavy kettle. Put on rack; add 1 cup reserved pickling liquid and half the onions and spices from liquid. Cover tightly and simmer very slowly for 3½ hours, or until tender, adding more liquid as needed. Remove meat to hot platter. Strain liquid in pan and return to heat; strain in additional pickling liquid to make about 2 cups. Skim off excess fat. Thicken gravy with a little flour mixed with cold water, or thicken with 6 crumbled gingersnaps. Serve with sliced meat, mashed potatoes, rice, or potato dumplings. Makes about 6 servings.

SWISS STEAK

3 pounds boneless chuck steak, about 1½ inches thick
  Salt and pepper
  All-purpose flour
2 onions, sliced
4 cups (two 1-pound cans) tomatoes

Remove excess fat from steak and cut meat into 6 pieces. Season meat and put it on a well-floured cutting board. Cover steak with 1 cup flour; pound with a meat hammer or edge of a heavy saucer. Continue to turn, flour, and pound meat until 1 cup flour is taken up. Melt a little fat from steak in skillet. Brown onion in hot fat, remove, and brown steak on both sides. Put onion on top of steak. Add tomatoes, cover, and simmer for 2½ to 3 hours, or until fork-tender. Or cover and bake in preheated moderate oven (350°F.). Remove steak with onion to hot serving dish. Serve with gravy made by thickening drippings in skillet with a little flour blended with cold water. Makes 6 servings.

PEPPER STEAK

2 pounds chuck roast, cut into thin strips about 2 inches x 1 inch (about 4 cups)
3 tablespoons cooking oil
  Water
2 beef bouillon cubes
2 each of red and green peppers, cut into eighths
3 tablespoons cornstarch
2 tablespoons soy sauce
  Hot cooked rice

Brown meat in hot oil. Add 2 cups water and bouillon cubes and bring to boil. Cover and simmer for 1 hour, or until meat is tender. Add peppers and simmer for 5 minutes. Blend cornstarch, soy sauce, and ½ cup water. Add to meat mixture and cook, stirring, until thickened. Serve with rice and additional soy sauce, if desired. Makes 4 servings.

BEEF ROULADES WITH CARROTS AND LIMA BEANS

4 slices chuck roast, ½ inch thick
1 dill pickle
¼ cup all-purpose flour
2 tablespoons cooking oil
2 cups water
2 beef bouillon cubes
8 small carrots
1 package (10 ounces) frozen Fordhook Lima beans

Cut each slice of chuck into halves. Pound each piece until very thin. Cut pickle into 8 lengthwise pieces. Place a piece of pickle in the center of each slice of meat. Roll and fasten with toothpicks. Roll in flour. Brown rolls on all sides in hot oil. Add water and bouillon cubes. Bring to a boil, cover, and lower heat. Simmer for about 1½ hours. Add carrots and Lima beans. Cover and simmer for 30 minutes longer. Makes 4 servings.

OLD-FASHIONED BEEF STEW

2 pounds beef chuck, cubed
3 tablespoons all-purpose flour
3 tablespoons shortening
 Salt
¼ teaspoon pepper
6 cups water
12 small white onions, peeled
2 cups diced, peeled yellow turnip
6 carrots, peeled and cut into chunks
4 medium potatoes, peeled and cut
 into quarters
½ cup cooked peas

Dredge meat with flour and brown on all sides in shortening in kettle. Add 2 teaspoons salt, pepper, and water. Bring to boil; simmer, covered, for 1½ hours, or until meat is almost tender. Add remaining ingredients, except peas, and simmer for 45 minutes, or until vegetables are tender. Season with salt to taste, and sprinkle with peas. Makes 6 servings.

HUNGARIAN GOULASH

3 pounds boneless beef chuck
 or 3½ pounds bone-in chuck
3 pounds large onions, cut in wedge-
 shape pieces (about 7 cups)
1 tablespoon salt
½ teaspoon black pepper
 Paprika
 Parsley
 Cooked noodles
 Dairy sour cream

Cut meat into 1-inch cubes, discarding excess fat and bone. Put meat, onions, salt, pepper, and 2 tablespoons paprika in large heavy kettle. (No water is needed.) Cook over medium heat for about 20 minutes, stirring often. Simmer, covered, for 2 hours, stirring occasionally. Uncover and simmer until liquid cooks down to gravy consistency. Garnish with parsley and serve with noodles and a generous dollop of dairy sour cream topped with a sprinkling of paprika. Makes 6 servings.

DAUBE OF BEEF, BÉARNAISE

2½ pounds beef, either rump or chuck
 Bones and trimmings (see below)
3 ounces salt pork
2 tablespoons minced parsley
1 small garlic clove, pureed
¼ teaspoon ground thyme
 Brandy
½ large onion, chopped
1 carrot, chopped
2 cups red wine
 Herb bouquet (bay leaf, 2 parsley
 sprigs, thyme sprig)
2 cups beef stock or bouillon
2 teaspoons salt
 Pepper
2 garlic cloves, sliced
3 onions, sliced
3 carrots, sliced
3 tablespoons rendered beef fat or
 shortening
¼ pound sliced raw or cooked ham
¼ cup all-purpose flour

ENCYCLOPEDIA OF COOKERY

Sauerbraten

Hungarian Goulash

Beef à la Mode

Swiss Steak

Bones and trimmings—When you purchase the meat, tell your butcher that you want 2½ pounds of boneless lean meat, plus some fat and bone. He can tell you how large a piece to buy.

Daube of Beef, Béarnaise—Trim off fat from meat and remove bones. Cut lean meat into 2-inch cubes (large pieces are the secret of a good stew). Cut fat into pieces and put it into a preheated moderate oven (350°F.) until it renders; strain and reserve melted fat. Cover bones and any small trimmings with water and simmer to make a stock.

Larding: Here's where a larding needle is convenient. But first cut salt pork into ¼-inch-thick strips, about 2½ inches long, to make lardoons. Mix together the minced parsley, puréed garlic, thyme, and 1 tablespoon brandy, and roll the lardoons in the mixture. Let stand at least an hour. To lard the meat, insert a lardoon in the open end of your larding needle, pushing it in as far as it will go, then pierce the meat with the pointed end. Carefully draw the needle through the meat; the lardoon should stay in the meat. If it doesn't, try again. (If you don't have a larding needle, make a hole through each cube of meat with a boning knife or strong vegetable knife, or a knitting needle, and poke the lardoon through the hole.)

When all the meat is larded, put it in a bowl with the chopped onion, chopped carrot, wine, herb bouquet, and ¼ cup brandy. Let stand for 2 hours, turning the meat occasionally. Remove meat from marinade and dry carefully on paper towels. Reserve marinade. Add stock, salt, a few grindings of pepper, and the garlic to the marinade, and simmer for 30 minutes. In the meantime, lightly brown the sliced onions and carrots in the rendered fat. Cut ham into squares and arrange on the bottom of a 2½- or 3-quart casserole. Dredge the dry beef in flour and arrange in the casserole in layers, with the browned vegetables. Strain the marinade and stock over the meat, add the herb bouquet, cover casserole closely, and cook in preheated moderate oven (350°F.) for 2 hours. Uncover, discard herb bouquet, skim off every vestige of fat, and taste. Season with more salt if needed and serve with boiled potatoes or crusty bread. Makes 4 to 6 servings.

Note: To remove the fat use a baster or a spoon, tipping the casserole so that the fat collects at one side. Some people use paper towels to blot up the last of it.

PANBROILED ROUND STEAK

2 pounds round steak, 1 inch thick
¼ cup each of cider vinegar and cooking oil
½ teaspoon salt
⅛ teaspoon pepper
All-purpose flour
Fat

Put steak in bowl. Mix all ingredients except last 2 and pour over steak. Let stand for about 5 hours in cool place, turning several times. Drain steak and dredge with flour. Pound well with dull side of knife. Heat small amount of fat in skillet and brown steak quickly on both sides. Makes 6 servings.

CHINESE BEEF WITH MUSHROOMS

2 tablespoons minced onion or 4 green onions, sliced
3 tablespoons cooking oil
1½ pounds lean beef, cut into ¼-inch slivers
2 tablespoons soy sauce
2 cans (4 ounces each) sliced mushrooms, drained, or ½ pound fresh mushrooms, sliced thin

Sauté onion in hot oil until soft. Add beef. Sauté beef for 3 minutes, stirring constantly. Push meat to side of skillet; stir in soy sauce. Add mushrooms and sauté in pan juices until tender. Mix with meat. Cook, covered, over moderate heat for 3 minutes longer. Makes 4 servings.

BRISKET OF BEEF IN HORSERADISH SAUCE

4- pound piece boneless fresh brisket
2 medium onions, sliced
2 carrots
1 celery stalk
2 bay leaves
Salt and pepper
Horseradish Sauce
Chopped parsley

Put meat in heavy kettle. Add onions, carrots, celery, bay leaves, and salt and pepper. Just about cover meat with boiling water. Cover kettle and simmer for 3 to 4 hours, or until meat is tender. Remove, slice, and serve in Horseradish Sauce with a sprinkling of parsley. Makes 6 servings.

Horseradish Sauce

1 onion, chopped
¼ cup butter or margarine
2 tablespoons all-purpose flour
2 cups strained meat stock
½ cup prepared white horseradish
1 cup cider vinegar
2 whole cloves
¼ cup sugar

Sauté onion in butter until golden. Stir in flour. Gradually stir in meat stock. Cook over low heat, stirring constantly, until thick and smooth. Gradually stir in remaining ingredients. Simmer for 10 minutes. Remove cloves and serve.

BRAISED SHORT RIBS OF BEEF, JARDINIÈRE

3 pounds beef short ribs, cut into 3-inch pieces
All-purpose flour
Salt and pepper
2 tablespoons fat
1 cup meat stock or water
2 carrots, diced
½ small rutabaga, diced
4 small onions
½ pound green beans, cut up
Chopped parsley

Dredge meat with flour. Season. Brown on all sides in fat in Dutch oven. Add stock; cover and bake in preheated slow oven (300°F.) for 2 to 3 hours, or until meat is very tender. Baste frequently with liquid in pan. During last hour of cooking, add vegetables. When meat and vegetables are tender, put meat on a hot platter. Arrange vegetables around it; sprinkle with parsley. Makes 4 servings.

BEEF CASSEROLE

2 cups diced, cooked beef
1 can (10¾ ounces) beef gravy
1 can (1 pound) onions, drained
1 package (10 ounces) frozen peas and carrots, cooked
½ cup grated Cheddar cheese

Combine meat, gravy, onions, and peas and carrots. Put in casserole and sprinkle with cheese. Bake in preheated moderate oven (350°F.) for 35 minutes. Makes 4 servings.

SHEPHERD'S BEEF PIE

Combine cut-up cooked beef with gravy. Add cooked peas, carrots, or green beans. Pour hot into a casserole. Make a ring of seasoned mashed potatoes around the edge of the casserole. Bake in preheated hot oven (400°F.) for about 20 minutes.

GROUND BEEF

COCKTAIL MEATBALLS

½ pound ground beef
1 small onion, minced
Dash of garlic salt
½ teaspoon salt
Dash of pepper
1 teaspoon Worcestershire
1 teaspoon soy sauce
1 teaspoon mustard pickle relish
Small pickled onions

Mix all ingredients, except pickled onions. Shape in ½-inch balls. Fry in lightly greased skillet until browned, shaking pan often. Serve with pickled onions on toothpicks. Makes about 3 dozen.

■ **Variation**—Meatballs can be dipped into toasted sesame seeds before serving.

STEAK TARTARE

For each serving allow 6 ounces freshly ground lean round or sirloin steak. Have

Shepherd's Beef Pie

butcher grind meat twice. Handle as little as possible, but arrange each serving in a mound. Make an indentation in each and drop in a raw egg yolk. Garnish with capers or anchovy fillets. Have available Worcestershire sauce, mustard, salt, a pepper mill, bottled thick meat sauce, ketchup, and separate dishes of capers, caraway seeds, and finely chopped onion. Let each guest season his beef to taste. Serve plenty of thinly sliced buttered rye bread or crisp toast.

BASIC MEAT LOAF

2 pounds lean ground beef
2 teaspoons salt
¼ teaspoon pepper
2 eggs
½ cup soft bread crumbs
½ cup milk or other liquid
¼ cup chopped onion

1 teaspoon fresh chopped
  or ¼ teaspoon dried herbs (basil, marjoram, rosemary, sage, savory)
3 or 4 slices of bacon or salt pork
  (optional)

Mix all ingredients except bacon thoroughly, using hands or a heavy-duty electric mixer. If you prefer to use a spoon, beat eggs slightly before adding. Pack into a lightly greased loaf pan (9 x 5 x 3 inches), or form into a loaf on a cookie sheet, top with bacon, and bake in preheated moderate oven (350°F.) for 1 hour, or until the loaf shrinks slightly from the sides of the pan. If you have not covered the top with bacon, it is a good idea to baste it occasionally with equal amounts of melted butter and wine, water, or stock. Serve with a sauce such as mushroom,

tomato, or sour cream, or serve plain. Makes 6 to 8 servings.

BEEF LOAF WITH WINE

2 pounds lean ground beef
½ cup soft bread crumbs
½ cup chopped onion
1 garlic clove, pureed (optional)
2 eggs
2 teaspoons salt
¼ teaspoon pepper
2 teaspoons fresh or ½ teaspoon
  dried tarragon or basil, crushed
¼ cup melted butter
  Red wine

Mix first 8 ingredients together with ¼ cup wine. Pack into a loaf pan lined with wax paper and chill. Turn out on a cookie sheet and score top with the back of a knife. Mix together melted butter and ½ cup wine. Bake loaf in preheated moderate oven (350°F.) for 1 hour,

basting occasionally with butter-wine mixture. Good with mushroom sauce or sour cream. Makes 6 to 8 servings.

INDIVIDUAL BEEF LOAVES
1½ pounds ground beef
1 egg
1 cup soft bread crumbs
½ green pepper, chopped
1 medium onion, chopped
1½ teaspoons salt
¼ teaspoon pepper
¾ cup tomato juice
2 tablespoons all-purpose flour
2 tablespoons fat
2 medium onions, sliced
2 parsley sprigs, chopped
1 beef bouillon cube
½ cup boiling water

Cook loaves on top of the stove. Mix meat, egg, crumbs, green pepper, chopped onion, salt, pepper, and tomato juice. Shape into 6 loaves. Sprinkle with flour. Heat fat in kettle and brown loaves on all sides. Remove loaves and pour off fat. Put sliced onions and parsley in kettle and arrange loaves on top. Dissolve bouillon cube in boiling water. Pour over contents of kettle. Cover kettle and simmer for 30 minutes. Put loaves on hot platter and pour drippings over top. If desired, thicken drippings with flour-and-water paste. Makes 6 servings.

HAMBURGER STEAK
Shape 3 pounds ground beef into an oval steak about 2 inches thick. Put in a shallow pan. Broil top for about 5 minutes. Finish cooking in preheated hot oven (425°F.) for 10 to 20 minutes, or until of desired doneness. To test for doneness, carefully cut into steak. Season with salt and pepper to taste. Makes 8 to 10 servings.

Note: If desired, serve with one of the following sauces: **Curry Butter**—Cream butter and beat in curry powder. **Sour Cream-Horseradish**—Mix dairy sour cream with prepared horseradish and sprinkle with chopped parsley. **Sweet-and-Sour Bacon Relish**—Heat equal parts of vinegar and brown sugar to boiling point. Add chopped drained cooked bacon. Serve hot.

BEEF PATTIES PARMIGIANA
1½ pounds ground beef
1 teaspoon salt
½ teaspoon pepper
1 egg, beaten
2 tablespoons milk
Fine dry bread crumbs
3 tablespoons butter or margarine
1 can (8 ounces) tomato sauce
4 slices Mozzarella cheese
Grated Parmesan cheese

Mix meat, salt, and pepper. Form into 4 patties. Mix egg and milk. Dip patties into mixture, then into crumbs. Fry in butter in broilerproof skillet over medium heat until browned on both sides. Pour tomato sauce over patties and top each with a slice of Mozzarella and a sprinkling of Parmesan. Put under broiler until Mozzarella melts and is slightly browned. Makes 4 servings.

KÖTTBULLAR (Swedish Meatballs)
¼ pound veal
¼ pound fresh pork
1 pound ground beef
1 egg, slightly beaten
1 cup milk
½ cup fine dry bread crumbs
2 tablespoons minced onion
3 tablespoons butter or margarine
1½ teaspoons salt
½ teaspoon pepper
¼ teaspoon ground nutmeg
2 tablespoons all-purpose flour
¾ cup light cream

Have butcher grind veal and pork, or force through a food chopper 3 or 4 times, using medium blade. Grind beef 2 times. Combine egg, milk, and bread crumbs; let stand for a few minutes. Sauté onion in 1 tablespoon butter until brown. Combine soaked crumbs, meats, salt, pepper, and nutmeg. Beat with spoon or with hand until smooth. Shape into 3 dozen balls about 1 inch in diameter. Brown in remaining butter. Pour off most of fat. Sprinkle meatballs with flour and shake pan. Add 1 cup hot water, stirring to loosen all particles and blend well. Cover and simmer for 35 to 40 minutes. Add cream and heat. Serve meat with the gravy. Makes 6 servings.

BEEF AND NOODLES WITH SOUR CREAM AND PAPRIKA
2 tablespoons butter
1 pound ground beef
1 tablespoon instant minced onion
1 garlic clove, minced
½ pound mushrooms, sliced
¼ cup dry red wine
Juice of 1 lemon
2 beef bouillon cubes
1 cup water
2 cups uncooked wide noodles
Salt and pepper
1 cup dairy sour cream
Paprika
Chopped parsley

Melt butter; add beef, onion, garlic, and mushrooms. Sauté until meat loses red color, stirring with fork to break up meat. Add wine, lemon juice, bouillon cubes, and water. Simmer, uncovered, for 10 minutes. Add noodles, cover, and simmer for 15 minutes, or until noodles are tender, adding more water if necessary. Season with salt and pepper. Stir in sour cream and heat gently. Sprinkle with paprika and parsley. Makes 4 servings.

CURRIED BEEF
4 medium onions, minced
1 garlic clove, minced
2 tablespoons butter or margarine
1 pound lean chuck, ground
1 tablespoon all-purpose flour
2 tablespoons chopped raisins
¼ cup chopped blanched almonds
1 teaspoon ground ginger
3 teaspoons curry powder
1 beef bouillon cube
1¼ cups water
1 cup cooked peas
Seasoned salt and pepper to taste
Hot cooked rice

Cook onions and garlic in butter until golden. Add meat and brown lightly, breaking up with fork. Blend in flour. Add next 6 ingredients. Bring to boil and simmer, covered, for 15 minutes, stirring occasionally. Add peas, salt, and pepper, and reheat. Serve on rice. Makes 4 to 6 servings.

VARIETY MEATS

PARSLEY HEARTS OF BEEF
2 beef hearts (about 3 pounds each)
Butter or margarine
2 cups chopped parsley
¾ cup all-purpose flour (about)
½ teaspoon salt
Water or beef bouillon
¼ cup cream
½ cup currant jelly

Cut hearts into halves lengthwise. Carefully remove fat, arteries, veins, blood, and sinews. Wash thoroughly and dry. Cream 6 tablespoons butter. Work in parsley. Stuff hearts with parsley mixture. Sew hearts together. Roll in flour. Melt 6 tablespoons butter. Brown hearts on all sides in hot butter. Add salt and enough water to cover half the hearts. Simmer, covered, for 3 hours, turning occasionally. Remove hearts when tender. Remove thread. Cut into medium-size slices and keep hot. Add or remove enough water to make 2 cups. Stir in 3 tablespoons flour blended with cream until smooth. Cook over low heat, stirring constantly, until thick and smooth. Stir in currant juice. Reheat. Serve sauce over heart slices. Serve with sugar-browned potatoes and vegetables, or pickled beets, or pickled cucumbers. Makes 6 to 8 servings.

Note: The hearts may also be stuffed with a mixture of peeled and cored apples and/or chopped prunes. A 3-pound beef heart will take about 2 cups stuffing. Since the hearts are dry, add 4 tablespoons butter to 2 cups fruit stuffing.

BEEF KIDNEY STEW
1 beef kidney
2 cups water
3 tablespoons cider vinegar
All-purpose flour
Salt and pepper
¼ cup butter or margarine
3 tablespoons olive oil

2 garlic cloves, finely chopped
½ cup onion, finely chopped
1 teaspoon crumbled dried rosemary
1 bay leaf
1 cup red wine

Remove all membrane from kidney and soak kidney in water with vinegar added for 2 hours. Drain kidney and cut into thin slices. Dredge slices with flour seasoned with salt and pepper. Heat butter and olive oil and sauté kidney slices quickly, browning them on both sides. Add garlic and onion and continue cooking for 5 minutes. Add rosemary, bay leaf, and wine. Simmer for 15 minutes, or until kidney slices are tender. Serve with boiled potatoes. Makes 4 servings.

BROILED BEEF LIVER AND BACON

Cut liver ½ inch thick. Brush slices with melted butter or margarine. Place on a rack 3 inches from broiler heat source. Broil for 5 to 6 minutes on each side, using tongs to turn liver slices. Bacon can be broiled at the same time, allowing 3 to 4 minutes for each side. Serve immediately.

PAN-FRIED BEEF LIVER

1 pound beef liver
¼ cup all-purpose flour
2 tablespoons fat
Salt and pepper

Have liver sliced thin. Dip pieces of liver into flour. Heat fat in a skillet. Brown liver slices in hot fat. Season with salt and pepper. Reduce heat and cook over low heat for 10 to 15 minutes. Serve with browned onions and crisp bacon strips. Makes 4 to 6 servings.

■ **To Brown Onions**—Sauté 2 or 3 large sweet onions in ¼ cup bacon fat or shortening. Stir onions occasionally and sauté until they are an even brown color.

VENETIAN BEEF LIVER WITH ONIONS

1½ pounds beef liver
¼ cup butter
2 tablespoons olive oil
4 medium onions, minced
¼ cup dry white wine
Salt and pepper
1 teaspoon fresh lemon juice
2 tablespoons chopped parsley

Cut liver into paper-thin 2-inch slices while partially frozen. In skillet, heat together butter and olive oil. Sauté onions until soft and golden. Add wine and cook for 2 minutes. Add liver and fry quickly over high heat until browned on both sides. Season with salt and pepper. Add lemon juice. Sprinkle with parsley. Serve immediately. Makes 4 servings.
Note: ¼ cup bouillon may be used instead of the wine. In this case, increase lemon juice to 1 tablespoon.

POTTED LIVER, DANISH STYLE

2 large carrots, thinly sliced
3 medium-size onions, sliced
¼ pound salt pork or Danish bacon, cubed
1¼ pounds liver, cut into ½-inch slices
All-purpose flour
¼ cup butter or margarine
Salt and pepper
1 cup heavy cream
½ cup chopped parsley

Cook carrots and onions with salt pork or bacon until tender, stirring occasionally. Do not brown. Dredge liver with flour. In another pan, heat butter and cook liver in it until browned on all sides, about 5 minutes. Add salt and pepper to taste. Combine vegetables, liver, and the pan juices in one skillet. Simmer, covered, over low heat for about 10 minutes. Add cream and bring just to a gentle boil. Sprinkle with parsley and serve in casserole with boiled potatoes on the side. Makes 4 to 6 servings.

BEEF BONE MARROW, POACHED

Have large marrow bones split or cut into 1½-inch slices. With a sharp pointed knife carefully remove marrow. Cut marrow into ½-inch slices. Poach in a small amount of stock or salted water for 1½ to 2 minutes, or until marrow is translucent. Do not overcook, since the high fat content will cause it to disintegrate.

Or, without removing marrow, simmer pieces or slices of bones in salted water or stock until marrow pulls away from the bone. Remove gently and cut into slices. Serve marrow slices on toast sprinkled with salt and pepper, or serve as a garnish with meat.

BEEF BONE MARROW, ROASTED

Have marrow bones split and cut into 4-inch lengths. Put in a shallow baking pan and roast in a preheated slow oven (300°F.) for 1 hour. Serve on a napkin with slices of hot toast. Or carefully remove marrow, slice, and serve as suggested in Beef Bone Marrow, Poached.

MARROW BALLS

¼ cup fresh marrow
2 tablespoons butter, softened
3 eggs, beaten
¼ teaspoon salt
⅛ teaspoon paprika
Cracker crumbs

Beat marrow until creamy. Beat in butter. Stir in eggs, salt, and paprika. Add enough cracker crumbs, about ½ cup, to make mixture stiff enough to shape into balls. Roll mixture into small balls about the shape of a walnut. Drop balls into simmering soup and simmer for 15 minutes, or until balls rise to surface of soup. Use as soup garnish. Makes about 4 servings.

OXTAIL SOUP

1 oxtail
1 large onion
1 tablespoon fat
2 carrots, chopped
½ cup chopped lean ham or beef
1 thyme sprig
1 parsley sprig
1 bay leaf
3 whole cloves
1 garlic clove
1 tablespoon all-purpose flour
2 quarts beef consomme or water
3 tablespoons pearl barley
Salt, pepper, cayenne
2 tablespoons sherry

Cut oxtail into joints. Chop onion and sauté in hot fat until golden. Add oxtail pieces and brown slowly. Add carrots and ham. When mixture browns, add thyme, parsley, bay leaf, cloves, and garlic, all chopped very fine. Continue to brown; stir in flour. Add consommé and barley. Lower heat and simmer, covered, for about 4 hours, or until meat is tender. Season to taste with salt, pepper, and cayenne. Add sherry when ready to serve. Makes about 8 to 10 servings.

OXTAILS À LA BOURGEOISIE

2 oxtails
2 onions, chopped
1 tablespoon butter
½ cup chopped cooked ham
2 carrots, diced
1 white turnip, diced
1 garlic clove, minced
Pinch of thyme
1 bay leaf
2 beef bouillon cubes
2 cups water
Salt and pepper to taste
1 cup cooked peas

Have oxtails cut up. Brown with onion in hot butter. Add ham, carrots, and turnip. Cook until lightly browned. Add remaining ingredients except peas. Cover and simmer over low heat for about 3 hours, or until meat is tender. Add peas and reheat slightly. Makes 6 to 8 servings.

BOILED TONGUE

1 tongue, corned or smoked
1 onion stuck with 3 whole cloves
2 bay leaves
3 celery stalks with leaves
1 slice of parsnip
Few parsley sprigs
10 peppercorns

Soak tongue overnight in enough water to cover. Drain. Add enough water to cover tongue. Add remaining ingredients. Bring to a boil, cover, and simmer until tongue is tender, 45 minutes to 1 hour per pound. Smoked tongue requires a longer cooking time than corned tongue. Cool tongue in stock. Trim off bone and gristle at thick end. Slit skin down length of tongue and pull off skin. Slice tongue and serve with a sauce. Makes 6 to 8 servings.

COLOMBIAN TONGUE

1 smoked beef tongue, about 3 pounds
  Water
1 bay leaf
1 garlic clove
½ teaspoon peppercorns
1 onion, minced
1 tablespoon butter
1 tablespoon all-purpose flour
1 can (3 ounces) chopped
  mushrooms, drained
  Few parsley sprigs, chopped
¾ cup red wine

Simmer tongue, covered, in water to cover with seasonings for 3 hours, or until very tender. Remove tongue from liquid and discard skin and bones. Keep tongue hot in liquid, or cool and reheat. Sauté onion in butter until golden. Blend in flour. Gradually stir in 1 cup tongue broth. Add remaining ingredients. Cook over low heat, stirring constantly, for 10 minutes. Serve as a sauce for sliced tongue. Makes 8 to 10 servings.

TRIPE LYONNAISE

1 pound tripe
½ teaspoon salt
¼ teaspoon white pepper
  Butter
3 medium onions, sliced
1 tablespoon vinegar
1 tablespoon chopped parsley

Wash tripe and place in Dutch oven or large heavy saucepan. Cover with water. Add salt and pepper. Bring to a boil, lower heat, and simmer for 4 hours, or until tripe is tender. Drain and cut tripe into pieces. Melt 1 tablespoon butter in large skillet. Add tripe pieces to hot butter. Sauté for 20 minutes, or until tripe is well browned. In another skillet melt 1 tablespoon butter. Add onions and sauté until lightly browned. Combine tripe and onions in a serving dish. Add vinegar to pan in which tripe was cooked and cook, stirring constantly, for 3 minutes over medium heat. Pour over tripe. Sprinkle with chopped parsley. Makes 4 servings.

CURED BEEF

CORNED BEEF

8 cups water
1 cup salt
¼ cup sugar
1 bay leaf
6 peppercorns
1 garlic clove, minced
1 tablespoon whole mixed pickling
  spices
5 to 6 pounds beef brisket or rump

Mix all ingredients except meat in a crock. Add meat, cover with a plate, and put a heavy weight on top. Let meat stand in brine for 36 hours. Beef brisket is best for this, but rump can be used.

BAKED SPICY CORNED BEEF

4 pounds corned brisket of beef
1 tablespoon whole mixed pickling spice
1 celery stalk
1 onion
1 carrot
⅓ cup firmly packed light brown sugar
1 tablespoon prepared mustard
½ cup sweet-pickle juice or fruit juice

Wash corned beef and put in large kettle. Cover with boiling water. Add pickling spice, celery, onion, and carrot. Cover and simmer for 4 to 4½ hours, or until tender. Cool beef in broth; then put in shallow roasting pan and score fat layer. Mix brown sugar and mustard; pat on beef. Pour pickle juice into pan. Bake in preheated slow oven (300°F.) for 1 hour, basting from time to time with some of the drippings in pan. Slice, and serve hot or cold. Makes 8 servings.

Corned Beef Baked in Sherry

Follow recipe above, substituting ½ cup sherry for the sweet-pickle juice.

QUICK HASH PATTIES

2 cans (1 pound each) corned-beef or
  roast-beef hash
  Chili sauce or ketchup
½-inch strips of processed American
  cheese

Chill hash. Then remove both ends from cans. Push out hash and cut into 6 slices. Put slices on lightly greased shallow pan and broil until browned. Spread with chili sauce or ketchup and crisscross 2 strips of cheese over top of each. Broil until cheese is slightly melted. Makes 3 or 4 servings.

RED-FLANNEL HASH

2 cups chopped cooked corned beef
  or 1 can (12 ounces) corned beef,
  chopped
1 cup chopped cooked peeled potatoes
1 cup chopped cooked beets
1 tablespoon instant minced onion
¼ cup meat stock
  Salt and pepper
2 tablespoons butter or margarine

Mix all ingredients except butter. Melt butter in heavy skillet. Add hash mixture and spread evenly. Cook slowly, covered, until browned on the bottom, for about 30 minutes. Fold and turn out on platter. If browning is not desired, stir hash during the cooking. Makes 4 servings.

HASH LYONNAISE

1 tablespoon fat
2 medium onions, sliced
2 cans (1 pound each) corned-beef or
  roast-beef hash

Melt fat in skillet; add onions and cook for a few minutes. Add hash, mix well, and sauté until brown. Makes 4 servings.

CREAMED DRIED BEEF ON BOILED POTATOES

4 medium potatoes, peeled
1 jar (5 ounces) dried beef
¼ cup butter or margarine
¼ cup all-purpose flour
⅛ teaspoon pepper
2 cups heavy cream

Cook potatoes in boiling salted water until tender; drain. Meanwhile, sauté beef in butter in skillet for 3 minutes. Blend in flour and pepper. Remove from heat and stir in cream gradually. Return to low heat and cook until thickened, stirring constantly. Serve on hot potatoes. Makes 4 servings.

SAUCES

MEAT SAUCE FOR SPAGHETTI

2 onions, chopped
2 garlic cloves, minced
2 tablespoons cooking oil
½ pound ground beef
½ pound ground pork
4⅔ cups (two 1-pound, 3-ounce cans)
  tomatoes
1½ cups tomato puree
¼ cup chopped parsley
1 green pepper, chopped
2 leaves fresh or dried basil
½ teaspoon grated lemon rind
½ teaspoon crumbled dried thyme
2 to 3 teaspoons salt
¼ teaspoon pepper
¼ teaspoon crushed red pepper

In large saucepan sauté onions and garlic in hot oil until golden. Add beef and pork and cook until lightly browned but still red inside, stirring to break up meat. Add tomatoes and purée; bring to boil and simmer for 20 minutes. Add remaining ingredients and simmer, uncovered, for 1½ hours, stirring occasionally. Makes enough sauce for 1 pound spaghetti, cooked, or for 8 servings.

STEAK SAUCES (for 4 servings)

Butter and Cream Sauce—Melt ⅓ cup butter or margarine and add ½ cup heavy cream, ⅓ cup steak sauce, ½ teaspoon salt, dash of cayenne, ¼ cup chopped parsley, and ¼ teaspoon onion salt or garlic salt.

Herb Butter—Combine ½ cup softened butter or margarine, 2 tablespoons each of minced parsley, celery tops, green onion tops, or chives, and one of the following: 1 teaspoon minced fresh (or ½ teaspoon dried) rosemary, marjoram, basil, savory, dill, or thyme.

Mushroom Sauce—Lightly brown ½ pound sliced mushrooms in 3 tablespoons butter or margarine. Stir in 2 tablespoons flour; let brown slightly. Add 1¼ cups cold water, or vegetable cooking water, 2 bouillon cubes, ⅛ teaspoon pepper. Cook until slightly thickened, stirring often. Add salt if needed.

Red and Green Sauce—Heat together ½ cup margarine or butter, 3 tablespoons cider vinegar, 3 tablespoons tomato paste, ¼ teaspoon cayenne, 2 teaspoons dry mustard, ¼ teaspoon garlic salt, ½ teaspoon salt, 1 tablespoon sugar, and ¼ cup minced parsley.

Savory Butter—Combine ½ cup softened butter or margarine, 2 tablespoons ketchup, 1 tablespoon Worcestershire, dash of hot pepper sauce, and 1 tablespoon grated onion.

Spiked Chili Sauce—Heat 1 bottle chili sauce with 2 tablespoons prepared horseradish, ¼ teaspoon hot pepper sauce, 1 tablespoon Worcestershire, and 2 tablespoons lemon juice.

THREE SAUCES FOR TONGUE

Prepare one of these spirited sauces in a skillet; add tongue slices and simmer just enough to heat through

Sauce Indienne

½ cup mango chutney
1 can (10½ ounces) beef gravy
1 tablespoon fresh lemon juice
½ tablespoon sugar
½ teaspoon curry powder
1 teaspoon Worcestershire

Combine all ingredients. Taste and season as you like. Sauce should be spicy, not fiery. Mix well, bring to boil, and simmer for a few minutes, to blend the flavors. Makes about 1¾ cups.
Note: This English classic is good hot or cool.

Cumberland Sauce

1 cup red currant jelly
¼ cup red wine
    Juice of 1 lemon
    Grated rind of 1 orange
1 teaspoon paprika
½ teaspoon ground ginger
½ teaspoon dry mustard

Combine all ingredients. Cook over low heat until jelly melts, stirring to blend thoroughly. Garnish with pineapple slices and whole canned apricots. Makes about 1½ cups.

Sauce Polonaise

2 tablespoons butter
2 tablespoons all-purpose flour
2¼ cups beef bouillon or consomme
¼ cup slivered blanched almonds
¼ cup raisins
2 teaspoons bottled sauce for gravy
    Juice of 1 small lemon
1 tablespoon sugar
½ cup red wine
    Salt and pepper to taste

Melt butter; stir in flour; gradually stir in liquid. Cook over low heat, stirring constantly, until smooth and thickened. Add remaining ingredients. Simmer for 10 minutes, stirring frequently. Makes about 3 cups.

BEER—A foamy, fermented beverage brewed from a malted cereal, with hops added. The introduction of hops came in the 15th century in England, whereas the brewing of beer goes back for thousands of years. Beer can be and has been brewed from a great variety of grains, such as wheat, millet, barley, and rice.

Brewing is one of the oldest occupations of mankind, and we have records that beer was enjoyed as long as 5,000 years ago by the ancient Babylonians, Egyptians, and Chinese. Egyptian papyri of around 1300 B.C. tell us of beer-shop regulations by the authorities to prevent overindulgence. Columbus, when he came to America, was presented with a form of beer made from corn. In England, beer was the common drink of all classes when tea was not yet known. Every household brewed its own, and old cook books give us the rules for small beer, for cottagers' beer, etc. But let us not make the mistake of thinking of the people of the past as nothing but imbibers. Imbibe they did, enjoying the process, but they also needed a beverage that could be used in lieu of water, which was seldom fit to drink in towns and villages. Beer fulfilled this need before tea or coffee, just as tea with its boiled water was the way the Chinese purified their water.

Beer was the common drink of the Anglo-Saxon and Scandinavian countries, where the grape would not grow because of the northern climate, and it was their substitute for wine, the ordinary drink of the southern countries. Beer is so much part of the life, the folklore, the literature, and the arts of these countries that volumes could be filled quoting examples, from the heroic feasts of the Vikings to the extremely scientific brewing methods of our day.

Today's American beer is brewed from barley which has been germinated in water and dried, and cereal adjuncts such as corn or rye, and hops, the dried cones of the hop vine. In addition, cultured yeast is needed for the fermentation which creates beer's characteristic sparkle, as is pure filtered water which, by volume, makes up about nine tenths of the finished beer. The importance of the water is not to be underestimated; the fame of Irish Guinness stout is due, so it is said, to the excellence of Dublin water. Local beers in various countries also rose to fame because of the water with which they were made.

There are many varieties of beer, including ale, porter, and stout. By far the most popular one, accounting for ninety per cent of America's beer production, is lager. The word lager comes from the German and means "to store," and that is exactly what lager beer is, namely, beer stored for various periods of time to age or mellow. The alcoholic content of the majority of American beers is on the average three and one half per cent by weight, and seldom more than five per cent by weight, which is a low alcoholic content compared to spirits or to wines.

Beer is sometimes used in cooking, interchangeably with ale, especially in dishes with cheese and with certain seafoods and meats. When cooked, the alcohol evaporates completely.

SHRIMPS COOKED IN BEER

Shell and devein shrimps before cooking. Drop shrimps into boiling beer and water, using 3 parts stale beer to 1 part water. Use 1 tablespoon salt for each quart water, a few peppercorns, 1 or 2 bay leaves, and a sprinkling of celery seed. Simmer, covered, for 2 to 5 minutes, or until shrimps are pink. Drain, cool, and serve. No sauce is needed when shrimps are cooked this way.

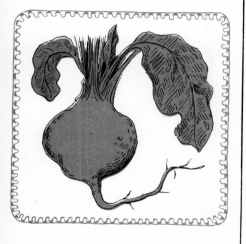

BEET—This vegetable is the enlarged red root of a plant which is a member of the *Beta* genus and first cousin to chard. In their wild state, beets seem to have originated in the Mediterranean, where they have been known since Christian times. Beet greens, the tops of the plants, are also edible, and some varieties are purposely grown for this. Beets are also grown for sugar.

Availability—The peak season is June, July, August. Available in smaller amounts the rest of the year. The chief sources are California, New Jersey, Ohio, Pennsylvania, Colorado.

Beets are available canned and in jars, whole, diced, and sliced in various ways. Harvard beets and pickled beets are also available.

Purchasing Guide—Sold in small bunches with tops, or with tops removed, or completely trimmed and wrapped in plastic.

Look for beets with a good globular shape, which are smooth and firm to the touch. Small and medium-size beets are usually the most tender.

Beet tops, frequently taken from young plants and sold for greens, should be fresh and unwilted.

Storage—Put beets, with or without tops, in refrigerator. Do not pack tightly.

☐ Refrigerator shelf or vegetable compartment, uncooked: 1 month
☐ Refrigerator frozen-food compartment, prepared for freezing: 1 month
☐ Freezer, prepared for freezing: 9 to 12 months

Nutritive Food Values—Beets have small amounts of vitamins and minerals. Beet greens are an excellent source of vitamin A and calcium.

☐ Greens, 3½ ounces, cooked, boiled, and drained = 18 calories
☐ Beets, 3½ ounces, cooked, boiled, and drained = 32 calories
☐ Canned beets, 3½ ounces = 34 calories

Basic Preparation—Cut off the tops about 2 inches from the beets (to keep color loss at a minimum during cooking). Young fresh tops that are in good condition may be washed and saved to use in salads or to cook for greens.

☐ **To Boil**—Cook whole and unpeeled, covered, in boiling salted water to cover until tender, for 30 to 40 minutes, depending on size. Then drain, but save a little of the cooking water for future use. Cool slightly, or let a little cold water run over them, and slip off the skins, stems, and roots by rubbing with the fingers. Beets may then be served whole (small ones), or sliced, diced, or cut into shreds. Season to taste and reheat in a little of the cooking water, adding butter or margarine and lemon juice or vinegar. Or, use in preparing other recipes such as Pickled or Glazed Beets, Beets in Orange Sauce, or Harvard Beets.

☐ **To Bake**—Place beets as prepared for boiling in a shallow pan; brush beets with oil. Bake in preheated moderate oven (350°F.) for 1 hour, or until tender. Peel beets as above. Season with salt, pepper, butter or margarine, and a little lemon juice.

The red pigment in beets is more stable when an acid is added. That's why vinegar or lemon juice is sometimes used. This adds flavor, too.

☐ **To Cook Beet Tops**—Use washed young tender greens in salad.

Cut older leaves into shreds. Add just enough water to cover the greens. Sprinkle with salt. Cook, covered, for 15 to 20 minutes, or until greens are tender. Drain and serve with butter.

☐ **To Freeze**—Use smooth tender beets of small to medium size. Remove green tops and wash thoroughly. Cook beets in boiling water until tender. Drain and chill in ice water. Remove skins. Slice and dice. Package, allowing ½-inch headspace, and freeze.

POLISH BORSCH

1½ pounds beef chuck, cut up
1½ quarts water
4 medium beets, cooked and sliced
2 celery stalks, diced
1 onion, minced
  Salt and pepper
¼ cup dairy sour cream
2 tablespoons all-purpose flour
1 egg

Put meat in kettle and add water. Bring to boil and simmer, covered, for 1½ to 2 hours, or until meat is almost tender. Add beets, celery, and onion; cook for about 30 minutes longer. Season to taste. Blend sour cream, flour, and egg. Stir into soup; bring again to boil. Serve in soup bowls and pass boiled potatoes. Makes 4 servings.

BEETS AND GREENS

8 small beets with leaves
½ cup boiling water
1 teaspoon salt
1½ tablespoons bacon fat
1 tablespoon vinegar
⅛ teaspoon pepper

Beets should be young and tender. Wash beets and leaves thoroughly. Cut out tough parts of stems; keep leaves whole. Put beets in saucepan with leaves on top. Add boiling water and salt; cover and cook for 10 to 15 minutes, or until beets are tender. Peel beets and leave whole. Add to greens. Add fat, vinegar, and pepper. Makes 4 servings.

GLAZED BEETS

Melt 3 tablespoons butter in saucepan. Add 2½ cups drained cooked baby beets and shake pan to coat beets. Cook over low heat for about 3 minutes. Sprinkle with about 1 tablespoon sugar and shake again. Makes 4 servings.

SCANDINAVIAN PICKLED BEETS

½ cup cider vinegar
1 onion, sliced
¼ cup sugar
¼ teaspoon salt
¼ teaspoon peppercorns
1 bay leaf, crumbled
2 cups (one 1-pound can) beets, sliced

Combine all ingredients except beets with ½ cup liquid drained from beets. Add beets and bring to boil. For a sweeter pickle, add more sugar. Serve hot or cold. Makes 6 servings.

BEIGNET—This is the French word for fritter. *Beignets* may be of many different kinds. Some *beignets* are bits of meat, poultry, fish, vegetables, fruits, rice, etc., which are dipped into a batter and then fried in deep fat. Other *beignets* (sweet or not) are made from the same kind of batter of which éclairs are, with or without flavorings such as cheese, and then dropped by the spoonful into deep fat and fried. Yet another kind of *beignet* is a molded little sweet cookie, which is baked.

CHEESE BEIGNETS

½ cup water
3 tablespoons butter
½ cup all-purpose flour
2 eggs
4 tablespoons grated Parmesan, Swiss, or sharp Cheddar cheese
1 teaspoon salt
⅛ teaspoon pepper
1 egg white, stiffly beaten
Fat for deep frying

Combine water and butter in saucepan and bring to a boil. Remove from heat. Add flour, all at once. Beat until glossy and dough clears sides of pan. Beat in eggs, one at a time, beating well after each addition. Add cheese, salt, and pepper. Fold in beaten egg white. Drop from teaspoon into hot deep fat (365°F. on frying thermometer). Brown on all sides. Remove from fat and drain on paper towel. Serve very hot. Excellent with drinks, soups, or salads. Makes about 3 dozen small *beignets*.

Belgian Cookery

A rich, varied, and distinctive national cuisine proclaims a robust love of life

BELGIAN COOKERY— Belgium nestles between France, Germany, the Netherlands, and the Duchy of Luxembourg, and has a coastline on the North Sea. Two peoples live in it, the Flemish and the Walloons, each with separate traditions, and each great contributors to European civilization by way of paintings, architecture, and marvelous food. Belgian food reflects these two strains, as well as the best foods of the surrounding countries. On every level of life, food has an enormous importance; this has not changed since Brueghel and the Flemish still-life painters of the 16th and 17th centuries heaped their canvases with lovingly painted fruits and vegetables, shellfish, meats, and game.

Belgian food has an opulence of its own. It is richer and more varied than French food, proclaiming a robust love of life. Among the meats, you find the smoked ham of the Ardennes, the *carbonnades flamandes*, the pork and beer stews of Ghent, Bruges, and all of Flanders, and the savory ways of cooking tongue. Game and poultry are popular. Fish, lobsters, and oysters, and all the foods of the sea, appear constantly on Belgian tables. Eel and mussels might be called the national favorites, and mussels and French-fries are as Belgian as Brussels sprouts. French-fries are the staff of life for many a citizen, and are eaten out-of-hand from pushcarts every hour of the night or day.

Belgian vegetables, also found in our American markets, both fresh and canned, enjoy well-deserved worldwide fame. No visitor to Belgium should fail to feast his eyes on the still lifes in the windows of Belgium's luxury food shops. Tender, pale asparagus from Mechlin, juicy from ivory stem to jade tip, tiny Brussels sprouts, large blue or green grapes, peaches, pears, and strawberries from Belgium's miles of hothouses are presented like jewels in individual boxes. And Belgian endives—one of the finest of all vegetables known to man—abundant in our markets, can be grown only in Belgium with success.

The number of pastries, cakes, and cookies is great, and they are usually made in bakeries and *confiseries*. Gingerbread is molded for St. Nicholas' Day in antique wooden molds, sometimes as high as six feet. Whatever their size, many of them are museum pieces.

The national drink of Belgium is beer —many varieties of beer—and you can sit for hours in a *brasserie,* reading a paper or a book, sipping beer or the strong, pungent coffee which is an integral part of Belgian life.

GENTSCHE WATERZOOI (Fish Soup)
1 pound fish (carp, perch, etc.)
1 pound eel
1 quart water
2 cups white wine
1 carrot, cut up
1 medium onion, diced
3 cloves
1 bay leaf
1 parsley sprig
1 tarragon sprig (optional)
Dash of white pepper
Salt to taste
1 lemon, sliced and seeded

Cut fish and eel into equal-size pieces about 1 inch square. Put water and wine into kettle with carrot, onion, cloves, bay leaf, parsley, and tarragon, if desired; bring to boil and simmer for 30 minutes. Strain, add fish, and simmer for 20 minutes, or until fish is done. Season with white pepper and salt. Five minutes before the soup is done, add lemon slices. Serve with thin bread-and-butter sandwiches. Makes 6 servings.

MORUE OU CABILLAUD À LA FLAMANDE
(Codfish or Halibut, Flemish Style)
8 dried codfish steaks or 8 halibut steaks
2 lemons, peeled and sliced
2 medium onions, sliced
Salt and pepper
⅛ teaspoon ground allspice
½ cup dry white wine
2 tablespoons fine dry bread crumbs
3 tablespoons grated cheese
½ cup butter
2 tablespoons chopped parsley

If dried codfish steaks are used, soak in cold water overnight. Place fish in a well-greased oblong baking dish. Steaks should lie side by side, overlapping slightly. Top fish with lemon and onion slices. Season with salt and pepper to taste. Dried codfish steaks will require less salt. Sprinkle with allspice. Pour wine over fish. Combine bread crumbs with grated cheese and sprinkle over fish. Dot with butter. Bake, uncovered, in preheated moderate oven (350°F.) for 25 minutes, or until fish flakes. Sprinkle with parsley before serving. Makes 6 servings.

PORC À LA FLAMANDE (Flemish Pork)
1 tablespoon butter
2 pounds pork shoulder, diced
Salt and pepper
2 cups beer
½ cup boiling water
1 teaspoon crushed dried rosemary
4 onions, halved
2 cups bouillon
2 packages frozen Brussels sprouts
2 cups cooked sliced potatoes
1¾ cups cooked sliced carrots
¼ cup all-purpose flour
2 tablespoons water

Melt butter in large kettle and brown pork shoulder in it. Sprinkle with salt and pepper. Add beer, water, and rosemary. Simmer, covered, for 45 minutes. Add onions and cook for 30 minutes. Stir in bouillon and Brussels sprouts. Cover and cook until sprouts are tender, about 10 minutes. Add potatoes and carrots. Blend flour and water to a smooth paste. Slowly stir into pork mixture. Cook until liquid is thickened,

stirring occasionally. Makes 6 to 8 servings.

CARBONNADE FLAMANDE
(Flemish Beer Stew)
1 pound onions, thinly sliced
¼ cup butter
2½ pounds round steak, cubed
1 garlic clove, minced
⅛ teaspoon each of ground nutmeg and thyme
1 teaspoon salt
½ teaspoon pepper
1 quart light beer
2 tablespoons butter
2 tablespoons all-purpose flour
1 tablespoon sugar

In Dutch oven or flameproof casserole, sauté onions in half the butter until soft and golden. Remove onions and reserve. Melt remaining butter in the same Dutch oven or casserole. Brown beef on all sides; it must be a deep brown. Return onions to cooking pot. Add garlic, nutmeg, thyme, salt and pepper, and beer. Bring to a boil. Reduce heat and simmer, covered, for 1½ hours, or until meat is tender. Place meat in another saucepan and keep hot. Knead butter and flour together with fingertips to make balls the size of a pea. Drop into pan juices and stir until thoroughly blended. Stir in sugar. Cook, uncovered, over medium heat for about 5 minutes, stirring frequently. Return meat to sauce and heat through. Serve with boiled potatoes. Makes 6 servings.

WATERZOOI DE POULET (Chicken Stew)
1 veal bone
2 medium onions
1 leek
3 celery stalks
1 bay leaf
2 quarts water
1 stewing chicken (about 4 pounds)
2 tablespoons butter or margarine
2 tablespoons all-purpose flour
2 egg yolks
½ cup light cream
Salt and pepper
1½ cups cooked tiny onions
1 cup cooked julienne carrots
8 small boiled potatoes
Minced parsley

Cook veal bone with onions, leek, celery, and bay leaf in water for 1½ hours. Cut chicken into serving pieces and add. Simmer for 1½ hours, or until tender. Remove chicken and keep warm. Strain stock. If there is more than 2½ cups, cook it down to that amount. Melt butter and blend in flour. Gradually stir in stock and cook over low heat, stirring constantly, until thickened. Mix egg yolks into cream, add a little sauce, mix well, then stir into remaining sauce. Do not allow this to boil. Season to taste. Add onions, carrots, and potatoes. Place chicken on hot dish and pour sauce with vegetables over it. Sprinkle with parsley. Makes 4 servings.

CANARD À LA BRUXELLOISE
(Duck à la Brussels)
One 4- to 5-pound duck

BELGIAN COOKERY

¼ pound bacon, thickly sliced and diced
1 pair sweetbreads, blanched and chopped
1 tablespoon butter
1 teaspoon salt
¼ teaspoon pepper
1 tablespoon minced parsley
1 tablespoon minced chives or onion
¼ cup canned mushrooms, drained and chopped
½ cup dry white wine
1 carrot
1 medium onion
1 tablespoon all-purpose flour
1 tablespoon butter

Wash and dry duck, inside and out. Combine bacon, sweetbreads, butter, salt, pepper, parsley, chives, and mushrooms. Stuff duck with mixture. Truss duck. Place in roasting pan. Add white wine, carrot, and onion. Roast duck to desired doneness. Allow 1¼ hours for rare duck, 1½ hours for medium rare, and about 2 hours for very well-done duck. Most people prefer their duck medium-rare. Prick skin often during roasting to drain off excess fat.

Remove duck to heated platter. Carve and keep hot. Skim excess fat from pan juices. Place pan over direct heat. Reduce pan liquid to about half. Knead flour and butter together with fingertips to make balls the size of a pea. Drop into pan juices and stir until thoroughly blended. Cook, uncovered, for 3 minutes, stirring constantly. Pour sauce over carved duck. Garnish platter with carrots, peas, and cauliflowerets. Makes 4 servings.

OEUFS À L'OIGNON (Eggs and Onions)

3 tablespoons butter or margarine
2 large onions, thinly sliced
2 tablespoons all-purpose flour
1 cup chicken bouillon
1 teaspoon salt
½ teaspoon pepper
⅛ teaspoon ground nutmeg
2 tablespoons heavy cream or undiluted evaporated milk
1 tablespoon fresh lemon juice
6 hard-cooked eggs, cut into quarters lengthwise

Heat butter in heavy skillet. Add onions and cook over lowest possible heat until tender, stirring constantly. Do not allow onions to brown. Stir flour into onions. Increase heat and brown onions and flour slightly. Gradually stir in chicken bouillon. Cook, stirring constantly, until sauce thickens. Add salt, pepper, and nutmeg. Cook for 3 minutes, stirring constantly. Remove from heat and add cream, lemon juice, and eggs. Place mixture in greased shallow baking dish. Bake in preheated moderate oven (350°F.) for 15 minutes. Serve with home-fried potatoes. Makes 4 servings.

SALADE AUX ENDIVES ET BETTERAVES (Endive and Beet Salad)

4 large Belgian endives, cut into ½-inch pieces
2 large cooked beets, peeled and shredded
½ cup French dressing

Pain d'Amandes
(Brussels Almond Bread Cookies)

Salade Aux Endives
et Betteraves
(Endive and Beet Salad)

Porc à la Flamande
(Flemish Pork)

Just before serving, combine all ingredients and toss well. Makes 4 to 6 servings. **Note:** Do not assemble salad before serving time, or endives will discolor.

SALADE LIÈGEOISE
(Hot Green-Bean Salad with Potatoes)
4 large Idaho potatoes
1 pound fresh green beans
2 tablespoons butter
1 cup beef bouillon
¼ pound sliced bacon
1 tablespoon minced onion
⅛ teaspoon dried rosemary
¼ teaspoon pepper
2 tablespoons vinegar
½ pound Canadian bacon, cooked

Peel and wash potatoes. Slice as for French-fries. Break green beans into 2-inch pieces. Melt butter in heavy saucepan. Add potatoes, beans, and bouillon. Simmer, covered, over low heat for 45 to 60 minutes, or until vegetables are very tender. Stir frequently. Cook bacon slices and drain; reserve ½ cup bacon fat. Heat bacon fat and add onion, rosemary, pepper, and vinegar. Pour over vegetables. Crumble bacon slices and sprinkle over mixture. Toss like a salad. Serve surrounded by Canadian bacon. Makes 6 servings.

GAUFRES BRUXELLOISES
(Brussels Beer Waffles)
3½ cups sifted all-purpose flour
½ teaspoon salt
½ cup cooking oil
1½ pints light beer
2 eggs
2 tablespoons grated lemon rind
1 teaspoon fresh lemon juice
½ teaspoon vanilla extract

Combine all ingredients in a deep bowl. Beat until smooth. Let stand at room temperature for 2 hours to rise slightly. Or, if for breakfast, store unrisen in refrigerator overnight and use without further rising. Spread batter on waffle iron; use only a small quantity to insure crispness. Watch while baking; waffles brown quickly. The beer acts as a leavening and leaves no trace whatsoever in these light, crisp waffles. Good with sour cream and brown sugar. Makes 14 to 16 waffles.

POIRES CUITES (Baked Pears)
8 large Seckel or Bosc pears
¼ cup butter or margarine, softened
Vanilla Sugar

Wash and dry pears. Rub skins all over with softened butter. Place on a baking sheet. Bake in preheated slow oven (300°F.) for about 40 minutes, or until soft. Sprinkle with Vanilla Sugar. Serve hot or cold, with a custard sauce, or plain. Makes 8 servings.

Vanilla Sugar
Combine 2 whole vanilla beans with 1 pound granulated or confectioners' sugar. Place this in an airtight container and cover. Let stand for 1 week. The sugar will have a delightful vanilla fragrance and taste.

PAIN D'AMANDES
(Brussels Almond Bread Cookies)
4½ cups sifted all-purpose flour
1 teaspoon baking powder
1 teaspoon ground cinnamon
⅛ teaspoon salt
2 cups blanched almonds, grated
1¼ cups firmly packed light brown sugar
⅓ cup brandy
⅔ cup milk
½ pound butter or margarine, melted

Sift flour, baking powder, cinnamon, and salt into a mixing bowl. Add grated almonds and brown sugar. Pour in brandy, milk, and melted butter. Mix thoroughly with the hands until dough feels like clay. Shape into a roll. Wrap in wax paper. Chill overnight. Slice cookies ¼ inch thick and place on buttered cookie sheet. Bake in preheated moderate oven (375°F.) for 10 minutes. Remove from pan immediately. Cool on wire rack. Makes about 60 cookies.

BERGAMOT—The name is used for three very different plants: 1—A native American herb, *Monarda,* which belongs to the mint family. It is a perennial with soft foliage and dense clusters of purple flowers and grows to two to three feet. The leaves have a pleasant lemon scent. There are several varieties of the herb bergamot, and the best known one is the *Monarda didyma,* a native of our eastern states commonly known as "Oswego tea," from the tribe of Indians that used it extensively. It is also called fragrant balm, Indian plume, bee balm, red balm, and mountain balm. Oswego tea is said to be the beverage used by our patriotic colonists instead of tea when they were boycotting British tea. The herb bergamot is still used as a tea when dried. When fresh, it makes a pleasant addition to wine drinks, fruit compotes, punches and lemonades, or in soups and stews. 2—A pear, one of the oldest to be cultivated in the British Isles, where the Romans may well have introduced it. The bergamot pear is a winter pear, and there are several varieties. There are numerous references to it in literature; in fact, up to the 19th century, bergamot in English literature meant the pear. 3—A tree of the citrus family cultivated in Italy for the essential oils of the rind of its small, pear-shaped orange. These oils are only used commercially either as a flavoring or, chiefly, in perfumes.

BERRY—The word describes not only the fruits that have berry as part of their names, but also cherries, tomatoes, and even the hips of roses, for the definition says that berries are *any* kind of small, pulpy fruit, no matter what its structure may be. They are one of nature's most dramatic proofs that good things do indeed come in small packages. In cookery, there are certain fruits we think of as strictly berries. Their names alone are a delight: barberries, bilberries, blackberries, blueberries, cloudberries, cranberries, currants, elderberries, gooseberries, loganberries, mulberries, raspberries, rowanberries, and strawberries conjure visions of a pleasant land under wide skies, where nature's jeweled bounty is there for the taking.

Berries grow in a wide variety of climates, but generally speaking, they are northern fruit; some, like the cloudberry of Scandinavia, even require Arctic latitudes. Though many berries, especially strawberries, are cultivated commercially, berries still have the feeling of the wild about them. Many wild berries taste incomparably better than their tamed brothers; nothing equals the flavor of the tiny wild strawberries of France, the wild raspberries of Maine, and the lingonberries of the vast silent woods of Norway, Sweden, and Finland.

Berries have been a wilderness food, helping many a lost man to survive. They have provided the necessary vitamins to people living when vitamins had not yet been discovered and named as such, yet were no less necessary to good health. Berries have given variety and joy to the monotonous diet of colonists, often providing the only fruit. They have inspired poets through the ages; the 16th-century poet Thomas Tusser sings in his "Septembers Husbandrie" as follows: "The Barbery, Respis (raspberry) and Goosebery too, Look now to be planted as other things doo; The Goosebery, Respis and Roses, al three, With Strawberies under them trimly agree." And Tusser's admonition: "Set strawberies, wife, I love them for life" is as valid now as when the words were written.

In cooking, berries are generally interchangeable in recipes. Specific information will be found under the name of each berry.

Storage
☐ Fresh, refrigerator shelf, in moisture-proof wrapping: 1 to 2 days
☐ Canned, refrigerator shelf, opened and

Fresh Gooseberries, Raspberries, and a Blackberry Roly-Poly

covered: 2 to 4 days

☐ Refrigerator frozen-food compartment, prepared for freezing: 2 months

☐ Freezer, prepared for freezing: 9 to 12 months

Frozen berries should be kept solid during storage. Thawing time for berries varies. Follow package directions. Or, in general, allow 2 to 2½ hours at room temperature, 4 to 6 hours on shelf in refrigerator.

Home Freezing—Blackberries, blueberries, boysenberries, cranberries, currants, gooseberries, raspberries, and strawberries are most suitable for home freezing. Wash and drain thoroughly. Freeze as quickly as possible.

☐ **Loose pack**—Spread berries in a single layer on a cookie sheet. Freeze until firm and then pour into moistureproof bags or containers.

☐ **Dry sugar pack**—Mix ¾ cup sugar for every quart of fruit. Let stand with occasional stirring until juice is formed and sugar is dissolved. Pack in containers, leaving ½-inch headspace.

☐ **Syrup pack**—Cook 4 cups water with 4¾ cups sugar until sugar is dissolved and syrup is clear. Pack berries into containers. Cover with syrup, allowing ½-inch headspace.

BEURRE MANIÉ—"Manipulated butter" is the literal translation of this French culinary term. *Beurre manié* is a thickening agent for sauces and it is composed of butter and flour kneaded or blended together into a paste. The thickening agent must be used at the end of the cooking process, and a sauce should not boil after it has been thickened with *beurre manié*.

The advantage of using *beurre manié* is that a sauce thickened with it will not lump, and that it will also be enriched. It is the standard and wholly admirable and easy French way for making sauces of a desired consistency, and it is highly recommended to American cooks.

Beurre manié is made by blending flour and butter together with the fingertips and rolling the mixture into balls the size of a pea. Then the heat under the sauce to be thickened is turned very low, and the *beurre manié* is dropped, a little at a time, into the sauce, and stirred until thoroughly blended into it. The sauce should simmer only a few minutes after this, to dispel the starchy taste of the flour.

Beurre manié can be made in any proportions of flour and butter to suit the cook and the purpose. Usually, however, there are two basic proportions, one French, which uses twice as much flour as butter, and one American, which uses equal parts of flour and butter, and thus makes for a richer sauce.

Beurre manié can be made in larger quantities and kept covered in the refrigerator, to be used as needed.

FRENCH BEURRE MANIÉ

1½ teaspoons butter and 1 tablespoon flour will thicken 1 cup liquid to a *thin sauce* consistency.

1 tablespoon butter and 2 tablespoons flour will thicken 1 cup liquid to a *medium sauce* consistency.

1½ to 2 tablespoons butter and 2 tablespoons flour will thicken 1 cup liquid to a *thick sauce* consistency.

AMERICAN BEURRE MANIÉ

1 tablespoon butter and 1 tablespoon flour will thicken 1 cup liquid to a *thin sauce* consistency.

2 tablespoons butter and 2 tablespoons flour will thicken 1 cup liquid to a *medium sauce* consistency.

3 to 4 tablespoons butter and 3 to 4 tablespoons flour will thicken 1 cup liquid to a *thick sauce* consistency.

BEVERAGE—The word comes from the Latin *bibere,* "to drink." Literally, it covers all liquids drunk by human beings, from water through milk to alcoholic drinks. By implication, beverages are man-made drinks, including coffee, tea, carbonated waters, fruit drinks, wine, beer, spirits, alcoholic punches, etc.

BIGARADE—This French culinary term means that a dish has been flavored with the rind and juice of the Seville, or bitter, orange. In American usage, *bigarade* means that a dish has been cooked with ordinary oranges, since Seville oranges are not readily available.

Bigarade is also the name of a sauce made with the Seville orange. It is never a dessert sauce. It is used mainly with roast duck, since the flavors complement each other in an excellent manner.

ROAST DUCK BIGARADE

1 large duck (about 5 pounds) or 2 small ducks (2 to 3 pounds each)
1½ cups water
  Salt and pepper
1 large orange, unskinned, coarsely chopped
1¾ cups fresh orange juice
½ cup honey
½ cup orange sections

Cut wing tips off duck. Cook wing tips, giblets, and neck in water for 30 minutes. Strain; reserve broth. Rub duck inside and out with salt and pepper. Fill duck cavity with chopped orange. Place duck on rack in baking pan. Roast according to desired doneness. Allow 1¼ hours for rare duck, 1½ hours for medium-rare, and about 2 hours for very well-done duck. Combine orange juice and honey. Baste duck frequently with mixture during baking time. Also prick skin during roasting to allow excess fat to escape. Remove roasted duck to hot serving platter and keep hot. Skim excess fat off pan juices. Place baking pan over direct heat. Add strained broth and cook over high heat for 5 minutes. Add orange sections and heat through. Pour sauce over duck or serve separately. Makes 4 servings.

SAUCE BIGARADE

  Rind of 1 large orange, preferably a Seville orange
1 cup hot chicken bouillon or stock made from duck, goose, or game
1 teaspoon cornstarch
¾ cup hot orange juice
1 tablespoon vinegar
1 tablespoon sugar
1 teaspoon fresh lemon juice
2 tablespoons Curacao (optional)
  Salt and pepper

Remove the yellow part only of the orange peel in regular strips. Cut strips into matchlike slivers. Pour boiling water over orange strips and let stand for 5 minutes. Drain. Thicken bouillon or game stock with cornstarch. Stir in orange slivers, hot orange juice, vinegar, sugar, lemon juice, and, if desired, Curaçao. Season to taste with salt and pepper. Simmer over low heat for 5 minutes, stirring occasionally. Serve immediately with fowl garnished with orange sections. Makes about 2 cups sauce.

BIND—In cookery this term means to hold separate solids or liquids together by adding an ingredient which serves as the cohesive agent, or by cooking. A bound dish is a thickened dish. Eggs are used to bind mayonnaise, stuffings, and custards. For croquettes, a cooked, thickened sauce holds the mixture together.

Sauces or soups are bound by flour or rice flour, cornstarch or rice starch, crackers or bread crumbs.

Jellied dishes are bound or set by gelatins, agar, or pectin.

Puddings are bound with cornstarch, flour, tapioca, or potato flour.

Pastry, either dough or crumb-crust type, is bound by shortening, and cakes by eggs and milk.

BIRCH BEER—The sap of the Sweet Birch, also called Black Birch or Cherry Birch, can be fermented into a mild or potent beer. Birches are tapped like maples and their sap is delightful to drink, faintly sweet and tasting of wintergreen. Birch beer was one of the traditional beverages of the American frontier and the early settlers.

BIRD—In culinary language the word is used to describe two things: 1—Meat birds, a feature of most European cuisines, are a flavorful way of making meat go further. Their name dates back to the days when chicken and other birds were luxury fare, but they, because of their shape, were called a poor man's "bird." Thin slices of raw or cooked meat, most usually veal steak or cutlet, are spread with a bread or meat stuffing and rolled up. These "birds" are sautéed and simmered in cream, stock, or gravy. Meat birds are often called "rolls" or "roulades." 2—The word is also used, of course, for winged, feather-covered, warm-blooded vetebrates that can fly and which belong to the *Aves* family. Any wild or domesticated birds can be eaten by man, and they have been eaten at one time or another, either by choice, or for survival reasons, with varying degrees of pleasure or pain.

VEAL BIRDS

Cut thin slices of veal shoulder steak into pieces 2 or 3 inches wide and about 4 inches long. Place a tablespoon of well-seasoned bread stuffing on each strip of veal, roll carefully, and skewer in place with toothpicks. Brown meat on all sides in a little fat in a skillet; transfer to a baking dish. Rinse out skillet with a little water and pour liquid over meat. Cover and cook in preheated moderate oven (350°F.) for about 45 minutes, or until meat is tender. Thicken gravy with flour.

BISCUIT—A term that includes a great many varieties of baked doughs and batters. The word is French and means "twice cooked," applying originally to thin, flat breads used by travelers and soldiers and on shipboard. These breads had to be baked twice to expel as much moisture as possible to increase their keeping qualities.

In ordinary usage, biscuit means one thing in the United States and another in the British Isles and on the European continent. American biscuits are usually home-baked quick breads made with baking powder or baking soda or are such specialties as beaten biscuits. In Great Britain and Europe, the word biscuit refers to every variety of cookie and cracker. Sometimes, the variety is specified: there are sweet biscuits, or cream biscuits, or cheese biscuits.

In French culinary language, the word

biscuit is also used to describe ice cream cut into portions that look like biscuits.

BISCUIT TORTONI—An Italian cook created and named this frozen dessert which is made with whipped cream, toasted almonds, sherry, and macaroon crumbs. Biscuit Tortoni is always frozen and served in individual baking cups.

BISCUIT TORTONI

2 eggs, separated
½ cup confectioners' sugar
2 tablespoons sherry or rum
½ teaspoon vanilla extract
1 cup heavy cream, whipped
¾ cup crushed almond macaroons
¼ cup maraschino cherries, drained and chopped

Beat egg yolks with sugar until fluffy. Stir in sherry and vanilla. Beat egg whites until stiff and in peaks. Fold egg mixture into whites. Fold in whipped cream. Stir in ½ cup almond macaroons and the cherries. Put mixture in paper dessert dishes holding 4 ounces. Sprinkle each with a little of the remaining crushed macaroons. Freeze until firm. Serve in paper dishes. Makes 6 to 8 servings.

BISQUE—The term is of French origin and is used to describe two very different

types of dishes. One is a rich cream soup, nowadays usually made with fish or shellfish. Originally a bisque was a soup made with boiled meats, poultry, or game, garnished with bread crumbs.

Bisques are rich fare, and the Victorians and Edwardians, lovers of rich food, were great admirers of them. Bisques carry with them the aura of long, luscious dinners eaten in dining rooms with rich, heavy furnishings, plush draperies, and enormous mirrors in gilt frames.

A bisque may also be a frozen dessert with fruits, nuts, or macaroons. Here, too, the term denotes a rich dish.

CHILLED SEAFOOD BISQUE

1 can (10 ounces) tomato soup
1¼ cups milk
1 can (4½ ounces) small shrimps, drained
1 can (6½ ounces) crabmeat, flaked
Salt and pepper
Lemon juice and slices
Chopped chives

Beat soup and milk until smooth. Add shrimps and crabmeat. Season to taste with salt, pepper, and lemon juice, then chill. Top with lemon slices and chives before serving. Makes 4 servings.

CHESAPEAKE OYSTER BISQUE

1 pint oysters
Milk
2 tablespoons butter

Chilled Seafood Bisque

2 tablespoons all-purpose flour
1 egg, slightly beaten
¼ cup heavy cream
Dash of cayenne
Salt to taste
Sherry
Parsley

Heat oysters in their liquor, but do not boil. Drain; reserve liquid. Cut oysters into small pieces. Add enough milk to liquid to make 2 cups. Melt butter, blend in flour, and add the liquid. Stir and cook until thickened. Add egg mixed with cream and seasonings. Add oysters; heat but do not boil. Serve in heated cups with a dash of sherry; put a parsley sprig on top of each serving. Makes 4 servings.

BITTERS—Bitters are liquids flavored with the essences of aromatic and/or bitter roots, herbs, barks, and plants, such as orange rind, myrrh, quinine, juniper, cloves, cassia, and gentian, to quote a few of the ingredients. Bitters are used to stimulate the appetite, to aid digestion, and to flavor and season foods and drinks of all kinds. Many bitters have an alcoholic content.

The bitters best known in America takes its name from the town of Angostura, in Venezuela, later renamed as Ciudad Bolivar. It was first made there in 1824. It does not contain bitter bark of the angostura tree, but aromatic substances such as cardamom, mace, cinnamon, and gentian. Bitters of all kinds are also made in Europe and sold under their trade names as *apéritifs*.

In America, bitters are used to flavor cocktails such as Old Fashioneds. In cooking, a dash or two of bitters can work wonders in pepping up a soup, a ground meat, or a creamed dish, and surprisingly, fresh fruit or vanilla ice cream.

CARIBBEAN GRAPEFRUIT

Sprinkle 1 teaspoon sugar and 2 dashes of bitters over each prepared chilled grapefruit half. Let bitters seep through sugar before serving.

BLACKBERRY—An oblong, conical fruit composed of many small fruits called drupelets. Blackberries are also called brambles, since they are the fruit of various brambles of the *Rubus* genus. When the ripe fruit is picked, the stem or receptacle holding it remains part of the shrub. Ripe blackberries are a lustrous purple-black in color. As for the unripened fruit, what seems like a paradox puts it this way: blackberries are red when they are green. They may be wild or cultivated.

They are one of the finest and most abundant wild crops of America and well worth gathering. They have long been popular in England where until recently, every farmer's wife went "blackberrying" in September, to turn her crop into puddings, pies, jams, and even homemade wine.

Blackberries and their close realtive, dewberries, can be used in dozens of ways. They are delicious as fresh fruit with sugar and cream, they make fine jams and jellies, and their juice, squeezed from the raw crushed berries, tastes wonderfully good when mixed in equal quantities with lemonade. Blackberry wine and cordial used to be a precious homemade drink and the pride of a housewife. Blackberries and apples, stewed separately and then mixed, or baked together into a deep-dish pie, are a particularly happy flavor combination.

Availability—Season is in May, June, July, and August, with the peak of the season in June. Major sources are New Jersey and California.

Canned blackberries are also available.

Purchasing Guide—Select berries that are bright, fresh, plump, well shaped, and solid in color. They should be free of dirt and moisture with no adhering caps; caps may indicate immature fruit.

Avoid shriveled, wet, or leaky berries. A stained container often indicates overripe or damaged berries.

Sold by ½ pint, pint, and quart.

☐ 1 pint = 2 cups

Storage—Sort berries and keep in refrigerator. Cover lightly with moistureproof wrapping. Do not wash before storing. Use as soon as possible.

☐ Fresh, refrigerator shelf: 1 to 2 days
☐ Fresh, refrigerator frozen-food compartment, prepared for freezing: 1 month
☐ Fresh, freezer, prepared for freezing: 9 to 12 months
☐ Canned, kitchen shelf: 1 year
☐ Canned, refrigerator shelf, opened and covered: 1 to 2 days

Nutritive Food Values—Berries contribute to the vitamin and mineral content of the diet. Iron is fair and the vitamin C content is fair to good, depending on amount eaten.

☐ Fresh, 3½ ounces, raw = 58 calories

☐ Canned, 3½ ounces, light syrup = 72 calories
☐ Canned, 3½ ounces, heavy syrup = 91 calories

Basic Preparation—Wash berries just before they are to be used. Run water over them gently; do not allow fruit to soak in water.

Sprinkle with sugar and serve plain or with cream. Add to fruit cups and salads. Use in puddings, gelatin dishes, pies, tarts, flummeries, jam, and sherbet.

☐ **To Freeze**—Wash berries in cold water; use hands to lift berries out of water to prevent crushing. Pack berries in a sugar syrup (3 cups sugar to 4 cups water), or dry pack without sugar, or sugar pack adding ¾ cup sugar to each 4 cups berries. Freeze with ½-inch headspace in container.

BLACKBERRY PATCH SALAD

For each serving, arrange salad greens on a plate. Place two canned, or peeled fresh, pear or peach halves, cut side down, in center. Frost each with soft cream cheese whipped with a little milk. Stud the cheese with as many blackberries as desired. Serve with tart French dressing. Garnish with watercress or fresh mint.

BLACKBERRY PIE

1 quart fresh blackberries, washed and drained
1½ cups sugar
⅛ teaspoon salt
1½ tablespoons all-purpose flour
Pastry for 2-crust 9-inch pie, unbaked
1 tablespoon butter

Mix blackberries with sugar, salt, and flour. Fill pastry-lined pie pan. Dot with butter. Adjust top crust. Bake in preheated very hot oven (450°F.) for 10 minutes. Reduce heat to moderate (350°F.) and bake 25 minutes longer. Makes 6 to 8 servings.

BLACKBERRY ROLY-POLY

Sugar
¼ cup all-purpose flour
Pinch of salt
Juice of 1 lemon
1 quart blackberries
Biscuit Dough
2 tablespoons melted butter
½ teaspoon ground cinnamon
Whipped cream

Mix ¾ cup sugar, flour, salt, lemon juice, and 3½ cups blackberries. (Reserve ½ cup for decorating.) Roll Biscuit Dough on floured board to form a rectangle 16 x 9 inches. Brush with butter and sprinkle with 2 tablespoons sugar and the cinnamon, mixed together. Put blackberry mixture down center of dough, roll up and shape in a ring on greased cookie sheet. (If roll breaks, just pull together again.) Pinch ends. With scissors, make cuts in ring at 2-inch intervals, not cutting completely to center. Bake in preheated hot oven (425°F.) for 25 to 30 minutes, or until browned. Heap reserved berries in center and top with whipped cream and a berry. Serve at once. Makes 6 to 8 servings.

Biscuit Dough

3 cups all-purpose flour
3 teaspoons baking powder
1½ teaspoons salt
½ cup shortening
1 cup milk (about)

Sift flour, baking powder, and salt. Cut in shortening until mixture resembles coarse cornmeal. Add enough milk to make a soft dough.

BLACKBERRY WHIP

2 egg whites
Dash of salt
¼ cup sugar
1 tablespoon fresh lemon juice
Grated rind of 1 lemon
1 pint blackberries
Custard sauce

Beat egg whites with salt until stiff. Gradually beat in sugar, 1 tablespoon at a time. Beat until thick and glossy. Fold in lemon juice, rind, and washed, well-drained blackberries. Chill. Serve with a custard sauce or plain. Makes 4 servings.

SPICED JELLIED BLACKBERRIES

1 box (3 ounces) blackberry or other berry-flavored gelatin
1½ cups boiling water
Dash each of ground cinnamon, nutmeg, and cloves
½ cup fresh orange juice
1¼ cups blackberries

Dissolve gelatin in boiling water; add spices and orange juice. Chill until of the consistency of unbeaten egg whites. Stir in berries and chill until set. Serve with custard sauce, or whipped or plain cream. Makes 4 to 6 servings.

BLANCH—The word comes from the French word meaning "white." In cooking it refers to a brief cooking of foods in boiling water or steam: for example, blanching vegetables before freezing and canning, or blanching almonds, peaches, or tomatoes to remove skins.

Certain plants, such as asparagus or celery, may be blanched, that is, kept white, during growth by excluding light. Earth is heaped up around the growing stalks to keep them from turning green in the sunlight.

BLANCMANGE—The name of this cold pudding is French and means "white food." Blancmange is made with milk, sugar, cornstarch, flour, or arrowroot as a thickener, and a flavoring. The original, true blancmange is a delicate, snow-white pudding. However, modern blancmange comes in many colors, depending on the flavoring: plain, coconut, chocolate, fruit, nut, or maple. Though blancmange goes back to the 16th century and even earlier, its heyday was during Victorian and Edwardian times. Quivering blancmange puddings, molded into extravagant and fantastic shapes, were the delight of ladies whose delicate bearing belied their robust appetites, if we are to judge from the ample menus of the times.

BLANCMANGE

2½ cups milk
1 teaspoon grated orange rind (optional)
5 tablespoons cornstarch
¼ cup sugar
⅛ teaspoon salt
1 teaspoon vanilla extract (optional)
Chocolate sauce

Scald 2 cups of the milk and orange rind (if used) in top part of double boiler. Combine cornstarch, sugar, and salt. Mix with remaining ½ cup milk to a smooth paste. Gradually stir into scalded milk. Cook, stirring constantly, over boiling water until smooth and thickened. Cover pan and cook for 10 minutes longer, stirring frequently. Add vanilla (if used) and pour into custard cups or molds. Chill. Unmold and serve with chocolate sauce. Makes 4 to 5 servings.

CHOCOLATE BLANCMANGE

Scald milk with 2 ounces unsweetened chocolate. Follow directions for Blancmange.

COCONUT BLANCMANGE

Follow directions for Blancmange. Add ½ cup shredded or flaked coconut to scalded milk.

PINEAPPLE BLANCMANGE

Follow directions for Blancmange. Add ¾ cup crushed pineapple to Blancmange just before serving.

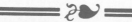

BLANQUETTE—This French culinary term is derived from the word *blanc* or *"white."* It denotes a meat dish, lamb, veal, or chicken, which is kept white while cooking in a sauce. The sauce is thickened with egg yolks beaten with cream and sharpened with a little lemon juice. A typical *blanquette* should contain small boiled white onions and mushrooms.

Blanquettes, especially of veal, are very old and traditional dishes and the glory of the *cuisine bourgeoise,* that is, "home cooking" and they would not be found on a formal French dinner menu. They are a superb dish when properly made, and are suited for buffet and dinner entertaining.

BLANQUETTE DE VEAU
(Veal Stew, French Style)

3 pounds shoulder or leg of veal, cut into 1¼-inch cubes
1 onion, stuck with 2 cloves
1 garlic clove
1 carrot
¼ teaspoon ground thyme
Salt
24 mushroom caps
½ cup water or white wine
2 teaspoons fresh lemon juice
18 small white onions
¼ cup butter
¼ cup all-purpose flour
2 egg yolks
½ cup cream

Put veal, onion stuck with cloves, garlic, carrot, thyme, and 1 teaspoon salt in boiling water to cover. Simmer, covered,

over low heat for 1½ hours, or until meat is tender. Remove meat. Cook broth down to 1½ cups. Blanch mushroom caps in water with 1 teaspoon lemon juice. Cook for 5 minutes, or until just tender. Poach onions in water until just tender. Drain, season with salt, and add a little butter. Keep warm. Add liquids to broth. Melt rest of butter; stir in flour. Gradually add broth from meat. Cook, stirring constantly, until sauce is smooth and thick. Remove sauce from heat. Season to taste. Beat egg yolks and cream together and slowly add to sauce, stirring constantly. Blend until smooth and creamy. Season with 1 teaspoon lemon juice. Return to low heat and heat through. Do not let sauce boil. Heap veal on a hot platter, surround with onions and mushroom caps and pour sauce over all. Makes 8 servings.

BLEND—To mix two or more ingredients so thoroughly that they cannot be separated. This can be done by hand with a rotary egg beater, or by mechanical means, as in an electric mixer or an electric blender.

Blend is also a term used to describe mixtures of tobacco, tea, coffee, cocoa, spices, etc.

BLEU—A classic French method of cooking freshwater fish, especially trout, which turns them blue. It consists of plunging the fish into boiling water, or water mixed with vinegar, salt, and pepper, and sometimes spiced with thyme and a bay leaf. To cook *au bleu* works only if the fish is absolutely fresh and has been caught just before cooking. Connoisseurs say that the fish should still be alive. Fish cooked this way is served with melted butter, served separately, and accompanied by a boiled, parsleyed potato. The fish is usually placed on a clean napkin which absorbs excess moisture.

Trout *au bleu* is one of the greatest culinary treats. All good European restaurants keep a tank with live trout for *au bleu* cooking.

BLINI—This is the Russian and Polish version of pancakes. (In Polish the word is *bliny.*) They are usually small, made with buckwheat flour and raised with yeast. They are served as appetizers with various stuffings, such as salmon, cottage cheese, and best of all, caviar. When stuffed, they are called *blinchiki.*

Blini have been made in Russia since time immemorial, especially during Shrovetide, which is pancake time in Europe. An expert says that from the humblest cottage to the richest palace, all Russians had their *blini* at least twice a day during Shrovetide, and that the greatest importance was attached to their preparation.

QUICK BLINI

1 cup buckwheat flour
1 teaspoon baking powder
1 teaspoon sugar
⅛ teaspoon salt
1 egg, slightly beaten
  Dairy sour cream
1 tablespoon butter, melted
¾ cup lukewarm milk
  Caviar

Sift first 4 ingredients 3 times. Mix egg, 2 tablespoons sour cream, butter, and milk. Add to first mixture and beat well. Drop by tablespoon onto hot greased griddle, making each cake no larger than 2 inches in diameter, and brown on both sides. Put on hot platter and top each cake with 1 tablespoon sour cream, then 1 teaspoon caviar. Also good with apricot or strawberry jam. Makes about 2 dozen.

RAISED BLINI

1 package active dry yeast or 1 cake compressed yeast
1¼ cups water*
¾ cup sifted all-purpose flour
1¼ cups buckwheat flour
1 cup milk, scalded
2 eggs, separated
½ teaspoon salt
1 teaspoon sugar
  Melted butter or margarine
¼ cup heavy sweet cream or dairy sour cream
  Caviar, smoked salmon, or sturgeon

* Use very warm water (105°F. to 115°F.) for dry yeast; use lukewarm (80°F. to 90°F.) for compressed. Sprinkle dry yeast or crumble cake into water. Let stand for a few minutes; then stir until dissolved. Add all-purpose flour and ¼ cup buckwheat flour. Mix well, cover, and let stand in a warm place for 2½ to 3 hours. Add remaining 1 cup buckwheat flour and mix well. Let rise again for about 1½ hours. Beat in lukewarm milk. Beat egg yolks, salt, and sugar. Gradually beat in 2 tablespoons melted butter. Whip cream until fluffy but not stiff. Beat egg whites until stiff and fold into cream. Add all ingredients to first mixture and let stand for 1½ hours longer. Without stirring batter, spoon out by tablespoon from top of batter onto hot greased griddle. When browned on underside, sprinkle with melted butter, turn and brown other side. Serve very hot with melted butter, dairy sour cream, and caviar. Or serve with thin slices of smoked salmon or sturgeon. *Blini* can also be served with preserves or syrup. Makes 20 to 25 *blini*.

Note: Stuff any leftover *blini* with ground cooked meat seasoned with cooked onion, roll up, and sauté in butter. Or fill with preserves, roll up, and sauté as above.

BLINTZ—Blintzes are the Jewish version of pancakes, commonly attributed to Russian cookery where they are called *blini* or *blinchiki* (see preceding entry). They are most popularly filled with cheese, but fruits, such as blueberries and cherries, can be used as fillings.

CHEESE BLINTZES

1½ cups sifted all-purpose flour
1 teaspoon salt
1¼ cups water
5 eggs
⅔ cup milk
  Shortening
1 pound cottage cheese
  Dairy sour cream

Combine flour and salt. Add water and mix until smooth. Add 4 eggs and beat well. Add milk and mix to a thin batter. Heat a small amount of shortening in a 6-inch skillet. Pour in ¼ cup batter. Cook slowly until pancake is lightly browned on bottom and set on top. Turn out with browned side up. Repeat, making about 18 pancakes. Mix cheese with remaining egg. Put a spoonful of cheese in center of each pancake, fold in ends, and roll up. Brown in small amount of hot shortening. Serve with sour cream. Makes 6 to 8 servings.

BLUEBERRY—This is the edible berry of a plant of the same name. Blueberries belong to the *Vaccinium* genus, and there are many varieties of them, ranging in color from purplish-blue to blue-black. They grow singly, or in clusters, on bushes from one to twenty feet high, on mountains and in swamps, and they need an acid soil. In their wild state, blueberries are found from the northern tip of Alaska down to Florida. They also grow profusely on other continents, even above the Arctic Circle, and they are much prized wherever they grow. Bilberries and whortleberries are blueberry varieties.

There is much confusion about the difference between blueberries and huckleberries, since the words are used interchangeably. Generally speaking, the lighter berries are called blueberries, and the darker, blackish ones, huckleberries. Outside of New England, they are often lumped together as huckleberries. But blueberries (*Vaccinium*) have tiny, unnoticeable seeds, whereas huckleberries (*Gaylussacia*) have ten hard, seedlike nutlets. Huckleberries are always wild, but blueberries are cultivated for commercial crops, reaching the size of a small green olive.

Blueberries are old Indian food. They were a major food supply for many tribes who ate them fresh, or cooked with meat, or dried them in large amounts for winter use.

Blueberries are the only pleasant aftermath of a forest fire, because they will grow in abundance on burnt-over ground. Picking wild blueberries is a delightful occupation, which many of us remember with nostalgia, both for the picking and for the incomparable pies and desserts made from fresh wild berries. A good way of picking an abundant berry patch is to put a plastic or cloth sheet on the ground under the bushes and shake down the berries. To clean a large amount of wild berries, pour them into a large-holed sieve. The small green berries will fall through it, along with the pieces of stems, odd leaves, etc.

Availability—Peak crop in June, July, and August with small amounts available in May and September. Major sources are New Jersey, Massachusetts, Michigan, and Washington.

Canned blueberries are available packed in water or sugar syrup.

A muffin mix with canned berries and canned blueberry pie fillings are also available. Frozen berries are available with and without syrup. Allow 6 to 8 hours to defrost in refrigerator or 3 hours at room temperature.

Purchasing Guide—Select clean, plump, dry berries with a deep blue or black color. Berries may be covered with a light-colored bloom.

☐ One pint = 2 cups

Storage

☐ Fresh, room temperature: 1 to 2 days
☐ Fresh, refrigerator shelf, in moisture-proof wrapping: 1 to 2 days
☐ Fresh, refrigerator frozen-food compartment, prepared for freezing: 2 months
☐ Fresh, freezer, prepared for freezing: 1½ years
☐ Canned, kitchen shelf: 1 year
☐ Canned, refrigerator shelf, opened and covered: 2 to 4 days
☐ Wild berries, kitchen shelf, dried and in jars: 1 month

Nutritive Food Values—Fair amounts of vitamin C and iron.

☐ Fresh, 3½ ounces = 62 calories

Blueberry Lattice Pie

Blueberry Parfait

Blueberry Muffins

Blueberry Deep-Dish Pie

Blueberry Tart

Blueberry Shortcake

Blueberry Cottage-Cheese Cake

Blueberry-Orange Bread

...eberry Flummery

Fresh Blueberry Sauce

Blueberry Peach Meringue

Blueberry Pancakes

BLUEBERRY

- ☐ Canned, 3½ ounces, water = 39 calories
- ☐ Canned, 3½ ounces, extra heavy syrup = 101 calories
- ☐ Frozen, 3½ ounces, in syrup = 105 calories

Basic Preparation—Wash berries before using. Do not allow them to soak in water. Look over and remove any stems. Serve with sugar and cream. Add to fruit cups; serve with melon. Add to muffins, pancakes, coffeecake, shortcake, cereal, gelatin, puddings, pies, tarts, cobblers, meringues, blintzes, ice cream, jam, and flummeries.

☐ **To Freeze**—Use firm, fully ripe berries. Wash and drain well. Pour unsweetened berries into freezer containers allowing ½-inch headspace.

☐ **To Freeze, Dry Sugar Pack**—Fill leak-proof freezing containers with blueberries. Use 1 pound sugar to 4 pounds berries. Continue, alternately adding berries and sugar until the container is filled, allowing ½-inch headspace at the top for expansion. Seal, freeze immediately, and store at 0°F. or below. This is a good method for freezing blueberries to be used in pies.

☐ **To Dry**—Spread in a single layer on a tray in the sun during the day and place in a warm room at night until berries are dry and hard.

Pack berries into sterilized jars. Heat at lowest oven temperature for 20 minutes. Cool, cover, and store in a cool place. Use as you would raisins or currants.

NORWEGIAN BLUEBERRY SOUP
- 1 envelope unflavored gelatin
- ¼ cup cold water
- 4 cups fresh orange juice
- 3 tablespoons fresh lemon juice
- ¼ cup sugar
- 2 cups fresh blueberries, washed
  Fresh mint

Soften gelatin in cold water in a custard cup. Place in a pan of hot, not boiling, water until melted and ready to use. Combine orange and lemon juices, sugar, and melted gelatin. Stir until sugar and gelatin are dissolved. Chill until mixture begins to thicken. Fold blueberries into mixture. Chill until ready to serve. Spoon into chilled bouillon cups. Garnish with fresh mint. Makes 6 to 8 servings.

FRESH BLUEBERRY AND LIME MOLD
- 2 envelopes unflavored gelatin
- 1 cup cold water
- 1½ cups hot water
- ½ cup sugar
- ¼ teaspoon salt
- ½ cup fresh lime juice
- 3 cups fresh blueberries, washed
  Salad greens
  Mayonnaise

Soften gelatin in cold water. Let stand for 5 minutes. Add hot water, sugar, and salt and mix well to dissolve gelatin. Blend in lime juice. Chill until mixture is about as thick as fresh egg whites. Fold in blueberries. Turn into a 5-cup mold and chill until firm. Turn out onto serving plate. Garnish with salad greens. Serve with mayonnaise. Makes 6 to 8 servings.

BLUEBERRY TARTS
- All-purpose flour (about 1¼ cups)
  Dash of salt
  Granulated sugar (about ¾ cup)
- ½ cup butter or margarine
- 1 tablespoon cider vinegar
  Dash of ground cinnamon
- 2½ cups fresh blueberries, washed
  Confectioners' sugar
  Whipped cream

Mix 1 cup flour, salt, and 2 tablespoons granulated sugar. Blend in butter and add vinegar. Line four 4½-inch scalloped tart pans with foil, allowing 1 inch of foil to extend over pan sides. Press tart mixture on bottoms and sides of pans and crimp edges. Mix ½ cup granulated sugar, 1½ tablespoons flour, and cinnamon. Stir into 1¼ cups berries and divide among pans. Bake in preheated hot oven (400°F.) for 20 to 25 minutes. Cool and carefully pull off foil. Put remaining berries on tarts and top with confectioners' sugar. Serve with whipped cream. Makes 4 servings.

BLUEBERRY LATTICE PIE
- ¼ cup quick-cooking tapioca
- ¼ cup granulated sugar
- 2 tablespoons brown sugar
- ¼ teaspoon salt
- ⅛ teaspoon ground cinnamon
- ½ cup blueberry syrup
- 2 packages (12 ounces each) frozen sweetened blueberries, thawed and drained
- 1 tablespoon fresh lemon juice
  Pastry for 8-inch lattice-top pie, unbaked
- 1 tablespoon butter

Mix all ingredients except last 2. Roll out half the pastry, line an 8-inch pie pan, and trim. Pour in berry mixture and dot with butter. Roll out rest of pastry. Cut ½-inch strips with pastry cutter or knife. Lay across pie, lattice fashion. Seal edges and press together with fork. Bake in preheated hot oven (400°F.) for 45 minutes. Makes 6 servings.

FRESH BLUEBERRY PIE
- 1 cup sugar
- ¼ cup all-purpose flour
- ¼ teaspoon salt
- ½ teaspoon ground cinnamon
- ½ teaspoon grated lemon rind
- 4 cups fresh blueberries, washed
- 1 tablespoon fresh lemon juice
  Pastry for 2-crust 9-inch pie, unbaked
- 2 tablespoons butter

Combine the first 7 ingredients. Turn into a 9-inch pie pan lined with pastry rolled ⅛ inch thick. Dot with butter or margarine. Cover with the remaining pastry rolled ⅛ inch thick. Trim, turn under, and flute edge. Cut a gash in top crust to allow for escape of steam. Bake in preheated hot oven (425°F.) for 40 minutes, or until crust is brown. Makes 6 servings.

BLUEBERRY DEEP-DISH PIES
- Pastry (2 cups flour recipe), unbaked
- 1 egg yolk
- 2 tablespoons quick-cooking tapioca
- 2 tablespoons sugar
  Dash of lemon juice
- ⅛ teaspoon salt
- 2 cans (15 ounces each) blueberries in heavy syrup

Roll out pastry and cut 4 rounds to fit tops of serving dishes. Put on ungreased baking sheet, prick with fork, and brush with egg yolk beaten with a little cold water. Bake in preheated hot oven (425°F.) for 10 minutes. Mix tapioca, sugar, lemon juice, salt, and berries. Cook, stirring, until thickened. Pour into 4 dishes and top with crusts. Makes 4 servings.

BLUEBERRY TURNOVERS
- ¼ cup sugar
- ⅛ teaspoon salt
- ⅓ cup all-purpose flour
- 2 tablespoons fresh orange juice
- 1 can (15 ounces) blueberries with syrup
  Pastry (2½ cups flour recipe), unbaked
  Fat for shallow frying

In saucepan mix sugar, salt, and flour. Stir in orange juice and blueberries with syrup. Cook, stirring, until very thick; cool. Roll out pastry on a lightly floured board. Cut out twelve 4½-inch rounds. Put 2 tablespoons blueberry mixture on half of each round, moisten edges, and fold over. Seal edges with a fork. Fry in small amount of fat until golden brown on both sides. Makes 12.

BLUEBERRY BUCKLE
- ¼ cup butter or margarine
- ¾ cup sugar
- 1 egg
- 2 cups sifted all-purpose flour
- 2 teaspoons baking powder
- ½ teaspoon salt
- ½ cup milk
- 2 cups fresh blueberries, washed
  Crumb Topping

Cream butter; add sugar and beat until light. Add egg and beat well. Add sifted dry ingredients alternately with milk, beating until smooth. Fold in berries. Pour into greased pan (9 x 9 x 2 inches). Sprinkle with Crumb Topping. Bake in preheated moderate oven (375°F.) for about 35 minutes. Makes 6 to 9 servings.

Crumb Topping
Blend ¼ cup soft butter, ½ cup sugar, ⅓ cup all-purpose flour, and ½ teaspoon ground cinnamon.

BLUEBERRY BETTY
- 2 cups washed fresh, or drained thawed frozen, blueberries
  Juice of 1 lemon
- ½ cup firmly packed light brown sugar
- 4 cups ½-inch white bread cubes, without crusts
- ¼ cup granulated sugar
- 1 teaspoon ground cinnamon
  Cream

Mix berries, lemon, and sugar; spread half in shallow baking dish. Mix bread cubes, sugar, and cinnamon and put half over berries. Sprinkle with rest of berries and top with rest of bread cubes. Bake in preheated moderate oven (350°F.) for 25 to 30 minutes. Serve warm with cream. Makes 4 to 6 servings.

BLUEBERRY PANDOWDY

2 cups washed fresh, or drained thawed frozen, or canned, blueberries
⅓ cup sugar
 Juice of ½ lemon
 Cake batter
 Cream or hard sauce

Combine berries, sugar, and juice in saucepan and cook, uncovered, stirring occasionally, for 5 minutes. Pour into well-greased baking pan (9 x 9 x 2 inches). Spread with Cake Batter and bake in preheated moderate oven (375° F.) for about 20 minutes. Spoon out servings, hot or cold, and serve with cream. Makes 6 servings.

Cake Batter

½ cup butter or margarine
½ cup sugar
1 egg
1½ cups sifted all-purpose flour
2 teaspoons baking powder
½ teaspoon salt
½ cup milk

Cream butter until light and fluffy. Gradually beat in sugar. Stir in egg. Sift dry ingredients and add alternately with milk, beating until smooth. Spread on berries.

STEAMED BLUEBERRY PUDDING

3 tablespoons butter or margarine
¼ cup sugar
1 egg
1 cup sifted all-purpose flour
1 teaspoon baking powder
¼ teaspoon salt
⅓ cup milk
1 cup blueberries, washed
 Foamy Blueberry Sauce

Cream butter and sugar. Add egg; beat well. Add sifted dry ingredients alternately with milk. Fold in blueberries. Fill greased 6-ounce custard cups or other individual molds ⅔ full. Cover tops with wax paper; tie on firmly with cord. Place on rack in steamer or large kettle containing 1 inch of boiling water. Cover kettle and steam for 1 hour, adding more boiling water if necessary. Unmold and serve with Foamy Blueberry Sauce. Makes 4 servings.

FOAMY BLUEBERRY SAUCE

¼ cup butter or margarine
1 cup sugar
1 cup blueberries, crushed
1 tablespoon fresh lemon juice
¼ teaspoon salt
1 egg white

Cream butter and sugar. Add blueberries and lemon juice and beat well. Cook in top part of double boiler over boiling water for 5 minutes. Add salt to egg white; beat until stiff. Fold into warm berries and serve at once on pudding.

GINGERED FRESH BLUEBERRY COMPOTE

2 cups fresh blueberries
1 cup fresh orange juice
1 tablespoon fresh lemon juice
¼ cup confectioners' sugar
2 tablespoons minced preserved gingerroot
 Fresh mint leaves

Wash blueberries and place in a serving bowl. Combine next 4 ingredients and pour over blueberries. Chill for 1 to 2 hours. Serve in sherbet glasses or fruit dishes. Garnish with fresh mint leaves. Makes 6 servings.

FRESH BLUEBERRY FLUFF

1 envelope unflavored gelatin
1¼ cups cold water
2 cups fresh blueberries
½ cup sugar
1 tablespoon fresh lemon juice
1 egg white, unbeaten
 Whipped cream or custard sauce

Soften gelatin in ¼ cup cold water and set aside. Place 1 cup blueberries in a saucepan with ½ cup water. Cover and cook until skins burst, 3 to 5 minutes. Remove from heat and strain; there should be ¾ cup. Stir in softened gelatin, sugar, lemon juice, and remaining ½ cup water. Chill until mixture begins to thicken. Add egg white and beat with an electric or rotary beater until fluffy. Fold in remaining whole blueberires. Chill. Serve in sherbet glasses; top with whipped cream. Makes 6 servings.

BLUEBERRY-PEACH MERINGUE

6 egg whites
¼ teaspoon salt
1½ teaspoons cream of tartar
¼ teaspoon vanilla extract
1½ cups sugar
 Almond Cream Filling
2 cups sliced peaches
 Juice of 1 lemon
2 cups fresh blueberries, washed

Let egg whites stand until warmed to room temperature; beat until frothy. Add salt, cream of tartar, and vanilla. Beat until whites begin to hold their shape. Very gradually beat in sugar and continue to beat until stiff but not dry. On 12-inch heatproof chop plate spread about ⅓ of meringue to within 1 inch of edge. Pile remaining meringue around edge to height of about 2½ inches, leaving center unfilled. Bake in preheated very slow oven (250°F.) for 1¼ hours. Turn off heat and leave in oven for 15 minutes. Cool. Pour Almond Cream Filling carefully into center. Chill for several hours. Just before serving, sprinkle peaches with lemon juice, and sweeten. Arrange peaches and berries on pie. Makes 8 servings.

Almond Cream Filling

In top part of small double boiler, mix 2 tablespoons flour, ⅓ cup sugar, and a dash of salt. Gradually stir in 1¼ cups milk. Cook, stirring, over boiling water until thickened. Gradually stir mixture into 6 beaten egg yolks. Return to dou-

ble boiler, and cook, stirring, until mixture coats a metal spoon. Remove from heat and add ½ teaspoon each of vanilla and almond extracts. Chill; fold in ¾ cup heavy cream, whipped.

BLUEBERRY PARFAIT

Put a spoonful of Blueberry Sauce, page 210, in each parfait glass. Fill with vanilla ice cream or lemon sherbet. Freeze until firm. Just before serving, top with fresh blueberries.

BLUEBERRY FLUMMERY

2 cups fresh blueberries, washed
 Water
¼ cup cornstarch
¾ cup sugar
⅛ teaspoon salt
 Juice of ½ lemon
 Dairy sour cream

Put blueberries in saucepan with 1 cup water and simmer for 5 minutes. Put through sieve. Add water to make 2½ cups. Mix cornstarch, sugar, and salt. Stir in sieved berries. Cook, stirring, until thickened and clear. Add lemon juice. Cool, stirring occasionally. Chill. Serve with sour cream. Makes 4 servings.
Note: Thicken without sieving, if desired. Reduce cornstarch to 3 tablespoons.

BLUEBERRY MUFFINS

 All-purpose flour (about 2⅔ cups)
2½ teaspoons baking powder
¼ teaspoon salt
 Sugar
1 cup buttermilk
2 eggs, beaten
½ cup butter or margarine, melted
1½ cups fresh blueberries, washed

Sift 2½ cups flour, baking powder, salt, and ½ cup sugar. Add next 3 ingredients, and mix only until dry ingredients are dampened. Mix berries with 2 tablespoons flour. Fold in berries. Spoon into greased muffin pans, filling two thirds full. Sprinkle with sugar. Bake in preheated hot oven (400°F.) for 20 to 25 minutes. Serve hot with lots of butter. Makes 16 to 24 muffins.

BLUEBERRY WAFFLES

2 eggs, separated
1½ cups milk
½ cup melted butter or margarine
2 cups sifted all-purpose flour
2 teaspoons baking powder
1 tablespoon sugar
¾ teaspoon salt
1 cup fresh blueberries, washed
 Syrup

Beat egg whites and set aside. Beat egg yolks; add milk and butter. Sift dry ingredients; add egg mixture; mix until smooth. Fold in egg whites and berries. Bake in hot waffle iron. Serve with syrup or hot Blueberry Sauce, page 210. Makes 6 waffles.

BLUEBERRY PANCAKES

1½ cups sifted all-purpose flour
2½ teaspoons baking powder
3 tablespoons sugar
¾ teaspoon salt

2 eggs, separated
1 cup milk
3 tablespoons melted butter or margarine
1 cup fresh blueberries, washed
Blueberry Sauce

Sift dry ingredients. Beat egg yolks; combine with milk and butter. Add to dry ingredients; mix until smooth. Stir in berries. Then fold in stiffly beaten egg whites. Bake on hot greased griddle. Serve with Blueberry Sauce, page 210. Makes 12 pancakes.

BLUEBERRY-ORANGE BREAD

2 tablespoons butter
1/4 cup boiling water
Orange juice (about 2/3 cup)
4 teaspoons grated orange rind
1 egg
1 cup sugar
2 cups sifted all-purpose flour
1 teaspoon baking powder
1/4 teaspoon baking soda
1/2 teaspoon salt
1 cup washed fresh, or drained thawed frozen, blueberries
2 tablespoons honey

Melt butter in boiling water in small bowl. Add 1/2 cup orange juice and 3 teaspoons rind. Beat egg with sugar until light and fluffy. Add sifted dry ingredients alternately with orange liquid, beating until smooth. Fold in berries. Bake in greased fancy 1½-quart baking dish or loaf pan (9 x 5 x 3 inches) in preheated slow oven (325°F.) for about 1 hour and 10 minutes. Turn out on rack or tray. Mix 2 tablespoons orange juice, 1 teaspoon rind, and honey; spoon over hot loaf. Let stand until cold. Makes 1 loaf.

FRESH BLUEBERRY CAKE

1½ cups sifted all-purpose flour
2 teaspoons baking powder
1/2 teaspoon salt
1 cup sugar
1/2 cup shortening
1 teaspoon vanilla extract
1 egg
2/3 cup milk
1½ cups fresh blueberries, washed
2 tablespoons all-purpose flour
1 tablespoon sugar
Lemon Sauce

Sift flour with baking powder and salt. Gradually blend sugar with shortening and vanilla. Beat in egg. Add flour mixture alternately with milk. Combine blueberries, 2 tablespoons flour, and 1 tablespoon sugar and fold into the batter. Turn into a well-greased lightly floured cake pan (9 x 9 x 2 inches). Bake in preheated moderate oven (350°F.) for 1 hour, or until cake tester or toothpick inserted in center comes out clean. Turn out on wire rack. Serve warm or cold, cut into squares, with Lemon Sauce. Makes 9 servings.

■ **Variation**—For blueberry cupcakes, bake the above batter in cupcake pans.

Lemon Sauce

1/2 cup sugar
1 tablespoon cornstarch
1/4 teaspoon salt
1/4 cup cold water
3/4 cup boiling water
3 tablespoons fresh lemon juice
1 teaspoon grated lemon rind
1/2 teaspoon vanilla extract
2 tablespoons butter

Combine sugar, cornstarch, and salt. Gradually stir in cold water. Gradually stir in boiling water and cook for 3 minutes, or until smooth, clear, and thickened slightly. Stir in remaining ingredients. Serve over Fresh Blueberry Cake. Makes 1½ cups.

BLUEBERRY SHORTCAKE

3 cups sifted all-purpose flour
4½ teaspoons baking powder
1 teaspoon salt
1/3 cup sugar
3/4 cup shortening
2 eggs, beaten
2/3 cup light cream or milk
2 tablespoons melted butter or margarine
Fresh Blueberry Sauce
Heavy cream, whipped

Sift dry ingredients. Cut in shortening. Stir in eggs and enough cream to moisten dry ingredients. Divide dough and pat half into 9-inch layer-cake pan. Brush with butter. Roll out remaining dough and put on top. Bake in preheated hot oven (425°F.) for about 25 minutes. Split and fill with half the sauce. Spoon remaining sauce over top and garnish with whipped cream. Makes 6 to 8 servings.

Fresh Blueberry Sauce

In a small saucepan mix 8 teaspoons cornstarch with 2 cups water until smooth. Add 2 cups fresh blueberries and 1 cup sugar and cook over low heat until thick and transparent, stirring constantly. Blend in 2 tablespoons butter or margarine and 2 teaspoons fresh lemon juice. Makes 3 cups sauce.

BLUEBERRY COTTAGE-CHEESE CAKE

1 tablespoon soft butter
4 cups blueberries, washed
2 envelopes unflavored gelatin
3/4 cup sugar
1/4 teaspoon salt
1 egg, separated
3/4 cup milk
1 teaspoon grated lemon rind
3 cups cottage cheese, sieved
2 tablespoons fresh lemon juice
1 teaspoon vanilla extract
3/4 cup heavy cream, whipped

Spread butter on bottom and sides of shallow 1½-quart dish. Arrange 3½ cups berries in dish to form a shell. In top part of double boiler mix gelatin, sugar, and salt. Beat egg yolk and milk; add to gelatin mixture. Cook over boiling water, stirring, until gelatin is dissolved, about 6 minutes. Add lemon rind, and cool. Stir in next 3 ingredients. Chill until slightly thickened to the consistency of unbeaten egg whites. Fold in stiffly beaten egg white and cream. Pour into shell; put 1/2 cup berries in center; chill until firm. Makes 8 to 10 servings.

BLUEBERRY SAUCE

2 cups fresh blueberries
1/3 cup sugar
1 tablespoon fresh lemon juice
1/4 teaspoon salt
1/2 teaspoon vanilla extract

Wash and crush blueberries. Add sugar, lemon juice, and salt. Mix well. Place in a saucepan. Bring to boiling point and boil for 1 minute. Add vanilla. Chill. Serve over puddings, cakes, or ice cream. Makes 1½ cups.

BLUEBERRY RELISH

2 cans (15 ounces each) cultivated blueberries or equal amount of frozen blueberries
1 apple, peeled and diced
1/2 cup sugar
1 cinnamon stick
1 teaspoon whole cloves
2 teaspoons cider vinegar
4 teaspoons fresh lemon juice
1/2 teaspoon aromatic bitters

Empty blueberries into large saucepan. Add diced apple, sugar, cinnamon, and cloves. Bring to a boil, reduce heat, and simmer for 3 minutes. Add vinegar, lemon juice, and bitters. Stir carefully just to mix; remove from heat and let cool. Pour through large strainer to drain off juice. Reserve syrup; discard cinnamon and cloves. Chill blueberry-apple mixture and serve as relish. Makes 1½ cups. Use syrup to baste and glaze small ham during baking.

Potato-Stuffed Bluefish

BLUEFISH—A vivacious and spirited fish, bluish above and silvery below, highly esteemed as important food along the Atlantic coast. Bluefish get to be as large as ten pounds, but those sold in fish markets usually weigh from three to six pounds. Bluefish are meaty fish, delicate in flavor. They can be broiled, sautéed, baked, or fried.

Storage

☐ Refrigerator shelf, raw: 1 day

☐ Refrigerator shelf, cooked and covered: 1 to 2 days

☐ Refrigerator frozen-food compartment, prepared for freezing: 1 month

☐ Freezer, prepared for freezing: 6 months

Nutritive Food Values—A good source of protein and phosphorus

☐ 3½ ounces, baked = 159 calories

☐ 3½ ounces, fried = 205 calories

☐ **To Freeze**—Scale and clean fish. Remove head and fins. Dip fish into a solution of 1½ teaspoons ascorbic acid and 4 cups water for 20 seconds. Wrap tightly in moisture-vaporproof paper, excluding as much air as possible. Seal, tape, and date.

BROILED BLUEFISH, MAÎTRE D'HÔTEL

Have medium-size bluefish, about 3 pounds, split for broiling. Brush with cooking oil or melted fat, sprinkle with salt and pepper, and lay it, skin side down, on greased broiler rack. Broil under medium heat until well browned. Remove to hot platter and spread with Maître d'Hôtel Butter. Makes 4 servings.

Maître d'Hôtel Butter

Cream 2 tablespoons butter or margarine. Add ¼ teaspoon salt, dash of cayenne, 1 tablespoon fresh lemon juice, and 1 teaspoon finely chopped parsley.

POTATO-STUFFED BLUEFISH

3 potatoes, boiled
2 onions, boiled
  Butter or margarine
½ teaspoon salt
¼ teaspoon pepper
½ teaspoon ground sage
½ teaspoon ground thyme
1 bluefish (about 3 pounds)

Finely chop potatoes and onions together; add 2 tablespoons butter and seasonings. Wash fish; fill with stuffing and sew together. Brush with butter; place in baking pan and bake in preheated slow oven (300°F.) for 40 minutes. Makes 4 servings.

BAKED BLUEFISH CUTLETS

½ cup grated Parmesan cheese
1 cup fine dry bread crumbs
¼ cup chopped parsley
1½ teaspoons salt
⅛ teaspoon pepper
1 bluefish (about 3 pounds)
1 egg
2 tablespoons milk
2 tablespoons butter or margarine
  Vinegar

Mix cheese, crumbs, parsley, salt, and pepper. Cut fish into pieces and dip into beaten egg mixed with milk; then roll in dry crumb mixture. Cook in hot butter only until lightly browned on both sides. Put in shallow baking pan and bake in preheated moderate oven (350°F.) for 20 minutes. Serve with a little vinegar. Makes 4 servings.

BONELESS BLUEFISH
    1 bluefish (about 3 pounds)
    Salt and pepper
    Juice of 1 lemon
    ¼ cup olive oil
    Chopped parsley
    1 garlic clove (optional)

Have fish cleaned; place in skillet and cover with boiling water seasoned with salt and pepper. Simmer gently for 10 to 15 minutes, or until tender. Carefully lift fish onto ovenproof platter. When cold, split fish with spatula; remove bones. Mix lemon juice, oil, parsley, and salt and pepper and pour over fish. Put pieces of garlic on top, if desired. Place in broiler under medium heat until thoroughly heated. Makes 4 servings.

BOCKWURST—A fresh, whitish sausage of German origin, made with a mixture of ground pork and veal and seasoned with cloves, mace, sage, and other spices. Some bockwurst also contains raw egg. The word in German means literally "buck sausage." Bockwurst has been eaten for centuries as a traditional accompaniment for beer.

Bockwurst is perishable and must be thoroughly cooked before being eaten. To cook it, fry slowly in a pan as is done with any fresh sausage.

BOIL—The word describes the movement of a liquid heated to reach the vaporizing stage, characterized by bubbles that break constantly on the surface. Water boils at a temperature of 212°F. at sea level, but the temperature decreases as altitude increases. When a liquid is boiling, the temperature remains constant.

In cooking terms "to boil" is perhaps the most basic of all cooking processes, and means to cook in liquid that is boiling and continuously bubbling. Many cooks seem to think that the harder a food boils, the quicker it will be cooked. This is not true. There are various stages of boiling:

To simmer is to cook just below the boiling point. This is done over very low heat. The food must cook so slowly that no bubbles at all appear on its surface, which just quivers gently, as if it were breathing. To simmer is an extremely important cooking process since it brings out the flavors of foods, makes tough meats tender, and prevents delicate foods, such as fish, from falling apart as they would do if boiling.

To bring to a boil is to heat the liquid to the point where bubbles rise to the top

from the bottom of the liquid, when a vapor rises, and all the liquid is in motion.
To boil is to cook at boiling point. When this is reached, adjust heat to keep constant; higher heat won't make your food boil more quickly.

To boil rapidly means that the liquid is in rapid motion and breaks into small waves. It does not cook food more quickly, but it is better for some cooking: to prepare cereals, for example, since it keeps the particles separated, to evaporate a sauce or a jam, or to concentrate candy.

A full rolling boil is the stage at which the liquid rises in the pan and falls in great waves that won't lie down. This is only used for heavy sugar mixtures, such as in frostings, candies, and jelly-making.
To parboil is to cook foods partially in boiling water and finish them off in some other way. This is done to soften foods, or to lighten them, to remove pronounced flavors, and to prepare them for canning and freezing since the boiling water kills bacteria.

BOLOGNA—A mildly seasoned sausage made of finely ground beef, pork, or veal. The meat is packed into a casing and smoked. It originated in Bologna, Italy, during the Middle Ages. There are several varieties: large and small bologna, ham bologna, all-beef bologna (seasoned with garlic), and Lebanon bologna (all-beef bologna which originated in Lebanon, Pennsylvania, and requires long, slow smoking). In Bologna, Italy, the sausage is known as *mortadella*.

Bologna is available in bulk and sliced in vacuum-sealed packages. Bologna is generally used as a sandwich filling, cut into cubes for casseroles or salads, rolled around asparagus or broccoli spears and covered with a cheese sauce, or barbecued in one chunk on a rotisserie.

Storage
☐ Refrigerator shelf, wrapped: 3 to 5 days
☐ Refrigerator frozen-food compartment, wrapped for freezing: 3 months
   Freezing in a deep freeze is not recommended because of the high fat content.

Nutritive Food Values—Good source of protein and fat with small amounts of thiamine, riboflavin, and niacin.
☐ 3½ ounces, all meat = 277 calories

BOMBE—The name of this elegant, molded frozen dessert is French and means literally "bomb." This goes back to the days when a *bombe* was molded in a round shape, the shape of the bomb of the times. Modern *bombes* are classically molded in tall, conical molds, or in melon-shaped molds.

A *bombe* consists of an outer layer, usually of ice cream, sherbet, or whipped cream, and a softer filling, such as a custard or a mousse. The dessert is then frozen in its mold. To loosen from mold, put a cloth wrung out of hot water on bottom of mold and invert over serving plate.

Bombes are festive desserts, and they should be brought to the table in their entirety, to be admired by the guests before being divided into servings.

RASPBERRY BOMBE
    1½ quarts raspberry sherbet
    1 cup heavy cream
    ¾ cup confectioners' sugar
    2 teaspoons vanilla extract
    1 tablespoon Cointreau or Grand Marnier liqueur
    Raspberries

Chill a 2-quart mold and line quickly with sherbet. Put in freezer. Whip cream until stiff. Add sugar, vanilla, and liqueur. Force enough berries through sieve to make 1 cup, and add to cream. Fill center of mold with cream mixture and freeze until firm. Unmold on serving plate. Decorate with fresh berries and whipped cream, if desired. Makes 6 to 8 servings.
Note: Vanilla ice cream can be substituted for the cream mixture in the above recipe.

ITALIAN COFFEE BOMBE
    Sugar
    ⅛ teaspoon salt
    1 teaspoon all-purpose flour
    2 egg yolks, beaten
    ½ cup milk
    ⅓ cup Italian coffee or very strong coffee
    1 tablespoon Cointreau or other liqueur
    ½ teaspoon vanilla extract
    2 cups heavy cream

Combine ¼ cup sugar, salt, and flour in small saucepan. Add egg yolks, milk, and coffee; mix well. Cook over low heat, stirring constantly, until slightly thickened. Remove from heat and chill. Add Cointreau and vanilla. Whip cream until stiff and add 2 tablespoons sugar. Line a 1-quart mold with half of the cream. Freeze until firm. Fold remaining cream into coffee mixture and pour into center of mold. Freeze until firm. Unmold on serving plate and cut into wedges. Makes 6 to 8 servings.

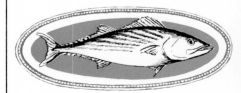

BONITO—This relative of the mackerel, tuna, and kingfish lives in both the Atlantic and the Pacific. A saltwater fish, it is caught commercially on a large scale; more of it is canned in flakes and chunks than is sold fresh.

Fresh bonito may be poached, broiled, panbroiled, baked, or fried; canned bonito is good in salads and casseroles.

Storage

☐ Fresh, refrigerator shelf, raw: 1 day
☐ Fresh, refrigerator shelf, cooked and covered: 1 to 2 days
☐ Fresh, refrigerator frozen-food compartment, prepared for freezing: 1 month
☐ Fresh, freezer, prepared for freezing: 6 months

To freeze, wrap pieces of fresh bonito tightly in freezer paper. Seal ends, tape, and date.

☐ Canned, kitchen shelf: 2½ years
☐ Canned, refrigerator shelf, opened, and covered: 1 to 2 days

Caloric Values

☐ Fresh, 3½ ounces, raw = 168 calories
☐ Canned, drained and oil removed, 3½ ounces = 198 calories

DEVILED FRESH BONITO STEAKS

2 tablespoons prepared mustard
1 tablespoon cooking oil
2 tablespoons chili sauce
2 tablespoons horseradish
1 teaspoon salt
4 fresh bonito steaks (about 2 pounds)

Mix all ingredients except bonito. Spread half the mixture on steaks. Place on greased broiler rack and broil for about 6 minutes under medium heat. Turn fish; spread with remaining sauce and broil for 5 to 6 minutes. Makes 4 servings.

BORAGE (Borago officinalis)—This sturdy annual grows to a height of one and one-half to two and one-half feet and it is a lovely addition to any garden. Its oval leaves have a grayish-green appearance due to a covering of grayish hairs. In spite of the fuzzy coarseness of its foliage, borage is a beautiful plant with its clusters of blue, star-shaped flowers. Ancient herbalists loved to illustrate these delicate blossoms. Although this herb is native to Asia Minor, Greece, Italy, the Mediterranean coasts, Persia, and Sicily, it has spread to many parts of the world. Growing best in temperate and warm climates, it is chiefly found in the eastern part of our country.

Borage became known very early as a dispeller of melancholy and bearer of courage. The Greeks put it in their cups of wine to bring good cheer. Pliny describes how the cooling, tender leaves could be crushed and added to red wine. "I, Borage, bring courage," rhyme the English. In Queen Elizabeth's time the flowers, as well as the leaves, were used in salads. From Europe the herb traveled to this country. It was among the plants cultivated on Isabella Island by the companions of Columbus.

Fresh borage leaves, when very young and not yet too fuzzy, may be cooked and eaten like spinach or added to tomato and cucumber salads. Fresh or dried, borage flavors soups, stews, green peas, green beans, and many other vegetables. The leaves may also be used instead of parsley. The flowering tips and leaves add interest to fruit dishes and iced drinks, and the flowers can be candied or crystallized for confections and decorations.

COUNTRY SALAD BOWL

Slice 3 large unpeeled tomatoes, 1 peeled and scored cucumber, 1 medium green pepper, and 1 sweet onion. Arrange in a colorful serving bowl; add fresh borage leaves. Serve with your favorite dressing. Makes 4 servings.

BORDEAUX—The name covers a region and a city in southwestern France which are famous for their superlative cooking and wines. The city of Bordeaux, a beautiful one, is a gourmet's fondest dream come true, due to its combination of great wines and great hospitality. Bordeaux cookery is on the delicate side, with many famous local foods, such as a variety of mushrooms called *cèpes*, crayfish, and Arcachon oysters from the nearby Atlantic.

Bordeaux has produced incomparable wines ever since the Romans planted grapes there during the 3rd century. The wines are shipped all over the world, and wine-making has given origin to many legends and ancient traditions which live on to this day. There are red, white, and *rosé* Bordeaux wines. The red ones are dry and also known as "clarets." The white ones range from dry to very sweet. The most famous red Bordeaux wines are called Médoc, St. Émilion, and Pomerol, and the white ones, Graves and Sauternes. Many Bordeaux wines sold in America bear a gold and black seal on the bottle necks. This seal is a guarantee that the wine has passed stringent tests and is of the highest standard of quality within its own class and price range.

CHICKEN BORDEAUX

6 tablespoons all-purpose flour
1 teaspoon salt
¼ teaspoon pepper
1 broiling chicken (2½ to 3 pounds), quartered
¼ cup salad oil
1 teaspoon sugar
½ cup canned tomatoes
1 cup dry white wine
½ cup sliced mushrooms, fresh, or canned and drained

Combine 4 tablespoons flour, salt, and pepper. Dredge chicken with seasoned flour. Heat salad oil in large skillet. Cook chicken in it until well browned on all sides. Simmer, covered, over lowest possible heat for 25 minutes. Stir remaining flour and sugar into tomatoes to make a smooth paste. Add mixture to chicken. Add wine and mushrooms. Simmer, covered, over low heat for 20 to 30 minutes, or until chicken is tender. Makes 4 servings.

LOBSTER BORDELAISE

¼ cup butter
2 medium carrots, sliced
1 small onion, minced
4 rock lobster tails, in the shell
1 tablespoon olive oil
½ teaspoon salt
⅛ teaspoon cayenne
½ cup dry white wine
3 tablespoons tomato sauce
2 tablespoons fish bouillon or bottled clam juice

Heat 2 tablespoons butter in a small heavy saucepan. Add carrots and onion. Cook, covered, over lowest possible heat for 20 minutes, stirring frequently. Cut lobster into 2-inch pieces. In a large skillet, heat 1 tablespoon butter and olive oil. Add lobster and cook rapidly until shell turns red. Add salt and cayenne. Transfer carrots and onions from saucepan to skillet; add wine, tomato sauce, and bouillon. Bring to a boil. Lower heat and cook, covered, over low heat for 10 minutes. Remove lobster to heated serving dish and keep hot. Cook liquid in uncovered skillet until it is reduced to about half. Remove skillet from heat. Stir remaining butter into sauce and blend thoroughly. Pour over lobster. Serve with rice and a bottle of white Bordeaux wine if you want to be authentically French. Makes 4 servings.

Note: The original dish is made in Bordeaux with crayfish, but it is equally delicious with fresh or frozen rock lobster.

BORDELAISE

BORDELAISE—A classic French sauce which takes its name from the town of Bordeaux. It belongs to the family of brown sauces, is made with red wine and is rather highly seasoned. It is a sauce for meat, usually served with steak.

SAUCE BORDELAISE
2 tablespoons butter
2 tablespoons minced shallots or 1 tablespoon minced onion
¾ cup dry red wine
1½ cups Brown Sauce (see page 246) or canned beef gravy
2 tablespoons fresh lemon juice
3 tablespoons minced parsley
Salt and cayenne
¾ cup sliced mushrooms, sauteed in 1 tablespoon butter

Melt butter and sauté shallots in it until soft and transparent. Add wine and simmer until reduced to half its volume. Stir in Brown Sauce, lemon juice, parsley, salt and cayenne to taste, and mushrooms. Heat through before serving. Makes about 2 cups sauce.

BORSCH—This is a dark-red Russian or Polish soup. The characteristic ingredient is beets. Borsch can contain other vegetables and also meat. It can be a thin soup or a substantial meal in itself. It can be served hot or cold. Borsch is usually served with sour cream.

Borsch is the basic soup of the Russians and Poles, and of many of the people whom they have influenced, such as the Ukrainians, the Lithuanians, and the Jews, all of whom have their own versions of borsch. There are probably as many ways to make borsch as there are home cooks. Some Ukrainian borsch lovers feel that ordinary water will not do for this soup, but that it needs *kvas*, a slightly fermented infusion made with dark rye bread and beets which has a pleasant, slightly acid taste. Whatever the borsch, it is one of the most inspired of soups and a glowing example of how to make little do much.

MEATLESS BORSCH
4 large beets
2 onions, minced
1 quart water
1 teaspoon salt
1 teaspoon sugar
About ¼ cup fresh lemon juice
½ cup dairy sour cream

Wash beets; peel and chop fine. Place in kettle, add onion and water, and bring to boil. Reduce heat, cover, and simmer for about 35 minutes, or until beets are tender. Force through coarse sieve and add salt, sugar, and lemon juice to taste. Serve hot or cold, topped with sour cream. Makes about 1 quart or 4 servings.

UKRAINIAN BORSCH
1 pound beef chuck, in one piece
8 cups beef bouillon
Salt and pepper

1 bay leaf
2 tablespoons butter
1 onion, chopped
2 carrots, sliced
3 medium raw beets, shredded
½ medium cabbage, shredded
1 tablespoon minced parsley
1 8-ounce can tomato sauce
1 tablespoon vinegar
2 medium potatoes, cubed
Dairy sour cream

Place beef and cold beef bouillon in deep kettle. Add salt and pepper to taste and bay leaf. Bring to a boil, and skim. Simmer, covered, for about 30 minutes. In another pan melt butter and sauté in it onion, carrots, beets, cabbage, and parsley for 3 minutes. Add tomato sauce and vinegar and simmer over low heat for 10 minutes. Add to soup with potatoes. Simmer, covered, for about 1 hour, or until meat is tender. Skim when needed. Correct seasonings. Remove beef to platter, slice, and serve separately. Serve with sour cream. Makes 6 to 8 servings.

BOUILLABAISSE—This is a highly seasoned fish stew of the French Mediterranean coast and one of the world's great soups. It is the French version of a universal dish: a fish chowder, which is made wherever people catch fish, from New England to Polynesia.

The true bouillabaisse of Marseilles is made of a large variety of fish fresh from the Mediterranean or, as local people say, of a "netful of fish." It should contain at least eight different kinds of fish; a passable job can be done with less but the result will not be as interesting. Of course the traditional bouillabaisse contains varieties of fish not available here, but fair substitutions can be made.

If you eat bouillabaisse in its native region, it will most likely contain *langouste* or rock lobster, *rascasse, grondin, roucaou, Saint-Pierre, vaudreuil, merlin*, and always eel. But no matter what the variety, the stew should contain some shellfish, some eel, and a fairly even choice of heavy-meated and delicate types of fish. Best choices for shellfish are lobsters and mussels. For heavy-meated fish try cod, haddock, sea bass; for more delicate fish use sole, red snapper, flounder, or sea perch.

BOUILLABAISSE
3 pounds mixed fish (including eel)
2 pounds lobster
3 dozen clams
3 leeks
2 large onions
3 garlic cloves
3 tomatoes
⅓ cup olive oil
Bouquet garni (cheesecloth bag of thyme, bay leaf, parsley, celery, rosemary)
Pinch of saffron
Salt, pepper, and cayenne
Fish stock or water
1 pound uncooked, deveined, shelled shrimps

Skin eel first. Cut skin around head of eel. With a sharp knife, cut under skin slowly to loosen a small flap. Hold head in one hand and grasp skin with the other hand. Or use a pair of pliers. Strip the skin off as you would a glove, in one motion. Cut off head. Cut eel into 3-inch lengths. Cut fish into serving pieces; keep heavy-meated fish separate from delicate fish. Split lobster down the middle from head to tail, on the under side. Remove intestines. Break off claws and crack them. Cut tail and body into pieces. Wash and clean clams. Wash leeks thoroughly, being certain they contain no sand. Cut white portions into small pieces. Peel and chop onions and garlic. Peel and seed tomatoes. Heat olive oil in a large kettle and add vegetables. Cook them for a few minutes; add *bouquet garni*. Arrange heavy-meated fish and eel on the vegetables and cook for about 8 minutes. Add delicate fish, lobster, and saffron. Season to taste with salt, pepper, and cayenne; cover with fish stock. Bring to a boil and simmer for 15 minutes. Add clams and shrimps and cook just until the clam shells open. Spoon fish out into large bowls and pour broth on top. Makes 6 servings.

BOUILLON—The word is French, and comes from *bouillir*, literally, "to boil." A bouillon is a broth made by simmering meat, fish, or vegetables in water to extract their flavors. When a clear broth is desired, the bouillon must be clarified, and a clarified bouillon is generally called "consommé." Bones, both animal and fish bones, are often added to give strength and taste to the broth.

Bouillon must be the oldest of all soups, since it is a by-product of cooking other foods. The French and other Europeans dote on it, both as soup and in cooking, and there are many recipes for the various kinds of bouillon. Very often, the original amount is cooked down considerably to obtain a more concentrated product. Or for festive occasions, such as wedding feasts, four different meats might be combined, including a chicken and a turkey. Italian cooking cannot be imagined without *il brodo*, the daily soup of millions, made nourishing with rice, pasta, and/or vegetables.

Bouillon, though practically nil in caloric values has, by association with its ingredients, led people to believe that in concentrated form it will give strength and have therapeutic results. The present Duke of Bedford tells how his grandfather invariably drank one cup of bouillon for the first course of his dinner. Precisely nine and one-half pounds of the best beef shin were required to make this precious brew fresh daily.

Bouillon greatly enhances the flavor of

WOMAN'S DAY

most cooking. Today's canned bouillon and bouillon cubes are excellent.

How to clarify bouillon—Before clarifying bouillon, all fat must be removed. Several methods are used. Chill the soup and then remove the hard layer of fat. After stock has been degreased, cool to room temperature. For every 5½ cups stock, beat 2 egg whites slightly and add with the broken-up egg shells to the stock. Stir well. Cook over very low heat until broth just simmers. *Do not boil.* Simmer for 10 to 15 minutes over a very low heat. A white scum will rise to the top. Remove pan from heat and let stand for 30 minutes. Push scum carefully to one side. Spoon liquid from underneath and strain through several layers of cheesecloth.

BEEF BOUILLON

1 to 2 pounds cracked
    beef marrow bones
6 pounds beef shin or other stew meat
3 quarts cold water
8 peppercorns
6 whole cloves
1 bay leaf
    Pinch each of dried thyme
    and marjoram
    Few parsley sprigs
½ cup each of diced carrot, turnip,
    onion, and celery
1 tablespoon salt

Scrape the marrow from bones and put in large kettle. Cut meat into 1-inch cubes. Melt the marrow, add half the meat, and brown. Add bones, remaining meat, and water. Bring slowly to boil, and skim. Add remaining ingredients and bring to boil; cover and simmer for about 3 hours, skimming occasionally. Strain and cool quickly. Makes about 2½ quarts.

CHICKEN BOUILLON

1 stewing chicken (about 4 to 5 pounds)
6 cups cold water
1 carrot, sliced
1 onion, sliced
2 celery stalks with leaves
½ bay leaf
6 whole peppercorns
1 teaspoon salt

Put all ingredients in kettle. Bring slowly to boil, cover, and simmer for 2 hours. Remove chicken. Cool bouillon, skim off fat, and strain bouillon. Makes about 1 quart.

Note: Use the chicken meat for salad, à la king, or in other dishes.

FISH BOUILLON

2 pounds lean fresh fish
    (halibut, whiting, or flounder)
1 onion, thinly sliced
1 teaspoon fresh lemon juice
¼ teaspoon salt
1 cup dry white wine
    Cold water to cover

Combine all ingredients and simmer, covered, for about 30 minutes. Strain and season to taste. Makes about 2 cups.

Note: If fish trimmings (heads, bones, and tails) are used, discard. If fillets are used, the fish may be eaten in patties, fritters, or casseroles. Use only 1 pound fish if bouillon is to be used for poaching fish or for fish soup.

TOMATO BOUILLON

2 cups tomato juice
2 cups beef bouillon
  Small piece of bay leaf
  Slice of onion
  Few celery leaves
1 tablespoon fresh lemon juice
  Salt and pepper

Mix tomato juice, bouillon, bay leaf, onion, and celery leaves in saucepan. Bring to boil and simmer, uncovered, for 10 to 15 minutes. Strain; add lemon juice and season to taste. Serve hot, or chill and serve cold. Makes 4 cups.

JELLIED BOUILLON

Soften 2 envelopes unflavored gelatin in ½ cup cold water in saucepan for 5 minutes. Heat, stirring, until gelatin is dissolved. Stir in 1 tablespoon fresh lemon juice, 4 cups homemade chicken or beef bouillon or diluted canned bouillon or bouillon made from paste, cubes, or granules. Season to taste. Chill until set. Just before serving, break up jelly with a fork. Serve in bouillon cups with a garnish of chopped chives or parsley. Makes 4 servings.

BOUQUET GARNI—The literal translation of this French cooking term is a "varied bouquet." A *bouquet garni* consists of a number of herbs and sometimes spices tied together in a muslin or cheesecloth bag so that they may be easily discarded after cooking. *Bouquets garnis* are generally used in slow-cooking dishes such as soups and stews. They are basic to French cooking.

The composition of a *bouquet garni* varies, depending on the use to which it is to be put. It may be as simple as a few parsley sprigs and some celery tops. Usually, a *bouquet garni* contains parsley, thyme, and bay leaf. However, depending on the dish to be flavored, any one or combination of other herbs and spices (such as basil, celery, garlic, onion, chervil, chives, rosemary, tarragon, or whole cloves) may be added to the

basic *bouquet garni.* It is well to season lightly with the strong-flavored herbs such as basil and thyme.

A *bouquet garni* should include at least one fresh herb. If a *bouquet garni* made from dried herbs only is used, add a few sprigs of fresh parsley to the bouquet. To make a *bouquet garni,* cut a triple layer of cheesecloth into a 3- to 4-inch square. Place herbs in the middle. Fold over and tie with strings, or sew.

BOUQUET GARNI FOR BOUILLON

6 small bay leaves
6 whole cloves
½ cup (⅜-ounce package) celery flakes
1 tablespoon ground marjoram
⅓ cup parsley flakes
¾ teaspoon peppercorns
1½ teaspoons ground savory
2 tablespoons ground thyme

Put 1 bay leaf and 1 clove in each of 6 small cheesecloth bags. Mix remaining ingredients well, divide equally, and pack in the bags. Each bag will season 2 quarts of liquid. Store bags in airtight containers. Use for flavoring stews.

BOUQUET GARNI FOR SOUP

¼ cup each of ground marjoram
  and thyme
¼ cup parsley flakes
2 tablespoons ground savory
1 tablespoon ground sage
1 tablespoon crumbled bay leaf
½ cup (⅜-ounce package) celery flakes

Mix all well; pack in small cheesecloth bags. This recipe will make 24 bouquets, each of which will season 2 quarts of liquid. The bags should be dropped into the boiling soup toward the end of the cooking and should not be left in more than 1 hour. Store bags in airtight containers until used. Good for flavoring meat gravies, too.

FRENCH LAMB OR VEAL STEW

2 pounds lamb or veal stew meat,
  cut into 1-inch pieces
½ cup all-purpose flour
½ teaspoon salt
¼ teaspoon pepper
3 tablespoons salad oil
1 medium onion, sliced
4 thin lemon slices
1 bouquet garni
  (3 parsley sprigs,
  1 small garlic clove,
  1 tablespoon chopped celery,
  and ½ teaspoon dried
  rosemary leaves)
3 tablespoons tomato sauce
  Boiling water or beef bouillon
12 green or black olives, pitted
⅓ cup chopped parsley

Trim meat free of excessive fat and gristle. Combine flour, salt, and pepper. Dredge meat with seasoned flour. Heat oil in heavy saucepan or Dutch oven. Brown meat in it on all sides. Add onion and cook over low heat until soft. Add lemon slices, *bouquet garni,* tomato sauce, and just enough water to cover meat. Bring to a boil. Reduce heat. Simmer, covered, over low heat for 45 minutes. Add olives and parsley and simmer for

20 minutes longer, or until meat is tender. Stir frequently and, if necessary, add a little more water to prevent sticking. Serve with boiled noodles and a tossed green salad. Makes 4 to 6 servings.

AIGO-SAU
(Fish Stew)

1½ to 2 pounds fresh fish
6 potatoes
2 large tomatoes
1 medium onion
2 garlic cloves
  Salt and pepper
1 bouquet garni (bay leaf, parsley,
  celery, fennel, and strips of
  orange peel)
⅓ cup olive oil
  Boiling water
  Small loaf of French bread
  Garlic cloves, cut

Cut fish into serving pieces and arrange these on the bottom of a large skillet. Peel and slice potatoes and place them in a layer on top of fish. Peel and chop tomatoes, onion, and garlic and put these on top of potatoes. Season to taste with salt and freshly ground black pepper; add *bouquet garni.* Pour olive oil over all and add enough boiling water barely to cover fish and vegetables. Boil quickly for 20 minutes, or until potatoes and fish are just tender. Slice French bread and toast it lightly. Rub each slice with a cut garlic clove; place a slice of toast in the bottom of each soup bowl. Pour the broth over this. Serve the fish and vegetables separately. Makes 4 to 6 servings.
Note: Aigo-Sau is often served with a hot condiment called *rouille.* To make *rouille,* pound or chop 2 garlic cloves with 2 hot red peppers. Mix in 3 tablespoons bread crumbs and 3 tablespoons olive oil and blend with 1 cup of the fish broth. Serve in a sauceboat.

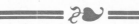

BRAINS—This is the name of the edible brain substance of an animal when used for human consumption. Brains are considered an easily digested food and thus often given to children and invalids.

After precooking, the brains can be scrambled with eggs, served with a rich sauce, sautéed in butter, dipped into eggs and crumbs and fried in deep fat, used in salads, or dipped in melted butter and broiled.

Purchasing Guide—Brains should be absolutely fresh when purchased; this means firm and with a bright color. Allow ¼ pound per serving:
Beef brains average ¾ pound each
Lamb brains average ¼ pound each
Pork brains average ¼ pound each
Veal brains average ½ pound each

Storage—Brains are very perishable and should be used immediately. They may be precooked by simmering in water and then kept covered in the refrigerator, but they should be used within 24 hours. If frozen, they may be dropped into hot water to thaw.

Basic Preparation—Brains should be thoroughly washed before cooking, either under running cold water or by soaking in salted cold water (1 tablespoon salt for each quart of water) for 30 minutes or longer, up to 1½ hours. The soaking firms their soft texture. Drain brains and carefully remove the membrane with the tip of a paring knife.

It is possible to cook brains without precooking. But precooking, or blanching, adds to their texture and flavor. Time required after precooking in water, on top of range or in a slow oven (300° F. to 325°F.): to broil, 10 to 15 minutes; to braise, 20 to 25 minutes; to cook in liquid, 15 to 20 minutes.

☐ **To Precook**—To each quart of water, add 1 teaspoon salt, 1 tablespoon lemon juice or mild vinegar. Bring liquid to boiling point. Pour carefully over brains and cover by 2 inches. Bring to just below simmering point and keep at this point, on lowest possible heat. Simmer lamb brains for 15 minutes, veal or calf or pork brains 20 minutes, and beef brains for 25 minutes. Let brains cool in liquid for 10 minutes and drain. Or else, drain precooked brains and plunge in cold water and then drain again. If they are not to be used immediately, keep them in the cooking liquid in the refrigerator.

SCRAMBLED EGGS WITH BRAINS
    1 pound beef brains
      Salt
      Water
    1 tablespoon vinegar or lemon juice
    6 eggs
    ⅛ teaspoon white pepper
    2 tablespoons butter
      Chopped parsley
      Paprika

Soak brains in salted cold water for 15 minutes; drain and carefully remove membrane with tip of paring knife. Cover with boiling water; add 1 teaspoon salt and vinegar; simmer for 15 minutes. Drain, plunge into cold water, and drain again. Chop coarsely. Beat eggs slightly; add ½ teaspoon salt, pepper, and brains. Melt butter in frying pan; add egg mixture. Cook over low heat, stirring often, until set. Sprinkle with chopped parsley and paprika. Makes 4 servings.

BRAINS WITH WINE SAUCE
    1 pound veal or beef brains
      Salt
      Water
    1 tablespoon vinegar or lemon juice
    ½ cup chicken bouillon or 1 chicken
      bouillon cube and ½ cup water
    ½ cup white wine
      Dash of cayenne
    1 onion, minced
    1 tablespoon chopped parsley
    1 egg, beaten
    ½ cup fine dry bread crumbs
    3 tablespoons cooking fat

Soak brains in salted cold water for 15 minutes; drain and carefully remove

membrane with tip of paring knife. Cover with boiling water; add 1 teaspoon salt and the vinegar; simmer for 15 minutes. Drain, plunge into cold water, and drain again. Put brains in saucepan; add chicken bouillon, wine, cayenne, ½ teaspoon salt, onion, and parsley. Cover; bring slowly to boil and simmer for 20 minutes. Drain. Save liquid and boil to reduce to about ½ cup. Cut brains into small pieces, dip into beaten egg, then into crumbs. Brown in fat in skillet; cover and cook over low heat for 8 to 10 minutes. Remove from pan. Pour reduced broth into skillet; stir well and strain. Serve over brains. Makes 4 servings.

BRAIN BATTER CAKES
    1 pound brains
      Salt
      Water
    1 tablespoon vinegar or lemon juice
    ⅛ teaspoon pepper
    1½ teaspoons sugar
    1 teaspoon Worcestershire
    2 teaspoons curry powder
    1 medium onion, finely chopped
      Batter
      Cooking fat

Soak brains in salted cold water for 15 minutes; drain and carefully remove membrane with tip of paring knife. Cover with boiling water; add 1 teaspoon salt and vinegar; simmer for 15 minutes. Drain, plunge into cold water, and drain again. Chop brains fine. Add 1 teaspoon salt, pepper, sugar, Worcestershire, curry powder, and onion. Fold into Batter and drop by tablespoonfuls into hot fat. Fry until brown; drain on absorbent paper. Makes 4 servings.

Batter
    1 cup sifted all-purpose flour
    1 teaspoon baking powder
    ½ teaspoon salt
    2 eggs
    1 cup milk

Sift flour, baking powder, and salt. Beat eggs well, combine with milk, and add gradually to dry mixture, beating until smooth.

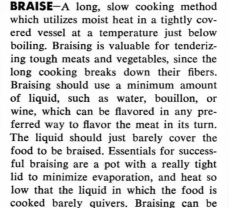

BRAISE—A long, slow cooking method which utilizes moist heat in a tightly covered vessel at a temperature just below boiling. Braising is valuable for tenderizing tough meats and vegetables, since the long cooking breaks down their fibers. Braising should use a minimum amount of liquid, such as water, bouillon, or wine, which can be flavored in any preferred way to flavor the meat in its turn. The liquid should just barely cover the food to be braised. Essentials for successful braising are a pot with a really tight lid to minimize evaporation, and heat so low that the liquid in which the food is cooked barely quivers. Braising can be done on top of the stove or in the oven.

How to Cook Superbly: Braising

By Helen Evans Brown

TWO BRAISED BEAUTIES, chicken (in the pot) and pork (on the platter), are each browned,

Once you've learned the art of braising, I'm willing to bet that you'll use it often. This method of cooking is especially recommended for the less tender cuts of meat, poultry, or game, as it combines browning and cooking with a small amount of liquid to add moisture. The meat, be it roast or fowl, may be left whole or cut into pieces. It can be done partly on top of the stove and finished in oven, or cooked entirely on top of the stove, or entirely in the oven. In other words, it's versatile.

Briefly, the procedure is this: the meat is browned, either in a hot oven or in fat on top of the stove. It is then laid on a bed of vegetables and herbs, *aromatique,* the French call this; sometimes the bones, also browned, are included.

The liquid, stock, wine, tomatoes, or a combination of two or three, is added, and the meat is covered and cooked slowly until tender. And that's the way to make inexpensive meat a dish to serve the most exacting epicure.

Equipment—The one thing you must have for proper braising is a heavy pan with a cover. In France they use a *braisière,* which has a concave lid used to hold hot coals or water, but a Dutch oven, a deep roasting pan with cover, or a casserole that will take top-of-the-stove heat will do nicely. Lacking this equipment, the meat can be cut into pieces and cooked in a heavy covered pan such as a chicken fryer. Other special gadgets called for in these recipes are a larding needle and a ball cutter, both of which can be dis-

pensed with. (See Larding and Vegetable Balls.)

Herb Bouquet or Bouquet Garni—This usually consists of 2 or 3 sprigs of parsley, a bay leaf, and a sprig of thyme tied together. If you don't have a pot of thyme for sprigs, use ½ teaspoon dried leaf thyme and either put it in a tea ball or tie in a bag made of cheesecloth. Sometimes celery or other herbs such as basil or rosemary are included.

Beurre Manié—Equal parts of butter and flour are kneaded together, formed into small balls, and added one at a time, until the desired thickness has been reached. If any are left over they store nicely in a jar in the refrigerator.

Larding—Slice fresh pork fat ¼ inch thick, then cut slices into strips ¼ inch

then combined with liquid, vegetables and herbs to cook slowly to delicious, tender doneness.

wide. Insert in end of a larding needle and take a large "stitch" in the meat, pulling the fat through, then releasing it so that it stays in the meat with the ends of fat sticking out. When it is desirable to have the fat run through the center of the meat, use another type of larding needle. Push this through the meat, fasten the strip of fat, called a lardon, on the end; and then withdraw the needle, pulling the fat into the meat. Both these methods take practice, and if you have neither time nor a larding needle, try poking holes in the meat with an ice pick or skewer and poking the fat into the holes with your finger.

Vegetable Balls—These are a nicety that require a ball cutter or *cuillier* (spoon) for scooping. One that is about an inch in diameter is a good size. The spoons come as small as ⅜ inch, but those are for garnishing. Peel the potatoes, turnips, or what have you, the larger the vegetable the better, then press the spoon, hollow concave side down, into it, turning until the vegetable reaches the bottom of the spoon; this you can see, as each scoop is equipped with a tiny hole. Then continue to turn and twist, scooping out a perfect, or near-perfect, ball. You'll be surprised how easy it is. Drop at once into cold water until all are made. As you scoop, trim away the scraps of potato that are obviously too small for a ball, giving your, eyes a chance to gauge where the next scoop should be made. A really large potato will yield 12 balls, but if you use more, don't worry, the scraps

are fine for mashing, hashing, or potato soup. And if all this twisting and scooping is too much for you, cut your vegetables with an apple corer, then slice into 1-inch pieces. You'll have cylinders rather than balls, but they are mighty impressive.

BRAISED CHICKEN

1 roasting chicken (4 to 5 pounds)
  Salt and pepper
2 tablespoons chicken fat
2 tablespoons butter
1 cup sliced carrots
1 cup sliced onions
1 cup sliced celery
½ pound small mushrooms, sauteed
  Herb Bouquet
1 cup white wine
1 cup chicken bouillon
  Beurre Manie

Sprinkle chicken with salt and pepper,

inside and out, and tie legs close to body. Render chicken fat (you can usually pull plenty from a chicken of this size) in the oven or in a heavy pan on top of the stove. Combine with the butter, or use all butter or all chicken fat, as you prefer, and brown chicken in it, turning so that it is colored on all sides. Add vegetables, Herb Bouquet, wine, and bouillon to the pan, cover, and cook in preheated moderate oven (350°F.) for 1 hour, until the chicken is fork-tender, or until the juice runs clear when pricked with a fork. Remove chicken to a platter; surround with vegetables; strain sauce and thicken with *Beurre Manié*. Serve sauce separately. Makes 5 to 6 servings.

BRAISED LOIN OF PORK

1 loin of pork (4 to 5 pounds)
½ teaspoon oregano
  Seasoned all-purpose flour
¼ cup each of chopped onion and carrot
1 garlic clove, crushed
20 boiling onions (1 pound)
24 potato balls (2 pounds
  or 3 to 4 large potatoes)
  Beurre Manie (page 218)

Sprinkle meat with oregano, then rub with seasoned flour (¼ cup flour, 1 teaspoon salt, ¼ teaspoon pepper). Put meat in a braising pan, deep roaster, or Dutch oven and bake in preheated very hot oven (450°F.) for 30 minutes, or until brown all over. Add onion, carrot, and garlic and bake for 15 minutes longer. In the meantime, peel onions. Make potato balls (see Vegetable Balls, page 219). Reduce heat to moderate (350°F.) and cook meat for 30 minutes more. Remove from oven, place meat on a pan or platter, and pour off fat from pan. In the fat, brown the onions and potato balls; remove from pan and keep warm. Add 2 cups water to the meat pan and stir over heat until all the brownings are dissolved. Strain, pushing chopped vegetables through, and reserve. Return meat to pan, add browned onions and potato balls, the strained sauce, and enough boiling water to half cover the vegetables. Cover and roast in a moderate oven (350°F.) for 1 hour; uncover and continue cooking, turning and basting the vegetables to glaze and brown on both sides. When the meat is fork-tender, or the meat thermometer reads 180°F., it is done. Arrange meat on a platter, surround with the vegetables, and thicken the sauce slightly with *Beurre Manié*. Correct seasoning and serve with the pork. A green salad with this, and the meal will mark you as a really good cook. Makes 6 to 8 servings.

BRAISED LAMB SHANKS

6 lamb shanks
1 garlic clove
  Salt, pepper, flour
⅓ cup shortening (butter,
  bacon fat, or olive oil)
2 onions, sliced
1 carrot, sliced
1 cup red wine

  Herb Bouquet (page 218)
½ teaspoon rosemary
2 tablespoons all-purpose flour

Don't have shanks cut if you have a pan large enough to hold them whole. Cut the garlic and rub the shanks with it on all sides; then rub with salt, pepper, and flour; brown in the shortening. Remove from the pan; brown the onions and carrots in the same fat, adding a little more if necessary. Return the meat, add the wine, Herb Bouquet, rosemary, and 1 cup of boiling water. Cover and bake in preheated moderate oven (350°F.) for 2 hours, or until the meat is fork-tender. Remove shanks to a platter and keep warm. Pour surplus fat from pan and add 2 tablespoons flour to the vegetables. Mix well; add 1 cup water; simmer for 4 to 5 minutes, stirring until smooth. Strain, correct seasoning, and serve with shanks. Makes 6 servings.

BRAISED DUCK WITH TURNIPS

1 duck (about 5 pounds)
  Salt and pepper
12 small onions (1 pound)
2 bunches large turnips
2 tablespoons butter
1 teaspoon sugar
2 tablespoons all-purpose flour
½ cup sliced onions
½ cup sliced carrots
2 cups chicken bouillon
  Herb Bouquet (page 218)

Put duck in a deep roasting pan or casserole, sprinkle with salt and pepper, and brown in preheated very hot oven (450°F.), turning to color on all sides. Peel onions and cut turnips into balls with the French scooping spoon previously described. Cook in butter, turning to color on all sides. When brown, sprinkle with the sugar and continue cooking until glazed and shiny; reserve. Remove duck from pan. Pour off all but 2 tablespoons of fat, sprinkle with flour, add sliced vegetables, and return duck to pan. Add bouillon and Herb Bouquet, cover, and continue baking in a moderate oven (350°F.) until the duck is tender, about 1½ hours, adding onions and turnips 30 minutes before the duck is done. When done, the juice runs clear when duck is pricked with a fork. Makes 3 to 4 servings.

BRAISED BEEF À LA MODE

5 pounds boneless rump or beef
  (and bones)
½ pound pork fat
2 teaspoons salt
  Pepper
¼ cup chopped onion
¼ cup chopped carrot
¼ cup chopped celery
  Herb Bouquet (page 218)
2 garlic cloves, peeled
1 cup red wine
3 tablespoons Cognac (optional)
3 tablespoons fat
1 cup water or stock
2 cups canned tomatoes
1 veal knuckle, cracked
24 baby or French carrots
24 small onions, peeled

2 cups sliced celery
2 tablespoons butter

Tie meat in a compact form and lard through center with pork fat, according to directions on page 219. Combine salt and pepper, vegetables, herbs, garlic, and red wine. Add Cognac or not, as you please. Marinate meat in this mixture for 6 hours or overnight, turning occasionally. Drain, saving marinade, and dry; then brown in the fat. Put in braising pot or casserole, add bones, marinade, water, tomatoes, and veal knuckle. Cover and bake in preheated moderate oven (350°F.) for 1½ hours. Discard bones; remove meat and veal knuckle. Strain sauce and skim off all fat. In the meantime, peel the vegetables and parboil. Drain. Brown parboiled onions in the butter. Return meat to the casserole which has been wiped clean. Cut the meat from the veal knuckle and add along with the vegetables and strained sauce. Cover and continue cooking until tender, about 1 hour, or longer if the meat was not tender to begin with. Arrange meat on a platter; surround with vegetables. Correct seasoning of the sauce, skim off fat if any remains, and serve with the meat. Makes 8 to 10 servings. It is delicious cold, by the way.

BRAN—The outer layers of food grains, obtained during flour-making, are called by this name. Bran contains carbohydrates, vitamins, and minerals. It adds bulk to the diet and has a laxative effect.

Bran is used as a breakfast food and as an ingredient in baking. Pure bran is dark brown in color and sold in the shape of flour, small strips, curls, and buds. Pure bran is often combined with another cereal such as wheat, and then pressed into flakes or little strips. The percentage of bran in these combinations is generally 40 per cent.

Nutritive Food Values—Bran cereal is a good source of carbohydrates, has fair amounts of calcium and phosphorus.

☐ 3½ ounces, flakes, 40% bran = 303 calories

BRAN BREAD

2 cups sifted all-purpose flour
4 teaspoons baking powder
½ teaspoon salt
⅔ cup sugar
1½ cups raisins
1⅓ cups milk
¼ cup molasses
2 cups shredded bran cereal
1 egg
⅓ cup melted butter

Sift flour, baking powder, salt, and sugar into mixing bowl. Add raisins and coat well. Combine remaining ingredients, add to dry ingredients, and mix well. Pour into greased loaf pan (9 x 5 x 3 inches) and bake in preheated moderate oven (350°F.) for 45 to 50 minutes, or until done.

BRAN MUFFINS

⅓ cup shortening
½ cup firmly packed brown sugar
1 egg
1 cup sifted all-purpose flour
1 teaspoon baking powder
½ teaspoon baking soda
1 teaspoon salt
3 cups shredded bran cereal
1 cup buttermilk

Beat together shortening, sugar, and egg. Sift flour, baking powder, soda, and salt into mixing bowl. Add bran and mix well. Mix dry ingredients alternately with buttermilk into shortening mixture. Fill greased muffin pans ⅔ full. Bake in preheated hot oven (400°F.) for about 20 minutes, or until done. Serve hot with butter and jam. Makes 1 dozen.

BRANDY—This colorless spirituous liquid is obtained by the evaporation, by distillation, of most of the watery portion of wine. The alcohol content is usually fifty to sixty per cent. The wine can be made from grapes and other fruits, although the word brandy implies the use of the fruit of the grape. The word itself comes from the middle English "brandywine" or "brandwine," which means burnt wine, or wine distilled by high heat.

Brandy is made from rather thin wines and it is matured in casks for many years where it becomes amber in color. Dark brandy is artificially colored with a caramel solution. A certain amount of brandy evaporates from the cask every year or is drawn off, and this is replenished. Brandy can mature only in the cask, and the right maturing is one of the fine points, of which there are many, in making brandy.

Good brandy is judged by its bouquet, or aroma, and by its smoothness, as well as its taste, which differs with different brandies, making the choice a personal one, as with whiskies. Good brandy is never cheap, since it cannot be hurried in the making.

All wine-producing countries, the United States, France, Italy, Spain, Portugal, Greece, Israel, and Australia, make brandies with definite tastes and characteristics. But most connoisseurs of the subject believe that the best brandy in the world is made in France, and that the best brandy in France is made in and around the town of Cognac. Though the words Cognac and brandy are often used interchangeably, this is incorrect, since French law specifies that only the brandy of the Cognac region can be called by this name. Brandy shippers have their own designation for the quality of their product. One star on a bottle of Cognac denotes a standard quality, and the letters V.S.O.P. stand for Very Superior Old Pale.

Brandies are also made from the fermented mash of fruits such as peaches, apples, plums, cherries, raspberries, pears, and blackberries. Brandies produced from fruit and wine other than grape must be labeled as such, that is, "peach brandy," etc. They are not to be confused with liqueurs made from these fruits, which are not pure spirits like true brandy.

Cooking with brandy is an art much in favor in France. It gives meats, fish, and poultry a subtle distinguished flavor all its own. Most often, the brandy used in cooking is flamed (flambé), that is, heated, poured onto the food and lighted, or poured onto the food already lighted. To flame successfully with brandy or any other spirit, the liquor must be warmed. This can be done by pouring it into either a spoon or a ladle and holding it over direct heat. All alcohol evaporates during flaming and only the taste remains. It would be a waste of the very finest brandy to flame it. Nevertheless, a good quality should be used in cooking or the dish won't be flavored properly.

CHICKEN FLAMBÉE

1 broiling chicken (about 2 pounds), quartered
Salt and pepper
3 tablespoons butter or margarine
⅓ cup dry white wine
1 tablespoon all-purpose flour
½ cup water
3 tablespoons brandy

Season chicken with salt and pepper. Brown in butter. Add wine. Cover and simmer for 45 minutes, or until tender. Stir flour into drippings in pan. Add water and bring to boil. Heat brandy in spoon. Add to sauce. Flame immediately. Spoon over chicken. Makes 4 servings.

BRANDIED FRUIT

Fill jars with drained canned fruits (peaches, apricots, pineapple, Royal Ann cherries, and maraschino cherries). Pour equal parts of drained fruit syrup and brandy over fruits. Refrigerate.

BRATWURST—The word comes from the German and means literally a "frying sausage" to distinguish it from ready-to-eat sausages. It is a fresh link sausage which is usually made from ground veal, to which pork or beef may have been added. Bratwurst is mildly spiced with salt, pepper and/or coriander, ginger, and mustard. It must be kept refrigerated.

Bratwurst is found in all European countries in one form or another, though the real Bratwurst belongs to Germany where it is a common food, and to Switzerland and the Scandinavian countries. As with all locally made food products, its flavor varies from place to place, but it is always a mild sausage.

Bratwurst is slowly fried in a pan until gently browned on all sides. It may also be browned first and then simmered in enough beer to cover. Or it may be grilled in the kitchen or outdoors. Brat-

wurst is served with potatoes, and horse-radish is a good accompaniment.

BRAZIL NUT—Botanically speaking, Brazil nuts are not nuts at all, but the edible seeds of *Bertholletia excelsa,* the rough-barked giant tree of the Amazon forest of South America. The fruit is globular, four to six inches in diameter, hard-walled, and contains eight to twenty-four seeds, arranged like the sections of an orange. These seeds are what we know as Brazil nuts. The shell of the individual nut is triangular, dark brown, and very rough. The kernels are white with a rich flavor and are quite oily.

The trees grow wild in the tropics and attempts to cultivate them in the southern United States have failed because the climate is not warm enough.

Availability—Available all year round.

Purchasing Guide—Brazil nuts are graded only according to size: jumbo, extra-large, large, large-medium, and medium. Certain brand names indicate in-the-shell nuts which have been specially inspected, cleaned, hand-picked, and polished. Shelled nuts are sold both blanched and unblanched.

A rule of thumb: Nuts in the shell are half shell and half nut.

☐ 1 pound nuts in the shell = 1½ cups shelled = 7.7 ounces

When choosing Brazil nuts in the shell, look for those which are clean, free from scars, and well filled, so the kernel does not rattle. They are sold in bulk and in film bags.

When choosing shelled Brazil nuts, look for those which are plump, meaty, crisp, and brittle. Limp, shriveled nut-meats indicate staleness. Shelled Brazil nuts are packaged in bags.

Storage—Keep shelled Brazil nuts, tightly covered, in a cool dry place. Brazil nuts remain fresh longer in larger pieces and uncooked.

☐ Unshelled, kitchen shelf: 6 months
☐ Unshelled, refrigerator shelf: 8 to 10 months
☐ Unshelled, freezer: 1 to 2 years
☐ Shelled, refrigerator shelf: about 1 year
☐ Shelled, freezer: at least 2 years

Nutritive Food Values—Brazil nuts provide some protein, iron, and thiamine.

Because of their high fat content, they are high in calories.

☐ 4 average or 3 large = 97 calories

Basic Preparation

☐ **To Shell**—Cover with cold water, bring to a boil, and boil for 3 minutes. Drain; cover with cold water for 1 minute, drain, and crack. **Alternate method**—Place nuts in freezer for several hours; crack while frozen.

☐ **To Slice**—Cover shelled nuts with cold water. Bring slowly to a boil, simmer for 2 to 3 minutes, drain, and slice with a vegetable peeler.

Whole Brazil nuts may be salted or sugared or eaten as is.

Slices may be used to decorate baked goods and desserts, or as a crunchy ingredient in main dishes and sauces.

Chopped nuts may be added to cakes, cookies, candies, breads, and stuffings.

BRAZIL-NUT PILAF

3 tablespoons butter or margarine
½ cup coarsely chopped Brazil nuts
1 can (3 or 4 ounces) sliced mushrooms
1 cup diced celery
2 chicken bouillon cubes
½ teaspoon salt
1 cup uncooked rice

Melt butter in heavy saucepan or skillet. Add nuts and cook slowly, stirring occasionally, until nuts are a delicate brown. Drain mushrooms, measure liquid, and add water to make 2½ cups. Add to skillet with celery, bouillon cubes, and salt. Bring to boil and slowly add rice. Cover; reduce heat and simmer for 25 minutes, or until rice is tender. Serve as an accompaniment for the main course. Makes 6 servings.

TOASTED BRAZIL-NUT CHIPS

Cover 1½ cups shelled Brazil nuts with cold water in saucepan. Bring slowly to boil and simmer for 5 minutes. Drain, cut into thin lengthwise slices. Spread out in shallow baking pan. Dot with 2 tablespoons butter; sprinkle with 1 teaspoon salt. Bake in preheated moderate oven (350°F.) for 12 to 15 minutes; stir occasionally. Makes 2 cups.

BRAZIL-NUT PIE SHELL

¾ cup ground Brazil nuts
2 tablespoons sugar
½ cup flaked coconut

Mix together Brazil nuts, sugar, and coconut in 9-inch pie pan. Press mixture with the back of a tablespoon against bottom and sides, up to rim of pan. If toasted flavor is desired, bake in preheated hot oven (400°F.) for 6 to 8 minutes, or until lightly browned. Good for coconut, cream, and other pies requiring a pre-baked crust.

BREAD COOK BOOK

BREAD—Defined simply as a food made from flour or meal by moistening, kneading, and baking, bread, in its various forms, has been one of the most universal foods, indeed the staff of life, since prehistoric times. It has inspired prayer and poetry. The Puritans admitted that "Brown bread and the Gospel is good fare." For sheer love of life who could want more than, "A Book of Verses underneath the Bough, A Jug of Wine, a Loaf of Bread and Thou." And we all know Little Tommy Tucker, who sang for his supper and got white bread and butter.

Bread has made history, too. Bread riots unseated emperors in ancient Rome. The French revolutionists of 1789 cried for bread and received the unthinking reply: "Let them eat cake." In more recent times Mussolini asked his people to "love bread, the heart of home." In all ages, governments in time of stress have hesitated before taking the final, desperate step of rationing bread.

The bread of primitive man was unleavened and perhaps, as the story goes, the discovery of a leavening agent by a cook of ancient Egypt was pure chance. However it came about, the Egyptians baked some of the finest bread in the ancient world in cone-shape ovens. Flattened and perhaps coarse to present-day taste, the ancient round or triangular loaves unearthed at Deir-el-Bahari were a great improvement over the open-air baking of earlier times. Bread, the symbol of the bounty of the Nile, was cast upon its waters as a tribute to the gods; it was placed in tombs to feed the departed spirits. Egyptians literally earned their daily bread: workers were given bread at the end of the day as wages.

It was the practical-minded Romans who developed the circular millstone and enlarged the baking oven to mass-production capacity. The commercial baker, in business by 168 B.C., carefully put his mark on each loaf. The ruins of Pompeii reveal beehive-shape ovens, as well as the remains of bread baked in them. Pliny states that bread *sine pondere* (without heaviness) is best, revealing an early preference for light, white bread.

In the Middle Ages, as the cities and towns grew, trade guilds were established for bakers. Millers and bakers were not always highly respected, for they were suspected, and in many cases rightly so, of taking some of the grain or dough for themselves. A London baker devised a method for taking dough under the watchful eyes of his customers. His kneading board had a small hole in the middle through which pieces of dough were pulled by a boy hidden under the table.

During the Revolutionary War, bread was so important a part of our diet that the Continental Congress appointed a "Superintendent of Bakers and Director of Baking in the Grand Army of the United States." Latecomers though we were in the long history of bread-making, we were fast to learn, and a breakfast menu for first-class passengers, at the height of riverboat luxury, offered a choice of twelve kinds of hot bread. Yet Greece cf the 2nd century A.D. offered as many as fifty different breads, including a cheese bread similar to our modern cheese bread.

It wasn't until 1834 that the roller mill was invented to crush grain more rapidly and economically between its revolving cylinders, completely removing the outer covering and germ. The customers were happier with their snow-white bread and millers and bakers were happier, too, because without the germ the flour kept longer. It wasn't until recently that we realized that nutritional elements were lost in the process, necessitating the enrichment of bread with additional B vitamins and iron.

There are two basic kinds of bread: yeast breads, which are leavened by yeast and quick breads which are leavened by baking soda or baking powder.

YEAST BREADS AND ROLLS

Yeast breads are made from non-sweet or sweet doughs. The former are used to make what we commonly call bread. The sweet doughs are made into sweet loaves, coffeecakes, kuchens, and buns of many different kinds.

Yeast comes in two types: dry granular

Man cannot live by bread alone, but he certainly cannot live without it.
Bread was indisputably the first prepared food for prehistoric man soon learned
to bake, on a hot stone, a crude bread of ground wild seeds and water.
Today, women pride themselves on their bread recipes.

Potato Rolls

Cinnamon Rolls

Squash Rolls

French Bread

Finnish Coffee Braid

Sennebec Hill Bread

Dark Rye Bread

or compressed. Each requires a different temperature of water in which to dissolve properly. For best results, use a small room thermometer or a candy thermometer to test the temperature.

In making a yeast bread, sugar, warm water, and salt are added to the yeast, stimulating its growth and starting fermentation. During the process of fermentation a gas is released which is trapped within the elastic structure which flour gives to dough, causing the bread to rise. Kneading the dough causes the development of these elastic strands, formed from the gluten in the flour. Extra milk, eggs, sugar, butter or fat add tenderness, color, and flavor to the bread.

Since yeast hates the cold, all ingredients used should be heated slightly or be at room temperature, and bread doughs should be allowed to rise in a warm .draft-free spot. Breads should be baked quickly in a hot oven and allowed to cool on a rack away from drafts.

Baked breads can be stored in moistureproof wrappings and freeze well.

Making Yeast Breads—The amount of all-purpose flour used is variable, depending on variations in the size of eggs and the amount of moisture in the flour itself. Add flour to the dough until, after beating well, the dough pulls off the spoon cleanly. Knead on a lightly floured board, adding more flour until dough no longer sticks. Kneading is simple. Fold the dough toward you and push the outer edge of the dough down, into, and away from you with the heel of your hand. Keep repeating until dough is smooth and feels bouncy.

Let dough rise in a greased bowl, turning the dough or slightly greasing the top to keep surface of dough from drying out. Allow to rise until double in bulk, or until, when the top is pressed, a dent remains. If you wish a finer, more even-textured loaf, push dough down firmly and allow to rise once again.

To shape a loaf of bread, roll out dough into an oblong, *three inches* wider than the length of the pan and *three times* longer than the width of the pan (a pan 9 x 5 x 3 inches requires an oblong 12 x 15 inches). Starting at the narrow edge, roll up as for a jelly roll. Seal ends and fold over one inch at either end. Place in a greased loaf pan and allow to rise until double in bulk.

Brush loaf with beaten egg for a shiny crust, and with milk or butter for a soft crust.

When baked, the loaf has a hollow sound when tapped and is well browned.

Freezing Yeast Breads and Rolls

All freezing must be done in freezer, since refrigerator frozen-food compartment temperatures are not cold enough. It is preferable to freeze baked yeast breads and rolls rather than unbaked ones.

☐ **To Freeze, Unbaked**—Plain yeast dough, prepared as usual, does not rise well even after a short time in the freezer. Consequently, if yeast dough is to be prepared for freezing, double the amount of yeast in the recipe and make a rich dough with additional sugar, shortening, and egg (depending on the kind of bread or roll made). Divide the dough into proper amounts to use at one time. Shape, if desired. Pack or wrap dough in any moisture-vaporproof wrapping material or container, excluding as much air as possible. Freeze quickly to stop yeast action.

To bake dough which has been frozen, leave freezer package in refrigerator overnight to thaw. Or unwrap and place in a greased bowl to thaw. Then knead dough, shape it, and allow to rise until double in bulk, as for fresh dough. Punch down. Bake as directed in recipe.

Storage life: 2 weeks

☐ **To Freeze, Baked**—Cool baked breads or rolls thoroughly on a rack. Wrap in moisture-vaporproof wrapping material, excluding as much air as possible. Thaw in wrapper for 15 to 30 minutes. To freshen or warm, heat in preheated slow oven (300°F.) for 15 to 20 minutes. If original wrapper is unsuited to oven heat, transfer to paper bag and heat.

Storage life: 3 to 6 months, depending on bread.

QUICK BREADS

The person who first named these popular members of the bread family remains a mystery. *Why* they are so-named is obvious; they are easier to make and take less time than the ones made with yeast. *What* they are requires some special definition, for there are so many of them and they are also called "hot breads," or by the name of the specific recipe in mind.

Quick breads can be classified by the type of leavening agent used. For example: *biscuits, griddle cakes, scones,* and *shortcake* are leavened by baking powder or baking soda. *Popovers* and *Yorkshire pudding* are leavened by steam.

Quick breads can also be grouped according to the thickness or thinness of the batter used to make them. There are "pour" batters, "drop" batters, and "soft" doughs which are to be rolled, patted out, or shaped. *Popovers* and *waffles* are made with pour batters. *Corn bread, loaves, spoon breads,* and *dumplings* are made from drop batters, while some *muffins* and *gingerbread* are made from pour batters, others from drop.

Scones, coffeecakes, tea breads, and *doughnuts* are made from soft doughs, and *biscuits* can be made from either drop batters or soft doughs.

Although these result in completely different breads, all are made of almost the same ingredients. They vary only because of the proportions used, and the way they are mixed and baked or cooked.

Further variety in quick breads comes from the diversity of cereal products used: wheat, whole-wheat, rye, and corn flours, and bran, oatmeal, or cornmeal. Any of these can be made into muffins, for example, yet the final baked products will taste and look different.

Mixing Quick Breads

There are two methods used for mixing quick breads:

1. The Muffin Method. Most instructions in recipes follow a pattern. The dry ingredients are mixed together and sifted into a mixing bowl, and a depression or "well," as it is often called, is made in the center of this. Then the liquid specified in the recipe is combined with melted fat, and with beaten eggs if they are required. This, in turn, is poured into the "well" and the batter stirred *only enough* to mix it. About 15 strokes is usually sufficient. This caution is almost always included in the recipe, for overmixing will result in disappointments: tunnels, tough texture, and crust with high peaks in muffins, for example. Popovers are an exception to this rule because although they are mixed by the muffin method too, they do not contain baking powder or soda (the leavening depends on eggs) and they must be well beaten so the mixture will have enough gluten to hold the steam which forms during baking and makes them "pop."

2. The Biscuit Method. For light, flaky biscuits, a solid fat is "cut" into the flour and the other dry ingredients in the mixing bowl, with a pastry blender, two knives, or the fingers. When the mixture looks fine and even, the liquid is added all at once. This is stirred until all ingredients are wet, then turned out on a floured board, formed into a ball with floured fingers, and folded over and over or kneaded 10 to 20 times, until the dough is smooth and uniform. Finally, it is patted or rolled out, cut into the desired shapes, and baked.

Biscuits—The standard for baking biscuits is doubled volume, straight sides, level tops, uniform browning, smooth tender crust, flaky layers with fine even cells, and a creamy white color free from yellow or brown spots.

Drop biscuits have a crispier crust and crumblier texture than rolled biscuits;

Bacon Batter Bread

Butter Braid

Coconut Bread

Potato Bread

more liquid is used in the recipe and biscuits are dropped from a spoon onto a cookie sheet.

Biscuits made with soda differ in flavor and texture from those made with baking powder. Fortunately, there are enough recipes to give everyone a biscuit to his taste.

Popovers—Thin hollow shells, crisp, yet tender, and moist inside, popovers are golden brown with enlarged, rounded peaked tops, rather like a chef's hat in shape. The flavor is mild and the pleasure of eating is partly this, partly the crisp crust. Although mixed by the muffin method, the batter requires more liquid and more beating, and the eggs in the mixture allow the batter to expand with the steam formed. A very hot oven is required to do this and to set the batter before the steam escapes.

Griddle Cakes—These should be evenly browned on both sides, of fairly even shape and uniform thickness, with a smooth and tender crust. Inside they should be moist but not sticky, evenly grained, and pleasantly flavored. Much of the success in griddle or pancakes lies in correct recipe proportions, proper mixing, uniformity of griddle temperature, and freshly mixed batter.

Waffles—Crisp, light buttercakes with a tender crust, waffles are imprinted with the crisscross of the iron in which they are baked to a golden brown. When mixing, be sure not to overstir; this will make them tough and heavy. When baking, watch the temperature of the iron and measure the batter carefully; then pour.

Muffins—These delicate quick breads have an evenly rounded and browned top with a slightly pebbly appearance. The crust is crisp and tender, and inside they should be moist, evenly fine-grained with no long tunnels. They are tender and have a fine flavor. There are many kinds of muffins and many recipes for them. In making them watch out for overmixing; the batter is mixed only enough to blend the dry and the moist ingredients.

Freezing Quick Breads

All storage must be done in freezer, because refrigerator frozen-food compartment temperatures are not cold enough.

☐ **To Freeze, Unbaked**—Make doughs as usual. Wrap in moisture-vaporproof wrapping material, excluding as much air as possible. If a batter, freeze in baking container such as paper cups. Unmold and then wrap for freezing. See below for additional directions for the quick breads most frequently frozen unbaked.

Storage life of frozen unbaked biscuits and muffins: 2 weeks

Biscuits

Shape dough into biscuits. Wrap as above, separating the biscuits with a double layer of wrapping material.

To bake unthawed: Remove wrapping. Put frozen biscuits on greased cookie sheet. Bake in preheated hot oven (425°F.) for 15 to 25 minutes, depending on thickness of biscuit, or until golden brown.

To bake thawed: Unwrap to make sure the biscuits won't stick together during thawing. Thaw at room temperature. Bake thawed biscuits in preheated hot oven (425°F.) for 10 to 12 minutes or until golden brown.

Muffins

Spoon batter into paper baking cups and put cups in freezer. When batter is frozen, keep in paper baking cups and wrap in moisture-vaporproof wrapping material, excluding as much air as possible. Return to freezer.

To bake unthawed: Unwrap. Put paper cups with frozen batter into ungreased muffin pans. Bake in preheated slow oven (300°F.) until well risen. Finish baking in hot oven (425°F.) for 5 to 10 minutes, or until golden brown.

To bake thawed: Unwrap. Put paper cups with frozen batter into ungreased muffin pans. Thaw for 1 hour at room temperature. Bake in preheated hot oven (425°F.) for 15 to 25 minutes, depending on size of muffins, or until golden brown.

☐ **To Freeze, Baked**—Bake as usual. Cool thoroughly on a rack. Wrap in moisture-vaporproof wrapping material, excluding as much air as possible. See below for additional directions for the quick breads most frequently frozen baked.

Storage life of frozen baked biscuits, muffins, and waffles: 2 months

Biscuits

Do not thaw frozen baked biscuits. To heat them: Unwrap. Bake in preheated slow oven (300°F.) for 20 minutes or until golden brown.

Muffins

When ready to use, frozen baked muffins can be heated unthawed or thawed.

To heat unthawed: Unwrap. Put muffins into greased muffin pans. Heat in preheated slow oven (300°F.) for 10 to 25 minutes, depending on size of muffins, or until golden brown.

To heat thawed: Unwrap and thaw at room temperature. Put muffins into greased muffin pans. Heat in preheated slow oven (300°F.) until warmed through. Baking time depends on size of muffins.

Waffles

Waffles are always baked before being frozen. To freeze baked, see general directions above. When wrapping, separate waffles with double layers of wrapping material.

To heat: Unwrap. Put in waffle iron or toaster until heated through.

YEAST BREADS

WHITE BREAD

1 package active dry yeast
  or 1 cake compressed yeast
¼ cup water*
2 cups milk, scalded
¼ cup butter or margarine
2 tablespoons sugar
2 teaspoons salt
6 cups sifted all purpose flour

*Use very warm water (105°F. to 115°F.) for dry yeast; use lukewarm (80°F. to 90°F.) for compressed. Sprinkle dry yeast or crumble cake into water. Let stand for a few minutes; then stir until dissolved. Pour hot milk over butter, sugar, and salt in large mixing bowl. Cool to lukewarm and add yeast and 3 cups flour. Beat well. Add remaining flour and mix well. Turn out on floured pastry cloth or board and knead until smooth and satiny. Put in greased bowl; turn once, cover, and let rise until doubled, about 1½ hours. Punch down; let rise for 30 minutes. Shape into 2 loaves and put in greased pans (9 x 5 x 3 inches). Let rise until doubled, about 45 minutes. Bake in preheated hot oven (400°F.) for about 35 minutes.

Individual Loaves

Use recipe for White Bread above. After first rising, cut half of dough into 6 pieces. Shape into small loaves and put in greased pans (4¾ x 2⅝ x 1½ inches). Let rise until doubled, about 30 minutes. Brush with melted butter and bake in preheated hot oven (425°F.) for about 20 minutes. Shape remaining dough into 1 loaf and put in greased loaf pan. Let rise and make as in directions for White Bread.

FRENCH BREAD

1 package active dry yeast
  or 1 cake compressed yeast
  Water*
1 cup boiling water
1 tablespoon shortening
2 teaspoons salt
1 tablespoon sugar
6 cups sifted all-purpose flour
1 egg white

*Use very warm water (105°F. to 115°F.) for dry yeast; use lukewarm (80°F. to 90°F.) for compressed. Sprinkle dry yeast or crumble cake into ¼ cup water. Let stand for a few minutes; then stir until dissolved. Pour boiling water over shortening, salt, and sugar in large mixing bowl. Add ¾ cup cold water and cool to lukewarm. Add yeast and gradually beat in enough flour to form a stiff dough. Turn out on floured pastry cloth or board and knead until smooth and satiny. Put in greased bowl; turn once, cover, and let rise until doubled, about 1½ hours. Shape into 2 oblong loaves about 14 inches long. Put on greased cookie sheets. Let rise until doubled, about 1 hour. Brush with beaten egg white and, with knife, make 3 slashes across top. Bake in preheated hot oven (425°F.) for 30 minutes. Reduce heat to moderate (350°F.); bake for 20 minutes more.

WHEAT-GERM BREAD

2 packages active dry yeast
  or 2 cakes compressed yeast
  Water*
3 tablespoons sugar
2½ teaspoons salt
  Butter or other shortening
⅓ cup molasses
¾ cup milk, scalded
1 cup wheat germ
4 cups unsifted whole-wheat flour
2 cups all-purpose white flour

Measure ¼ cup water into large bowl. *Use very warm water (105°F. to 115°F.) for dry yeast; use lukewarm (80°F. to 90°F.) for compressed. Sprinkle dry yeast or crumble cake into water. Let stand a few minutes; then stir until dissolved. In saucepan mix 1¼ cups water, sugar, salt, ⅓ cup butter, and molasses. Heat until butter melts. Cool to lukewarm. Pour scalded milk over wheat germ. Let stand until liquid is absorbed and mixture is lukewarm. To yeast, stir in the lukewarm molasses mixture and the lukewarm wheat-germ mixture. Mix whole-wheat and white flours. Add half to yeast mixture and beat until smooth. Stir in the remaining flour mixture. Turn the dough out on a lightly floured board. Knead quickly and lightly until smooth and elastic. Place in a greased bowl and brush the top lightly with melted shortening or butter. Cover with a clean damp towel. Let rise in a warm place, free from draft, until doubled in bulk, about 1½ hours; punch down and divide into 2 equal portions. Shape into loaves and place in 2 greased loaf pans (9 x 5 x 3 inches). Cover with a clean damp towel. Let rise in a warm place, free from draft, until doubled in bulk, for about 1¼ hours. Bake in preheated hot oven (400°F.) for about 50 minutes.

INDIVIDUAL WHOLE-WHEAT BATTER LOAVES

1 package active dry yeast
  or 1 cake compressed yeast
1¼ cups water*
2 tablespoons honey, brown sugar,
  or molasses
1 cup whole-wheat flour
2 cups sifted all-purpose flour
2 teaspoons salt
2 tablespoons soft shortening

*Use very warm water (105°F. to 115°F.) for dry yeast; use lukewarm (80°F. to 90°F.) for compressed. In large bowl of electric mixer, sprinkle dry yeast or crumble cake into water. Let stand for a few minutes; then stir until dissolved. Add honey, about half of each of the flours, the salt, and shortening. Blend at low speed, then beat for 2 minutes at medium speed. (Or beat by hand.) Stir in remaining flours with spoon. Cover and let rise until doubled, about 30 minutes. Stir down and spread evenly in 6 greased pans (4¾ x 2⅝ x 1½ inches). Smooth and shape tops of loaves with floured hand. Let rise until batter reaches tops of pans, about 40 minutes. Bake in preheated moderate oven (375°F.) for about 30 minutes. Cool.

DARK RYE BREAD

1 cup dark molasses
4 cups water*
2 packages active dry yeast
  or 2 cakes compressed yeast
  Cooking oil (about ⅔ cup)
2 tablespoons salt
4 egg yolks
2 cups riced hot cooked potato
2 cups nonfat dry-milk solids
2 cups rye meal or rye flour
7 cups dark rye flour
3½ to 4½ cups all-purpose flour

* Add molasses to warm water (105°F. to 115°F.) for dry yeast or lukewarm (80°F. to 90°F.) for compressed yeast. Sprinkle or crumble yeast over this and let stand for 10 minutes. Beat ½ cup oil, the salt, egg yolks, and potato together and add to yeast mixture. Mix in dry ingredients, adding enough white flour to make a stiff dough that pulls from the spoon after it has been beaten. Brush top lightly with oil and allow to rise until double. Punch down and let rise again. Shape into 4 round loaves and put in well-greased 2-quart heatproof glass casseroles. Let rise until double in size. Bake in preheated hot oven (400°F.) for 15 minutes. Reduce heat to moderate (350°F.) and bake for about 40 minutes more. **Note:** Recipe can be halved, if desired. Or, if four 2-quart casseroles are not available, bread can be baked in loaf pans (9 x 5 x 3 inches).

WHITE BATTER BREAD

2 packages active dry yeast
  or 2 cakes compressed yeast
2¾ cups water*
6½ cups sifted all-purpose flour
3 tablespoons sugar
3 teaspoons salt
2 tablespoons soft shortening

* Use very warm water (105°F. to 115°F.) for dry yeast; use lukewarm (80°F. to 90°F.) for compressed. In large bowl of electric mixer, sprinkle dry yeast or crumble cakes into water; let stand for a few minutes, then stir until dissolved. Add 3¼ cups flour, the sugar, salt, and shortening. Blend at low speed; then beat

for 2 minutes at medium speed (or beat by hand). Beat in remaining flour by hand. Cover and let rise until doubled, about 45 minutes. Stir batter, beating hard for half minute. Spread in 2 greased loaf pans (9 x 5 x 3 inches). Let rise until doubled, about 20 minutes. Bake in preheated moderate oven (375°F.) for 40 to 50 minutes.

HOT CASSEROLE BREAD
1 package active dry yeast
  or 1 cake compressed yeast
  Water*
4 cups sifted flour (preferably
  unbleached)
1 tablespoon sugar
2 teaspoons salt
  Butter

*Use very warm water (105°F. to 115° F.) for dry yeast; use lukewarm (80°F. to 90°F.) for compressed. Sprinkle dry yeast or crumble cake into 1 cup water. Let stand a few minutes; then stir until dissolved. Combine flour, sugar, and salt in bowl. Add water and yeast, and mix. Add more water, ¼ to ½ cup, to make a soft dough. Cover and let rise until doubled. Beat down and divide dough between two round 1-quart heatproof glass casseroles that have been buttered generously. Let rise until doubled; then bake in preheated hot oven (400°F.) for 40 minutes. Remove from casseroles and brush crust with butter.

PUMPERNICKEL
1½ cups cold water
¾ cup yellow cornmeal
1½ cups boiling water
1½ teaspoons salt
2 tablespoons sugar
2 tablespoons shortening
1 tablespoon caraway seeds
2 packages active dry yeast
  or 2 cakes compressed yeast
¼ cup water*
2 cups mashed potatoes
4 cups rye flour
4 cups whole-wheat flour

Stir cold water into cornmeal in a saucepan, add boiling water, and cook, stirring constantly, until thick. Add salt, sugar, shortening, and caraway seeds and let stand until lukewarm. * Use very warm water (105°F. to 115°F.) for dry yeast; use lukewarm (80°F. to 90°F.) for compressed. Sprinkle dry yeast or crumble cakes into water. Let stand for a few minutes; then stir until dissolved. Add yeast and mashed potatoes to the cornmeal; mix well. Stir in flours. Turn out on floured pastry cloth or board and knead until smooth and satiny. Put in greased bowl; turn once, cover, and let rise until doubled. Divide dough into 3 portions, form into balls, and let rest for a few minutes. Roll each loaf twice as long and twice as wide as the pan in which it is to be baked. Fold ends into center and overlap slightly. Press sides to seal and then fold over in similar fashion

to fit pan. Put each one in a greased pan with seam side down. Let rise until doubled. Bake in preheated moderate oven (375°F.) for about 1 hour.

ONION BREAD
1 package active dry yeast
  or 1 cake compressed yeast
1 cup water*
2 teaspoons sugar
2 teaspoons salt
3¼ cups sifted all-purpose flour (about)
2 tablespoons melted butter
  or margarine
½ cup coarsely chopped onion
2 teaspoons paprika

* Use very warm water (105°F. to 115° F.) for dry yeast; use lukewarm (80°F. to 90°F.) for compressed. Sprinkle dry yeast or crumble cake into water; stir until dissolved. Add sugar, 1 teaspoon salt, and 2 cups flour. Stir, then beat well. Stir in ½ cup more flour, reserving ½ cup for kneading. Sprinkle about ¼ cup flour on pastry cloth or board. Turn dough out on flour; knead until smooth and satiny, adding remaining flour as needed. Put in greased bowl; turn once, cover, and let rise until doubled, about 1 hour. Punch down and divide. Pat each half into a greased 9-inch round layer-cake pan or 8-inch square pan. Brush with butter and sprinkle with onion. Punch onion down into dough so surface looks dented. Let rise until doubled, about 45 minutes. Sprinkle each with ½ teaspoon salt and 1 teaspoon paprika. Bake in preheated very hot oven (450° F.) for about 20 minutes. Cut into wedges or strips and serve hot with butter. (Good with roast beef.)

CHEESE BREAD
1 package active dry yeast
  or 1 cake compressed yeast
¼ cup water*
2 tablespoons sugar
1½ cups liquid skim milk
2½ cups shredded sharp Cheddar cheese
¼ cup grated raw carrot
3 tablespoons cooking oil
1¼ teaspoons salt
5 to 6 cups sifted all-purpose flour

* Use very warm water (105°F. to 115° F.) for dry yeast; use lukewarm (80°F. to 90°F.) for compressed. Sprinkle dry yeast or crumble cake into water. Let stand for a few minutes; then stir until dissolved. Heat remaining ingredients except flour to lukewarm. Pour over yeast. Add about half of flour and mix well. Add enough more flour to make a stiff dough that will not stick to bowl. Turn out on floured pastry cloth or board and knead until smooth and satiny. Put in greased bowl; turn once, cover, and let rise until doubled. Punch down and shape into 2 loaves. Put in greased loaf pans (9 x 5 x 3 inches). Let rise until doubled. Bake in preheated moderate oven (350°F.) for about 40 minutes.

LIMPA BREAD
1 package active dry yeast
  or 1 cake compressed yeast
  Water*
¼ cup firmly packed brown sugar
2 teaspoons caraway seeds
2 tablespoons shortening
2 teaspoons salt
4 cups sifted all-purpose flour
2 cups unsifted rye flour (about)

* Use very warm water (105°F. to 115° F.) for dry yeast; use lukewarm (80°F. to 90°F.) for compressed. Sprinkle dry yeast or crumble cake into ½ cup water. Let stand a few minutes; then stir until dissolved. In saucepan mix ½ cup cold water, sugar, caraway, shortening, and salt. Bring to boil and simmer for 5 minutes. Pour into large mixing bowl and add 1 cup cold water. Stir in 2 cups all-purpose flour. Add yeast and mix well. Stir in remaining all-purpose flour. Add 1½ cups rye flour and mix well. Sprinkle ¼ cup rye flour on pastry cloth or board. Turn dough out and knead until smooth and satiny, using more rye flour as necessary. Put in greased bowl; turn once, cover, and let rise until doubled, about 1½ hours. Punch down. Divide; shape each half into a ball. Put on greased cookie sheet. Make 3 cuts, ½ inch deep, in tops. Let rise until doubled. Bake in preheated hot oven (400°F.) for 35 minutes.

ANADAMA BATTER BREAD
1 package active dry yeast
  or 1 cake compressed yeast
¼ cup water*
¾ cup boiling water
½ cup yellow cornmeal
3 tablespoons shortening
¼ cup light molasses
2 teaspoons salt
1 egg
2¾ cups sifted all-purpose flour

* Use very warm water (105°F. to 115° F.) for dry yeast; use lukewarm (80°F. to 90°F.) for compressed. Sprinkle dry yeast or crumble cake into water. Let stand for a few minutes; then stir until dissolved. In large bowl of electric mixer stir together boiling water, cornmeal, shortening, molasses, and salt. Cool to lukewarm. Add yeast, egg, and about half of flour. Blend at low speed, then beat for 2 minutes at medium speed. Stir in remaining flour. Spread in greased loaf pan (9 x 5 x 3 inches). Let rise until batter reaches 1 inch from top of pan. Bake in preheated moderate oven (375° F.) for 35 minutes.

Oatmeal Batter Bread
Use recipe for Anadama Batter Bread, substituting ½ cup rolled oats for the cornmeal.

SALLY LUNN
1 package active dry yeast
  or 1 cake compressed yeast
½ cup water*
1 cup milk, scalded

½ cup sugar
2 teaspoons salt
½ cup butter or margarine
3 eggs, well beaten
4½ cups unsifted all-purpose flour

*Use very warm water (105°F. to 115° F.) for dry yeast; use lukewarm (80°F. to 90°F.) for compressed. Sprinkle dry yeast or crumble cake into water. Let stand for a few minutes; then stir until dissolved. Pour milk over ¼ cup sugar, the salt, and butter in large bowl. Cool to lukewarm and add yeast, eggs, and flour. Beat until smooth. Cover and let rise until doubled, about 1 hour. Stir down; pour into 2 well-greased 8-inch square cake pans. Cover and let rise until doubled, about 30 minutes. Sprinkle each loaf with 2 tablespoons sugar and bake in preheated hot oven (400°F.) for 25 minutes. Makes 2 loaves.

SENNEBEC HILL BREAD

2 packages active dry yeast
    or 2 cakes compressed yeast
2 cups water*
½ cup molasses
4 egg yolks
2½ teaspoons salt
⅓ cup cooking oil
1 cup nonfat dry-milk solids
½ cup regular rolled oats
½ cup yellow cornmeal
½ cup wheat germ
1 cup rye meal or rye flour
2 cups whole-wheat flour
3 cups all-purpose flour (about)

* Use very warm water (105°F. to 115° F.) for dry yeast; use lukewarm (80°F. to 90°F.) for compressed. Sprinkle dry yeast or crumble cakes into water in large bowl of electric mixer; add molasses. Let stand for a few minutes; then stir until dissolved. Add egg yolks, salt, oil, dry milk, oats, cornmeal, and wheat germ. Beat on low speed until well mixed. (Or beat with rotary beater.) By hand, add rye meal, whole-wheat flour, and enough all-purpose flour to make a stiff dough. Mix well and brush lightly with

oil. Cover and let rise until doubled. If punched down and allowed to rise again, this bread will have a finer texture, but this is not necessary. Turn out on floured pastry cloth or board and knead gently. Shape into 4 loaves. Put in 4 greased pans (7½ x 3½ x 2½ inches), or two pans (9 x 5 x 3 inches). Let rise until doubled. Bake in preheated moderate oven (375°F.) for 25 minutes. Reduce heat to 350°F. and bake for about 20 minutes longer. This bread is excellent for toast. Makes 4 medium or 2 large loaves.

OATMEAL BREAD
- 1 cup quick-cooking rolled oats
- 2 cups milk, scalded
- 1 package active dry yeast
  or 1 cake compressed yeast
- ½ cup water*
- ½ cup molasses
- 2 teaspoons salt
- ¼ teaspoon ground ginger
  All-purpose flour

Put oats in large bowl and cover with milk. Stir and let stand until lukewarm. Sprinkle or crumble yeast into water. * Use very warm water (105°F. to 115° F.) for dry yeast; use lukewarm (80°F. to 90°F.) for compressed. Let stand a few minutes; then stir until dissolved. Add yeast mixture, molasses, salt, and ginger to oat mixture. Stir in 4½ cups unsifted flour. Cover and let rise in warm place until double in bulk, about 1 hour. Knead down on well-floured board and put into 2 greased loaf pans (9 x 5 x 3 inches). Let rise until almost double, about 45 minutes. Bake in preheated moderate oven (350°F.) for 45 to 50 minutes. Makes 2 loaves.

POTATO BREAD
- ½ cup butter
- 1½ cups cooked potato,
  put through a sieve
- 2 tablespoons sugar
- 2 teaspoons salt
- 1 cup milk, scalded
- 2 packages active dry yeast
  or 2 cakes compressed yeast
- ⅓ cup water*
- 5½ cups sifted all-purpose flour
- 1 egg white
  Sesame seeds

Add butter to hot potatoes and stir until melted. Add sugar, salt, and milk. Sprinkle or crumble yeast into water. * Use very warm water (105°F. to 115°F.) for dry yeast; use lukewarm (80°F. to 90° F.) for compressed. Let stand a few minutes; then stir until dissolved. Add to milk mixture. Stir in 3 cups of flour and beat until smooth. Gradually stir in remaining flour, or enough to make a firm dough. Knead for 10 minutes. Put in a greased bowl, cover, and let rise until double in bulk. Punch down and let rise again. Punch down and shape dough into a large braid, or into 2 smaller braids. Put on greased cookie sheet or into 2

greased loaf pans (9 x 5 x 3 inches). Cover and let rise. Brush with egg white which has been slightly beaten with 1 tablespoon of water. Sprinkle heavily with sesame seeds. Bake in a preheated hot oven (400°F.) for 10 minutes. Lower heat to moderate (350°F.) and bake for 30 to 35 minutes longer. Makes 1 large braid or 2 smaller braids.

BUTTER BRAID
- 1 cup milk
- ½ cup butter
- ⅓ cup sugar
- 2 teaspoons salt
- 2 packages active dry yeast
  or 2 cakes compressed yeast
- ¼ cup water*
- 3 eggs, beaten
- 6 to 7 cups sifted all-purpose flour
  Poppy or sesame seeds
- 1 egg white

Scald milk and pour it over butter, sugar, and salt. Sprinkle or crumble yeast into water. * Use very warm water (105°F. to 115°F.) for dry yeast; use lukewarm (80°F. to 90°F. for compressed. Let stand a few minutes, then stir until dissolved. Stir into the cooled milk mixture. Add beaten eggs and 3 cups of flour. Beat until smooth. Stir in rest of the flour to make a stiff dough. Turn onto a lightly floured board and knead well. Put in a greased bowl. Cover and let rise until double in bulk. Punch down and turn out onto board. Divide in half. Cut one half of dough into 3 equal pieces and roll out into strips about 18 inches long. Braid. Place on greased cookie sheet. Divide two thirds of the remaining dough into 3 equal pieces, and braid. Place over the first braid. Form remaining dough into braid and lay over the first two. Brush all with melted butter and sprinkle with poppy seeds. Let rise until double. Brush with a mixture of 1 egg and 1 tablespoon water. Bake in preheated moderate oven (375°F.) for 30 to 35 minutes, or until done. Brush twice with egg and water mixture while baking.

BACON BATTER BREAD
- 1½ cups milk, scalded
- 2 teaspoons salt
- ¼ cup firmly packed brown sugar
- 2 tablespoons bacon fat
- 2 packages active dry yeast
  or 2 cakes compressed yeast
- ½ cup water*
- 1 egg, beaten
- 4 cups sifted all-purpose flour
- 1 cup whole wheat flour
- ¼ teaspoon ground coriander
- ⅓ cup crumbled cooked bacon

* Use very warm water (105°F. to 115°F.) for dry yeast; use lukewarm (80°F. to 90°F.) for compressed. Combine milk, salt, 2 tablespoons brown sugar, and bacon fat. Cool. Combine yeast, 2 tablespoons brown sugar, and water. When bubbly add to the cooled milk mixture. Add egg and flours. Beat

thoroughly for 3 minutes. Put in greased bowl. Cover and let rise for about 45 minutes. Stir in coriander and crumbled bacon. Beat for 2 minutes and pour into greased 2-quart glass casserole or two greased glass loaf pans (9 x 5 x 3 inches). Let rise until the batter reaches top of the pans. Score top with knife. Bake in preheated moderate oven (375°F.) for 35 to 40 minutes.

COFFEECAKES AND RINGS MADE WITH YEAST

STREUSEL COFFEECAKE
- 1 package active dry yeast
  or 1 cake compressed yeast
- 2 tablespoons water*
  Sifted all-purpose flour
  (about 2½ cups)
  Sugar (about 1⅓ cups)
- 1 teaspoon salt
  Butter or margarine (about ⅔ cup)
- 3 eggs
- ½ cup dairy sour cream
- 1 teaspoon vanilla extract
  Cinnamon

* Use very warm water (105°F. to 115° F.) for dry yeast; use lukewarm (80°F. to 90°F.) for compressed yeast. Sprinkle dry yeast or crumble cake into water. Let stand for a few minutes; then stir until dissolved. Sift 2½ cups flour, ½ cup sugar, and the salt into bowl. Cut in ½ cup butter. Add yeast, eggs, sour cream, and vanilla. Beat hard for 3 minutes. Let rise until bubbly, about 30 minutes. Beat hard one or two minutes, and chill overnight. Roll to a rectangle ¼ inch thick. Sprinkle with a mixture of ½ cup sugar, 1 tablespoon cinnamon, and the raisins. Roll up and fit into buttered 9-inch tube pan. Don't worry if roll breaks. Sprinkle with mixture of 2 tablespoons flour, 2 tablespoons butter, 5 tablespoons sugar, and ½ teaspoon cinnamon. Let rise until light, about 1½ hours. Bake in preheated slow oven (325°F.) for about 45 minutes.

GERMAN COFFEE BRAID
- 1 package active dry yeast
  or 1 cake compressed yeast
- 2 tablespoons water*
- ¾ cup milk, scalded
  Butter or margarine (about ½ cup)
- ¾ cup sugar
- 1 teaspoon salt
- 1 egg
- 3 cups sifted all-purpose flour
- 1½ teaspoons ground cinnamon
- ¼ teaspoon ground nutmeg
  Confectioners' Sugar Frosting
  Candied cherries
  Chopped walnuts

* Use very warm water (105°F. to 115° F.) for dry yeast; use lukewarm (80°F. to 90°F.) for compressed. Sprinkle dry yeast or crumble cake into water. Let stand for a few minutes; then stir until dissolved. Pour hot milk over ¼ cup butter, ¼ cup sugar, and the salt; cool to

lukewarm. Add yeast, egg, and 1½ cups flour. Beat until smooth; then beat in remaining flour. Turn out on floured pastry cloth or board and knead until smooth and satiny. Put in greased bowl; turn once, cover, and let rise until doubled, about 1 hour. Punch down and let rise again. Divide into 3 equal parts. Roll each into a rectangle 12 x 17 inches. Brush with soft butter. Mix ½ cup sugar, the cinnamon, and nutmeg. Sprinkle on dough. Roll each piece up tightly from narrow side. Put on greased cookie sheet and braid tightly, pinching ends together. Brush with soft butter and sprinkle with sugar. Let rise until doubled, about 30 minutes. Bake in preheated moderate oven (350°F.) for about 30 minutes. Cool, and decorate with Confectioners' Sugar Frosting, cherries, nuts.

Confectioners' Sugar Frosting

Combine ½ cup sifted confectioners' sugar with about 1 teaspoon milk or light cream, or enough to make a thick pouring consistency. Stir in a few drops of vanilla flavoring.

APRICOT-PEANUT SQUARES

    2 packages active dry yeast
       or 2 cakes compressed yeast
    ½ cup water*
    2 tablespoons sugar
    1 teaspoon salt
    ½ cup butter or margarine, melted
    2 eggs
    2 cups all-purpose flour
    ¾ cup chopped salted jumbo peanuts
    1 cup apricot preserves
    1 teaspoon vanilla extract

*Use very warm water (105°F. to 115°F.) for dry yeast; use lukewarm (80°F. to 90°F.) for compressed. Sprinkle dry yeast or crumble cake into water. Let stand a few minutes; then stir until dissolved. Stir in the sugar, salt, ¼ cup melted butter, eggs, and 1 cup flour. Beat until smooth. Add remaining flour. Cover. Let rise in a warm place, free from draft, until doubled in bulk, about 45 minutes. Meanwhile mix peanuts, apricot preserves, remaining melted butter, and the vanilla. Blend well. When the batter has doubled in bulk, stir down. Spread in a well-greased jelly-roll pan (15 x 10 x 2 inches). Spread the apricot-peanut mixture over the batter. Let rise in a warm place, free from draft, until doubled in bulk, about 25 minutes. Bake in a preheated moderate oven (350°F.) for 30 to 35 minutes, or until done. Cut into 24 squares.

APPLE DANISH PASTRIES

    2 packages active dry yeast
       or 2 cakes compressed yeast
    ¼ cup water*
    ¾ cup milk, scalded
       Sugar
    2 teaspoons salt
    1⅓ cups butter or margarine

    ½ teaspoon lemon extract
    3 eggs, beaten
    4½ cups all-purpose flour
    1 can (1 pound, 4 ounces) sliced apples
    3 teaspoons cinnamon

*Use very warm water (105°F. to 115°F.) for dry yeast; use lukewarm (80°F. to 90°F.) for compressed. Sprinkle dry yeast or crumble cake into water. Let stand a few minutes; then stir until dissolved. Pour hot milk over ⅓ cup sugar, the salt, and ⅓ cup butter. Cool to lukewarm. Add the yeast mixture. Stir in the lemon extract and eggs. Add the flour gradually. Place the dough in a greased pan (13 x 9 x 2 inches). Chill for 1 to 2 hours. Turn the chilled dough out onto a floured board. Roll into a rectangle 16 x 12 inches. Spread ⅓ cup butter or margarine over two thirds of the dough. Fold the unspread portion of the dough over half the covered portion. Fold the third section over the first two. Roll the dough to its original size and repeat this process twice, using the remaining butter. Return the dough to the refrigerator and chill overnight. Next day, divide the dough in half. Roll each half into a rectangle 14 x 9 inches. Cut into strips 14 x ¾ inches. Twist and form each strip into a spiral roll. Put a few drained apple slices in center of each. Sprinkle with the cinnamon mixed with ½ cup sugar. Cover. Let rise in a warm place, free from draft, until doubled in bulk. Bake in preheated moderate oven (375°F.) for about 12 minutes. Makes about 2 dozen.

FINNISH COFFEE BRAIDS

    1 package active dry yeast
       or 1 cake compressed yeast
    2¼ cups water*
    1 cup sugar
    4 egg yolks
    2½ teaspoons salt
       Melted butter or margarine
   10 cardamom seeds, finely ground,
       or 1 teaspoon ground cardamom
    ⅔ cup nonfat dry milk solids
    7 cups unsifted all-purpose flour

* Use very warm water (105°F. to 115°F.) for dry yeast; use lukewarm (80°F. to 90°F.) for compressed. Sprinkle dry yeast or crumble cake into water in large bowl of electric mixer; add sugar. Let stand for a few minutes; then stir until dissolved. When lukewarm, add 2 egg yolks, salt, ½ cup butter, the cardamom, and milk. Beat with electric mixer on low speed while adding 3 cups flour. (Or beat with rotary beater.) Add remaining flour or enough to make a stiff dough, mixing well by hand. Cover and let rise until doubled. Roll out on floured board to rectangle 18 x 12 inches and cut into nine strips 12 x 2 inches. Dough will be soft. Brush each strip with melted butter. On lightly greased cookie sheet, braid 3 strips into a long (about 12-inch) coffee

loaf. Repeat, making 3 loaves. Bake in preheated hot oven (400°F.) for 10 minutes. Remove from oven and quickly brush loaves with 2 egg yolks beaten with 1 teaspoon water. Sprinkle with sugar. Bake in moderate oven (375°F.) for about 15 minutes.

TURBAN COFFEECAKE

    2 packages active dry yeast
       or 2 cakes compressed yeast
    ¼ cup water*
    ½ cup milk, scalded and cooled
    2¾ cups sifted all-purpose flour
    ½ cup soft butter
    ½ cup granulated sugar
    3 eggs
    1 tablespoon grated lemon rind
    1 teaspoon salt
    ¼ teaspoon ground mace
    2 tablespoons grated nuts
       Confectioners' sugar

Sprinkle or crumble yeast into water. * Use very warm water (105°F. to 115° F.) for dry yeast; use lukewarm (80°F. to 90°F.) for compressed. Let stand a few minutes; then stir until dissolved. Add milk and 1 cup flour; beat well. Cover and let rise until doubled (about 30 minutes). Cream butter and granulated sugar until light. Add eggs one at a time, beating well after each addition. Add lemon rind. Add yeast mixture and remaining flour, sifted with salt and mace. Grease well a 9-cup turban mold and sprinkle nuts to cover the inside. Put dough into mold, cover and let rise until doubled, about 1½ hours. Bake in preheated slow oven (325°F.) for about 45 minutes. Turn out on rack and cool. Sift confectioners' sugar lightly over top.

CINNAMON LOAF

    1 package active dry yeast or
       1 cake compressed yeast
    2 tablespoons water*
    ⅔ cup milk, scalded
    ½ cup sugar
    1 teaspoon salt
       Butter or margarine
    2 eggs
    3 cups sifted all-purpose flour
    1½ teaspoons ground cinnamon
    2 tablespoons melted butter or
       margarine

* Use very warm water (105°F. to 115°F.) for dry yeast; use lukewarm (80°F. to 90°F.) for compressed. Sprinkle dry yeast or crumble cake into water. Let stand for a few minutes; then stir until dissolved. Pour hot milk over ¼ cup sugar, the salt, and ¼ cup butter; cool to lukewarm. Add eggs, yeast, and half of flour. Beat with rotary beater or electric beater until smooth. Beat in remaining flour with spoon. Cover and let rise until doubled, about 1 hour. Punch down and knead lightly. Roll out on floured pastry cloth or board to a rectangle 18 x 9 inches. Spread with 2 tablespoons butter; sprinkle with ¼ cup sugar mixed with the cinnamon. Roll up tightly from narrow end and put in greased loaf pan

(9 x 5 x 3 inches). Brush with melted butter and let rise until doubled, about 45 minutes. Bake in preheated moderate oven (350°F.) for about 30 minutes. Cool.

SWEDISH CARDAMOM BRAID

2 packages active dry yeast
  or 2 cakes compressed yeast
½ cup water*
½ cup milk, scalded
½ cup, plus 2 tablespoons sugar
1 teaspoon salt
1½ cups butter or margarine
2 eggs, beaten
5 cups all-purpose flour
1½ teaspoons ground cardamom
½ cup seedless raisins
1 egg white

*Use very warm water (105°F. to 115°F.) for dry yeast; use lukewarm (80°F. to 90°F.) for compressed. Sprinkle dry yeast or crumble cakes into water. Let stand a few minutes; then stir until dissolved. Pour hot milk over ½ cup of the sugar, the salt, and butter. Cool to lukewarm. Add yeast mixture, beaten eggs, 3 cups flour, and the cardamom and raisins. Beat until smooth. Stir in an additional 2 cups sifted flour (about). Turn the dough out on a lightly floured board. Knead until smooth and elastic. Place in a greased bowl; brush the top with soft shortening. Cover. Let rise in a warm place, free from draft, until doubled in bulk, about 1 hour. Punch down and turn out on a lightly floured board. Divide the dough into thirds. Roll each part into a strand 10 inches long, tapering the ends. Braid loosely. Place on a greased cookie sheet. Cover. Let rise in a warm place, free from draft, until doubled in bulk, about 1 hour. Before baking, brush with the slightly beaten egg white mixed with 2 tablespoons sugar. Bake in a preheated moderate oven (350°F.) for about 35 minutes.

RAISED FRUITCAKE

2 packages active dry yeast
  or 2 cakes compressed yeast
½ cup water*
⅓ cup milk, scalded
½ cup sugar
1 teaspoon salt
3½ cups all-purpose flour
½ cup butter
2 eggs, beaten
1½ teaspoons grated orange rind
1 cup raisins
1 cup chopped walnuts
1 cup chopped mixed candied fruit
1 teaspoon cinnamon
1 teaspoon ginger
½ teaspoon nutmeg
  Orange Glaze

*Use very warm water (105°F. to 115°F.) for dry yeast; use lukewarm (80°F. to 90°F.) for compressed. Sprinkle dry yeast or crumble cake into water. Let stand a few minutes; then stir until dissolved. Pour hot milk over ¼ cup sugar and the salt. Cool to lukewarm. Add yeast mixture and 1 cup flour; beat until smooth. Cover and let rise in a warm place, free from draft, until light, about 20 minutes. Cream but-

ter until light and fluffy. When yeast mixture is light, beat in butter, remaining sugar, eggs, and orange rind. Stir in remaining 2½ cups flour; beat hard. Add remaining ingredients, except Glaze. Turn into a well-greased 3-quart bundt mold. Cover and let rise in a warm place, free from draft, about 1½ hours. Bake in preheated moderate oven (375°F.) for 40 to 45 minutes. Cool and top with Orange Glaze.

Orange Glaze

Mix thoroughly 1 teaspoon grated orange rind, 2 tablespoons orange juice and 1 cup confectioners' sugar.

YEAST ROLLS

SQUASH ROLLS

1 cup warm water
¾ cup sugar
1 package active dry yeast or
  1 cake compressed yeast
  Cooking oil
2 teaspoons salt
1 cup strained, cooked winter squash
½ cup nonfat dry-milk solids
5 cups sifted all-purpose flour (about)

Put warm water and sugar into large bowl of electric mixer. Sprinkle dry yeast or crumble cake into this and allow to stand for 5 minutes. Add 3 tablespoons oil, salt, squash, and dry milk. Beat well at low speed. Gradually beat in 2 cups of the flour. (Or beat with rotary beater.) Scrape beaters and add the rest of flour by hand, mixing well. Let rise. Knead gently on a floured board. Roll to 1-inch thickness. Cut with floured 2½-inch biscuit cutter. Roll edges lightly in oil so that the baked rolls will separate readily. Put into greased pan (13 x 9 x 2 inches) and allow to double in size. Bake in preheated hot oven (400°F.) for about 20 minutes. Makes about 15.

POTATO ROLLS

1 package active dry yeast
  or 1 cake compressed yeast
1 cup water*
2 eggs
⅓ cup sugar
1 tablespoon salt
  Cooking oil
1½ cups riced warm cooked potato
½ cup nonfat dry-milk solids
4½ to 5 cups sifted all-purpose flour

Sprinkle or crumble yeast into water. * Use very warm water (105°F. to 115° F.) for dry yeast; use lukewarm (80°F. to 90°F.) for compressed. Let stand for 10 minutes; then stir until dissolved. Into large bowl of electric mixer put the eggs, sugar, salt, ⅓ cup oil, potato, milk, and yeast mixture. Beat at low speed until well blended. (Or beat with rotary beater.) Gradually add 2 cups flour and beat well. Add remaining 2½ to 3 cups flour by hand. Mix until the dough forms a ball away from the sides of the bowl.

Let rise until double in size. Roll out on a floured board until about 1½ inches thick. Cut with floured 2¼-inch biscuit cutter. Roll edges lightly in oil and put into baking pan (13 x 9 x 2 inches). Allow to rise again. Bake in preheated hot oven (400°F.) for about 25 minutes. Makes about 20.

PARKERHOUSE ROLLS

1 package active dry yeast
  or 1 cake compressed yeast
½ cup water*
⅔ cup butter or margarine (about)
¼ cup sugar
½ cup boiling water
1 egg, beaten
3 cups unsifted all-purpose flour
1 teaspoon salt

* Use very warm water (105°F. to 115° F.) for dry yeast; use lukewarm (80°F. to 90°F.) for compressed. Sprinkle dry yeast or crumble cake into warm water. Let stand for a few minutes; then stir until dissolved. Put ½ cup butter, the sugar, and boiling water in bowl and stir until butter is melted. Cool to lukewarm; then add yeast and egg. Add flour and salt; mix well, cover and put in refrigerator for at least 24 hours. Roll on lightly floured board to ¼-inch thickness and cut with floured 2½-inch cutter. With handle of wooden spoon, make a crease in each circle to one side of center; flatten smaller half of round slightly by rolling handle of spoon toward edge. Brush with melted butter; fold thicker half over thinner half; press edges together. Put on cookie sheets and brush again with butter. Bake in preheated hot oven (400°F.) for 12 to 15 minutes. Makes about 3 dozen.

BUTTERHORNS

1 package active dry yeast
  or 1 cake compressed yeast
½ cup water*
½ cup milk, scalded
½ cup butter or margarine
⅓ cup sugar
¾ teaspoon salt
1 egg, beaten
4 cups sifted all-purpose flour

* Use very warm water (105°F. to 115° F.) for dry yeast; use lukewarm (80°F. to 90°F.) for compressed. Sprinkle dry yeast or crumble cake into water. Let stand for a few minutes; then stir until dissolved. Pour hot milk over butter, sugar, and salt. Cool to lukewarm; add yeast, egg, and half of flour. Beat well. Add enough more flour to make a dough that will not stick to bowl. Turn out on floured pastry cloth or board and knead lightly. Put in greased bowl, cover, and let rise until doubled, about 1 hour. Divide dough into halves. Roll each half out on floured board to form a circle 12 inches in diameter. Cut each into 12 pie-shape pieces. Roll up from wide end and put, pointed side down, on greased

Apricot-Peanut Squares

Quick-Rising Sweet Rolls

Wheat-Germ Bread

Swedish Cardamom Braid

Apple Danish Pastries

Herb Breadsticks

White Bread

Raised Fruitcake

cookie sheets. Let rise until doubled, about 30 minutes. Bake in preheated hot oven (400°F.) for 15 minutes. Unraised dough can be refrigerated overnight; let stand at room temperature to soften enough to roll. Then proceed as directed. Makes 24 rolls.

Cloverleaf Rolls

Follow recipe for Butterhorns. After first rising, cut dough into 24 pieces. Cut each piece into thirds and roll into a ball. Put 3 balls in each of 24 greased 2¼-inch muffin cups. Proceed as directed. Makes 24 rolls.

CHEESE-FILLED ROLLS

1 package active dry yeast
  or 1 cake compressed yeast
2 tablespoons water*
  Milk (about ⅔ cup)
  Sugar (about ½ cup)
½ teaspoon salt
⅓ cup butter or margarine
2 eggs
1 teaspoon grated lemon rind
3¼ cups sifted all-purpose flour
4 ounces cream cheese
1 teaspoon ground cinnamon

* Use very warm water (105°F. to 115°F.) for dry yeast; use lukewarm (80°F. to 90°F.) for compressed. Sprinkle dry yeast or crumble cake into water. Let stand for a few minutes; then stir until dissolved. Scald ½ cup milk and pour over ⅓ cup sugar, the salt, and butter. Cool to lukewarm. Stir in yeast, 1 whole egg, 1 egg yolk, and lemon rind. Beat in 1½ cups flour; then stir in 1¾ cups. Cover and let rise until doubled, about 1½ hours. Punch down. Roll on floured surface to form a rectangle, 14 x 10½ inches. Cut into twelve 3½-inch squares. Mix cheese and 1½ tablespoons milk. Spread 2 teaspoons on each square; fold into triangles. Put on greased cookie sheets and let rise until light, about 30 minutes. Brush with 1 egg white beaten with 2 teaspoons water. Sprinkle with 2 tablespoons sugar and the cinnamon, mixed. Bake in preheated moderate oven (350°F.) for 10 to 15 minutes. Makes 12 rolls.

HERB BREADSTICKS

1 package active dry yeast
  or 1 cake compressed yeast
1¼ cups water*
3 tablespoons sugar
1½ teaspoons salt
1 tablespoon butter
3 teaspoons caraway seeds
1 teaspoon ground sage
3½ cups sifted all-purpose flour (about)

* Use very warm water (105°F. to 115°F.) for dry yeast; use lukewarm (80°F. to 90°F.) for compressed. Sprinkle dry yeast or crumble cake into water in large bowl. Let stand for a few minutes; then stir until dissolved. Add sugar, salt, butter, 2 teaspoons caraway seeds, sage,

and flour; mix well. Turn out on lightly floured board and knead until smooth and elastic, about 10 minutes. Put in greased bowl; turn once, cover, and let rise until doubled, about 1 hour. Punch down, turn out on floured board, and divide. Roll each half into a rectangle 12 inches long. Cut each into 12 pieces. Roll each piece on the board with palms of hands to form a rope about ⅓ inch thick and 12 inches long. Put on greased cookie sheet; sprinkle lightly with remaining caraway seeds. Cover and let rise until doubled, about 1 hour. Bake in preheated hot oven (400°F.) for 15 to 20 minutes. Makes 24 sticks.

BUTTERSCOTCH PECAN ROLLS

1 package active dry yeast
  or 1 cake compressed yeast
¼ cup water*
½ cup milk, scalded
¾ teaspoon salt
¼ cup granulated sugar
3 cups minus 2 tablespoons sifted
  all-purpose flour
  Butter or margarine, melted and cooled
1 egg
  Light brown sugar (about 1½ cups)
  Pecan halves

* Use very warm water (105°F. to 115°F.) for dry yeast; use lukewarm (80°F. to 90°F.) for compressed yeast. Sprinkle dry yeast or crumble cake into water. Let stand for a few minutes; then stir until dissolved. Pour hot milk over salt and granulated sugar. Cool to lukewarm. Add yeast and 1 cup flour; beat until smooth. Add remaining flour, 2 tablespoons melted butter, and egg; mix well. Turn out on floured pastry cloth or board and knead until smooth and satiny. Put in greased bowl, cover, and let rise until doubled, about 1 hour. Meanwhile, boil 1 cup plus 2 tablespoons brown sugar and ¾ cup water for 5 minutes. Put 1 tablespoon syrup in each of 18 greased 2¾-inch muffin cups. Arrange 3 or 4 pecan halves, rounded side down, in each cup. Roll dough to form a rectangle 18 x 8 inches. Brush with melted butter and sprinkle with ⅓ cup brown sugar. Roll up from the long side and seal edges. Cut into eighteen 1-inch slices. Put, flat side down, in prepared cups. Cover and let rise until doubled, about 30 minutes. Bake in preheated hot oven (400°F.) for 12 to 15 minutes. Let stand in pans for 1 minute before turning out. Makes 18 rolls.

CINNAMON ROLLS

1 package active dry yeast or
  1 cake compressed yeast
½ cup granulated sugar
2¼ cups water*
2 egg yolks
  Cooking oil
2½ teaspoons salt
1 cup nonfat dry milk solids
7 to 8 cups sifted all-purpose flour
1½ cups firmly packed light brown sugar
1 tablespoon ground cinnamon

* Use very warm water (105°F. to 115°F.) for dry yeast; use lukewarm (80°F. to 90°F.) for compressed. Sprinkle sugar and dry yeast or crumble cake into water in large bowl of electric mixer. Let stand for a few minutes; then stir until dissolved. Add egg yolks, ⅓ cup oil, the salt, milk, and 2 cups flour. Beat at low speed. (Or beat with rotary beater.) Add enough remaining flour to make a stiff dough. Mix well. Cover and let rise until doubled. Divide dough into halves and roll each half on a floured board to form a rectangle 14 x 10 inches. Using a pastry brush, brush with oil. Sprinkle half the brown sugar and cinnamon over each rectangle. Roll up as for jelly roll. Pinch dough firmly together. Cut into 1-inch slices and lightly roll in a shallow dish of oil so that the finished rolls will separate more readily. Put in two greased pans, one 13 x 9 x 2 inches, the other 11 x 7 x 2 inches. Cover and let rise until doubled. Bake in preheated hot oven (400°F.) for about 20 minutes. Makes about 28 rolls.

GEORGIA RAISED BISCUITS

1 package active dry yeast or
  1 cake compressed yeast
1½ cups water*
4½ cups unsifted all-purpose flour
2 tablespoons salt
1 tablespoon sugar
  Butter or margarine (about ⅔ cup)
1 egg yolk

* Use very warm water (105°F. to 115°F.) for dry yeast; use lukewarm (80°F. to 90°F.) for compressed. Sprinkle dry yeast or crumble cake into water. Let stand for a few minutes; then stir until dissolved. Sift dry ingredients into large bowl. Cut in ½ cup soft butter. Add yeast and mix well. Roll about ¼ inch thick on floured board. Cut with floured 2-inch cutter and put half on cookie sheets. Brush with melted butter. Top with remaining biscuits. Beat egg yolk and 1 tablespoon water together. Brush on biscuits. Cover and let rise until doubled, about 1 hour. Bake in preheated hot oven (425°F.) for about 10 minutes. Makes about 3 dozen biscuits.

GOLDEN GLORY KNOTS

2 packages active dry yeast or
  2 cakes compressed yeast
¼ cup water*
  Sugar
¾ cup milk, scalded
½ cup butter or margarine
2 teaspoons salt
3 eggs
1 teaspoon vanilla extract
1 can (6½ to 7½ ounces) creamed
  carrots (junior baby food) or
  1 cup finely mashed cooked carrots
6 to 7 cups sifted all-purpose flour
  Orange Frosting

* Use very warm water (105°F. to 115°F.) for dry yeast; use lukewarm (80°F. to 90°F.) for compressed yeast. Sprinkle dry yeast or crumble cakes into

water. Add 1 tablespoon sugar; let stand for a few minutes; then stir until yeast and sugar are dissolved. Pour hot milk over ½ cup sugar, the butter, and salt in mixing bowl. Stir to melt butter. Beat in eggs, vanilla, carrots, and yeast. Gradually add flour to form a stiff dough, beating well after each addition. Turn out on heavily floured pastry cloth or board and knead lightly. Put in greased bowl, cover, and let rise until doubled, about 1 hour. Roll half of dough on floured surface to rectangle 20 x 12 inches. Spread half of dough along wide side with ¼ of Orange Frosting. Cut crosswise into 1-inch strips. Twist each 4 or 5 times, then tie loosely into a knot, tucking one end under. Put on greased cookie sheets. Repeat with remaining dough. Let rise until light, about 45 minutes. Bake in preheated moderate oven (375°F.) for 12 to 15 minutes. Spread warm rolls with remaining frosting thinned with a little water. Decorate with coconut and jam, if desired. Serve warm or cold. Makes 40.

Orange Frosting

Melt ¼ cup butter or margarine in saucepan. Blend in 2 tablespoons flour and ¼ teaspoon salt. Add ¼ cup fresh or undiluted frozen orange juice. Cook, stirring, until thickened. Beat in 2½ cups sifted confectioners' sugar.

PAN ROLLS

Use the basic White Bread recipe that appears on page 228. After first rising, cut half of dough into 18 pieces. Shape into balls and put close together in greased pan (11 x 7 x 1½ inches). Let rise until doubled, about 30 minutes. Brush with melted butter and bake in preheated hot oven (425°F.) for about 20 minutes. Serve hot. Let remaining dough rise, and bake in greased loaf pan as directed in White Bread recipe.

LITTLE BRIOCHES

    2 packages active dry yeast
      or 2 cakes compressed yeast
    ¼ cup water*
    ¾ cup milk, scalded
    1 cup butter or margarine
    ½ cup sugar
    2 teaspoons salt
    6½ cups sifted all-purpose flour
    5 eggs

Sprinkle or crumble yeast into water. * Use very warm water (105°F. to 115° F.) for dry yeast; use lukewarm (80° F. to 90°F.) for compressed. Let stand a few minutes; then stir until dissolved. Pour hot milk over butter, sugar, and salt; cool to lukewarm. Add 2 cups flour and beat well. Add yeast and beat. Cover and let rise until bubbly. Stir down. Add 4 eggs and beat well. Add enough more flour to make a soft dough. Turn out on floured pastry cloth or board and knead until smooth and satiny. Put into greased bowl, cover and let rise until doubled, about

1½ hours. Punch down and divide dough into 24 pieces. From each piece, cut a small piece. Shape large pieces into balls and put into well-greased 2¾-inch muffin cups. Shape small pieces in balls. Make indentation in center of each large ball by pressing with thumb. Press small balls into indentations. Let rise until doubled, about 45 minutes. Mix 1 egg and 1 tablespoon water. Brush rolls with mixture. Bake in preheated moderate oven (375°F.) for 15 minutes. To freeze, wrap in foil. Reheat, wrapped, in slow oven (300°F.).

QUICK-RISING SWEET ROLLS

    3 packages active dry yeast
      or 3 cakes compressed yeast
    ¾ cup water*
    ¾ cup milk, scalded
    ½ cup sugar
    1½ teaspoons salt
    ½ cup butter or margarine
    2 eggs, beaten
    5½ cups unsifted all-purpose flour (about)

*Use very warm water (105°F. to 115°F.) for dry yeast; use lukewarm (80°F. to 90°F.) for compressed. Sprinkle dry yeast or crumble cake into water. Let stand a few minutes; then stir until dissolved. Pour hot milk over sugar, salt, and butter. Cool to lukewarm. Stir in the yeast mixture, eggs, and 3 cups flour; beat until smooth. Stir in additional flour to make a soft dough. Turn dough out onto floured board; knead until smooth and elastic, about 8 minutes. Place the dough in a greased bowl; turn the dough to grease it on all sides. Cover; let rise in a warm place, free from draft, until doubled in bulk, about 30 minutes. Punch the dough down and turn out onto a lightly floured board. Proceed according to directions for the desired shapes (see below). Bake in preheated hot oven (400°F.) for 12 to 15 minutes. Makes 3 to 4 dozen, depending on the shape of rolls.

TO SHAPE ROLLS
Crescents
Roll a piece of dough into a 12-inch circle, ¼ inch thick. Cut into wedge-shaped pieces. Brush with butter and roll up from the wide end. Put on a cookie sheet with the pointed end underneath.

Twists and Circles
Roll the dough to ¼ inch thickness. Spread with butter. Cut into ½-inch strips and twist the strips into knots or circles.

QUICK BREADS

BUTTERMILK DOUGHNUTS
    2 tablespoons shortening
    ¾ cup sugar
    2 eggs
    4 cups sifted all-purpose flour
    2 teaspoons baking powder
    ½ teaspoon each of ground cinnamon, mace, and nutmeg
    ½ teaspoon each of salt and baking soda
    1 cup buttermilk
      Fat for frying

Cream shortening and sugar until light. Add eggs, one at a time, beating well after each addition. Sift dry ingredients and add alternately with buttermilk to first mixture, beating after each addition. Mix well and chill for 1 hour, or longer. Turn out on lightly floured board and roll out to ½-inch thickness. Cut with floured 3-inch cutter. Fry in hot deep fat (370°F. on a frying thermometer) until golden brown on both sides, turning once. Drain on absorbent paper. Makes about 2½ dozen doughnuts.

RICH MUFFINS
    2 cups sifted all-purpose flour
    2½ teaspoons baking powder
    2 tablespoons sugar
    ¾ teaspoon salt
    ½ cup shortening
    1 egg, well beaten
    ¾ cup milk

Sift dry ingredients together. Cut in shortening. Combine egg and milk and add all at once to flour mixture. Then stir only until dry ingredients are dampened. Turn into greased muffin pans, filling each about ⅔ full. Bake in preheated hot oven (400°F.) for about 25 minutes. Makes about 10 muffins.

Cranberry Muffins
Use recipe for Rich Muffins. Chop 1 cup cranberries, sprinkle with 2 tablespoons sugar, and fold into batter. Bake as directed. Makes 12 muffins.

Bacon Muffins
Use recipe for Rich Muffins. Add ½ cup crumbled crisp bacon to flour mixture. Bake as directed.

Apricot Muffins
Use recipe for Rich Muffins. Add ½ cup cut dried apricots to flour mixture. Bake as directed.

DOUBLE-CORN MUFFINS
    1⅓ cups unsifted all-purpose flour
    3 teaspoons baking powder
    1 teaspoon salt
    2 tablespoons sugar
    ¾ cup yellow cornmeal
    2 eggs, beaten
    1 cup milk
    ¼ cup butter or margarine, melted
    ¼ teaspoon crushed dried rosemary
    1 cup cut fresh corn

Sift first 4 ingredients. Add remaining ingredients and mix only enough to dampen dry ingredients. Fill 12 greased 2½-inch muffin-pan sections about ⅔ full of batter. Bake in preheated hot oven (400°F.) for about 25 minutes. Makes 12 muffins.

RAISIN BRAN MUFFINS
    3 tablespoons soft butter or margarine
    ¼ cup molasses
    1 egg
    1 cup shredded bran cereal
    ¾ cup buttermilk
    1 cup sifted all-purpose flour
    1 teaspoon baking powder

½ teaspoon each of baking soda and salt
⅓ cup seedless raisins

Cream butter and molasses. Add egg and beat well. Add bran and buttermilk and let stand for 5 minutes. Add to sifted dry ingredients and mix only enough to dampen. Add raisins. Fill greased 2¾-inch muffin pans ⅔ full. Bake in preheated hot oven (400°F.) for about 25 minutes. Makes 9 large muffins.

BAKING-POWDER BISCUITS

2 cups sifted all-purpose flour
2½ teaspoons baking powder
¾ teaspoon salt
⅓ cup shortening
¾ cup milk

Sift flour, baking powder, and salt together. Cut in shortening. Add milk and stir with fork until soft dough is formed. Turn out on lightly floured board and knead 20 turns. Pat or roll lightly to ½-inch thickness. Cut with floured 2-inch cutter. Bake on ungreased cookie sheet in preheated very hot oven (450°F.) for 12 to 15 minutes. Makes about 14 biscuits.

Cheese Biscuits

Use recipe for Baking-Powder Biscuits. Add 1 cup grated Cheddar cheese to dry ingredients with the shortening. Makes 16 to 18 biscuits.

FRUIT BUNS

2 cups biscuit mix
1 tablespoon sugar
⅛ teaspoon ground nutmeg
¾ cup milk
½ cup soft butter or margarine
Fruit Filling

Combine mix, sugar, and nutmeg. Add milk and stir until mixture stiffens. Turn out on floured board and roll to ⅛-inch thickness. Spread with ¼ cup butter, fold dough in half, and roll out again. Spread with remaining butter. Fold and roll into a rectangle 18 x 6 inches. Cut into twelve 3-inch squares. Put squares in greased large muffin pans and fill with Fruit Filling. Pull corners of dough together; pinch to seal. Bake in preheated moderate oven (375°F.) for about 25 minutes.

Fruit Filling

Beat 1 egg, ½ cup sugar, 1 teaspoon fresh lemon juice, and ½ teaspoon ground cinnamon. Stir in 6 chopped drained cooked dried apricots, 3 chopped pitted cooked prunes, and 1 chopped cooked dried peach. (Or use ⅔ cup any drained stewed fruit.)

CURRANT SCONES

2 cups unsifted all-purpose flour
1½ teaspoons cream of tartar
¾ teaspoon baking soda
1 teaspoon salt
½ cup soft butter or margarine
½ cup dried currants
1 egg
1 cup buttermilk (about)
1 egg yolk
Sugar

Sift flour, cream of tartar, soda, and salt into bowl. Cut in butter. Add currants, whole egg, and enough buttermilk to make a soft dough. Mix and turn out on well-floured board. Knead a few times, then roll to ½-inch thickness. Cut into 2-inch diamonds. Put on cookie sheets and prick tops several times with fork. Beat egg yolk with a little cold water and brush on scones. Sprinkle with sugar. Bake in preheated hot oven (425°F.) for about 15 minutes. Makes about 2 dozen.

POPOVERS

2 eggs
1 cup milk
1 cup sifted all-purpose flour
¼ teaspoon salt

Beat eggs slightly; add milk. Then add flour and salt. Beat vigorously for 2 minutes. Pour batter into very hot greased custard cups or iron popover pans, filling ⅔ full. Bake in preheated hot oven (425°F.) for about 40 minutes. Serve at once. Makes 6 large popovers.

Cheese Popovers

Use recipe for Popovers. Sprinkle filled pans with ¼ cup grated sharp Cheddar cheese before baking.

Almond Popovers

Use recipe for Popovers. Add ⅓ cup ground blanched almonds to sifted flour and salt. Mix and bake.

Whole-Wheat Popovers

Use recipe for Popovers. Add 2 teaspoons melted butter to eggs and milk. Substitute ½ cup whole-wheat flour for half of white flour. Mix and bake.

BUTTERMILK WAFFLES

3 eggs, separated
1½ cups buttermilk
⅓ cup melted shortening
2 cups sifted cake flour
2 teaspoons baking powder
½ teaspoon baking soda
¾ teaspoon salt
1 tablespoon sugar

Beat egg yolks; add buttermilk and shortening. Add to sifted dry ingredients; mix only enough to dampen dry ingredients. Fold in stiffly beaten egg whites. Bake in hot waffle iron. Makes 6 servings.

Apple-Buttermilk Waffles

Use recipe for Buttermilk Waffles. Add to batter 2 finely chopped peeled apples and 1 teaspoon ground cinnamon. Serve with maple-flavored syrup or honey.

Bacon-Buttermilk Waffles

Use recipe for Buttermilk Waffles. Dice and cook 6 slices of bacon. Substitute bacon fat for equal part of shortening. Add bacon to batter. Serve with syrup.

PANCAKES

1¼ cups sifted all-purpose flour

1½ teaspoons baking powder
¾ teaspoon salt
1 tablespoon sugar
1 egg, well beaten
1 cup milk
3 tablespoons shortening, melted

Sift dry ingredients. Mix egg and milk; add to dry ingredients with the shortening. Mix only enough to dampen dry ingredients. Batter will be lumpy. Bake on hot greased griddle until browned on both sides. Turn only once. Serve hot with butter and syrup. Makes 10 to 12. For thinner pancakes, increase milk.

Cheese Pancakes

Use recipe for Pancakes. Add ½ cup grated Cheddar cheese to batter.

Bran Pancakes

Use recipe for Pancakes, but reduce flour to 1 cup and add ¾ cup bran flakes to dry ingredients. Makes 8 to 10 pancakes.

COCONUT BREAD

3 cups all-purpose flour, sifted twice
1 tablespoon baking powder
½ teaspoon salt
1 cup sugar
1 cup shredded coconut
1 egg, beaten
1 cup milk
1 teaspoon vanilla extract

Sift dry ingredients and add coconut. Mix thoroughly. Combine liquid ingredients and stir into the dry ingredients. Blend carefully. Let stand for 20 minutes. Pour into well-greased loaf pan (9 x 5 x 3 inches). Bake in preheated moderate oven (350°F.) for 45 to 50 minutes.

ORANGE NUT BREAD

2½ cups sifted all-purpose flour
3 teaspoons baking powder
1 teaspoon salt
1 cup sugar
¼ cup shortening
¾ cup milk
¼ cup fresh orange juice
1 egg
3 tablespoons grated orange rind
1 cup chopped nuts

Sift dry ingredients into bowl. Cut in shortening with pastry blender or 2 knives. Add milk, orange juice, and egg. Mix only enough to dampen dry ingredients. Add grated rind and nuts. Pour into greased loaf pan (9 x 5 x 3 inches), spreading batter to corners and leaving a slight depression in center. Let stand for 20 minutes. Bake in preheated moderate oven (350°F.) for about 1 hour. Let stand for 5 minutes; then turn out on rack to cool. Store overnight before slicing.

COMPANY GINGERBREAD

2½ cups sifted all-purpose flour
2 teaspoons baking powder
½ teaspoon baking soda
½ teaspoon salt
2 teaspoons ground ginger
1½ teaspoons ground cinnamon
½ teaspoon ground nutmeg
¼ teaspoon ground cloves
¾ cup shortening, melted
¾ cup firmly packed brown sugar

2 eggs, beaten
¾ cup molasses
1 cup boiling water

Sift dry ingredients. Combine shortening, sugar, and eggs and mix well. Blend in molasses and water. Add to dry ingredients and mix, beating until smooth. Mixture will be quite thin. Pour into greased 9-inch square pan. Bake in preheated moderate oven (350°F.) for about 45 minutes. Serve with butter or cream cheese.

CORN STICKS

1 cup sifted all-purpose flour
¾ cup cornmeal
2 teaspoons baking powder
¾ teaspoon salt
2 tablespoons sugar
1 egg, beaten
¾ cup milk
¼ cup melted shortening or cooking oil

Sift dry ingredients. Add egg, milk, and shortening. Stir until blended. Do not overmix. Mix only enough to dampen dry ingredients. Heat greased corn-stick pans; pour in batter. Bake in preheated very hot oven (450°F.) for about 20 minutes. Makes 8 large corn sticks.

CUSTARDY CORN BREAD

¾ cup white cornmeal
¼ cup sifted all-purpose flour
1 to 2 tablespoons sugar
½ teaspoon salt
1 teaspoon baking powder
1½ cups plus 2 tablespoons milk
1 egg, well beaten
2 tablespoons butter

Sift dry ingredients; stir in 1 cup plus 2 tablespoons milk and the egg. Mix only enough to dampen dry ingredients. Melt butter in 8-inch square pan and pour mixture into pan. Just before baking, pour remaining ½ cup milk over batter; do not stir. Bake in preheated hot oven (400°F.) for about 30 minutes. Serve as you would spoon bread. Makes 4 to 6 servings.

HUSH PUPPIES

2 cups water-ground cornmeal
1½ teaspoons salt
1 teaspoon sugar
2 teaspoons baking powder
1 tablespoon instant minced onion
2 eggs, beaten
½ cup milk
Fat for frying

Mix first 5 ingredients. Add eggs and milk; mix well. Shape into balls the size of a large walnut. Fry in hot deep fat (375°F. on a frying thermometer) until well browned and done, turning once. Drain on absorbent paper. Makes 4 servings.

PINEAPPLE COFFEECAKE

2 cups sifted all-purpose flour
2 teaspoons baking powder
½ teaspoon salt
Butter or margarine
¼ cup light corn syrup
1 egg, beaten
⅔ cup syrup, drained from 1 can (1 pound) crushed pineapple
¾ cup drained crushed pineapple

¼ cup firmly packed brown sugar
Cinnamon

Sift dry ingredients. Cut in 2 tablespoons butter. Mix corn syrup, egg, and syrup. Add to first mixture and mix only enough to dampen dry ingredients. Spread in greased 8-inch square pan; brush with melted butter. Cover with pineapple and sprinkle with brown sugar and cinnamon. Bake in preheated hot oven (400°F.) for about 30 minutes.

PINWHEEL ONION ROLLS

4 onions, thinly sliced
2 tablespoons butter
2¼ teaspoons salt
Dash of cayenne
2 cups sifted all-purpose flour
3 teaspoons baking powder
¼ cup shortening
⅔ cup milk
1 egg, beaten
⅓ cup evaporated milk, undiluted

Cook onions in the butter until golden; cool. Add ¾ teaspoon of the salt and the cayenne. Sift flour, baking powder, and 1 teaspoon of the salt. Cut in shortening. Add milk; mix only enough to dampen dry ingredients. Roll into rectangle 12 x 8 inches. Spread with onions; roll up as for jelly roll. Cut into eight 1-inch slices. Put flat side down, in greased pan (13 x 9 x 2 inches). Mix egg, evaporated milk, and remaining ½ teaspoon salt. Pour over rolls. Bake in preheated hot oven (400°F.) for about 25 minutes.

SESAME-SEED DIPS

2¼ cups sifted all-purpose flour
1 tablespoon sugar
3½ teaspoons baking powder
1½ teaspoons salt
1 cup milk
⅓ cup butter or margarine
Sesame seed

Sift dry ingredients into bowl. Add milk and mix well. Turn out on well-floured board and sprinkle lightly with flour. Knead about 10 turns. Roll out, making a rectangle about 12 x 8 inches. With floured knife, cut strips ½ x 4 inches. Meanwhile, melt butter in pan (13 x 9 x 2 inches) in preheated very hot oven (450°F.). Remove pan from oven and dip strips into butter, covering all sides. Lay in rows in the same pan, sprinkle with sesame seed, and bake for about 15 minutes. Makes 48.

BREAD, TO—To coat a food with bread or other crumbs, either directly or after dipping it first into beaten egg or milk. Breading is done prior to cooking the food; the cooking method is usually frying. Breading preserves the juices and provides a crust for texture. The crumbs used can be flavored with herbs, spices, cheese, etc., all ground fine. Some breading is done with dry crumbs, some with fresh crumbs, depending on the taste and texture desired.

BREAKFAST—The first meal of the day is meant, as the word itself says, "to break the fast." "Life within doors has few pleasanter prospects than a neatly arranged and well-provisioned breakfast table," wrote Nathaniel Hawthorne.

Breakfast means many things to many people. It may be nostalgia for the ample breakfasts of a rural New England or Midwestern childhood, it may be intense pleasure at the smell of bacon wafting through the house, or it may be the desire to drink one's coffee and read one's paper in utter peace and silence.

Not only people, but nations too, feel differently about breakfast. The people of cold northern Europe, in Norway for example, eat large, substantial breakfasts with fish, meats, and cheese. A Spanish farmer, on the other hand, may content himself with a bowl of soup or a piece of bread and sausage. Frenchmen invented one of the most delicious of all breakfast breads, the flaky, buttery *croissant*. Italians choose black coffee or *capuccino* and perhaps a quick brioche. The Swiss, Germans, and Austrians drink their *Milch-kaffee*, coffee with hot milk, and eat fresh rolls, butter, and jam. As for the people of the East, their breakfast foods are utterly different from ours. The English breakfast is closest to our American one, although today it is but a pallid image of what it was in the 19th century, when fish, ham, roast beef and grilled kidneys helped to sustain the folks until luncheon.

But breaking the fast is not the only function of breakfast. To be a good breakfast, the meal should be high in protein. The reason: protein is essential for building and maintaining healthy bodies and is best utilized when distributed evenly throughout the day. In addition to protein, a good breakfast should contain from one fourth to one third of all the other food values needed daily: carbohydrates, fats, vitamins, and minerals. Once upon a time, steak, fried potatoes, and apple pie launched Americans on their busy, hard-working days. Today the typical morning meal has become orange juice, bacon and eggs or cereal, buttered toast and jam, and milk or coffee. But there is no law that says this menu must be served morning after morning. In fact, where indifference to breakfast is a problem, variety may be the answer and it is up to the cook to provide it. Remember that any food enjoyed at lunch or dinner can be served at breakfast too: hamburger patties, vegetable soup, tuna fish, or peanut-butter sandwiches, even ice cream.

To give breakfast a new look, begin by varying the fruit one week, the cereal the next, etc., and gradually build up new menus.

BREAKFASTS, U. S. A.

By Helen Evans Brown and Philip S. Brown

We are breakfast buffs, and it is our hope that we may influence others to stop making light of the morning meal. A few years ago, breakfasts had fallen into a dismal decline. What should have been a happy morning treat had developed into a hastily gulped meal which had little chance of ending with a chorus of "Oh, What a Beautiful Mornin'!" We use the past tense warily, but ever so hopefully, for we believe that today's homemakers, heeding the warnings of doctors and nutritionists, are providing more nourishing breakfasts for their families.

To enliven your table in the mornings, we suggest a look at some American regional breakfasts, those which carry on the good-eating traditions of our forefathers in various parts of the country. In order to perform their mighty chores, these men who built America started their days with appropriately mighty meals, including favorite dishes from their homelands across the sea and also products local to their own regions.

WESTERN BREAKFAST
FRESH FRUIT COMPOTE*
BUTTERMILK PANCAKES*
BACON   HAM   SAUSAGE
MAPLE SYRUP   HONEY   SOUR CREAM
BOYSENBERRY SYRUP   PRESERVES
WHIPPED BUTTER   APPLE BUTTER
COFFEE, TEA, OR MILK

Fresh Fruit Compote—This is simply a combination of the fruits in season, cut up, lightly sugared, and served with all the juices. Oranges, pineapple, grapefruit, bananas, papayas, apples, pears, and summer fruits and berries can be used. Two or more fruits are usually included.

Buttermilk Pancakes—This recipe makes about 30 large pancakes. Sift together 4 cups sifted all-purpose flour, 1 teaspoon salt, 2 teaspoons soda, and 2 tablespoons sugar. Beat 4 eggs; add 1 quart buttermilk and ¼ cup melted butter. Combine with dry ingredients and stir just enough to blend. Cook by the tablespoonfuls on a buttered griddle or skillet over low heat. Turn when cakes rise and are bubbly.

Southern Breakfast
Western Breakfast

New England Breakfast

SOUTHERN BREAKFAST
LAMB OR VENISON CHOPS
SCRAMBLED EGGS
CREOLE SAUSAGE*   HOMINY GRITS*
BISCUITS   MUSCADINE JELLY
COFFEE

Creole Sausage—This is called *chaurice* in Louisiana, and is just like any home-made sausage except it is hotter. Combine 2 pounds ground lean pork, 1 pound ground fat pork, 1 large onion minced very fine, 1 garlic clove ground in a mortar with 1 tablespoon salt, 2 teaspoons hot pepper sauce, 2 teaspoons coarsely and freshly ground black pepper, 1 teaspoon ground thyme, 1 tablespoon minced parsley, 1 bay leaf crushed in the mortar, and ¼ teaspoon ground all-spice. Mix thoroughly and use to stuff well-washed casings (buy from your butcher) or to form into patties. In either case, panfry or bake on a rack until crisp but not dry. Makes 6 servings.
Note: For farm-style homemade sausage, omit hot pepper sauce and add 1 teaspoon each of ground cloves, mace, and coriander.
Hominy Grits—Follow package directions. Serve hot, with butter.
Muscadine Jelly—This is made from the muscadine grape, indigenous to the Gulf area. If you can't get it, substitute wild-grape jelly.

CHARLESTON BREAKFAST
PAPAYA WITH LIME
SHRIMP PASTE*   HOMINY GRITS*
WAFFLES, CREAMED CHICKEN,
AND VIRGINIA HAM (ALL OPTIONAL)
BEATEN BISCUITS   HONEY OR PRESERVES
COFFEE

Shrimp Paste—Put 4 cups small cooked and peeled shrimps through the grinder, then pound them in a mortar, or whirl in a blender, with 1 cup butter. When a smooth paste, season with freshly grated nutmeg, salt, and pepper or hot pepper sauce to taste. Pack in a well-buttered bread pan and bake in moderate oven (350°F.) for 30 minutes. Chill and serve cold, sliced. Makes 6 servings. (Some cooks don't bake it, merely pack the mixture in the pan and chill; easier and just as good.)
Hominy Grits—Follow package directions. Serve them very hot with butter.

NEW ENGLAND BREAKFAST
STRAWBERRIES AND COUNTRY CREAM
FRIED BROOK TROUT*   BACON
POPOVERS*   WILD HONEY   COFFEE

Strawberries—You'll probably have to settle for cultivated instead of tiny, wild ones, but do have them small, ripe, and *not* iced. As for the cream, just get the heaviest you can find.
Fried Brook Trout—Don't let anyone tell you that they're better any other way, and we include *truite au bleu!* Clean the fish, the smallest and freshest you can find, dip them into cornmeal, and sauté in butter or bacon fat until crisply brown on both sides. Serve with crisp bacon.
Popovers—Start oven at 400°F. Butter 12 large custard cups. Beat together 3 eggs, 1½ cups milk, 1 tablespoon melted butter, 1 teaspoon salt, and 1½ cups sifted all-purpose flour. When smooth, divide among the custard cups and bake for 45 minutes, or until well puffed. Serve at once. If you don't want them to collapse and to be dry inside, remove from oven after 40 minutes, slit for steam to escape, and return to oven for 5 to 10 minutes. This type of popover freezes well and needs only reheating in the oven. Makes 12.

PENNSYLVANIA-DUTCH BREAKFAST
CANNED OR STEWED PLUMS
SCRAPPLE*   CREAMED EGGS* (OPTIONAL)
FRIED APPLES*
SCHNECKEN* (CINNAMON ROLL)   COFFEE

Scrapple—Cook 4 fresh pigs' feet and 2 pounds of pork (shoulder, including bone or other inexpensive cut) in 2 quarts boiling water and 1 tablespoon salt, until the meat literally falls from the bones. Strain broth into a saucepan; pick meat from bones and grind. Bring broth to a boil and stir in ½ cup chopped onions and 1½ cups cornmeal. Cook for 2 minutes, add meat, and correct seasoning, adding salt and pepper to taste. Cook until thick, pour into a loaf pan, and chill. At serving time, slice ½ inch thick and fry crisp on both sides. (Add shortening to skillet only if needed.) Makes 6 servings.
Creamed Eggs—Hard-cook 10 eggs and dice the whites. Combine with 1 cup of cream sauce, and pour over 6 slices of buttered toast on a platter. Press the hard-boiled yolks through a sieve and drift over the creamed egg whites. Sprinkle with minced parsley. Makes 6 servings.
Cream Sauce—For each cup of cream sauce, melt 2 tablespoons butter, add 2 tablespoons flour, and cook, stirring, for 1 minute. Pour in 1 cup light cream and mix thoroughly. Season with salt and pepper to taste and turn heat very low, so that the sauce will cook, without burning, for at least 5 minutes. Or cook over hot water. This will remove any raw taste of flour. Add 2 tablespoons heavy cream and use as indicated for Creamed Eggs.
Fried Apples—Core apples and slice across about ⅜ inch thick. Fry in butter or bacon fat until brown on both sides, sprinkling with butter when they begin to color.

Schnecken—Use recipe for Basic Sweet Dough (see below) and, after the first rising, roll into a thin rectangle about 18 inches square. Spread lightly with melted butter; then sprinkle with the following mixture: 1 cup sugar, 1 tablespoon ground cinnamon, ½ cup seedless raisins, ½ cup chopped almonds, and ¼ cup chopped citron or glacéed fruits (the last is optional). Roll like a jelly roll and slice ½ inch thick. Put on buttered cookie sheets, flat side down, and let rise until double in bulk. Bake in preheated moderate oven (350°F.) for 20 minutes, or until nicely browned. Remove from the pan while still warm. Makes about 36.
Basic Sweet Dough—Crumble 1 yeast cake into ⅔ cup warm milk, and stir. Add 2 tablespoons sugar, ½ teaspoon salt, ¼ cup soft butter, 1 egg, and 1 cup sifted all-purpose flour. Beat well until elastic. Now add another 1 cup flour and work in well. If it's still sticky—and it probably will be—add more flour, up to 1 cup of it. The dough should be soft but easy to handle. Turn out on a lightly floured board and knead until the dough is smooth, shiny, and elastic. Put in a well-buttered bowl, turn mass upside down so that the top will be buttery, cover with a cloth, and let rise in a warm place until double in bulk. Knock down, turn onto a lightly floured board, knead for ½ minute or so, then use as directed to make Schnecken.

NORTHERN BREAKFAST
CANNED OR STEWED PRUNES
HAM WITH CREAM GRAVY*
CORN FRITTERS*
TOAST   APPLE BUTTER   BEVERAGE

Ham with Cream Gravy—This is a country dish. Have 1½ pounds uncooked or tenderized ham sliced thick or thin, as you like, and brown it on both sides in its own fat. Remove to a hot platter. To the skillet add 1½ tablespoons flour (there should be that much fat left) and 2 cups thin cream. Cook quickly, stirring, until slightly reduced and thickened; add pepper to taste and salt, if necessary, and pour over the ham. Makes 6 servings.
Corn Fritters—There are several kinds of corn fritters. Because this is a family breakfast, we give you the easiest, although none is difficult. Combine 2 cups chopped cooked or raw corn, ½ cup all-purpose flour, 1 teaspoon baking powder, 1 teaspoon salt, and 2 eggs, beaten until thick. Fry, by the tablespoonful, in hot butter, turning to brown both sides. Serves 6.

CALIFORNIA BRUNCH
STRAWBERRIES WITH ORANGE JUICE*
OR CURACAO
HANGTOWN FRY*   BACON

SMOTHERED ONIONS* CHERRY TOMATOES*
TOAST DATES AND CHEDDAR* COFFEE

Strawberries with Orange Juice—This is just what it says. Hull the berries and sugar them if they need it. Have them at room temperature, and pour over them cold orange juice.

Hangtown Fry—Drain 1 pint medium-sized oysters, dry them, dust them in flour, and then dip them into 1 egg beaten slightly with 1 tablespoon milk. Roll in cracker crumbs and allow to dry for at least 15 minutes. Melt 6 tablespoons butter in a large skillet and brown the oysters lightly on both sides. Add 8 eggs that have been beaten with ¾ teaspoon salt and a little pepper. Stir once or twice, then allow to set. Turn carefully onto a plate, then fold like an omelet, or reverse plate over the pan, and brown other side. Serve with smothered onions (or fried green peppers). Makes 6 servings.

Smothered Onions—Peel and slice 2 pounds onions and sauté very slowly in ¼ cup butter. When they begin to brown, "smother" them by covering. Cook until tawny all over.

Cherry Tomatoes—These may be served raw or (and we like them this way) they may be hulled and just heated in butter, then sprinkled with a whisper of thyme.

Dates and Cheddar—Fresh dates, preferably. Pit and stuff them with cheese, or just serve whole with cubed cheese.

BRIE—This is one of the finest of French cheeses, and one of the most famous. Brie is made from whole milk, and its shape is round and flat. The flavor varies from mild to pungent. The reddish crust is edible. Brie is fully ripened when the texture of the whole cheese is even: soft but not runny.

Brie is not a cooking cheese. It is excellent for appetizers and delicious eaten with fresh fruit. Brie should be allowed to stand at room temperature before serving, to bring out the full flavor of the cheese.

BRILLAT-SAVARIN—Jean Anthelme Brillat-Savarin (1755-1826) was a French magistrate and politician who became the most famous gastronome in the world.

His book *La Physiologie du Goût,* also translated into English (*The Physiology of Taste),* is a learned and witty treatise on food, drink, and people, and has been constantly quoted to this day for its amusing and profound comments.

BRINE—A strong salt solution used in the preservation of fish, meats, vegetables, and in pickling. To keep foods in brine is one of the very oldest methods of preservation.

BRIOCHE—A light, yet rich cake-bread made with yeast dough, butter, and eggs. The traditional shape of a brioche is round with a little hat, but there are also round, tall and slender, and ring brioches.

Brioche is a French cake-bread, and it goes back for hundreds of years. It is used as a sweet roll, as a cake combined with fruit, or as a shell to hold a hot entrée, such as creamed fish or meats.

A recipe for Little Brioches appears on page 237.

BROCCOLI—This dark green vegetable is a member of the *Brassica* family and is closely related to cauliflower, less closely to cabbage and Brussels sprouts. Broccoli has tight small heads called curds, which sit like buds on a thick stem. Both heads and stems are eaten. Broccoli should not be overcooked, but kept crisp.

Broccoli, of which more than one hundred million pounds are sold in fresh form each year, is very popular today, but recipe books printed at the turn of the century made little mention of it. Mrs. Hannah Glasse's *Art of Cookery* in 1774 included a recipe "To dress Brokala" and Mrs. Mary Randolph's *Virginia Housewife,* published in 1824, suggested cook-

ing broccoli "as asparagus" and dressing it "in the same manner as the cauliflower." Thomas Jefferson, it is said, grew broccoli at Monticello in the early 19th century.

In Greece and Italy, broccoli has been a favorite vegetable for some 2,000 years. It seems to have looked and tasted much as it does today. Italian families brought broccoli seeds to America and grew these handsome dark-green clusters of buds in the suburbs of New York and Boston long before the vegetable was known throughout the country as a whole. About 1920 commercial growers began producing and distributing broccoli.

Availability—Available all year round with peak crop from October to November. Major crop from California, also from Arizona, New Jersey, New York, Oregon, Pennsylvania, South Carolina, Texas, and Virginia.

Broccoli is also available frozen, in spears or chopped.

Purchasing Guide—It is sold by the bunch and by the pound, sometimes wrapped in transparent film. Look for dark-green or light-purplish heads with tightly closed buds. Stalks should be tender yet firm with unwilted leaves. Yellowish buds or leaves indicate poor quality or overmaturity.

Storage—Store in vegetable container or in moistureproof bag in refrigerator.
- ☐ Refrigerator shelf, raw: 3 to 5 days
- ☐ Refrigerator shelf, cooked: 1 to 4 days
- ☐ Refrigerator frozen-food compartment, prepared for freezing: 1 month
- ☐ Freezer, prepared for freezing: 6 months

Nutritive Food Values—One of the richest vegetable sources of vitamin C, if vegetable is cooked quickly in a small amount of water. Excellent source of vitamin A, riboflavin, iron, and calcium.
- ☐ 3½ ounces, raw = 32 calories

Basic Preparation—Wash; cut off only toughest part of stem and larger leaves. To insure quick cooking of stalks more than one inch in diameter, make lengthwise gashes starting at ends of stalks; they will then cook as quickly as the flowerets.

The head may be divided into individual flowerets: divide by slicing lengthwise, starting at base of flower and cutting straight down length of stem.

During cooking, remove cover several times to allow steam to escape. This will keep broccoli green.
- ☐ **To Boil**—Cook in skillet or large flat pan in 1 inch of boiling salted water, covered, for 10 to 15 minutes, cooking stem pieces for a few minutes before adding buds.

Broccoli Piquant
Broccoli-and-Chicken Soup

□ **To Steam**—Tie in a bunch and stand upright in deep kettle of boiling salted water which should come to base of flowerets. Cook quickly until stem near head is just tender, 10 to 15 minutes. Remove carefully from water.

□ **To Sauté**—Cut into thin diagonal slices and sauté quickly in hot oil or other shortening until tender-crisp. Cook stem pieces a little longer than bud pieces.

Season with salt, pepper, and butter. May be eaten hot or cold with hollandaise sauce. Good, too, with a French dressing or with plain lemon juice.

Sprinkle with Parmesan cheese, and a little butter; put under the broiler for a few minutes.

□ **To Freeze**—Use dark, compact heads. Cut off heavy stems and break or cut into flowerets. Wash thoroughly in water. Blanch in boiling water:

    Small flowerets for 3 minutes
    Medium flowerets for 4 minutes
    Large flowerets for 5 minutes

Chill in cold water for 4 to 5 minutes. Drain. Pack in containers with no headspace.

□ **To Cook, Frozen Broccoli**—Drop unthawed broccoli into ½ cup boiling salted water. Use a fork to break apart after block begins to thaw. When water returns to boil, cover; cook for 8 to 10 minutes, or until tender.

BROCCOLI-AND-CHICKEN SOUP

1 bunch broccoli
1½ cups boiling water
2 cans (10½ ounces each) cream of chicken soup
1 cup light cream
  Salt, pepper, cayenne

Cut off and discard large leaves and tough parts of stalks. Wash and chop broccoli coarsely. Add boiling water. Boil rapidly until tender. Using all the liquid, chop broccoli very fine in blender or force through coarse sieve. In saucepan mix soup, cream, and broccoli; season to taste. Heat to simmering. Top with crouton and grated Parmesan cheese. Makes about 1 quart.

CHICKEN DIVAN

1 frying chicken (about 2½ pounds), split
2 cups water
  Salt and pepper
1 package (10 ounces) frozen broccoli spears
2 tablespoons butter
3 tablespoons all-purpose flour
  Milk
2 tablespoons sherry
  Grated Parmesan cheese

Wash chicken. Simmer chicken, covered, in water with 1 teaspoon salt for 45 minutes, or until very tender. Save broth. Remove meat from bones in large pieces; then cut into long slices. Cook broccoli until just tender; drain and put in shallow casserole. Melt butter in top part of double boiler; stir in flour. Measure chicken broth and add enough milk to make 2 cups. Gradually stir into butter and flour. Cook over boiling water, stirring constantly, until thickened. Add salt, pepper, sherry. Cover broccoli with chicken, then with sauce. Sprinkle with cheese. Bake in preheated hot oven (400°F.) for about 12 minutes. Makes 4 servings.

BROCCOLI-AND-CHEESE CUSTARD

- 1 bunch broccoli
- 3 eggs
- ⅔ cup milk
- 1¼ cups grated sharp Cheddar cheese
  Salt and pepper

Cut off and discard large leaves and tough parts of stalks. Wash; split stalks into halves or quarters so they cook as quickly as flowerets. Cook, uncovered, in small amount of boiling salted water until barely tender. Drain and put in buttered shallow casserole. Beat eggs; add milk, cheese, salt, and pepper. Mix and pour over broccoli. Set casserole in pan with about 1 inch of hot water. Bake in a preheated moderate oven (350°F.) for 30 minutes, or until firm. Makes 4 servings.

BROCCOLI WITH SOUR CREAM

- 2 pounds fresh broccoli
  or 2 packages (10 ounces each)
  frozen broccoli spears
  Salt
- 1 cup dairy sour cream
- 2 tablespoons tomato paste
- ¼ teaspoon dried basil
- 2 teaspoons minced drained capers

Discard some of the larger leaves and a little of the stalk from fresh broccoli. Cook broccoli, covered, in 1 inch of boiling salted water for 10 to 15 minutes. (Cook frozen broccoli as directed on the box.) Drain and cool. Mix ¾ teaspoon salt and remaining ingredients; chill. Serve on cold cooked broccoli. Makes 4 servings.

BROCCOLI PIQUANT

- 1 package (10 ounces) frozen
  broccoli, cut up
- 2 slices of bacon, diced
- ½ garlic clove, minced
- 2 tablespoons cider vinegar
- ¼ cup soft bread crumbs
- 1 tablespoon butter

Cook broccoli according to package directions. Meanwhile, cook bacon and garlic until bacon is crisp. Add vinegar; heat. Brown bread crumbs in butter. Pour sauce over hot broccoli and sprinkle with crumbs. Makes 3 servings.

Note: Frozen chopped broccoli may be used.

BROCHETTE—This French word describes a small skewer on which meat, fish, or vegetables are cooked. The term *en brochette* means meats cooked, and often served, on a skewer. Like all skew-

Broccoli with Sour Cream
Broccoli-and-Cheese Custard

ered foods, *en brochette* foods can be grilled over an open fire or under a broiler, or cooked in the oven.

BROIL—To cook directly under or above a source of radiant heat, which may be gas, electricity, charcoal, or an open fire. To grill is the word used in the British Isles for broiling.

Broiling is one of the oldest cooking processes, since it requires little equipment. As new stoves and kitchen appliances became available during the last century, broiling lost its prominent place in the home kitchen. But today broiling has been reinstated in its full glory, not only because it preserves and brings out the natural flavor of foods, but also because it requires no additional fats or ingredients, a true boon to gourmet dieters.

To Broil—If using separate broiler, set regulator for broiling. Follow manufacturer's directions for operation of broiler. Place meat on rack of broiler pan. Adjust rack and pan so that top of meat is approximately 2 inches below heat for ¾- to 1-inch cuts, 3 inches for thicker cuts. Broil about half of the time indicated on timetable. Season. Turn. Complete broiling. Season and serve.

To Charcoal Broil—Use charcoal briquettes; start fire 20 to 30 minutes before cooking. Use only a small amount of charcoal and wait until coals are covered with a gray ash before cooking.

Knock gray ash off several times during cooking to achieve maximum radiant heat. Place foods high above coals so they cook slowly and thoroughly and do not burn.

BROTH—A thin liquid in which fish, meat, or vegetables have been cooked. Broth is often used interchangeably with bouillon, but it should not be confused with the word stock which denotes a richer extract.

QUICK MUSHROOM BROTH

 1 tablespoon butter
¼ pound mushrooms
 3 cups water
 3 cans (10½ ounces each) condensed beef consomme, undiluted
¼ cup sherry, if desired

Melt butter in a saucepan; add chopped mushrooms and cook slightly. Add water and simmer for 10 minutes. Add consommé and heat thoroughly. If sherry is used, add just before serving. Makes 6 servings.

BROWN—In cooking, to brown is to scorch the surfaces of a food, especially meat, in order to seal the juices within

and to add flavor. Browning can be done either by exposing the food directly to the heat or by cooking it in a small amount of fat. For browned toppings, place foods under the broiler or in a hot oven.

Butter and flour may be browned (for additional flavor and color in the finished dish) by cooking, while stirring, over low heat.

BROWNIE—This rich, moist chocolate cookie has a universal appeal. Brownies are easy to make and they keep and ship well. Brownies fall into two main categories: the fudge-type which is very chewy, and a true brownie, or cake-type, with a lighter texture. Many brownie recipes include nuts and fruits, and some are quite fanciful. Brownies are also sold ready-made, frozen and ready to eat, or as a mix.

BROWNIES
The fudge type

 1 cup soft butter or margarine
 2 cups sugar
 3 eggs
 1 teaspoon vanilla extract
 4 ounces (4 squares) unsweetened chocolate
 1 cup sifted all-purpose flour
½ teaspoon salt
 1 cup chopped nuts

Cream ½ cup of the butter with sugar. Add eggs and beat until light. Add vanilla. Melt remaining butter with chocolate; cool, and beat into first mixture. Add flour, salt, and nuts. Mix well and pour into greased and floured pan (13 x 9 x 2 inches). Bake in preheated moderate oven (350°F.) for about 45 minutes. Cool in pan and cut into small squares. Makes 5 dozen.

BLACK AND WHITE BROWNIES
The cake type

  1 cup butter or margarine
1½ teaspoons vanilla extract
  2 cups sugar
  4 eggs
  2 cups sifted all-purpose flour
 ½ teaspoon salt
  2 cups chopped nuts
  2 ounces (2 squares) unsweetened chocolate
    Chocolate frosting

Cream butter until light and fluffy. Beat in vanilla and sugar. Add eggs, one at a time, beating well after each addition. Add flour and salt and mix until blended. Stir in nuts; divide batter into halves; add cooled melted chocolate to one. Drop batters alternately by teaspoons onto greased, floured pan (13 x 9 x 2 inches). Run knife through batter several times to marbleize. Bake in preheated moderate oven (350°F.) for about 45 minutes. Turn out on rack to cool. Frost. At serving time, cut into bars

about 3 x 1½ inches. Makes 24 bars.

BROWN SAUCE—A dark basic sauce from which many other sauces are made. For this reason brown sauce, or *Sauce Espagnole*, as a similar sauce is called in French, is considered a *sauce mère*, a "mother sauce," in French cooking. Brown sauce can be made in various ways, some elaborate, some simple, but it should always cook very slowly to become properly flavorful.

Brown sauce freezes well. It will keep four to six weeks.

BROWN SAUCE

⅓ cup minced onions
⅓ cup minced carrots
⅓ cup minced celery
¼ cup boiled ham or raw bacon, finely chopped
¼ cup butter or cooking oil
¼ cup all-purpose flour
 6 cups beef bouillon, boiling
 2 tablespoons tomato paste
   Bouquet garni (see page 216)
   Salt and pepper

Cook onions, carrots, celery, and ham or bacon in hot butter or oil over low heat for 10 minutes. Stir flour into mixture. Cook over moderate heat, stirring constantly, for 10 minutes, until the flour is nut brown. Add bouillon all at once. Stir until smooth. Add tomato paste, *bouquet garni,* and salt and pepper to taste. Simmer, partly covered, over low heat for 2 hours or more. Skim when necessary. If sauce thickens too much, add a little more bouillon. Strain and degrease sauce. If not used at once, store covered in refrigerator, or freeze. Makes about 4 cups sauce.

Demi-Glace for Steaks
Combine ¼ pound mushrooms and ¼ cup sherry in a saucepan. Cook until sherry is reduced by half. Add 2 cups Brown Sauce and 1 tablespoon beef extract. Bring to a boil, reduce heat, and cook for 15 to 20 minutes.

Diable for Grilled Chicken
To 1 cup Brown Sauce, add 1 tablespoon each of Worcestershire, cider vinegar, and prepared mustard, a dash of hot pepper sauce, and ¼ cup beef bouillon. Simmer for 10 minutes. Stir in a little chopped parsley.

Fines Herbes for Meats, Poultry, and Eggs
To 1 cup Brown Sauce, add 1 teaspoon each of dried tarragon, chervil, and chives, 1 tablespoon minced parsley, 1 tablespoon chopped green onion, and juice of 1 lemon. Cook for 10 to 15 minutes.

BRUNCH—This meal is a combination of breakfast and lunch, and takes its name from the first two letters of *break-fast* and the last four of *lunch*. Brunches are a convenient form of entertaining, very popular on Sunday and holiday mornings, since they give hosts and guests a chance to sleep late, entertain and be entertained with little trouble (compared to a full-blown lunch or dinner), and still have a portion of the day for their individual pursuits.

BRUNCH, COUNTRY STYLE
Menu 1
RASPBERRY-RHUBARB COMPOTE*
HAM AND EGGS, FRENCH STYLE*
MUSHROOM SPOON BREAD*
HONEY PRESERVES
COFFEE   MILK

RASPBERRY-RHUBARB COMPOTE
1 package (1 pound) frozen rhubarb
1 package (10 ounces) frozen raspberries, thawed overnight in refrigerator
Dash of ground cinnamon
Few drops of almond extract

Cook rhubarb according to directions on package. Stir raspberries into rhubarb and add cinnamon and extract. Makes 4 servings.

HAM AND EGGS, FRENCH STYLE
2 tablespoons butter
4 thin slices of ham
4 eggs
  Pepper
  Salt (optional)

Melt butter in heavy skillet and dip each side of ham into it. Break 1 egg on each slice. Turn up heat so that white becomes solid; cook for about 10 minutes. Sprinkle with pepper, and salt if desired. Makes 4 servings.

MUSHROOM SPOON BREAD
1½ cups milk
1 can (10½ ounces) cream-of-mushroom soup
1 cup yellow cornmeal
4 eggs, separated
2 tablespoons butter

Mix milk and soup. Add cornmeal. Cook slowly, stirring, until of the consistency of mush. Beat egg yolks and add them with the butter to cornmeal mixture. Beat egg whites until stiff and fold into mixture. Bake in greased casserole in preheated moderate oven (350°F.) for 1 hour, or until done (top springs back at finger touch). Makes 4 servings.

Menu 2
PINEAPPLE-GRAPEFRUIT JUICE
SAUSAGE PATTIES   SAUTEED APPLES*
CRISP-FRIED NOODLES*
COFFEECAKE FROM MIX
COFFEE   MILK

SAUTÉED APPLES
1½ tablespoons butter
5 apples, peeled, cored, and sliced
2 tablespoons sugar
  Ground cinnamon

Melt butter in heavy skillet over low heat. Add apples, stirring, until all are covered with butter. Cover pan, shaking occasionally to keep apples from sticking. Keep on heat for 5 to 10 minutes, or until apples are mushy. Sprinkle with sugar and cinnamon. Makes 4 servings.

CRISP-FRIED NOODLES
4 teaspoons butter
½ package (8 ounces) broad noodles, boiled

Melt butter in heavy skillet over low heat. Cook noodles on one side, without stirring, until browned. Using dinner plate, invert noodles so that browned side is on top. Slip noodles back into pan; cook for another 5 minutes, or until bottom is browned. Makes 4 servings.

Menu 3
BROILED GRAPEFRUIT
SHAD ROE WITH BACON*
HOT BISCUITS WITH HONEY
COFFEE   MILK

SHAD ROE WITH BACON
2 large pairs shad roe
2 tablespoons butter
4 bacon strips
1 lemon
4 parsley sprigs

Dry roe between paper towels. Melt butter until it sizzles. Add roe and fry until golden brown on both sides. Be careful when turning roe not to break the skin. Fry bacon until crisp and break into small pieces. Put bacon over roe on hot platter. Garnish with lemon quarters and parsley. Makes 4 servings.

Menu 4
STRAWBERRIES WITH WHIPPED CREAM
MEAT PANCAKES*
BROILED ORANGE SLICES
BAKED FROZEN APPLE STRUDEL
COFFEE   MILK

MEAT PANCAKES
1 cup sifted all-purpose flour
1 teaspoon salt
2 eggs
1 cup milk
½ cup diced cooked ham, or other leftover cooked meat
½ cup each of 2 leftover cooked vegetables, diced
¼ cup butter or margarine
1 cup leftover or canned gravy

Sift flour and salt into bowl. Break in eggs. Add milk and mix all together with egg beater until batter is smooth and free of lumps. Add ham and vegetables. Melt 1 tablespoon butter in 9-inch skillet. Pour in one fourth batter, to cover bottom. When pancake is golden brown, flip over and cook other side. Repeat for remaining 3 pancakes, keeping them warm in oven until ready to serve. While preparing pancakes, heat gravy in saucepan. Serve one pancake to each person, adding gravy as desired. Makes 4 servings.

BRUSSELS SPROUTS—Brussels sprouts are a member of the cabbage family, and they look like miniature cabbages. The plant, instead of making one large cabbage head, produces a number of rows of small heads where the leaves are attached. By pulling away the lower leaves the little heads are given room to develop, attached as they are to the long stalk of the plant.

Brussels sprouts appear to be about 400 years old, and they are said, in a vague way, to have originated in Brussels, capital of Belgium. By 1793 they were an article of export from that country.

Until fairly recently, Brussels sprouts were a luxury vegetable, especially in Europe, where the tiny, fingernail-big sizes are prized for the delicacy of their taste. They should always be cooked in very little water. A dash of nutmeg is a good seasoning for a sauced or unsauced dish of sprouts.

Availability—Late August through March, with peak in November. Most of the crop comes from California and New York.

Brussels sprouts are also available frozen.

Purchasing Guide—Usually marketed in pint-size boxes and sold as a unit. Boxes should be refrigerated and should have air vents to prevent internal browning.

Sprouts should be firm, compact, and a true green color. Yellow leaves indicate poor quality and flavor. Small to medium-size sprouts are more desirable than large.

Storage—Keep boxes in film bags in refrigerator. Some of the loose or discolored outer leaves may be discarded before storing, but do not wash until ready to cook.
☐ Refrigerator shelf or vegetable compartment, wrapped: 4 days
☐ Refrigerator frozen-food compartment, prepared for freezing: 1 month

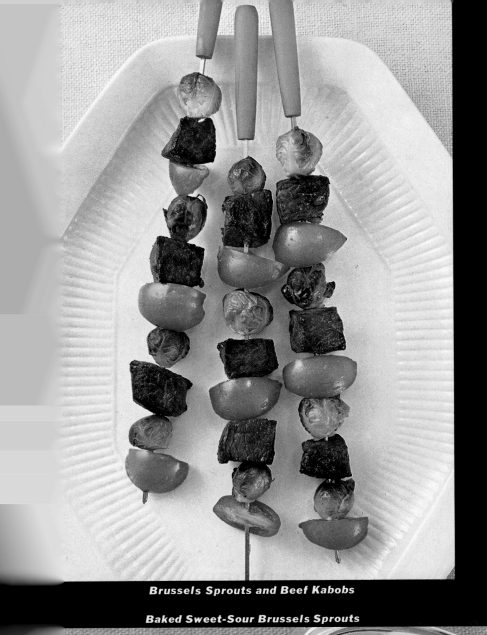

Brussels Sprouts and Beef Kabobs

Baked Sweet-Sour Brussels Sprouts

□ Freezer, prepared for freezing: 11 months

Nutritive Food Values—Brussels sprouts are high in vitamins A and C, and contain fair amounts of iron.

□ 3½ ounces, raw = 45 calories

Basic Preparation—Remove loose, discolored outer leaves. Trim off a bit of the stem. Wash thoroughly in cold water. Drop into a small amount of boiling salted water in a saucepan. Cover pan and cook for 5 to 10 minutes, or until just tender. Overcooking may produce strong flavor and cause loss of vitamins. Drain, add seasonings and butter or margarine, and serve.

□ **To Freeze**—Select firm, compact heads of good green color. Trim ends and remove coarse outer leaves. Wash and drain. Blanch in boiling water:

Small heads for 3 minutes

Medium heads for 4 minutes

Large heads for 5 minutes

Chill in cold water for 6 to 8 minutes. Drain. Pack in containers, leaving no headspace.

□ **To Cook, Frozen Brussels Sprouts**—Cook in a small amount of boiling salted water for 4 to 6 minutes, or until tender. Follow any additional directions on package.

BRUSSELS SPROUTS AND BEEF KABOBS

    1 pound beef sirloin
       cut into 1-inch cubes
    1 pint fresh, or 1 package (10 ounces)
       frozen, Brussels sprouts, cooked
    ½ cup French dressing
       Wedges of tomato

Combine beef, sprouts, and French dressing and marinate for 1 to 2 hours, turning occasionally. Arrange on skewers with tomatoes. Broil 3 to 4 inches from source of heat for 8 minutes, or until beef reaches desired degree of doneness. Makes 4 servings.

BRUSSELS SPROUTS IN BROWNED BUTTER

Cook and drain 2 pints fresh, or 2 packages (10 ounces each) frozen, Brussels sprouts. Brown ¼ cup butter or margarine slowly in a heavy skillet. Add juice of 1 lemon, sprouts, and salt and pepper; heat. Makes 4 servings.

BRUSSELS SPROUTS AND CHESTNUTS

Cook 1 package (10 ounces) frozen, or 1 pint fresh, Brussels sprouts until tender. Shell ½ pound chestnuts. To shell, gash end of each nut and cook in boiling water to cover for 15 to 20 minutes. Drain and remove shells and skins with a sharp knife. If not tender enough, cook in boiling salted water for 10 minutes longer. Combine Brussels sprouts and chestnuts and pour ¼ cup melted butter or margarine over them. Season to taste. Makes 4 servings.

BAKED SWEET-SOUR BRUSSELS SPROUTS

1 pint fresh, or 1 package (10 ounces)
 frozen, Brussels sprouts, cooked
2 tablespoons cooking oil
¼ cup cider vinegar
1 tablespoon sugar
½ teaspoon salt
¼ teaspoon pepper
2 tablespoons grated Parmesan cheese

Arrange sprouts in shallow baking dish. Combine oil, vinegar, sugar, salt, and pepper; blend. Pour over sprouts and sprinkle with cheese. Cover and bake in preheated moderate oven (350°F.) for 15 minutes, or until sprouts are tender. Makes 3 to 4 servings.

BUCKWHEAT—The triangular seeds of this plant are used as a cereal although, botanically speaking, it is an herb of the genus *Fagopyrum*. It is not a member of the family of cereal grasses to which wheat belongs. Buckwheat originates in Central Asia and Siberia, where it grows wild. Its use as a cereal is recent, compared to rice, barley, and millet; it is first mentioned in Chinese writings during the 10th and 11th centuries. Buckwheat was introduced into Europe during the early 15th century, and the first settlers brought it to the New World.

Buckwheat is a plant that likes a cool climate, and it will grow on the poorest and most arid soils. It is the staple grain of Russia and Poland, where millions of acres are put under buckwheat cultivation. The familiar Russian and Polish name for cooked buckwheat is *kasha*, and Jewish cookery, which uses buckwheat extensively, also uses this term.

Buckwheat is also consumed in Germany and France, the French name being *sayrasin*. In the United States, buckwheat is used mainly as flour for pancakes.

Purchasing Guide—Bran is removed and the remainder of the kernel is used to make flour or groats.

Buckwheat groats may be brown or white and also whole-kernel, coarse, medium, or fine; the medium is the most popular.

Storage

☐ Flour, kitchen shelf: 3 months
☐ Groats, kitchen shelf: 1 year
☐ Groats, refrigerator shelf, cooked, covered: 1 week

Nutritive Food Values—High in carbohydrates, with small amounts of vitamins and minerals.

☐ Dark flour, 3½ ounces = 333 calories
☐ Light flour, 3½ ounces = 347 calories
☐ Whole-kernel, 3½ ounces = 335 calories

Basic Preparation—Cook buckwheat groats as you would rice; follow package directions.

Buckwheat flour is used in combination with white flour; anything made of all-buckwheat flour would lack good color and texture.

KASHA

1 egg, beaten
1 cup buckwheat groats
1 teaspoon salt
¼ cup shortening
2 cups water

Combine egg, groats, and salt. Melt shortening in medium-size skillet. Stir in groat mixture and water; bring to a boil and cook, tightly covered, over low heat for about 15 minutes. Serve as a vegetable, in soups, or with gravy. Makes 4 servings.

COUNTRY-STYLE BUCKWHEAT GROATS

½ cup buckwheat groats
3 cups milk
½ teaspoon salt
 All-purpose flour
 Buttered maple syrup

Combine buckwheat groats, milk, and salt in a small saucepan. Bring to a boil, stirring occasionally. Spread evenly in an 8-inch square pan; chill. Unmold; cut into 2-inch squares; dredge with flour. Brown on both sides on lightly greased griddle, turning once. Serve with buttered maple syrup. Makes 4 servings.

BUCKWHEAT CAKES

1 package active dry yeast
 or 1 cake compressed yeast
 Water*
2 cups warm milk
¼ cup melted butter or sausage drippings
2 cups buckwheat flour
1 cup all-purpose flour
3 tablespoons sugar
2 teaspoons salt
½ teaspoon baking soda

* Use very warm water (105°F. to 115° F.) for dry yeast; use lukewarm water (80°F. to 90°F.) for compressed. Sprinkle yeast or crumble cake into 1 cup water. Let stand for a few minutes, then stir until dissolved. Add milk and butter.

Combine flours, sugar, and salt in a large bowl; add yeast and beat until smooth. Let rise overnight in a warm place; next morning dissolve soda in 1 tablespoon water and stir into raised mixture. Bake on hot griddle, lightly greased if necessary, turning once to brown both sides. Serve with butter and syrup. Makes about 36.

BAKED BUCKWHEAT PUDDING

2 eggs, beaten
½ cup buckwheat groats
6 cups milk
¾ cup molasses
6 tablespoons sugar
¾ teaspoon salt
1½ teaspoons ground ginger

Combine eggs and groats. Scald 2 cups milk in medium-size frying pan. Stir in groats, cover, and cook over low heat for 10 minutes, stirring occasionally. Blend in 2 cups milk and remaining ingredients. Pour into 1½-quart baking dish. Bake, uncovered, in preheated slow oven (325°F.) for about 1 hour. Stir in remaining milk; continue to bake for 1¼ hours. Serve warm with cream or ice cream. Makes 6 servings.

BUFFET—Literally translated, this French word means a "sideboard" or "cupboard." In French culinary language, a buffet indicates a good-size tiered table on which various dishes have been arranged in a decorative manner and, by implication, a restaurant that has such an arrangement. But even in French-speaking countries, the word is also used for an informal restaurant where a quick meal can be found, such as in *Buffet de la Gare,* "a station restaurant."

In America, the word buffet is used as a term for a meal where the guests help themselves from a table on which the foods are placed in a decorative array.

Buffet entertaining has become popular in recent years for three good reasons. First, fewer people have servants in this modern era, and when the food is good, the table attractive, and the company congenial, a buffet has all the graciousness of a meal that is formally served. The second point in favor of buffets: they permit a hostess to entertain more guests than she can seat comfortably at her dining-room table. And third, informality is the keynote of much of life today, and buffet entertaining, where guests serve themselves and, unconfined by a seating arrangement, can mingle with one another, fits in with this informality. But buffet meals, while they are easier on the hostess at the time of the party, do require careful planning and special equipment.

Planning the Menu—Consider casserole dishes: they come piping hot from oven to table and hold heat well.

Plan menus in terms of a main course that can be served on one plate.

Avoid foods that are hard to cut unless there are tables for all the diners.

Planning the Buffet Table—Make it as attractive as possible, and remember that food is part of the display so it should be considered as part of the color scheme.

Make it easy for guests to serve themselves. Arrange plates, napkins, silver, and serving dishes in the order in which they will be wanted.

Special Equipment—Chafing dishes, candle warmers, and electric warming trays keep hot foods hot.

Epergnes or other tiered serving dishes let you use space vertically if the buffet table is small.

CASSEROLE BUFFET
Menu
HAMBURGER CASSEROLE*

TOSSED SALAD   GARLIC BREAD*

MIXED-FRUIT BOWL*

COFFEE

HAMBURGER CASSEROLE
- 2 large onions, chopped
- 3 green peppers, sliced
- 1/3 cup butter or margarine
- 2½ pounds ground beef
- 3½ teaspoons salt
- ½ teaspoon pepper
- 5 cups fresh or canned whole-kernel corn
- 8 tomatoes, sliced
- 1 cup soft bread crumbs

Sauté onion and peppers in butter until brown. Add meat, break it up with fork, and cook for a few minutes, or until meat loses red color. Season with salt and pepper. In two 2-quart casseroles, arrange layers of half the corn, meat, and tomatoes. Repeat. Cover with crumbs. Bake in preheated moderate oven (350°F.) for 35 minutes. Makes 8 to 10 generous servings.

GARLIC BREAD
Cream ½ cup butter or margarine. Put 2 garlic cloves, halved, on toothpick and submerge garlic in butter; let stand for about 30 minutes. Remove garlic. Slice French bread loaf not quite through and spread slices with butter. Put slices together and spread a little butter over top; sprinkle with paprika. Heat in preheated hot oven (400°F.) for about 10 minutes.

MIXED-FRUIT BOWL
Chill pear halves, allowing 1 per serving. Add any other frozen or fresh fruit, such as grapefruit and orange sections, melon balls, or berries such as strawberries and blueberries.

ORIENTAL BUFFET
Menu
SWEET-AND-SOUR MEATBALLS*

CHINESE EGG ROLLS

PLUM SAUCE   MUSTARD

STEAMED RICE

CHINESE VEGETABLES*

FRESH-FRUIT BOWL

ALMOND COOKIES*

TEA

SWEET-AND-SOUR MEATBALLS
- ¾ cup fine dry bread crumbs
- 1 tablespoon instant minced onion
- 2 teaspoons salt
- ½ teaspoon pepper
  Water
- 3 pounds ground beef
- 1 pound bulk pork sausage meat
- 3 eggs, slightly beaten
  Cooking oil
- 1 bouillon cube
- 4 carrots
- 3 green peppers
- ¾ cup cider vinegar
- 1 cup firmly packed light brown sugar
- ¼ cup soy sauce
- 1/3 cup cornstarch

Add bread crumbs, onion, salt, and pepper to 1½ cups water; let stand a few minutes. Add to ground beef and pork with eggs and mix well. Shape into 36 balls. Brown in small amount of oil in skillet. Remove to roasting pan. Pour off fat in skillet; add 1½ cups water and bouillon cubes; heat, strain, and pour over meatballs. Cover and bake in preheated moderate oven (350°F.) for about 50 minutes. Cut carrots into strips and cook until almost tender; cut green pepper into wedges and cook for a few minutes. Make sauce by combining 4 cups water, vinegar, sugar, and soy sauce. Bring to boil; thicken with cornstarch mixed with a little cold water; cook until thick and clear. Pour liquid off meatballs and discard. Add carrots and green peppers to meatballs. Pour sauce over all and heat gently. Makes 12 servings.

CHINESE VEGETABLES
- 1 medium head of Chinese cabbage
- 2 celery stalks
- 3 green onions
- 2 tablespoons cooking oil
- ¼ cup water
- 1 package (10 ounces) frozen snow-pea pods
- 3 tablespoons soy sauce
- 2 pimientos, chopped

Slice cabbage, celery, and onions diagonally. Put vegetables in a large saucepan and add oil and water. Cover and steam for 5 minutes. Add pea pods and soy sauce. Cover and steam for a few minutes longer, or until all are tender but still crisp. Season with salt, if desired. Add pimientos. Makes 12 servings.

ALMOND COOKIES
- 1 cup margarine

- 1 cup sugar
- 1 egg
- ¼ cup honey
- 1½ tablespoons almond extract
- 4 cups sifted all-purpose flour
- 1½ teaspoons baking soda
- 1 cup sliced blanched almonds

Cream margarine until light and fluffy. Add sugar gradually and continue creaming. Add egg and beat well. Add honey and almond extract. Stir in flour sifted with soda. Form dough into 1-inch balls and put on greased cookie sheet. Flatten to about ¼ inch with finger tips. Sprinkle with nuts and press lightly into dough. Bake in preheated moderate oven (375° F.) for 7 to 8 minutes, until lightly browned. Makes about 5 dozen.

CHAFING-DISH BUFFET
Menu
SEAFOOD NEWBURG*

BEEF BALLS STROGANOFF*

CHEESE TOAST CUPS*

CARROT RICE*

ASPARAGUS OR BROCCOLI VINAIGRETTE*

FRESH STRAWBERRIES WITH

KIRSCH OR CREAM

NUT BUTTER COOKIES*

COFFEE

SEAFOOD NEWBURG
- 2 packages (6 ounces each) frozen king crabmeat
- 2 packages (10½ ounces each) frozen rock-lobster tails
- 2 packages (10 ounces each) frozen shrimps in shell
- 3 cans (10 ounces each) frozen shrimp soup
- 2 cans (10½ ounces each) cream-of-mushroom soup
- 1 cup heavy cream
- ¼ cup sherry
  Dash of pepper

Defrost frozen seafood and cook lobster tails and shrimps according to package directions. Shell lobster tails and shrimps. Cut seafood into bite-size pieces. Combine remaining ingredients and heat in chafing dish. Add seafood. Makes 12 servings.

BEEF BALLS STROGANOFF
- 2 eggs
- 1½ cups milk
- ¾ cup fine dry bread crumbs
- 1 tablespoon salt
- 1 teaspoon pepper
- 3 tablespoons chopped parsley
- 3 pounds ground beef chuck
- ½ cup butter or margarine

- 1½ cups chopped onions
- 1½ pounds fresh mushrooms, sliced
- 2 teaspoons paprika
- 6 tablespoons all-purpose flour
- 3 cups beef stock, bouillon, or consomme
- 1 tablespoon Worcestershire
  Salt and pepper
- ¾ cup dairy sour cream

Beat eggs; add milk, bread crumbs, salt, and pepper. Let stand for a few minutes.

Oriental Buffet

Add parsley and beef; mix thoroughly. Shape into 1-inch balls and brown in half of butter for about 10 minutes. Remove from pan. In same pan melt remaining butter; add onions, mushrooms, and paprika and brown slightly. Stir in flour to coat vegetables and brown for 2 to 3 minutes more. Gradually add beef stock, stirring constantly. Add Worcestershire and salt and pepper to taste. Return beef balls to sauce. Cover and cook slowly for 20 minutes. Add sour cream to sauce just before serving, or spoon sour cream on meatballs in serving dish to be stirred into sauce at the table. Makes 12 servings.

CHEESE TOAST CUPS

Cut crusts from slices of cheese bread. Melt butter and brush lavishly on slices. Press bread into muffin-pan cups and brown in preheated moderate oven (375° F.) for 10 to 15 minutes, or until crisped and browned. (Can be made ahead and reheated.)

Note: If cheese bread is not available, plain toast cups can be made with white bread.

CARROT RICE

Prepare either instant rice or the longer cooking rice according to package directions. Before cooking, add 3/4 cup coarsely shredded raw carrots to each 2 cups raw rice.

VINAIGRETTE SAUCE FOR ASPARAGUS OR BROCCOLI

1 teaspoon salt
1/8 teaspoon white pepper
Dash of cayenne
1/4 teaspoon paprika
3 tablespoons tarragon vinegar
1/2 cup olive oil
1 tablespoon minced green pepper
1 tablespoon chopped sweet pickle
1 tablespoon minced parsley
2 teaspoons chopped chives or green onions
Few drops of lemon juice
Asparagus for 12, cooked and cooled (4 pounds asparagus) or
Broccoli for 12, cooked and cooled (2 bunches fresh broccoli)

Mix and chill all ingredients except asparagus or broccoli. Pour sauce over vegetables just before serving. Toss lightly to coat vegetables. Makes about 3/4 cup sauce, or enough for 12 servings.

NUT BUTTER COOKIES

2/3 cup soft butter
6 tablespoons confectioners' sugar
1 teaspoon vanilla extract
2 cups sifted all-purpose flour
1/4 teaspoon salt
1/2 teaspoon almond extract
1 cup chopped nuts

Cream butter; add remaining ingredients gradually and mix well. Press into 2-inch-long finger-shape rolls. Squeeze each roll in the palm and fingers of one hand to obtain irregular shape. Place on ungreased cookie sheet and bake in preheated slow oven (325°F.) for 15 to 20 minutes. Makes about 3½ dozen.

BUN—This is a small, sweetened or unsweetened, round or oval cake or roll, and a very old form of baked food. Usually it is made with yeast. The best known buns are Bath buns, named after an English seaside city; hot cross buns, marked with a sugar cross (originally baked for Good Friday, although now baked throughout Lent); and Swedish saffron buns, served on St. Lucia Day (December 13). Young Swedish girls, dressed in white and wearing crowns with lighted candles, serve the saffron buns to their parents early in the morning. This custom inaugurates the Christmas season.

ENGLISH BATH BUNS

2 packages active dry yeast or 2 cakes compressed yeast
1/2 cup warm water*
1/2 cup milk
1½ cups sugar
1 teaspoon salt
3/4 cup butter or margarine
4 egg yolks
3 eggs
4½ cups sifted all-purpose flour
1/2 teaspoon lemon extract
1/2 cup chopped candied fruit
1/2 cup sliced blanched almonds
1 egg, beaten
1/2 cup milk

* Use very warm water (105°F. to 115° F.) for dry yeast; use lukewarm (80°F. to 90°F.) for compressed. Sprinkle dry yeast or crumble cakes into water in large bowl and let stand for a few minutes; stir to dissolve. Scald milk and add 1/2 cup sugar, salt, and butter; cool to lukewarm. Add milk mixture, egg yolks, eggs, flour, and lemon extract to yeast mixture. Beat until smooth, about 5 minutes. Cover and let rise until doubled, about 1¼ hours. Stir down, cover well, and chill in refrigerator overnight. Divide into small pieces; shape into balls and put on greased cookie sheets. Cover and let rise until doubled, about 50 minutes. Press fruit and almonds into the tops. Beat together egg and milk. Brush buns with mixture. Sprinkle remaining sugar over the tops. Bake in preheated moderate oven (350°F.) for 15 to 20 minutes. Serve warm. Makes about 24.

HOT CROSS BUNS

1 package active dry yeast or 1 cake compressed yeast
1/4 cup water*
1 cup milk, scalded
1 teaspoon salt
1/2 cup sugar
1/2 cup shortening
4½ cups sifted all-purpose flour
3 egg yolks, slightly beaten
1/2 teaspoon ground cinnamon
1/2 cup currants
Melted butter

* Use very warm water (105°F. to 115° F.) for dry yeast; use lukewarm (80°F. to 90°F.) for compressed. Sprinkle dry yeast or crumble cake into water. Let stand for a few minutes, then stir until dissolved. Pour hot milk over salt, sugar, and shortening and cool to lukewarm. Add yeast and 2 cups flour, beat well, and let rise until light. Add egg yolks, then remaining flour mixed with cinnamon. Add currants. Knead; put in large greased bowl. Brush top of dough with melted butter. Cover, and let rise until doubled in bulk. Shape into small round buns and place close together in greased pan. Let rise until doubled in bulk. With a very sharp knife or razor blade, cut a cross just through the top surface of each bun. Bake in preheated hot oven (400°F.) for 15 minutes, brush with melted butter, and continue to bake for 5 minutes more. Cool on a rack. If desired, brush each bun with a simple frosting made of confectioners' sugar moistened with water. Makes 1½ to 2 dozen.

SWEDISH SAFFRON BUNS

3/4 cup milk
1/3 cup sugar
1 teaspoon salt
1/4 cup butter or margarine
1 teaspoon powdered saffron
2 tablespoons boiling water
1/2 cup water*
2 packages active dry yeast or 2 cakes compressed yeast
1 egg, beaten
4 cups sifted all-purpose flour (about)
1/4 cup currants or seedless raisins

Scald milk; stir in sugar, salt, and butter; cool to lukewarm. Meanwhile add saffron to boiling water; let stand. Measure warm water into a large bowl. * Use very warm water (105°F. to 115°F.) for dry yeast; use lukewarm (80°F. to 90°F.) for compressed. Sprinkle or crumble in the yeast. Let stand for a few minutes; then stir until dissolved. Stir in lukewarm milk mixture, beaten egg, saffron water, and 2 cups flour; beat until smooth. Stir in currants, then enough remaining flour to make a soft dough. Turn out on floured surface; knead until smooth and elastic, about 8 minutes. Place in a greased bowl, turning to grease all sides. Cover; let rise in warm place, free from draft, until doubled in bulk, about 1 hour. Punch down. Turn out on floured board, cover, and let rest for 10 minutes. Cut off a piece of dough about 2 inches in diameter. Divide remaining dough into 16 equal pieces. Shape each piece into a ball; place in a well-greased small brioche mold or muffin cup. Divide the 2-inch piece of dough into 16 pieces; shape each into a small ball. Make a deep indentation in each bun; press a small ball into each indentation. Cover; let rise in a warm place, free from draft, until doubled in bulk, about 30 minutes. Bake in preheated moderate oven (375° F.) for about 15 minutes. Makes 16.

BURGUNDY—The name of a region of France which produces some of the greatest wines in the world. Outside of France, Burgundy is usually thought of as a red wine, but there are also superb dry white Burgundies, of which the best known is called Chablis. Good Burgundy is a rich, mellow wine, rather on the hearty side.

Burgundy as a region is also the home of some of the most glorious of all French cooking, famed throughout the world for the lusciousness of its foods and the care taken in their preparation. Especially well known are: the mustard from Dijon, made there since the days of the Romans; the sugar-coated Jordan almonds, still sold in the shop where they were first made nearly three and a half centuries ago; and the king of all beef stews, *boeuf bourguignon.*

BOEUF BOURGUIGNON

¼ cup finely diced salt pork or bacon
2 pounds lean stewing beef,
　cut into 1½-inch cubes
2 tablespoons brandy
1 teaspoon all-purpose flour
1 teaspoon salt
¼ teaspoon pepper
1½ cups dry red wine
1 tablespoon butter
2 medium onions, coarsely chopped
1 medium carrot, cut into pieces
1 garlic clove, minced or pressed
1 bouquet garni (see page 216)
　Water or beef bouillon
½ pound mushrooms, sliced

In heavy skillet cook salt pork or bacon until crisp. Brown meat in hot fat; the meat must be dark brown. Transfer meat to casserole. Heat brandy, pour over meat, and flame. When flame has died down, stir flour into meat. Season with salt and pepper and add red wine. Add butter to fat in skillet and heat. Brown onions in it. To meat in casserole, add onions, carrot, garlic, *bouquet garni,* and enough water or bouillon to cover meat. Simmer, covered, over lowest possible heat, or in preheated moderate oven (350°F.), for about 3 hours, or until meat is very tender and sauce dark brown. About 30 minutes before serving time, add mushrooms. Remove *bouquet garni* when dish is ready. Serve with boiled potatoes or buttered noodles. Makes 4 to 6 servings.
Note: This dish can be made ahead of time and refrigerated. Reheat slowly.

BUTTER—An edible animal fat, obtained from milk and cream which have been made solid by churning. Butter can be made from fresh or slightly acid milk (this affects the taste and spreading consistency); it can be salted or it can be sweet, that is, non-salted (Europeans prefer the latter kind). Good butter is the product of first-rate milk and cream, painstaking cleanliness, and skillful churning.

Butter has been a basic food since men began wandering to seek pasture for their animals: cattle, goats, sheep, asses, mares, and even camels. Probably butter originated spontaneously when the milk of these animals, carried in food containers, churned itself during the nomads' travels.

Butter was known to the ancient world as a symbol of goodness and plenty. The Bible is full of allusions to it: Judges 5:25, Job 29:6, Psalms 55:21, Proverbs 30:33, and Isaiah 7:15-22. The thought of butter and butter-making calls up charming visions of rural life in English butteries, where apple-cheeked lasses sat churning thick and satiny cream; or of the Swiss Alps, where the deep crocks of golden butter were cooled by crystal-clear glacier streams; or in the comfortable French farm kitchens ruled by bustling, aproned women.

The equipment used for making butter is often a fine token of the folk arts. It includes carved churns, painted cream containers, and carved butter molds and paddles.

Yet butter is not a universal product. In southern European countries oil, not butter, was used for fat since their climate made dairying impossible in less scientific days. In fact, European cooking can be classified in two broad ways: butter cookery and olive-oil cookery. The Chinese and Japanese do not use butter, but for the Tibetans and Indians it is a basic fat.

Perhaps the pleasure Western man takes in butter is not only a culinary one, but also one of nostalgia. Butter, basically a simple food, makes us feel that we still have a link with nature.

Availability—Sweet or salted butter is sold packaged in ¼-pound bars and 1-pound blocks. Whipped butter, salted and unsalted, is sold in 8- to 12-ounce round cartons. Whipped salted butter is also sold in bars, 6 to a 1-pound package.

Butter is also sold in combinations such as honey butter.

Purchasing Guide—Butter is graded on flavor, color, body, texture, and salt. Each category is rated a certain number of points to achieve the following scores:

U.S. Grade AA　(U.S. 93 Score)
U.S. Grade A　　(U.S. 92 Score)
U.S. Grade B　　(U.S. 90 Score)
U.S. Grade C　　(U.S. 89 Score)
U.S. Grade GG　(U.S. 89 or lower
　(or cooking　　　　Score)
　grade)

According to federal law, butter must contain not less than 80% milk fat; coloring may be added.
☐ 2 bars = ½ pound = 1 cup butter
☐ 1 cup butter = 1 cup margarine =
　⅞ cup vegetable shortening
☐ ⅓ cup butter = 5⅓ tablespoons
☐ ¼ cup butter = 4 tablespoons
Storage—Keep in refrigerator, tightly wrapped to prevent absorption of odors. Take out only as much as you need for one meal to prevent deterioration of flavor due to exposure to light and warmth.
☐ Refrigerator shelf: 1 to 2 weeks
☐ Refrigerator frozen-food compartment: 1 month
☐ Freezer: 1 year

Nutritive Food Values—High in fat with moderate amounts of vitamins A and D. Whipped butter contains ⅓ less calories than regular butter.
☐ Sweet or salted, 1 tablespoon = 100 calories. (One pat is ½ tablespoon)

Basic Preparation—Should be used at low heat during panfrying because it smokes and browns if temperature is too high.

Not suitable for deep frying because of its low smoking point.
☐ **To Make Decorative Butter**—Butter paddles, curlers, and molds can be bought in houseware stores. They can also be used for margarine.

Butter Curls—Begin at the far side of a 1-pound block of cold butter and draw a butter curler lightly and quickly toward you, making a thin shaving of butter which curls into a cylinder. Dip the curler into hot water each time.

Butter Balls—Scald and chill a pair of wooden butter paddles. Measure firm, but not cold, butter by teaspoons so that balls will be the same size. Roll lightly between paddles to shape into balls. Put on a chilled plate and store in refrigerator or drop into a bowl of ice water.

Butter Pats—Cut neat squares from a bar of cold butter with a sharp knife dipped into cold water or wrapped in wax paper. To add decoration, dip a fork in hot water and draw it diagonally across each square. Or garnish each square with a tiny parsley sprig.

Butter Molds—Use a special wooden butter mold and dip into ice water. Press firm butter into mold. Push to release butter. Chill until ready to serve.
☐ **To Clarify Butter**—This is often done when sautéing chicken, veal, and fish because it doesn't burn as easily as whole butter. It also adds richness to cakes. Put any quantity of sweet butter in a deep saucepan. Melt butter over low heat and continue to heat until foam disappears from top and there is a light-brown sediment in bottom of pan. The liquid butter should remain golden. When perfectly clear, remove from heat and skim any

brown crust from top. Pour off the clear butter, leaving sediment in pan. If a large amount of butter is being prepared, cool and strain through cheesecloth. Chill until ready to use.

Note: Salt butter can also be used, but it will yield slightly less clarified butter.

BLACK BUTTER

Stir ⅓ cup butter over low heat until melted and dark brown. Add 1 teaspoon lemon juice or mild vinegar and salt and pepper. For Almond Black Butter, add ⅓ cup slivered blanched almonds when butter is beginning to brown. Serve on fish or meat.

LEMON BUTTER

Cream butter until very light and fluffy. Add a few drops of lemon juice, or to taste.

MAÎTRE D'HÔTEL BUTTER

½ cup butter
½ teaspoon salt
⅛ teaspoon white pepper
2 tablespoons minced parsley
1 tablespoon lemon juice

Cream butter until fluffy. Beat in next 3 ingredients. Add lemon juice drop by drop. Makes about ½ cup.

Herb Butter

To Maître d'Hôtel Butter add 1 teaspoon ground thyme or marjoram and 1 teaspoon crumbled dried basil. Or use fresh herbs to taste. If desired, add ¼ teaspoon garlic salt. Good on broiled lamb chops, broiled steak, broiled fish.

BUTTER SPREADS FOR HOT BREADS

To ½ cup softened butter or margarine, add:

■ 1 cup grated Parmesan cheese, ⅓ cup mayonnaise, ⅓ cup minced green onion.
■ ¾ cup minced stuffed green olives, ½ cup ready-grated American cheese, 1 teaspoon scraped onion.
■ ½ cup honey, ¼ cup chunk-style peanut butter. Sprinkle spread slices with cinnamon.

BUTTERMILK—This is the milk that is left over after butter has been churned. It contains very little fat, since the fat has gone into the butter.

Real buttermilk is a thin liquid with little fat globules, whereas commercial buttermilk is a smooth, homogenized product which is far more appetizing to drink than the original product.

Buttermilk varies, depending on whether the milk and cream used for butter were fresh or slightly soured. Most of today's buttermilk is made from freshly skimmed milk that has been pasteurized, cooled, inoculated with a special culture, and allowed to ferment under suitable conditions. The concentration of butterfat and other milk solids is the same as for skimmed milk. Salt is sometimes added to accentuate the flavor.

Purchasing Guide—Available in 1-quart containers.

Storage—Store, covered, in refrigerator to preserve flavor. Since buttermilk acidity increases during storage, use as soon as possible after purchase.

Nutritive Food Values—A good source of protein, calcium, and riboflavin.
☐ 3½ ounces = 36 calories

Basic Preparation—Buttermilk is used in recipes for beverages, sherbets, baked products, and salad dressings. When buttermilk is substituted for fresh milk in a recipe, baking soda must be used instead of baking powder for leavening. The proportions to use are:

¼ teaspoon baking soda + ½ cup buttermilk = 1 teaspoon baking powder + ½ cup fresh milk

BUTTERMILK MERINGUE PIE

1 cup sugar
¼ cup all-purpose flour
½ teaspoon salt
1 whole egg
3 egg yolks
2 cups buttermilk
1 tablespoon butter
1 tablespoon lemon juice
9-inch pie shell, baked
Meringue

In top part of double boiler, mix sugar with flour and salt. Beat together whole egg, egg yolks, and buttermilk. Gradually stir into first mixture. Cook over boiling water until smooth and thickened. Cool slightly and add butter and lemon juice. Pour into cooled pie shell. Top with Meringue and bake in preheated hot oven (400°F.) for 5 minutes, or until slightly browned. Cool before serving. Makes 6 to 8 servings.

Meringue

Beat 3 egg whites with ¼ teaspoon salt until frothy. Gradually beat in 6 tablespoons sugar and beat until stiff and glossy. Pile lightly on pie, being sure to cover filling completely.

LOW-CALORIE BUTTERMILK DRESSING

3 tablespoons lemon juice
1¼ teaspoons seasoned salt
¼ teaspoon prepared mustard
1 cup buttermilk
Sugar

Combine all ingredients except sugar and blend well. Add sugar to taste. Good on lettuce-and-tomato or cottage-cheese salad. Makes 1 cup.

DANISH BUTTERMILK SOUP

2 eggs, well beaten
Juice and grated rind of 1 lemon
¼ cup sugar
1 teaspoon vanilla extract
4 cups buttermilk
1 cup heavy cream, whipped

Beat eggs with lemon juice, lemon rind, sugar, and vanilla. Whip buttermilk until frothy. Beat into egg mixture, a little at a time. Chill until frosty. Top with whipped cream. Serve with stewed fruit or preserves. A refreshing dessert for a hot-day supper. Serve with crisp cookies. Makes 4 servings.

BUTTERMILK SPOON BREAD

2 cups yellow cornmeal
1½ cups cold water
1 cup boiling water
2 tablespoons butter or margarine
2 teaspoons salt
2 eggs, beaten
1 teaspoon baking soda
1½ cups buttermilk

Stir cornmeal into cold water. Add boiling water and stir vigorously. Add remaining ingredients and mix well. Pour into buttered 2-quart casserole. Bake in preheated moderate oven (375°F.) for 45 minutes, or until firm and browned. Serve at once. Makes 6 to 8 servings.

BUTTERNUT—This native North American nut, also known as a white walnut, is used primarily in cakes and cookies. Butternuts are very difficult to shell, but do not need blanching. They grow in small clusters inside spongy, hair-covered husks. In colonial days in America, before the advent of commercial dyes, the husks were used to color homespun wools and cottons.

The ripe nuts are used in cooking as you would other nuts.

Availability—These nuts are not shipped commercially, but are available in the areas where they are grown. Butternuts are grown from New Brunswick to Georgia and westward to the Dakotas and Arkansas.

Storage—Store as you would other nuts: covered, in a cool, dry place.
☐ Refrigerator shelf, unshelled: 1 year
☐ Refrigerator shelf, shelled: 3 to 6 months

Nutritive Food Values—They contain some protein and iron and are high in fat.
☐ 3½ ounces = 629 calories

MAPLE BUTTERNUT CAKE

½ cup butter or margarine
½ cup sugar
1 cup maple sugar
2 eggs, well beaten
2½ cups sifted all-purpose flour
2 teaspoons baking powder
½ teaspoon baking soda
½ teaspoon ground ginger
½ cup hot water
½ cup chopped butternut meats
  Maple Sugar Frosting

Cream butter until light. Gradually add sugar. Stir in maple sugar and blend thoroughly. Beat in eggs. Sift together flour, baking powder, baking soda, and ginger. Add to batter alternately with hot water, beating well after each addition. Stir in nuts. Pour into well-greased loaf pan (9¼ x 5¼ x 2¾ inches). Bake in preheated moderate oven (350°F.) for 45 minutes. Cool and frost with Maple Sugar Frosting. Makes 1 loaf cake.

Maple Sugar Frosting

2 cups maple sugar
¼ teaspoon salt
1 cup light cream
½ cup butternut meats, chopped

Boil together maple sugar, salt, and cream until a little of the mixture dropped into cold water forms a soft ball (approximately 238°F. on a candy thermometer). Add nuts and beat until cooled and creamy. Spread immediately since frosting gets hard very quickly.

BUTTERNUT SQUASH—A winter squash, smooth and hard-shelled, long and slender, with seeds contained in a small hollow in the base. The squash gets its name from its color which, for most of the year, is light brown or dark yellow. The flesh is almost orange. Its flavor is sweet, it mashes smoothly, and is comparatively quick-cooking.

Availability—August to March, with peak season October through December.

Purchasing Guide—Weighs about 1 to 3 pounds. Look for squashes that seem heavy for their size, smooth-skinned with hard, tough rinds.

Storage—Keep in refrigerator or a cool place until ready to use.

☐ Refrigerator shelf, raw: 4 to 6 weeks
☐ Refrigerator shelf, cooked and covered: 1 to 4 days
☐ Refrigerator frozen-food compartment, prepared for freezing: 1 month
☐ Freezer, prepared for freezing: 2 years

Nutritive Food Values—Butternut squash is an excellent source of vitamin A and also provides fair amounts of vitamin C, iron, and riboflavin.

☐ 3½ ounces, raw = 171 calories

Basic Preparation—Wash, then peel with vegetable parer. Cut off the underlayer of green along with the skin. Cut into halves and scoop out seeds and stringy portion. Slice or cut into cubes.

☐ **To Steam**—Put cubes of squash in saucepan in about 1 inch of boiling salted water. Cover pan and cook for 20 to 30 minutes, or until tender. (A few slices of onion may be cooked with squash for additional flavor.)

Drain thoroughly, season; add a little butter or margarine. Return pan to heat and shake gently for about 1 minute to distribute seasonings and evaporate remaining liquid.

If squash is to be served mashed, follow directions above, then mash and serve.

To use leftover mashed butternut squash: melt a little butter in skillet; add 1 small onion, sliced, and fry until almost tender. Then stir in 2 to 3 tablespoons dark brown sugar. Add squash and blend well. Form squash into cakes and fry until brown on both sides.

☐ **To Bake**—Cut squash into halves; scoop out seeds. Place in a shallow baking pan, skin side down. Brush with melted butter or margarine and sprinkle with salt and pepper. If desired, may be sprinkled with a little brown sugar or molasses. Bake, covered, in preheated moderate oven (350°F.) for 30 minutes; bake, uncovered for 20 to 30 minutes longer, or until squash is tender. Serve in the shell or mash as above.

☐ **To Freeze**—Bake or steam squash as above until tender. Cool; mash pulp. Package, allowing ½-inch headspace.

ANISE BUTTERNUT SQUASH

4 cups mashed cooked butternut or other yellow winter squash
⅓ cup sugar
¼ cup butter or margarine
1½ teaspoons aniseed, crushed
½ teaspoon salt

Combine all ingredients. Turn into a buttered 1-quart casserole. Bake in preheated moderate oven (375°F.) for 45 minutes, or until top is well flecked with brown. Serve hot with pork, poultry, or ham. Makes 6 to 8 servings.

BUTTERSCOTCH—This popular flavor is obtained by combining butter and sugar, usually brown sugar, and by cooking the two together in a number of different ways.

Foods flavored with butterscotch, such as cakes, cookies, frostings, puddings, and sauces, take the name, and become butterscotch cake, butterscotch frosting, butterscotch pudding, etc.

Butterscotch is also a hard candy.

BUTTERSCOTCH SAUCE

2 cups firmly packed light brown sugar
½ cup evaporated milk, undiluted
¼ teaspoon salt
⅓ cup light corn syrup
⅓ cup butter or margarine

Combine all ingredients in a saucepan; bring to boil and cook for 3 minutes, or until 220°F. registers on a candy thermometer. Makes 2 cups. Allow ¼ cup for each serving.

Note: This sauce can be made a day ahead. Do not refrigerate.

BUTTERSCOTCH CREAM PIE

½ cup granulated sugar
⅓ cup hot water
2 cups milk
¼ cup butter or margarine
6 tablespoons all-purpose flour
¾ cup firmly packed dark brown sugar
½ teaspoon salt
2 eggs
9- inch pie shell, baked
1 cup heavy cream, whipped
  Toasted slivered almonds

Place granulated sugar in small heavy saucepan or skillet. Cook over low heat without stirring until sugar melts and becomes golden brown. Remove from heat. Add water slowly. Cook without stirring until sugar dissolves. Add milk. Heat to almost boiling. Melt butter in top part of double boiler. Remove from heat. Add flour, brown sugar, and salt. Beat in eggs and milk mixture. Cook over boiling water, stirring constantly, until thickened. Cover and cook for 10 minutes, stirring occasionally. Cool to room temperature. Pour into baked shell. Chill for several hours. Top with whipped cream and sprinkle with almonds. Makes 6 to 8 servings.

BUTTERSCOTCH FILLING

3 tablespoons butter or margarine
½ cup firmly packed dark brown sugar
1½ cups milk
¼ cup all-purpose flour
½ teaspoon salt
1 egg, beaten
½ teaspoon vanilla extract

Melt butter in top part of double boiler. Add sugar and cook for 2 minutes over direct heat. Add 1 cup milk and heat over boiling water. Mix flour, remaining milk, and salt until smooth. Gradually stir into hot mixture. Cook for 5 minutes, stirring constantly. Cover; cook for 10 minutes longer, stirring occasionally. Add mixture gradually to egg; return to double boiler and cook for 2 minutes. Cool; add vanilla. Use as filling in layer cake. Makes about 2 cups.

CABBAGE—*Brassica* is the Latin name of this leafy vegetable, which may be called man's best friend in the vegetable world. The word "cabbage" itself is an Anglicized version of the colloquial French word *caboche,* which means "head."

Cabbage comes in many varieties, some with loose heads, some with firm ones, and others with flat, conical, or egg-shape heads. Some cabbages are white, some green, some red; some have plain leaves and some curly ones. It grows in a large range of latitudes. Learned scholars have argued over its origin, which is both obscure and ancient. At least 4,000 years ago men were eating the leafy wild cabbage found on the coasts of Europe and northern Africa, and it appears that they also ate cabbage in China several thousand years ago. Egyptians, Greeks, and Romans adored cabbage, and Marcus Porcius Cato, the great Roman statesman, wrote five pages on it, anticipating the American taste for coleslaw: "It surpasses all other vegetables. It may be eaten either cooked or raw. If you eat it raw dip it into vinegar. . . . It promotes digestion marvelously."

The Celts, too, thought so highly of cabbage that they brought it into northern Europe. In Great Britain it became known through the centuries as the national flower of England.

Cabbage came to the North American continent via Jacques Cartier, who planted it in Canada on his third voyage in 1541-42. Though the early American colonists must have planted cabbage, if for nothing else but to feed their stock, there is no written record of it until 1669.

Cabbage is eaten in one form or another in most countries of the world. It is a favorite food of the Slavic and the Germanic peoples, and an important part of their daily diet.

The universality of cabbage is perhaps best illustrated by the number of legends that have sprung up around it. Babies were found in the cabbage patch, and in Scotland young women guessed at the figure and the size of their future husbands by drawing cabbages, blindfolded, on Halloween. To dream of cabbages meant sickness to loved ones and loss of money. And we are apt to forget that the man on the moon was sent there because he stole a cabbage from his neighbor on December 24. A child in white surprised him in this evil deed, and said: "Since you will steal on this holy night, let you and your cabbage go to the moon."

Sauerkraut is said to have originated in Asia, as a convenient way of preserving an essential food when no other food-preserving methods were available. All in all, it is certain that man would find it hard to live without cabbage.

Availability—Available all year round in different varieties.

Market Types

Danish—This is a compact, solid-headed, late-maturing cabbage. The leaves are tight and smooth around the top, and the heads are round and somewhat flattened or oval.

Domestic—The heads, somewhat angular in outline, are usually less compact than Danish, and the leaf tissues are more tender and brittle. The leaves are a little crumpled or curled and do not overlap as far at the crown as the Danish. They are largely an early or midseason crop.

Pointed (called "green" or "new" cabbage)—Smaller head than Danish and Domestic. Greener color.

Red—The leaves are relatively loose. Several varieties of this reddish-purple cabbage are common, especially in the New York area and in Wisconsin.

Savoy—It is readily identified by crinkled leaves that shade from dark to pale green, and heads that are loosely formed. This cabbage, a favorite with people of Latin descent, is becoming increasingly popular here. The flavor is a little mellower than that of other green cabbage.

Celery or Chinese (Pe-Tsai) Cabbage—Although it is called cabbage, this vegetable is a more distant member of the cabbage family. The long, firm tapering "stalks" (about 4 inches thick and 10 to 16 inches long) resemble a cross between oversize romaine lettuce and celery. Its tightly closed broad leaves are crisp, the color pale green to white. It is used mainly in salads, but many interesting cooked dishes are made with it.

Purchasing Guide—A head of cabbage should be solid and heavy for its size. New cabbage, which comes from southern areas during the winter, is usually not as solid as winter (stored) cabbage but is greener. Avoid heads showing injury, decay, or yellow leaves. If the base of some of the outer leaves is separated from the stem, the cabbage may be strong in flavor or coarse in texture when cooked. Celery cabbage should be firm, oval shape, and well blanched.

☐ 1 pound = 3½ cups raw = 2½ cups cooked

Storage—Remove any discolored leaves from head of cabbage. Place in a covered container or moistureproof bag, or wrap in foil or wax paper, and keep in the refrigerator.

☐ Refrigerator shelf or vegetable compartment, raw: 3 to 8 days
☐ Refrigerator shelf, cooked: 1 to 4 days
☐ Refrigerator frozen-food compartment, prepared for freezing: 2 to 3 months
☐ Freezer, prepared for freezing: 1 year

Nutritive Food Values—Raw cabbage is a very good source of vitamin C and some vitamin A; celery cabbage has a smaller amount. During the cooking process, however, there may be some vitamin loss.

☐ 3½ ounces, raw = 24 calories
☐ 3½ ounces, cooked = 20 calories
☐ 3½ ounces, celery, raw = 14 calories

Basic Preparation—Wash head well. Cut according to way it is to be used. If cabbage is old, cut round heads into wedges and remove center core; or shred it. *Never overcook cabbage.*

☐ **To Boil, Wedges**—Put about 1 inch of water in a saucepan; add about ½ teaspoon salt per pound of cabbage, and the wedges. Cook rapidly, uncovered, for 2 to 3 minutes; then cover pan, lower heat, and cook for 10 to 12 minutes more, or until tender but still crisp. Drain, season to taste, and add butter or margarine if desired.

☐ **To Boil, Shredded**—Follow same method as for wedges, but use only ½ inch of water and cook for only 5 to 8 minutes. Drain, season, and serve at once.

☐ **To Braise**—In a skillet melt enough butter, margarine, or bacon fat to cover the bottom of the pan. Add cabbage wedges or shreds; cook gently for 2 to 3 minutes, turning until the vegetable is coated with fat. Then cover tightly and let steam until tender, about 15 minutes for wedges, 8 to 10 for shreds.

Cook red cabbage by any of the methods above, but add a little vinegar or lemon juice or a few apple slices to help hold the color.

☐ **To Prepare Uncooked Cabbage**—Two methods are used to slice or shred cabbage for coleslaw and the many other ways of serving cabbage raw.

1. Coarse grating on a regular grater is preferred if the juice is to be drawn from cabbage, as in a coleslaw which is dressed with vinegar and seasonings only. Dressings also soak into grated cabbage more rapidly.

2. Slicing, paper-thin, is preferred when longer, drier shreds are desired. This is done with a slicing knife on a board or with a mechanical vegetable shredder. The resulting slaw or salad pieces have more form and the cabbage stays crisper.

☐ **To Freeze**—Use solid green and white heads. Trim all bruised pieces. Remove core and cut cabbage into pieces. Blanch in boiling water for 3 to 4 minutes, depending on size. Cool in ice water. Pack tightly to prevent air spaces, and allow ½-inch headspace.

Prepare celery cabbage in the same way, blanching pieces for only 70 seconds.

FRENCH CABBAGE SOUP

3 cups potatoes, peeled and chopped
1 pound lean bacon or ham, in one piece
3 quarts water
2 pounds cabbage, roughly sliced
6 peppercorns, crushed
6 parsley sprigs
1 bay leaf
½ teaspoon each of ground thyme and marjoram
2 garlic cloves, mashed
2 onions
2 carrots, quartered
2 celery stalks, sliced
2 turnips, peeled and chopped (optional)
1½ cups canned red or white beans, drained
Salt

Place potatoes and bacon in deep kettle. Add water. Bring to boil. Add all other ingredients except beans and salt. Simmer, covered, 2 hours, or until meat is tender. Remove meat; slice into serving pieces. Skim off excess fat from soup. Return meat to soup. Add beans. Season to taste with salt. Heat thoroughly. Serve with French bread. Makes 8 servings.

CABBAGE ALMOND SOUP

2 cups finely chopped cabbage
½ cup almonds, blanched and chopped
½ cup water
2 tablespoons butter
1 teaspoon caraway seeds
2 teaspoons salt
¼ teaspoon paprika
1 egg, well beaten
4 cups milk
¼ cup grated sharp Cheddar cheese

Cook cabbage and almonds in water for 10 minutes; add butter, caraway seeds, salt, and paprika. Mix egg with milk, add to cabbage mixture, and heat just to boiling, stirring occasionally. Top with cheese. Makes 4 servings.

CABBAGE ROLLS WITH SAUERKRAUT AND PORK

6 to 8 large cabbage leaves
2 cups cooked rice
½ pound sausage meat
2 tablespoons finely chopped onion
Salt and pepper
2 cups (one 1-pound can) sauerkraut
1 smoked pork hock
Paprika
Dairy sour cream

Cook cabbage leaves in small amount of boiling salted water for 3 to 4 minutes. Drain and dry on paper towels. Mix rice, sausage meat, onion, salt, and pepper. Fill and roll the cabbage leaves. Secure with toothpicks or poultry skewers. Place half of sauerkraut in a skillet. Top with cabbage rolls and pork hock. Cover with remaining sauerkraut. Add enough water to cover and simmer for 2 hours, adding more water when needed. Sprinkle with paprika and serve with sour cream. Makes 6 to 8 servings.

STUFFED WHOLE CABBAGE WITH BÉCHAMEL SAUCE

1 small whole green cabbage
1 pound ground beef chuck
¼ cup chopped onion
1 tablespoon butter or margarine
1 teaspoon salt
⅛ teaspoon pepper
Pinch of garlic powder
2 cups beef bouillon or 2 bouillon cubes dissolved in 2 cups boiling water
Bechamel Sauce

Trim coarse outside leaves from cabbage. Cut out the middle of cabbage (save cut portion for coleslaw). Brown meat with onion in butter. Add salt, pepper, and garlic powder. Spoon into cavity of cabbage. Tie cabbage in cheesecloth. Cook, covered, in boiling bouillon for 20 minutes, or until cabbage is tender. Serve hot with a Béchamel Sauce (see page 173). Makes 6 servings.

PANNED CHINESE CABBAGE

2 tablespoons butter
1 quart shredded Chinese cabbage
  Salt and pepper

Heat butter in skillet. Add cabbage, cover, and cook for about 3 minutes, stirring twice. Season with salt and pepper. Makes 4 servings.

CHINESE CABBAGE WITH EGG DRESSING

1 hard-cooked egg
2 tablespoons salad oil
2 tablespoons cider vinegar
1 pimiento, cut up
2 tablespoons chopped parsley
1 onion slice, minced
½ teaspoon salt
⅛ teaspoon pepper
  Chinese cabbage

Chop egg and add oil, vinegar, pimiento, parsley, onion, and seasonings. Mix well and pour over sliced cabbage.Toss lightly and serve at once. Makes 4 servings.

CABBAGE IN CREAM

2 quarts shredded green cabbage
  Salt
½ cup light cream
3 tablespoons butter
  Dash of ground nutmeg
  Pepper

Cook cabbage in ½ inch of boiling salted water for 5 to 8 minutes, or until tender. Drain. Add cream and butter; heat slowly, stirring gently with a fork. Add nutmeg, and salt and pepper to taste. Makes 4 to 6 servings.

CABBAGE, TOMATOES, AND GREEN PEPPER

3 onions, sliced
2 tablespoons butter
1 green pepper, cut into 1-inch pieces
2 large tomatoes
½ medium head of green cabbage
  Salt and pepper

Cook onions in butter for 3 minutes. Add green pepper; cover and cook for 5 minutes. Cut tomatoes into halves and cabbage into 4 wedges; add to onion and green pepper. Season to taste, cover, and simmer for about 15 minutes. Makes 4 servings.

WILTED CABBAGE

4 slices of bacon
½ cup cider vinegar
2 tablespoons sugar
1 teaspoon salt
⅛ teaspoon pepper
½ cup water
3 cups each of finely shredded red and green cabbage

Fry bacon in skillet until crisp; remove. To fat in skillet, add vinegar, sugar, salt, pepper, and water and bring to boil. Divide mixture, adding half to red and half to green cabbage. Cook quickly, about 5 minutes for green cabbage, and 8 to 10 minutes for red cabbage. Serve in 2-sectioned dish; crumble crisp bacon over top. Makes 4 servings.

SWEET-AND-SOUR RED CABBAGE

1 onion, chopped
3 tablespoons butter or margarine
9 cups shredded red cabbage
1 large tart apple, diced
3 tablespoons cider vinegar
1 cup water
3 tablespoons brown sugar
1 tablespoon caraway seeds
1¼ teaspoons salt
¼ teaspoon pepper
⅓ cup seedless raisins

Cook onion in butter for 5 minutes. Add cabbage; cover and cook for 5 minutes longer. Add remaining ingredients, cover, and simmer for about 10 minutes. Makes 6 servings.

SAVOY CABBAGE, POLONAISE

1 medium head savoy cabbage
1 teaspoon sugar
1 teaspoon salt
3 tablespoons butter or margarine
1 cup soft bread crumbs

Remove core. Shred cabbage medium fine. Cook in ½ inch of boiling water with sugar and salt in a covered saucepan for 6 to 8 minutes. Drain and turn into 1-quart baking dish. Melt butter, add bread crumbs, and mix well. Sprinkle on cabbage. Bake in preheated moderate oven (350°F.) for 20 minutes, or until crumbs are brown. Makes 6 servings.

CABBAGE WITH CHEESE SAUCE

¼ pound bacon
2 cups medium white sauce
1 medium head cabbage
¼ pound sharp Cheddar or process cheese, shredded
  Salt and pepper

Fry bacon until crisp; remove from pan. Use fat for making white sauce: use ¼ cup fat; stir in ¼ cup flour. Gradually stir in 2 cups milk. Cook over low heat, stirring constantly, until smooth and thick. Cut cabbage into wedges; cook in small amount of boiling salted water until tender, about 10 minutes. Add cheese to white sauce and heat until melted; season. Put drained cabbage on platter; cover with cheese sauce and sprinkle with crumbled bacon. Makes 4 servings.

BROWNED SAUERKRAUT

1 onion, chopped
2 tablespoons shortening, melted
1 quart sauerkraut, drained
1 medium potato, peeled and grated
1 teaspoon caraway seeds
  Boiling water

Cook onion in shortening until golden brown. Add sauerkraut. Cook over medium heat, stirring frequently, for 10 minutes. Add potato, caraway seeds, and boiling water to cover. Simmer, uncovered, over low heat for 30 minutes. Cover and simmer for 20 minutes longer. Makes 6 servings.

TWO-TONE CABBAGE SALAD

1 egg yolk
¾ teaspoon salt
¾ teaspoon powdered mustard
  Dash of cayenne
2 tablespoons cider vinegar
¾ cup evaporated milk, undiluted, heated
2 cups each of finely shredded red and green cabbage (separate)
  Lettuce

Beat egg yolk; add salt, mustard, cayenne, and vinegar. Gradually add milk, beating constantly. Add half of mixture to cabbage of each color and mix lightly. Put red mixture on lettuce leaf, top with green mixture. Chill. Makes 4 servings.

WESTERN PERFECTION SALAD

1 box (3 ounces) lemon-flavored gelatin
1 cup hot water
1 cup cold water
2 tablespoons wine vinegar
1½ teaspoons salt
¾ cup shredded or finely chopped carrots
¾ cup shredded or chopped green cabbage
¾ cup diced celery
  Salad greens
  Sour cream or other dressing, as desired

Dissolve gelatin in hot water. Stir in next 3 ingredients. Chill until thickened to the consistency of unbeaten egg whites. Fold in vegetables and pour into pan (8 x 8 x 2 inches). Chill until firm. Cut into 6 servings and put on greens. Serve with dressing. Makes 6 servings.

COUNTRY-STYLE COLESLAW

1 tablespoon cornstarch
1½ teaspoons salt
  Dash of cayenne
1 teaspoon powdered mustard
1½ tablespoons sugar
¼ teaspoon paprika
2 eggs
⅓ cup cider vinegar
1 cup milk
3 cups coarsely shredded green cabbage
  Parsley

In top part of double boiler, combine first 7 ingredients; beat well. Add vinegar and milk and mix well. Cook over boiling water, stirring constantly, until thickened. Cool and refrigerate. At serving time mix enough dressing with cabbage to just moisten; sprinkle with parsley. Makes 4 servings.

CABBAGE SLAWS

A collection of recipes that prove how successfully shredded cabbage combines with many different foods and flavorings

Two-Tone Cabbage Salad

Cabbage with Cheese Sauce

Chinese Cabbage with Egg Dressing

Cabbage Rolls with Sauerkraut and Pork

Red Cabbage Slaw

Toss 3 cups shredded red cabbage with plain French dressing. Season to taste with salt and pepper. Top with slices of white onion. Makes 4 servings.

Curried Pear Slaw

Combine ½ cup mayonnaise with 1 tablespoon curry powder and 1 tablespoon chutney. Mix with 3 cups shredded green cabbage, and season with salt and pepper. Top with slices of pear, sprinkled with lemon juice. Makes 4 servings.

Heavenly Slaw

Combine 2 cups shredded green cabbage with ½ cup cubed sharp Cheddar cheese, ½ cup miniature marshmallows, and ½ cup chopped nuts. Moisten with mayonnaise and a little pineapple juice; season with salt. Top each serving with a twisted slice of pineapple. Makes 4 servings.

Soy Ginger Slaw

Mix ¾ cup mayonnaise with 2 tablespoons soy sauce and ¼ teaspoon ginger. Combine 3 cups shredded green cabbage with slivers of green pepper and 2 chopped green onions. Add enough dressing to moisten. Top with remaining dressing and pieces of chutney if desired. Makes 4 servings.

Buttermilk Herb Slaw

Mix ¾ cup buttermilk with 1 tablespoon cider vinegar, 1 tablespoon sugar or 6 drops noncaloric sweetener, ½ teaspoon salt, and 2 teaspoons chopped fresh dill or marjoram (or ½ teaspoon dried). Mix with 3 cups chopped green cabbage. Top with slices of radish. Makes 4 servings.

Hot Bacon Slaw

Fry 4 slices of bacon until crisp. Remove from pan and crumble. Remove all but 2 tablespoons fat; add 3 tablespoons cider vinegar, 2 tablespoons water, ½ teaspoon powdered mustard, and a dash each of sugar, salt, pepper, and cayenne. Bring to boil; add 3 cups shredded green cabbage, toss, and heat for about 1 minute. Makes 4 servings.

Apple Horseradish Slaw

Mix 1 cup dairy sour cream with 2 tablespoons horseradish, 1 tablespoon cider vinegar, 1 tablespoon sugar, ½ teaspoon salt, and 1 teaspoon prepared mustard. Combine with 3 cups shredded green cabbage and 1 large diced unpeeled red eating apple. Makes 4 servings.

Dill Mustard Slaw

Combine ½ cup mayonnaise with 1 tablespoon dill-pickle juice and 2 tablespoons prepared mustard. Mix with 3 cups shredded green cabbage. Top with pickle and radish slices. Makes 4 servings.

Everyday Slaw

Combine 3 cups shredded green cabbage with slices of green onion and pieces of pimiento. Moisten with mayonnaise, vinegar, and salt and pepper to taste. Makes 4 servings.

Creamy Slaw with Carrots

Mix 2 cups finely chopped green cabbage with bottled coleslaw dressing or other creamy dressing; season with salt and pepper. Surround with shredded carrots. Makes 4 servings.

CABBAGE RELISH

    4 cups finely chopped green cabbage
    1 medium onion, chopped
    ½ green pepper, chopped
    2 pimientos, chopped
    1 tablespoon salt
    ½ cup cider vinegar
    ⅓ cup sugar
    ½ teaspoon celery seeds
    ¼ teaspoon mustard seeds
        Dash of cayenne

Combine vegetables with salt. Let stand for about 1 hour. Add remaining ingredients and mix well. Good with baked beans, fish, frankfurters, or hamburgers. Makes about 1 quart.

CABBAGE PALM—The name is given to several kinds of palm trees, which have edible parts. One of these is *Oreodoxa oleracea,* which can grow to more than 100 feet in height, but which is cut down for food when about three years old. The parts eaten are the tender central leaves, used as greens, and especially the terminal bud and the tender inside of its thick stem, the "hearts of palm." The taste of these is bland and delicate.

Fresh cabbage palm is available only in southern Florida and in the tropics. Canned hearts of palm are sold in specialty food stores.

HEARTS OF PALM WITH BUTTER SAUCE

    2 cans (14 ounces each) hearts of palm
    6 tablespoons butter
    ½ teaspoon fresh lemon juice
        Chopped parsley

Place hearts of palm and liquid in saucepan. If hearts are very thick, split lengthwise. Add 1 tablespoon butter. Simmer for 15 minutes. Meanwhile, melt remaining butter in a small saucepan; continue to heat until butter is lightly browned. Add lemon juice and ½ teaspoon parsley. Drain hearts of palm and serve with butter sauce and additional parsley. Makes 6 servings.

HEARTS OF PALM SALAD

    1 large head lettuce, torn into bite-size pieces
    1 small avocado, peeled and diced
    1 can (14 ounces) hearts of palm, drained
    ⅓ cup French dressing
        Salt and pepper

Toss lettuce and avocado in a large salad bowl. Cut hearts of palm into ¼-inch slices; add to bowl. Lightly mix in French dressing and seasonings to taste. Makes 4 to 6 servings.

CACTUS PEAR—Prickly pear is another name for this fruit of one of a group of plants known as succulents, which grow in arid hot climates, both in the Old and the New World. In the United States, they are indigenous to the Southwest. There are a number of edible varieties, with a water content that averages eighty-five per cent and a high sugar content. The two most common ones are the *Fiscus-indica* and the *Tuna*. The *Fiscus-indica* has an oval fruit about one and a half to three inches in diameter, with a yellowish skin and pink or reddish pulp. The fruit of the *Tuna* is pear-shape or roundish, and measures about one to one and a half inches in diameter.

Since the fruits are high in water content, thirsty animals (and people) often turn to them as lifesavers in drought times. The fruits grow the prickles to protect themselves against the onslaughts of animals so that they can mature their seeds in peace.

Cactus pears have a mild, sweet flavor and they are usually eaten raw.

Availability—The fruit is available from October to January.

Purchasing Guide—When buying cactus pears, select fruit that is bright in color, firm but not hard, with a thin skin and the fewest number of spines.

Storage—The fruit keeps best at moderate temperatures; it should not be refrigerated.

Caloric Value

☐ 3½ ounces, raw = 42 calories

Basic Preparation—Cacti are served peeled, which is best done by slitting the skin lengthwise so that it will come off easily. Slice them and remove the seeds. Chill and serve with lemon juice and sugar, or with cream. Cacti can also be made into bland preserves or candies.

CAKE COOK BOOK

A treasury of wonderful cake and frosting recipes
for any occasion: birthdays, anniversaries, holidays,
and just plain Sunday family gatherings

CAKE—However inspired, no written definition of the word cake could approximate the glories of sweetened dough, baked, filled, frosted, and made ravishing with edible decorations. Such creations can bring happiness to both our childhood and mature years, for few, if any, people are immune to their charm.

The word "cake" comes to us from Middle English, and may have had earlier origins in Old Norse. From the earliest days of civilization, man has always considered cake a food for the gods as well as for himself. The Egyptians made cakes in animal, bird, and human forms for their various gods; Greeks offered honey cakes to their gods; and in the North honey cakes were offered to Thor at the winter solstice to ensure a fruitful year to come.

Few pleasures are greater than turning out a perfect cake. And perfect cakes can be achieved by any cook who is careful and who is willing to follow recipe directions. Cake-making is an exact process; the ingredients and their relation to each other are balanced like a chemical formula; in fact, during the baking, a chemical process takes place, transforming the raw ingredients into a delicious new entity.

There are two main classifications of cake in American fare, those made with fat and those made without.

CAKES MADE WITH FAT

They are often called butter or shortened cakes and all of them can be filled and frosted. There are three types:

Standard cake—A layer, loaf, or cupcake, which is made with shortening, sugar, flour, and a chemical leavening agent. These cakes are baked in layer-cake, springform, loaf, or muffin pans. They include white, yellow or golden; chocolate, spice, and fruitcakes; and some tortes. A torte is a cake flatter and richer than an American layer cake.

Poundcake—As the name suggests, traditionally a poundcake contains a pound of sugar (2¼ cups), a pound of butter (2 cups), a pound of eggs (2 cups, about 8 large eggs), a pound of all-purpose flour (4 cups), a flavoring such as vanilla and/or mace, and no chemical leavening agent. Through the years this has been modified by varying the amounts of the ingredients and even adding chemical leavening and some liquid.

Chiffon cake—This is a relative newcomer to the world of cakes and it always contains some leavening agent such as baking powder. The distinguishing characteristic of the chiffon cake is that an oil instead of a solid fat is always used. This cake has a firmer texture than a conventional cake, and looks like a spongecake. It keeps well.

Mixing Cakes Made with Fat—There is more than one method for mixing these cakes. The four most popular follow:

Conventional Method—Butter or shortening is creamed until light and fluffy. The sugar is beaten into the creamed mixture. Eggs are separated and the yolks are beaten into this mixture, one at a time, followed by the flavorings. Then the dry ingredients, such as flour, baking powder, and salt, are sifted together and added to the batter alternately with the liquid ingredients, starting and ending with dry ingredients. Nuts and fruits, if any, are added next. Finally, the egg whites are beaten stiff and folded gently into the batter for additional leavening power.

Modified Conventional Method—This differs from the method described above inasmuch as the eggs are kept whole and are beaten into the creamed shortening. Proper long beating insures a fine texture. Poundcakes are made by this method.

Quick or One-Bowl Method—Recipes follow two patterns. In the Quick Method, dry ingredients are sifted into a bowl, then all the fat, liquid (or part of it), and flavorings are added. This is beaten for a specified time. In a last step, the eggs (with any remaining liquid) are added, and the whole again beaten for a specified time. Occasionally this method is varied by creaming the shortening first. This is done because one of the things on which the success of the method depends is soft shortening; one has to be able to combine completely by beating.

In the one-bowl method, all of the ingredients are put into a mixing bowl and beaten for a specified time. Again, as above, the shortening must be soft; in fact, all ingredients should be at room temperature before starting. This is the method used in most modern cake mixes. Electric mixers are great aids in this method.

Chiffon Cake Method—All the dry ingredients are sifted into a bowl. A well is made in the center and oil, egg yolks, liquid, and flavorings are added. This is beaten for a specified time. In turn this mixture is folded into very stiffly whipped egg whites.

CAKES MADE WITHOUT FAT

These include the angel foods and spongecakes. They use little or no chemical leavening; the air beaten into the egg whites acts as the principal leavening agent. In order to achieve their characteristic fine and tender texture, they should be prepared with special care. Since these cakes are delicate, it is better to use a thin glaze or a soft whipped frosting.

Angel-Food Cake—This is made by first sifting together cake flour and part of the sugar. Since so much depends on the beating of the egg whites, there is a specific procedure for this. First, the whites are beaten until they are just foamy, then an acid such as cream of tartar is added to hold the whites firm and increase the whiteness of the finished cake. Then the beating continues, with the rest of the sugar being added gradually, until the whites are stiff and will stand in sharply pointed peaks. The time at which sugar is added will vary according to the recipe. Generally, if an electric mixer is used, sugar is added earlier than when a whisk or hand beater is used. Finally, the first mixture of cake flour and sugar is slowly folded into the whites by sifting it over the whites while folding continues. As soon as the flour has disappeared into the whites, stop. Because the presence of any form of fat will prevent these cakes from reaching maximum height, an ungreased tube pan is always used for baking. After baking, the pan is turned upside down on a rack, on its own legs, or over a funnel, until the cake is absolutely cool. At this point it may have pulled away from the pan slightly, or it may have to be loosened with a knife.

Spongecake—The procedure is the same as in angel-food cakes, except that egg yolks are added. First, the egg whites are beaten until stiff. The egg yolks are beaten until light and lemon-colored. Next, the sugar is beaten in gradually, followed by the flavorings. Then, the egg-yolk mixture is beaten into the beaten egg whites. Finally, the flour is sifted over the batter and folded in carefully, until it has disappeared.

CAKE MIXES

Cake mixes are an important part of the cake picture and are available in an increasingly large number of varieties. Since they eliminate a large part of the work involved in cake-making, the homemaker can introduce her own imaginative, personal touches by adding spices, flavorings, finely chopped nuts and fruits, peels, coconut, grated chocolate, maraschino cherries; by using interesting frostings and fillings; and by cutting or baking the cake into unusual shapes. To

get the lightest cake possible, sift the mix before beating with liquid.

CAKE FROSTINGS, FILLINGS, GLAZES

These are sweet decorative coatings placed between layers or over the tops and sides of the cake to add to the flavor and appearance.

Frosting—Frosting or icing means the same thing. Frostings are both cooked and uncooked.

Cooked frostings, such as White Mountain Frosting, are made by beating a hot sugar syrup into beaten egg whites. Another method is to cook sugar, butter, and liquid into a candylike frosting such as in Fudge Frosting.

Uncooked frostings, such as Butter Frosting, are made by beating together butter, some liquid, flavoring, and confectioners' sugar. Decorators' Frosting is made by beating egg whites with confectioners' sugar.

Filling—Cooked fillings include liquid or fruit thickened with cornstarch, egg, or flour, such as Cream Filling or Pineapple Filling.

Uncooked fillings include those made with whipped cream, chopped fruit, jelly, or instant pudding.

Glaze—A glaze is a thin glossy coating with a firm consistency. It can be cooked or uncooked. Some are baked or broiled onto cakes, others are spread on hot cakes.

Frosting a Cake—Before frosting a cake, it must be thoroughly cooled. Brush off all loose crumbs. Place strips of wax paper on a platter. Place cake on top. Spread layer with cooled filling or frosting. Top with second layer. Frost sides of cake thinly with a small spatula. Allow to dry for a few minutes. Spread sides of cake again thickly and roughly with frosting. Spread top of cake decoratively with remaining frosting. Carefully pull out wax paper from under the cake, leaving the platter clean.

HINTS FOR SUCCESSFUL CAKE-MAKING

Use Accurate Equipment—Use nested aluminum measuring cups without dents. Use nested alumium measuring spoons. Avoid fancy measuring spoons since they may be inaccurate.

Have the Necessary Accessories—Have both a rubber and a straight-blade spatula handy; a timer is also desirable.

Read Recipe Completely—Assemble all ingredients and equipment and put on kitchen table or counter. Let shortenings, eggs, and milk reach room temperature. Sift flour *before* measuring. Unless speci-

fied differently, the flour used in these recipes is all-purpose flour.

Measure Precisely—Do not make any substitutions or guesses when measuring. Level off each measurement to be completely even. Use the sharp end of a spatula or knife.

Preheat Oven for 10 to 15 Minutes—The importance of this cannot be sufficiently stressed. Many cakes have been ruined by being placed in a barely warm oven. This causes them to fall before they can rise. Conversely, too hot an oven will cause cakes to rise in irregular peaks.

Place the Cake Correctly—Bake the cake on the middle shelf of the oven. Layer-cake pans should be arranged so as not to touch each other or the sides of the oven. If layers are baked on two shelves, stagger them so that one does not sit directly under the other. To bake properly, the heat must circulate evenly around the pans.

Check Your Oven—The best ovens will go off occasionally. Double-check yours with a portable oven thermometer. If you have any doubts, have the oven checked by a service man.

About Baking Pans and Cooling Racks—For best results, it is essential to use baking pans of the size specified in the recipe and to fill them no more than two-thirds full. Pans are measured across the top. Glass, enamel, or dark metal pans absorb and hold more heat than shiny pans. If shiny pans are used, oven temperature should be lowered by 25°.

Layer-cake pans come in standard sizes, with stationary or loose bottoms. The latter make all cake removing easier, especially when the cake is a spongecake. The standard sizes of round layer-cake pans are 8 x 1¼ inches, 9 x 1¼ inches, and 10 x 1¼ inches. Some come 1½ inches high, but there is hardly any difference in the finished product.

There are also loaf, rectangular, and square cake pans in various sizes. If storage space is limited, two loaf pans measuring 9 x 5 x 3 inches, one rectangular pan measuring 13 x 9 inches, and two square cake pans measuring 8 or 9 inches should be chosen.

Tube pans are needed for angel foods. Spring pans which have removable sides are very useful for baking large cakes and removing them easily. The best all-purpose spring pan measures 9 x 3 inches. A tube pan 10 x 4 inches is necessary for angel food, sponge-, and chiffon cakes.

Cake-cooling racks are made from heavy wire, set on little legs. They allow a cake to cool uniformly on all sides.

About the Phrases Used in Recipes—Since many recipes are written in condensed form, some reading between the lines may be helpful to the novice or unsuccessful cake maker. Here are explanations of some of the phrases used:

"Cream shortening and sugar until light and fluffy." The shortening specified may be butter, margarine, vegetable shortening, or lard. Let the fat soften to room temperature, then cream until it is fluffy, using the back of a spoon, your hand, or an electric mixer. Creamed shortening should have no lumps; it may change in color, becoming lighter. Now begin to add sugar; do it gradually, making sure the sugar is being absorbed. Give it plenty of fast beating at this stage, so that the whole looks very light and fluffy. You are now beginning to entrap, or incorporate, air, which gives lightness to the cake as well as the smooth, even texture called "fine-grained."

Much of a cake's success depends on proper creaming. This step should not be confused with mixing, which it definitely is not. When shortening and sugar are creamed together properly, the grainy appearance of the sugar has changed. Under-creaming produces a batter which results in a tough cake.

"Add flavorings, then egg yolks, one at a time, beating well after each addition." The latest theory is that flavoring that is creamed into the fat will be carried and held better throughout the batter. (Directions, however, may add this to liquid or at the end.) Again, as above, spend time and energy beating or creaming well after each egg yolk is dropped in and after all are added; the go-easy period comes later. (Follow same procedure if whole egg is added now.) Here, too, the importance of proper beating or creaming cannot be sufficiently stressed. This should produce a mixture that is smooth, fluffy, and satiny, and it should be done *before* the next step, the addition of the dry ingredients and liquid.

"Sift dry ingredients together and add to creamed mixture alternately with liquid, beginning and ending with dry ingredients. The batter is beaten until smooth after each addition." Always sift the flour before measuring (unless using an instantized flour). Spoon the flour lightly into a measuring cup; level off the excess with a straight-edge knife or spatula. Do not knock or tap the cup; it will

cause the flour to pack. Put flour in a sifter along with level measures of salt, baking powder, baking soda, and other dry ingredients specified, such as spices. The flour mixture is usually sifted into batter by thirds, the liquid poured in by halves; thus mixing will start and end with flour. Beat after each addition until smooth, with no lumps, and again at the end, but only until batter is well combined. Extensive beating here may toughen a cake, and an all-purpose flour batter is beaten less than cake-flour batter. In the modified conventional method, the mixing ends here.

"Fold in stiffly beaten egg whites." Egg whites should stand at room temperature until warmed. Beat egg whites until they are just stiff, with sharp, pointed peaks. Insufficiently beaten whites do not hold as much air, yet overbeating is a worse mistake. If small white flecks or clots form, it means the whites have passed beyond their capacity to hold air and are beginning to break down. Slide the whites from the bowl onto the top of the batter, then with a spatula or spoon gently fold them over and over from the center of the batter to edge of bowl, turning bowl as you do this, until all the egg whites have been absorbed.

"Grease and flour pans" or *"Line pans with wax paper"* or *"Line pan with paper and grease"* or *"Grease pans"* or *"Do not grease pans."* All these phrases for the preparation of the baking pans are found in recipes. Sometimes the kind of cake being baked determines the method; at other times the method may be a matter of personal preference. Pans that are greased and floured usually produce a thin brown crust on the layer or loaf. If this is not desirable, as may be the case for an all-white layer cake, one of the two paper methods may be preferable. A little of the crust always pulls off with the paper. A word about the pans: Use the size recommended, and do not fill it more than two-thirds full of batter.

As for greasing pans, it is not necessary to grease the sides; layer cakes rise better in pans with ungreased sides. The flouring is done by placing a small quantity of flour on the bottom of a *greased* pan and swirling it around to coat the bottom evenly. Many cooks find that it is easier to remove the cake when the pan is heavily greased and floured. However, if you are using a standard layer-cake pan (which has no loose bottom), you may find that a wax-paper lining in the ungreased pan makes cake removal easier.

In this case, be sure to grease the wax paper lightly on both sides.

Springforms can be treated like layer-cake pans. They present no problem since the sides come off anyway, leaving the cake loose. Fruitcake, which bakes for a long time, requires extra insulation at the bottom and sides of the cake or loaf pan in which it is to be baked. Line the bottom and sides of the pan with heavy, unglazed brown paper, and grease the paper on both sides. Angel foods and spongecakes are baked in totally ungreased and unfloured pans.

How to Tell When Cake Is Done—Press the middle of the cake lightly; if no imprint remains, and if cake pulls away a little from the side of the pan, the cake is done. Or stick a cake tester into the center; if it comes out clean, the cake is done.

About Removing Cakes from Pans—When removing cakes made with fat from the pans, let the cakes stand for a few minutes before trying to remove them. A little steam will form during this period which will help to push the cake out. Then put a cake rack over the top, invert the cake, still in the pan, and remove the pan. Cool cake thoroughly on a rack away from drafts before frosting or decorating. Cakes baked in ungreased pans should be cooled in the pan upside down on a rack. When cake is thoroughly cooled, cut it out of pan with a sharp knife.

About Cake Portions—The number of portions in cakes varies, depending on the kind of cake and the use it is put to: if it is to end a meal or to be served with a beverage, for example. The following table gives an approximate number of portions in cakes of a given size.

☐ 13 x 9 x 2 makes twenty-four 2-inch squares

☐ 13 x 9 x 2 makes twelve 3-inch squares

☐ 8-inch square loaf cake makes 6 servings

☐ 9-inch square loaf cake makes 6 to 8 servings

☐ 8-inch round layer cake makes 8 servings

☐ 9-inch round layer cake makes 8 to 10 servings

☐ 10-inch torte makes 10 to 12 servings

STANDARD CAKES

DELICATE WHITE CAKE
⅔ cup soft butter
1½ cups sugar
1 teaspoon vanilla extract
½ teaspoon almond extract
2½ cups sifted cake flour
2½ teaspoons baking powder
⅔ cup milk
4 egg whites
½ teaspoon salt
½ teaspoon cream of tartar

Cream butter until light and fluffy. Add sugar gradually, beating until light and fluffy. Add extracts. Sift together flour and baking powder and add to creamed mixture alternately with milk, beating until smooth, beginning and ending with dry ingredients. Beat egg whites until foamy; add salt and cream of tartar. Beat until stiff but not dry. Fold into first mixture. Pour into two 9-inch layer pans lined on the bottom with greased wax paper. Bake in preheated moderate oven (375°F.) for 20 to 25 minutes. Cool for 5 minutes. Turn out on rack; peel off paper. Cool, and frost as desired.

Rainbow Cake
Make Delicate White Cake. Divide batter into 3 parts. Leave one part plain, color one part pink and one green. Alternate 3 parts in layer pans and bake as directed. Make Fluffy White Frosting. Divide into 3 parts. Color ½ pink, ¼ yellow, and remaining ¼ green. Reserve half of pink for sides of cake. Alternate colors on bottom layer of cake and run a knife through colors to get a rainbow effect. Add top layer and repeat frostings. Spread pink frosting on sides, and decorate top with crushed peppermint candy.

Fluffy White (Seven-Minute) Frosting
2 egg whites
1½ cups sugar
⅛ teaspoon salt
⅓ cup water
2 teaspoons light corn syrup
1 teaspoon vanilla extract

In top part of double boiler combine egg whites, sugar, salt, water, and syrup. Put over boiling water and beat with rotary beater or electric mixer for 7 minutes, or until mixture will stand in stiff peaks. Blend in vanilla.

Strawberry Cream Cake
Make Delicate White Cake. Substitute ½ cup quick strawberry-flavored drink mix for ½ cup of the sugar. Spread sweetened whipped cream on one layer and top with sliced fresh strawberries; add more cream. Cover with other cake layer and top with cream and strawberries.

TWO-EGG CAKE
½ cup shortening
1 cup sugar
½ teaspoon vanilla extract

Almond Chiffon Cake   Devil's Food

2 eggs, separated
1¾ cups sifted cake flour
2 teaspoons baking powder
½ teaspoon salt
½ cup milk

Cream shortening; gradually add sugar and beat until light and fluffy. Add vanilla and egg yolks, one at a time, beating well after each. Sift together dry ingredients and add to creamed mixture alternately with milk, beginning and ending with dry ingredients. Beat egg whites until stiff but not dry and carefully fold into batter. Pour into two 8-inch layer pans lined on the bottom with greased wax paper. Bake in pre-heated moderate oven (375°F.) for about 25 minutes; cool on rack for 5 minutes; remove from pan. Remove paper and, when completely cooled, frost as desired.

GOLD BUTTER CAKE

½ cup butter
1 cup sugar
½ teaspoon lemon extract
Pinch of ground mace
1½ cups sifted cake flour

1½ teaspoons baking powder
½ teaspoon salt
4 eggs, well beaten
Orange-Lemon Glaze, or other glaze

Cream butter until light and fluffy. Add sugar gradually, beating until light and fluffy. Add lemon and mace. Sift together dry ingredients and add to creamed mixture alternately with eggs, beating well after each addition, beginning and ending with dry ingredients. Turn into greased and floured 8-inch tube pan, or greased and floured loaf pan (9 x 5 x 3 inches). Bake in pre-heated moderate oven (350°F.) for 50 minutes. Cool for 5 minutes. Turn out on cake rack. Cool, and cover with Orange-Lemon Glaze. When glaze has set, cake can be stored in tightly covered container.

Orange-Lemon Glaze

1¼ cups sifted confectioners' sugar
Grated rind of 1 orange
Grated rind of ½ lemon
2 tablespoons fresh orange juice
1 teaspoon fresh lemon juice

Combine sugar, fruit rinds, and juices. Stir until well blended. Spread over top and sides of cake. Let stand to set before cutting cake.

Orange-Honey Glaze

Combine ⅓ cup fresh orange juice, grated rind of ½ orange, and ⅓ cup honey. Mix well. Spread over top and sides of cake while it is still warm.

Apricot Glaze

Measure 1 cup drained canned or stewed apricots and press through sieve. Put in a saucepan with 1¼ cups sugar. Heat to boiling point, stirring constantly until sugar is thoroughly dissolved. Spread this, while still warm, over top and sides of cake.

CREAM-FILLED CHOCOLATE CAKE

2¼ cups sugar
3 tablespoons water
2 ounces (2 squares) unsweetened chocolate, melted
¾ cup butter
1 teaspoon vanilla extract
4 eggs, separated

Blitz Torte ▲   **Holiday Poundcake** ▼   **Butter-Pecan Angel Food** ▲

2¼ cups sifted cake flour
1 teaspoon cream of tartar
½ teaspoon baking soda
½ teaspoon salt
1 cup milk
    Cream Filling
    Chocolate Cream-Cheese Frosting

Add ¼ cup sugar and the water to chocolate. Cream butter; add remaining 2 cups sugar gradually, beating until light and fluffy. Add vanilla, then egg yolks, one at a time, beating well after each. Add chocolate mixture and blend thoroughly. Sift together dry ingredients and add to first mixture alternately with milk, beating until smooth, beginning and ending with dry ingredients. Fold in egg whites, beaten until stiff but not dry. Pour into three 9-inch layer pans lined on the bottom with greased wax paper. Bake in preheated moderate oven (350°F.) for about 50 minutes. Cool for 5 minutes. Turn out on racks and peel off paper. Cool, and put layers together with Cream Filling; spread top and sides of cake with Chocolate Cream-Cheese Frosting.

Cream Filling
½ cup sugar
3 tablespoons all-purpose flour
⅛ teaspoon salt
1½ cups milk
2 eggs, beaten
½ teaspoon vanilla extract

In top part of double boiler mix ¼ cup sugar, flour, and salt. Add ½ cup milk and stir until smooth. Pour in remaining milk and cook over boiling water, stirring constantly, for 10 minutes, or until smooth and thickened. Mix remaining sugar and eggs. Add hot mixture slowly, stirring constantly. Return to double boiler and cook for 5 minutes longer, or until very thick, stirring constantly. Cool, and add vanilla.

Chocolate Cream-Cheese Frosting
¼ cup butter or margarine
1 package (8 ounces) cream cheese
3 ounces (3 squares) unsweetened chocolate, melted
    Dash of salt
3 cups sifted confectioners' sugar
⅓ cup light cream
1 teaspoon vanilla extract

Cream butter. Add cheese, chocolate, and salt; blend. Add sugar alternately with cream, beating thoroughly after each addition. Add vanilla.

DEVIL'S FOOD
5 tablespoons cocoa
1 egg yolk
1½ cups milk
½ cup soft butter or margarine
2 cups sugar
1 teaspoon vanilla extract
2 eggs

2 cups sifted all-purpose flour
2 teaspoons baking powder
¼ teaspoon baking soda
½ teaspoon salt

In saucepan mix cocoa, egg yolk, and 1 cup milk. Cook over low heat, stirring, until smooth and thickened. Cream butter until light and fluffy. Add sugar gradually, beating until light and fluffy. Add vanilla, then eggs, one at a time, and beat well after each addition. Blend in cocoa mixture. Sift together dry ingredients and add alternately to creamed mixture with remaining milk, beginning and ending with dry ingredients. Beat until smooth. Pour into two 9-inch layer pans lined on bottom with greased wax paper. Bake in preheated moderate oven (350°F.) for about 25 minutes. Cool for 5 minutes. Turn out on rack and peel off paper. Cool, and frost as desired.

HONEY SPICE CAKE
½ cup soft butter
1 teaspoon grated lemon rind
¾ cup honey
2 cups sifted cake flour
2 teaspoons baking powder
¾ teaspoon salt
1 teaspoon ground cinnamon
¼ teaspoon each of ground nutmeg and cloves
2 eggs, separated
½ cup milk
⅔ cup raisins
¾ cup chopped filberts
    Butterscotch Frosting

Cream butter and lemon rind until light. Gradually beat in honey. Sift together dry ingredients. Add about one fourth to first mixture; beat until smooth. Add egg yolks, one at a time, beating well after each. Add remaining dry ingredients and milk alternately to first mixture, beginning and ending with dry ingredients. Beat until smooth. Stir in raisins and ½ cup nuts, and fold in stiffly beaten egg whites. Pour into two 8-inch layer pans lined on the bottom with greased wax paper. Bake in preheated moderate oven (375°F.) for about 25 minutes. Cool for 5 minutes. Turn out on rack and peel off paper. Cool, and frost with Butterscotch Frosting. Sprinkle with remaining nuts.

Butterscotch Frosting
1 package (6 ounces) butterscotch pieces
2 tablespoons water
1 package (8 ounces) cream cheese
⅛ teaspoon salt
1 tablespoon light cream
1 teaspoon vanilla extract
1 cup heavy cream, whipped

Melt butterscotch pieces in top part of double boiler over hot, not boiling, water. Stir in 2 tablespoons water and remove from heat; cool to lukewarm.

Beat until fluffy the cream cheese, salt, and light cream. Blend in first mixture and vanilla. Fold in whipped cream.

FROSTED MARBLE CAKE
½ cup shortening
1½ cups sugar
1¼ teaspoons vanilla extract
2 cups sifted cake flour
¾ teaspoon salt
2 teaspoons baking powder
½ cup milk
½ cup egg whites (about 4)
2¼ ounces (2¼ squares) unsweetened chocolate, melted
3 tablespoons water
    Chocolate Frosting
¼ cup chopped pecans

Cream shortening; add 1¼ cups of the sugar gradually, beating until light and fluffy. Add vanilla. Sift together dry ingredients and add alternately to creamed mixture with milk, beating until smooth, beginning and ending with dry ingredients. Fold in stiffly beaten egg whites. Divide batter into halves. Add remaining sugar to chocolate and water; heat and stir until blended and thick. Cool, and blend into half of batter. Alternate light and dark layers in greased, wax-paper-lined loaf pan (9 x 5 x 3 inches). Cut through with knife to improve marbling. Bake in preheated moderate oven (350°F.) for about 1 hour. Turn out on rack, remove paper, and cool. Frost with Chocolate Frosting and sprinkle with chopped nuts.

Chocolate Frosting
Melt 1 package (12 ounces) semisweet chocolate pieces and 3 tablespoons butter over hot water. Remove from heat; stir in ½ cup confectioners' sugar, ½ cup evaporated milk, 1 teaspoon vanilla, ¼ teaspoon salt. Beat until smooth.

BLITZ TORTE
4 egg whites
2 cups plus 2 tablespoons sugar
½ cup soft butter or margarine
1¾ cups sifted cake flour
2¼ teaspoons baking powder
¾ teaspoon salt
⅔ cup minus 1 tablespoon milk
1 teaspoon vanilla extract
2 eggs
¼ cup slivered blanched almonds
    Pineapple Filling
    Whipped cream or whipped topping

Beat egg whites until foamy. Gradually add 1 cup sugar, beating until stiff. Set meringue aside. Cream butter lightly. Sift in remaining 1 cup plus 2 tablespoons sugar, the flour, baking powder, and salt. Add milk and vanilla; mix until flour is dampened. Then beat for 2 minutes at low speed of electric mixer, or 300 vigorous strokes by hand. Add eggs and beat for 1 minute longer, or 150 strokes by hand. Pour into two 9-inch layer pans lined on the bottom with greased wax paper. (If convenient, use loose-bottomed pans.) Spread meringue on batter and sprinkle with nuts. Bake in preheated moderate oven (350°F.) for about 35 minutes. Cool for about 5 minutes. Cut around edge with a sharp knife. Turn out on a rack and remove wax paper. Quickly use another rack to turn meringue side up again. Cool, and spread Pineapple Filling between layers and whipped cream on sides.

Pineapple Filling
¼ cup sugar
1 tablespoon all-purpose flour
Dash of salt
2 egg yolks, beaten
⅔ cup milk
1 tablespoon butter
1 cup (one 9-ounce can) crushed pineapple, drained

In top part of double boiler mix sugar, flour, and salt. Stir in egg yolks and milk. Cook and stir over boiling water until thick. Stir in butter and pineapple.

TWO-MINUTE WHITE CAKE
⅓ cup shortening
1 cup sugar
2 egg whites
½ teaspoon vanilla extract
½ cup milk
1¾ cups sifted all-purpose flour
2 teaspoons baking powder
½ teaspoon salt

In mixing bowl put shortening, sugar, egg whites, vanilla, milk, and sifted dry ingredients. Beat vigorously for 2 minutes by hand or at medium speed of electric mixer. Pour into two 8-inch layer pans lined on the bottom with greased wax paper. Bake in preheated moderate oven (375°F.) for 20 minutes. Cool for 5 minutes. Turn out on rack and peel off paper. Cool, and frost as desired.

ONE-BOWL CHOCOLATE CAKE
½ cup soft shortening
1¾ cups sifted all-purpose flour
1½ cups sugar
1¼ teaspoons baking powder
½ teaspoon baking soda
1 teaspoon salt
1 cup milk
1 teaspoon vanilla extract
2 eggs
2 ounces (2 squares) unsweetened chocolate, melted
½ teaspoon red food coloring

Cream shortening. Sift dry ingredients into shortening. Add milk and vanilla; beat for 2 minutes. Add remaining ingredients and beat for 1 minute. Pour into 9-inch square pan lined on bottom with greased wax paper. Bake in preheated moderate oven (350°F.) for 1

hour. Cool for 5 minutes. Turn out on rack and peel off paper. Cool, and frost as desired.

AMERICAN APPLESAUCE CAKE
½ cup shortening
1 cup firmly packed light brown sugar
1 cup canned applesauce
2¼ cups sifted all-purpose flour
½ teaspoon baking soda
½ teaspoon salt
1 teaspoon baking powder
¾ teaspoon apple-pie spice
1 cup chopped nuts

Cream shortening; add sugar gradually, beating until light and fluffy. Add applesauce. Sift together dry ingredients and add to creamed mixture. Fold in nuts. Pour into loaf pan (9 x 5 x 3 inches) lined on the bottom with greased wax paper. Bake in preheated slow oven (325°F.) for about 1 hour. Cool for 5 minutes. Turn out on rack and peel off paper. Cool, and frost as desired.

PINEAPPLE UPSIDE-DOWN CAKE
3 tablespoons butter
¾ cup firmly packed dark brown sugar
6 slices pineapple or about 2½ cups (one 1-pound, 4-ounce can) chunks, well drained
Maraschino cherries and walnuts or pecans, halved
One-Egg Cake Batter

In 9-inch square cake pan melt butter and sprinkle with brown sugar. Arrange pineapple and cherry and nut halves on sugar mixture in a design. Cover with One-Egg Cake Batter. Bake in preheated moderate oven (375°F.) for about 35 minutes. Let cake stand for about 5 minutes before turning out on serving plate. Serve warm, with whipped cream, if desired. Makes 9 servings.

One-Egg Cake Batter
½ cup butter
½ cup sugar
1 egg
1½ cups sifted all-purpose flour
1½ teaspoons baking powder
½ teaspoon salt
½ cup milk

Cream butter; add sugar gradually and beat until light and fluffy. Add egg and beat well. Add sifted dry ingredients alternately with milk and beat until smooth, beginning and ending with dry ingredients.

ANNIVERSARY CAKE
1½ cups butter
3 cups sugar
5¼ cups sifted cake flour
5¼ teaspoons baking powder
1¼ teaspoons salt
1½ cups milk
1 tablespoon grated lemon rind
1½ cups grated fresh coconut or canned flaked coconut

9 egg whites
Orange Filling
Lemon-Orange Butter-Cream Frosting

Cream butter until light and fluffy. Add 2¼ cups sugar gradually, beating until light and fluffy. Sift together next 3 dry ingredients; add to creamed mixture alternately with milk, beating until smooth, beginning and ending with dry ingredients. Stir in lemon rind and coconut. Beat egg whites until foamy; gradually add remaining sugar and beat until stiff but not dry. Fold into batter. Pour into six 9-inch layer pans lined on the bottom with greased wax paper. Bake in preheated moderate oven (375°F.) for 15 to 20 minutes. Cool for 5 minutes. Turn out on racks and peel off paper. (If oven is not large enough, or you do not have enough pans, make as many cakes as you can, and while first cakes are cooling, repeat the baking procedure.) When all layers are baked and cooled, make a 6-inch cardboard circle and cut around 3 of the layers, thus making 6-inch layers. Use scraps for pudding or other desserts. Prepare Orange Filling and Lemon-Orange Butter-Cream Frosting.

■ **To Fill and Frost Cake**—Put one 9-inch layer on cake plate; spread with one third of filling. Add second 9-inch layer; spread with one third more of filling. Add last 9-inch layer and spread with frosting. Add 3 small layers, spreading remaining filling between. Frost top and sides of cake. Decorate with frosting, using pastry tube. Chill.

■ **To Serve**—Cut top tier into 6 wedge-shape pieces and put on serving plates. Then cut bottom tier into 10 to 12 servings.

Orange Filling
¾ cup cake flour
1½ cups sugar
¼ teaspoon salt
6 tablespoons water
2¼ cups fresh orange juice
6 tablespoons fresh lemon juice
3 tablespoons grated orange rind
Grated rinds of 1½ lemons
4 egg yolks, beaten

In heavy saucepan mix first four ingredients and blend until smooth. Add juices and rinds. Cook, stirring, until mixture thickens and becomes almost translucent. Stir a small amount of hot mixture into slightly beaten egg yolks. Stir into mixture in saucepan and cook, stirring, for a few minutes longer. Cool.

Lemon-Orange Butter-Cream Frosting
You need 1½ times this recipe. Do not make all at once. Prepare one recipe as below. Then make again, halving the amount of each ingredient listed and use

this batch for final decorating.

1 cup sugar
⅛ teaspoon cream of tartar
⅛ teaspoon salt
¼ cup water
2 egg whites
1 teaspoon grated lemon rind
⅔ cup softened butter
¼ cup fresh orange juice

In small saucepan mix sugar, cream of tartar, salt, and water. Cook until 240°F. registers on candy thermometer, or until a small amount of the syrup dropped into cold water forms a soft ball that holds its shape. Beat egg whites with rotary beater or electric beater until stiff but not dry. Add syrup very slowly to egg whites, beating constantly. Add grated lemon rind and cool thoroughly. Cream butter until light. Add egg-white mixture to butter, 2 to 3 tablespoons at a time, beating well after each addition. Beat in orange juice.

ORANGE-RUM CAKE

1 cup butter or margarine
2 cups sugar
Grated rind of 2 large oranges and 1 lemon
2 eggs
2½ cups sifted all-purpose flour
2 teaspoons baking powder
1 teaspoon baking soda
½ teaspoon salt
1 cup buttermilk
1 cup finely chopped walnuts
Juice of 2 large oranges
Juice of 1 lemon
2 tablespoons rum

Cream butter until light and fluffy. Gradually add 1 cup sugar, beating until light and fluffy. Add orange and lemon rinds. Add eggs, one at a time, beating well after each. Sift together next four ingredients and add to creamed mixture alternately with buttermilk, beating until smooth. Fold in nuts. Pour batter into greased 9- or 10-inch tube pan. (If using a fancy pan, be sure it holds at least 2 quarts when measured to brim with water.) Bake in preheated moderate oven (350°F.) for about 1 hour, or until done. Meanwhile, strain juices into saucepan. Add remaining sugar and rum. When cake is done, remove from oven. Bring mixture in saucepan to boil; pour slowly over cake in pan. If cake does not absorb all of mixture as it is poured, reserve remainder; spoon on later. Let cake stand for a day or two before serving.

FRUITCAKE

1 pound blanched almonds
3 pounds seedless raisins
2 pounds currants
1 pound candied cherries, halved
1 pound dried figs, chopped
1 pound dates, cut up
1 pound diced citron
½ pound each of candied orange and lemon peel
1 pound candied pineapple
6 cups sifted all-purpose flour
1½ pounds butter
3 cups firmly packed light brown sugar
13 eggs, separated
2 tablespoons each of ground cinnamon, mace, cloves, allspice, and nutmeg
3 teaspoons baking soda
1 cup brandy

Combine nuts and fruits with 1 cup flour. Cream butter well; add sugar and beat until creamy. Beat in egg yolks. Combine remaining flour with spices and soda. Add to creamed mixture with brandy. Add floured nuts and fruits. Fold in stiffly beaten egg whites. Line two deep spring-form pans (9 x 3 inches) with greased unglazed brown paper. Bake in preheated very slow oven (275°F.) for about 2 hours. Remove from oven and let stand for 10 minutes. Remove from pan and take off paper. When cold, wrap in cloths soaked in additional brandy. Store for at least 2 weeks to ripen. Moisten cloth as it dries out.

APRICOT-COCONUT TORTE

2 dozen coconut cookies
4 cups dried apricots
Water
2 envelopes unflavored gelatin
1½ cups unsalted butter
3 confectioners' sugar
6 eggs, separated
Grated rind of 1 orange
Grated rind and juice of 1 lemon
⅛ teaspoon salt
½ cup granulated sugar
1 cup heavy cream, whipped
1 can (17 ounces) unpeeled apricot halves, well drained
Chopped pistachio nuts

Crumble coconut cookies and sprinkle ½ cup on the bottom of deep 9-inch spring-form pan. Cook apricots in 3 cups water until tender and water is absorbed. Force through sieve or ricer, or purée in blender. Cool. Soften gelatin in ½ cup cold water. Dissolve over hot water or very low heat. Stir into apricots. Cream butter, add confectioners' sugar, and beat until blended. Beat in egg yolks, one at a time. Then beat in apricots, orange and lemon rinds, and lemon juice. Add salt to egg whites and beat until foamy. Gradually add granulated sugar and beat until stiff, but not dry. Fold into apricot mixture. Pour about one fourth of mixture into pan. Add a layer of crumbled cookies and continue alternating ingredients until all are used. Chill overnight. Remove to a serving plate, leaving cake on pan base, if preferred. Garnish

with whipped cream, apricot halves and chopped nuts. Makes 12 servings.

CHOCOLATE CHARLOTTE RUSSE

4 ounces (4 squares) unsweetened chocolate
¾ cup granulated sugar
⅓ cup milk
6 eggs, separated
1½ cups unsalted butter
1½ cups confectioners' sugar
⅛ teaspoon salt
1½ teaspoons vanilla extract
3 dozen ladyfingers, split
1 cup heavy cream, whipped
Shaved unsweetened chocolate

Melt chocolate squares in top part of double boiler over hot water. Mix granulated sugar, milk, and egg yolks. Add to chocolate, and cook until smooth and thickened, stirring constantly. Cool. Cream butter well. Add ¾ cup confectioners' sugar, and cream thoroughly. Add chocolate mixture, and beat well. Beat egg whites with salt until stiff; gradually beat in remaining ¾ cup confectioners' sugar. Fold into chocolate mixture. Add vanilla. Line deep 9-inch springform or loose-bottomed pan with split ladyfingers. Put in alternate layers of one third of mixture and remaining ladyfingers. Chill overnight. Remove to cake plate. Garnish with whipped cream and shaved chocolate.

MOLASSES SPICE CAKE

½ cup shortening
1 cup molasses
1 egg
2⅓ cups sifted all-purpose flour
1¼ teaspoons baking powder
¾ teaspoon baking soda
½ teaspoon salt
½ teaspoon each of ground ginger and allspice
¾ cup buttermilk
Fruit Filling
Fluffy White Frosting (see page 264)

Cream shortening. Beat in molasses and egg. Add sifted flour, baking powder, soda, salt, ginger, and allspice alternately with buttermilk, beating until smooth, beginning and ending with dry ingredients. Pour into two 8-inch layer pans lined on the bottom with greased wax paper. Bake in preheated moderate oven (375°F.) for about 30 minutes. Cool; spread Fruit Filling between layers and Fluffy White Frosting on top and sides.

Fruit Filling

Chop 1 cup pitted stewed prunes and ½ cup stewed raisins. Add ½ cup chopped nuts, 2 tablespoons citrus marmalade, ⅛ teaspoon salt, and 2 tablespoons prune juice.

Anniversary Cake

KENTUCKY JAM CAKE

1 cup soft butter or margarine
2 cups sugar
5 eggs
1 cup seedless blackberry jam
3 cups sifted all-purpose flour
1 teaspoon baking soda
½ teaspoon salt
½ teaspoon each of ground cloves and
  allspice
1 cup buttermilk
1 cup chopped nuts
1 cup chopped dates or raisins
  Caramel Frosting

Cream butter and sugar until light. Add eggs, one at a time, beating well after each addition. Add jam and beat well. Add sifted flour, soda, salt, cloves, and allspice alternately with buttermilk, beating until smooth, beginning and ending with dry ingredients. Stir in nuts and dates. Pour into four 9-inch layer pans lined on the bottom with greased wax paper. Bake in preheated slow oven (325°F.) for about 35 minutes. Cool; spread Caramel Frosting between layers and on top of cake.

Caramel Frosting

2 cups firmly packed light brown sugar
1 cup sugar
2 tablespoons light corn syrup
3 tablespoons butter
  Dash of salt
⅔ cup cream
1 teaspoon vanilla extract

Place all ingredients in a saucepan. Bring to a boil, cover, and cook for 3 minutes. Uncover and cook to 236°F. on a candy thermometer, or until a small amount of mixture forms a soft ball when dropped into cold water. Cool for 5 minutes, then beat until thick. If too stiff, add a little hot water.

POUNDCAKES

POUNDCAKE

2 cups butter
2¼ cups sugar
8 eggs (2 cups)
5 cups sifted cake flour
½ teaspoon salt
1 teaspoon ground mace

Cream butter; add sugar gradually, beating until light and fluffy. Add eggs, one at a time, beating well after each. Sift together dry ingredients and add to creamed mixture, a few spoonfuls at a time. Mix just enough to blend in flour mixture after each addition. Pour into one greased and floured loaf pan (9 x 5 x 3 inches) and one 1½-quart tube mold; or pour into two loaf pans. Bake in preheated very slow oven (275°F.) for about 2½ hours. Cool for 5 minutes. Turn out on rack to cool.

CHOCOLATE CHARLOTTE RUSSE

APRICOT-COCONUT TORTE

STRAWBERRY DREAM TORTE

CHOCOLATE POUNDCAKE
1 cup soft butter or margarine
1¼ cups sugar
1 teaspoon vanilla extract
5 eggs, separated
2 ounces (2 squares) unsweetened chocolate, melted
2 cups sifted all-purpose flour
½ teaspoon baking powder
½ teaspoon salt

Cream butter until light and fluffy. Add 1 cup sugar gradually, beating until light and fluffy. Add vanilla, then egg yolks, one at a time, beating well after each. Blend in cooled chocolate. Add sifted flour, baking powder, and salt; beat until smooth. Beat egg whites until stiff but not dry. Gradually beat in ¼ cup sugar. Fold into first mixture. Pour into loaf pan (9 x 5 x 3 inches) lined on bottom with greased wax paper. Bake in preheated slow oven (300°F.) for about 1¾ hours. Cool for 5 minutes. Turn out on rack and peel off paper. When cool, sift confectioners' sugar over top, if desired.

HALF-A-POUNDCAKE
1 cup soft butter
1½ cups sifted all-purpose flour
¼ teaspoon baking soda
1½ cups sugar
1½ tablespoons fresh lemon juice
1½ teaspoons vanilla extract
5 large eggs, separated
⅛ teaspoon salt
1 teaspoon cream of tartar

Grease a 9-inch tube pan or loaf pan (9 x 5 x 3 inches) with 1 tablespoon butter. Dust with flour and tap to remove excess. Sift flour, soda, and ¾ cup of the sugar into bowl. Add remaining butter and mix in well with fingers. Add lemon juice and vanilla, then egg yolks, one at a time, mixing with fingers until well blended. Beat egg whites with salt until stiff but not dry. Gradually beat in remaining sugar; fold in cream of tartar. Add to first mixture and fold in with hands or a rubber spatula until whites are thoroughly mixed in. Spoon into pan and spread evenly with back of spoon. Jolt pan on table to remove air bubbles. Bake in preheated slow oven (325°F.) for 1 hour, or until done. Then turn off heat and let stand in oven for 10 to 15 minutes longer. Loosen with spatula and turn out on wax-paper-covered rack; cool. Dust with confectioners' sugar, if desired. Store in an airtight container.

HOLIDAY POUNDCAKE
Follow Half-A-Poundcake recipe. Spread top of cooled cake with Glaze, allowing some to run down sides. Decorate with marzipan. **Glaze:** Mix 2 cups sifted confectioners' sugar, ½ teaspoon vanilla extract and enough milk to make glaze of spreading consistency.

Whitby Nun's Cake
Follow Half-A-Poundcake recipe, omitting vanilla. Add 1 tablespoon caraway seeds, 1 teaspoon ground cinnamon, 1 teaspoon rose water, and ½ teaspoon ground coriander (optional).

Antebellum Spice Cake
Follow Half-A-Poundcake recipe, adding the following spices: 1½ teaspoons ground cinnamon, ½ teaspoon ground allspice, ¾ teaspoon ground cloves, ¼ teaspoon ground nutmeg. If desired, frost with Seafoam Frosting.

Seafoam Frosting
In top part of double boiler combine 2 unbeaten egg whites, 1½ cups firmly packed light brown sugar, dash of salt, and ⅓ cup water. Beat for 1 minute with rotary or electric beater. Put over boiling water and beat constantly for 7 minutes, or until frosting will stand in stiff peaks. Remove from boiling water, add 1 teaspoon vanilla, and beat for 1 minute.

Canadian Orange-and-Lemon Poundcake
Follow Half-A-Poundcake recipe, adding grated rinds of 1 medium orange and ½ lemon. Omit vanilla and use 1½ tablespoons fresh orange juice; decrease lemon juice to 1½ teaspoons.

Nut Poundcake
Fold 1 cup coarsely chopped nuts into cake batter made from Half-A-Poundcake recipe. If desired, use 1 teaspoon almond extract and ½ teaspoon vanilla extract instead of the vanilla.

Traditional English Poundcake
Follow Half-A-Poundcake recipe, omitting lemon juice and vanilla and substituting 2 tablespoons brandy, ½ teaspoon ground nutmeg, and ¼ teaspoon ground mace.

Colonial Ginger Poundcake
Follow Half-A-Poundcake recipe, omitting lemon juice and vanilla and substituting 2 tablespoons brandy, ½ teaspoon ground nutmeg, ¼ teaspoon ground mace, and 2 teaspoons ground ginger.

STRAWBERRY DREAM TORTE
3 packages (8 ounces each) poundcake
4 envelopes unflavored gelatin
  Cold water
3 boxes (1 pound each) frozen sliced strawberries, thawed
⅛ teaspoon salt
3 cups heavy cream, whipped
1 quart fresh strawberries
¾ cup sugar
1½ tablespoons cornstarch
  Red food coloring

Cut cake in ¼-inch slices about 1½ inches wide and 4 inches long. (Have about 20 strips this size for sides of pan. Scraps can be used for layers.) Butter lightly a deep 9-inch springform or loose-bottomed pan. Line bottom and sides of pan with cake strips. Meanwhile, soften gelatin in ¾ cup cold water; dissolve over hot water or very low heat. Stir quickly into strawberries. Add salt, and fold in cream. Pour about one fourth of mixture on cake in pan. Add another layer of cake, and continue alternating ingredients until all are used. Chill overnight. Add glaze a few hours before serving. To make: Wash, and hull berries. Crush enough small uneven ones to make 1 cup. Keep remainder whole. Mix sugar and cornstarch in small saucepan. Add crushed berries and ¼ cup cold water; mix well. Cook, stirring, until thickened. Cool. Add a few drops red coloring. Arrange berries on cake and spoon glaze over fruit. Chill. Remove to serving plate, leaving cake on pan base, if preferred.

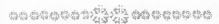

CHIFFON CAKE

ALMOND CHIFFON CAKE
2¼ cups sifted cake flour
1½ cups sugar
3 teaspoons baking powder
1 teaspoon salt
½ cup cooking oil
5 egg yolks
¼ cup cold water
½ cup milk
¾ teaspoon almond extract
1 cup egg whites (7 to 9 whites)
½ teaspoon cream of tartar
  Lemon-Orange Butter-Cream Frosting (see page 269)

Sift flour, sugar, baking powder, and salt together into a mixing bowl. Make a well in the center and add oil, yolks, water, milk, and almond extract. Beat until smooth. Beat whites with cream of tartar until they form very stiff peaks. Gradually add first mixture; carefully fold in until well blended after each addition. Pour into ungreased 10-inch tube pan. Bake in preheated slow oven (325°F.) for 55 minutes; then increase heat to moderate (350°F.) and continue to bake for 10 to 15 minutes longer. Invert cake, in pan, on cake rack to cool. Remove from pan and frost with Lemon-Orange Butter-Cream Frosting. Sprinkle frosted cake with ¼ cup slivered toasted blanched almonds, if desired.

ANGEL FOOD AND SPONGECAKES

CHERRY ANGEL-FOOD CAKE
1 cup sifted cake flour
1½ cups sugar
1½ cups egg whites (about 12)
1½ teaspoons cream of tartar
½ teaspoon salt
1 teaspoon vanilla or almond extract
⅓ cup well-drained finely minced
    maraschino cherries
    Pink Fluffy Frosting

Sift flour and ¾ cup sugar together. Beat egg whites until foamy; add cream of tartar, salt, and vanilla, and beat until mixture begins to hold its shape. Gradually add remaining sugar and beat until mixture is very stiff and glossy. Sift dry ingredients onto egg whites, a little at a time, and carefully fold in until well blended. Fold in finely minced cherries. Spoon into ungreased 10-inch tube pan and run knife through mixture to break up any large air holes. Bake in preheated slow oven (325°F.) for about 1 hour. Invert pan on cake rack until cold. Remove from pan and frost.

Pink Fluffy Frosting
1 cup sugar
6 tablespoons water
2 egg whites
¼ teaspoon cream of tartar
    Dash of salt
¼ teaspoon almond extract
½ teaspoon vanilla extract
½ teaspoon fresh lemon juice
    Red food coloring

Boil sugar and 5 tablespoons water until 232°F. registers on candy thermometer, or until syrup forms 2-inch threads (see page 284—Candy). Beat egg whites, cream of tartar, salt, and remaining water until stiff enough to form peaks. Add syrup gradually, beating constantly. Add extracts and lemon juice; continue to beat until mixture is thick enough to spread. Tint delicate pink with a few drops of red food coloring. Frost center, top, and sides of cake. Make peaks on frosting with tip of spatula.

BUTTER-PECAN ANGEL FOOD
Melt 2 tablespoons butter or margarine in small saucepan. Add ½ cup finely chopped pecans and ¼ teaspoon salt. Brown nuts lightly over medium heat for about 5 minutes. Drain on absorbent paper. Prepare angel food cake mix as directed on package. Add browned nuts with the last addition of dry ingredients. Bake in ungreased 10-inch tube pan. Cool as directed.

SPONGECAKE
1½ cups egg whites (about 12)
1 teaspoon cream of tartar
½ teaspoon salt
1⅓ cups sugar
1⅓ cups sifted cake flour
⅔ cup egg yolks (8 or 9 yolks)
    Grated rind of 1 orange
    or 1 teaspoon orange extract
    Confectioners' sugar

Beat egg whites until foamy. Add cream of tartar and salt and beat until whites begin to hold their shape. Gradually add sugar and beat until mixture is very stiff and glossy. Carefully fold sifted flour into whites. Combine egg yolks and orange rind and beat until thick and lemon-colored. Gradually fold into first mixture. Pour into ungreased 10-inch tube pan and bake in preheated slow oven (325°F.) for 1¼ hours. Invert on rack until cold. Remove and dust with confectioners' sugar.

DAFFODIL SPONGECAKE
1 cup egg whites (7 to 9)
1 teaspoon cream of tartar
½ teaspoon salt
1 teaspoon vanilla extract
1 cup sugar
1 cup sifted cake flour
4 egg yolks
    Grated rind of ½ orange
    Yellow Jacket Frosting

Beat egg whites until frothy. Add cream of tartar, salt, and vanilla and beat until whites begin to hold their shape. Gradually add sugar and beat until very stiff and glossy. Fold in flour in thirds. Beat egg yolks until thick and lemon-colored. Divide batter and fold egg yolks and rind into half. Put by tablespoons into ungreased 9- or 10-inch tube pan, alternating yellow and white mixtures. Bake in preheated slow oven (300°F.) for about 1 hour. Invert on rack to cool. Remove from pan. Spread top and sides with Yellow Jacket Frosting.

Yellow Jacket Frosting
1⅔ cups sugar
3 tablespoons light corn syrup
½ cup water
3 egg yolks
¼ teaspoon salt
    Grated rind of ½ orange
    Grated rind of ½ lemon
1 teaspoon fresh lemon juice

In saucepan mix sugar, corn syrup, and water. Cook without stirring until 250°F. registers on candy thermometer, or until a small amount of mixture dropped into cold water forms a hard ball. Beat egg yolks with salt until thick and lemon-colored. Gradually add syrup and beat until thick and of spreading consistency. Stir in grated rinds and juice.

CALORIE—This word, which has caused grief to so many weight-watchers, is used as a measuring unit for energy, just as ounces and pounds are used to measure weights, and pints and quarts to measure liquids. When used in connection with food, the calorie referred to is always the kilo calorie, and it is a measure of the potential energy of the carbohydrates, fats, and proteins when utilized by the body. The word does not indicate the nutritive value of foods, nor how the body utilizes the food: both are factors that belong to nutrition. When the body takes on more calories than it needs to perform its daily routine, it stores them away in the form of fat.

For the calorie-conscious reader who has wondered how this elusive unit of measurement is derived, we offer a simplified explanation of the scientific process:

A calorie is the amount of heat required to raise 1 kilogram of water 1° Centigrade. To determine this, a bomb calorimeter is used. A specific amount of food is placed in a sealed container with oxygen and is burned electrically. The container is surrounded with another specific amount of water whose temperature is raised as the food is burned. The temperature rise is recorded and the caloric value of that specific amount of food is determined. This method determines the caloric content of food as purchased (A.P.) and in the edible portions of food (E.P.).

The caloric values given in this Encyclopedia for various foods are based on 100 grams, about 3½ ounces edible portion.

CANADIAN COOKERY

Emerald Lake, British Columbia

CANADIAN COOKERY—This great and wonderful country sweeps across thousands of miles, from Atlantic to Pacific and northward to the Arctic. It is a land of towering beauty and fascinating contrasts. In Quebec, you will find an old walled city which might have been imported, intact, from France, and on the other side of the continent in Victoria, a replica of an English seaside town. The rugged seacoast of the east with its picturesque fishing villages is as much part of Canada as are the great wheat and oil-rich plains and the endless forests and numberless lakes of the north. There are cities as modern and bustling as any in the United States. And there are small picturesque villages where only French is spoken. A Moslem mosque graces Edmonton, a Hindu temple, Vancouver. A new Trans-Canada Highway spans the country for 5,000 miles, opening new worlds of beauty for all who travel on it and its connecting road links. National parks and camp sites make it possible for visitors to enjoy the vacation of their hearts' desire: fishing, hunting, swimming, boating, and sailing; reliving history and learning about Canadian ways from a friendly, hospitable people.

Food is plentiful in Canada and there is a wide variety. The fish and seafood on the east coast are superb; they are cooked much as we cook them. Among the delicious local specialties are the fiddleheads, the fern fronds as they emerge from the ground, before they uncurl, which are served like asparagus boiled with butter; and the wild dike mushrooms from the Fundy shore of Nova Scotia.

In Quebec, there is an interesting French cuisine and among the best known dishes, for instance, are a delectable pea soup and *Tourtière,* a main dish made from minced pork.

In Ontario, where Germans, Dutch, Irish, Chinese, and Hungarians made their new homes, you'll find the various specialties of their homelands. You'll also find the cookery of England and Scotland, the homelands of so many of Ontario's early settlers.

The golden plains that sweep westward for thousands of miles toward the provinces of Manitoba, Saskatchewan, Alberta, and the Rockies were settled toward the end of the 19th century and new settlers arrive every year: northern Europeans from Scandinavia, Scotland, and Germany, ten thousand Icelanders, eastern Europeans from the Ukraine, Russia, and Poland. Here you will find the borsch, the cabbage dishes, and the dumplings of the Slavic countries, and the smörgåsbord and open sandwiches of the Scandinavians.

This is the home of wild rice and of saskatoons, small berries that resemble firm blueberries crossed with wild currants, which grow wild near the rivers. Buffalo meat is often on sale in the stores.

On the Pacific coast, bountiful British Columbia, larger than the states of Washington, Oregon, and California combined, offers matchless fish from its tumbling rivers and calm lakes, game from its deep forests, and beautiful fruit. In the capital of Victoria, you'll catch nostalgic glimpses of England in ravishing gardens, teashops, and cricket matches followed by cricket teas.

In the Yukon Territory, along the highway that leads to Alaska, you are in great fishing country—and all fishing is great in Canada. Here, too, you are in "sourdough" country, for the men and women of the Klondike gold rush in 1898 needed starchy foods to sustain them on the long trail. Necessity taught the prospectors the art of the "sourdough" starter for their breads; some sourings are kept to make sponge for the next day and some again for the next and so on.

In the Yukon, as in the Northwest Territories, where the scenery is on the grandest scale, the fish and the game match the surroundings. Moose, caribou, and bear (whose paws are said to be delicious); snow goose, ptarmigan, and other Arctic birds; trout, salmon; cloudberries (the yellow delicacy of the North) abound here, practically for the taking.

To the American observer, Canadian food habits appear much like our own. Three meals a day is the pattern, and as many people eat a hot dinner at noon as at night. Most Canadians tend to serve meat, poultry, or fish at the noon meal, and they eat more potatoes with their main meal than Americans do.

Canadians are also partial to cakes and cookies at noon and evening meals and they serve tea far more often than do Americans.

SCALLOP BISQUE

1 pound scallops
1 tablespoon finely chopped onion
3 tablespoons butter or other fat
2 tablespoons all-purpose flour
2 cups milk
¼ teaspoon salt
⅛ teaspoon pepper
Spice bag with 6 peppercorns, 1 whole garlic clove, and 1 bay leaf

Rinse scallops to remove any grit and chop into ½-inch pieces. Cook onion in butter until tender. Blend in flour and gradually add milk. Cook and stir over low heat until slightly thickened. Add salt, pepper, spice bag, and scallops. Cook gently for 10 minutes. Remove spice bag and serve. Makes 4 servings.

CLAM BOUILLON DIGBY PINES

2 cups clam bouillon
2 cups chicken bouillon
¼ cup dairy sour cream
1 tablespoon chopped chives

Heat clam bouillon and chicken bouillon together. Top each serving with 1 tablespoon sour cream and a sprinkling of chives. Makes 4 servings.

HABITANT PEA SOUP

2 cups dried yellow peas
2 quarts plus 1 cup cold water
½ pound salt pork, blanched and minced
1 onion, minced
½ cup minced celery
2 carrots, chopped
¼ cup minced parsley
Salt and pepper
½ teaspoon ground allspice

Pick over peas and soak overnight or according to package directions. Boil for 10 minutes in water to cover. Drain; discard water. Place peas in deep kettle. Add cold water, salt pork, vegetables, salt and pepper to taste, and allspice. Simmer, covered, over lowest possible heat for 2 to 3 hours. Makes 6 to 8 servings.

SALT COD CHOWDER

1 pound salt codfish
½ cup diced onion
½ cup diced celery
1 small green pepper, diced
¼ cup butter or margarine
2½ cups water
2 cups (one 1-pound can) tomatoes
1½ cups (one 12-ounce can) tomato juice
1 can (10 ounces) condensed tomato soup
¼ cup tomato ketchup
2 tablespoons tomato paste
Spice bag: 1 bay leaf, 2 whole cloves, 3 parsley sprigs, 2 garlic cloves, quartered, ½ teaspoon crumbled dried tarragon, and ¼ teaspoon crumbled dried thyme
¼ teaspoon paprika
½ teaspoon hot pepper sauce
½ tablespoon Worcestershire
1 cup cooked white rice

Soak cod overnight. Bring to a boil with fresh water 4 times, washing cod several times as water is being changed between boilings. Sauté onion, celery, and green pepper in butter for about 5 minutes. Add next 6 ingredients with spice bag and boil vigorously for 20 minutes. Add paprika, hot pepper sauce, Worcestershire, and cod which has been flaked. Cover and simmer for 15 minutes. Remove spice bag and, just before serving, add cooked rice. Serve garnished with salted whipped cream and a sprinkling of chopped parsley, if desired. Makes 8 servings.

FILET PIQUANT (Spicy Fish Fillets)

2 pounds fish fillets
½ cup fine dry bread crumbs
1 tablespoon cider vinegar
1 tablespoon Worcestershire
1 tablespoon fresh lemon juice
½ cup melted butter or margarine
1 teaspoon prepared mustard
1 teaspoon salt

Habitant Pea Soup   **Tourtière**

⅛ teaspoon white pepper
  Paprika

Wipe fish with damp cloth. Place fish in greased shallow baking dish, the bottom of which is covered with bread crumbs. Mix together next 7 ingredients and pour over fish. Garnish with paprika and baste several times. Bake in preheated hot oven (450°F. to 500°F.), allowing 10 minutes per inch thickness for fresh fish and about 20 minutes per inch thickness for frozen fish. Makes 6 servings.

HALIBUT PAYSANNE (Country Halibut)
2 pounds halibut steaks, 1 inch thick
½ teaspoon salt
¼ teaspoon white pepper
¼ cup ketchup
1 can (6 ounces) sliced mushrooms
½ cup sliced green onions

Place steaks in greased baking dish and season with salt and pepper. Brush top of each steak with ketchup. Top with mushrooms and sprinkle with green onions. Bake in preheated hot oven (450°F.), allowing 10 minutes cooking time per inch thickness for fresh fish and about 20 minutes per inch thickness if fish is frozen. Makes 6 servings.

FISH AND POTATO SCALLOP
4 medium potatoes
1 pound cooked haddock or halibut
  Salt and pepper
½ cup chopped onion
2 tablespoons minced parsley
3 cups milk (about)
2 tablespoons butter
4 bacon strips

Peel potatoes and slice thin. Remove all bones and skin from fish and flake fine. In a greased casserole place a layer of potatoes, then a layer of fish. Sprinkle with salt, pepper, onion, and parsley. Continue layering, ending with potatoes. Add milk to almost cover. Dot top with butter and place bacon strips on top. Bake, covered, in preheated moderate oven (375°F.) for 30 minutes. Remove cover and bake for 15 minutes longer, or until potatoes are tender and browned on top. Makes 4 to 6 servings.

BOEUF DU POITOU (Poitou Beef)
3 to 4 pounds beef bottom round
  or chuck
3 onions, sliced thin
3 carrots, each cut into 3 pieces
1 bay leaf
½ teaspoon ground savory
1 tablespoon salt
1 teaspoon pepper
1 tablespoon honey

Place all ingredients in an earthenware bean pot and cover with cold water. Bake in preheated slow oven (300°F.) for 4 hours. Do not remove cover during cooking period. Serve hot or cold. Makes 6 servings.

LE JAMBON DE CAMPAGNE
(Country Ham)

¼ cup ham fat
1 slice (1 to 1½ pounds) ham
2 pounds potatoes

Melt ham fat in a large iron skillet. Brown fairly thick slice of ham on both sides. While it is browning, slice potatoes as for French-fries. Remove ham from pan and keep it hot. Put potatoes in melted ham fat and cook over high heat, stirring them often until they begin to brown. Put ham slice on top of potatoes. Cover and cook over low heat until potatoes are thoroughly cooked, about 30 minutes. To serve, turn like a pancake. The bottom will be golden brown and crusty. Makes 6 servings.

TOURTIÈRE (Pork Pie)

1 pound lean pork, ground
1 teaspoon salt
½ teaspoon pepper
¼ teaspoon ground nutmeg
⅛ teaspoon ground mace
2 teaspoons cornstarch
1 cup water
Pastry for 2-crust 8-inch pie, unbaked

Combine all ingredients except pastry. Blend thoroughly. Simmer, covered, for 30 minutes, stirring frequently. Roll out pastry and use half to line an ungreased 8-inch pie pan. Pour meat mixture into pan. Cover pie with remaining pastry and seal edge with water. Prick with a fork to allow steam to escape during baking. Bake in preheated hot oven (425°F.) for 10 minutes. Reduce heat to moderate (350°F.) and bake for 35 minutes longer, or until top is brown. Makes 6 servings.

Note: Some people flavor their *Tourtière* with ¼ teaspoon each of ground cloves, cinnamon, and marjoram instead of the nutmeg and mace.

RAGOÛT DE PATTES (Pork Hock Stew)

2 garlic cloves (optional)
3 pounds pork hocks
1 tablespoon salt
¼ teaspoon pepper
¼ teaspoon each of ground cloves,
cinnamon, and nutmeg
¼ cup drippings or other fat
2 medium onions, chopped
Water
¾ cup browned flour

If desired, poke a garlic sliver into each pork hock. Mix salt, pepper, and spices and sprinkle hocks with mixture, coating each well. Brown in fat. Add onions and water to cover. Cover pot and simmer for 2 to 3 hours, or until meat is *very* tender. Sprinkle browned flour over mixture and stir to blend. Cook for 20 minutes longer, stirring frequently. Makes 6 servings.

Note: To brown flour spread it evenly on baking sheet and place in hot oven (400°F.) for about 10 minutes, or until brown; or place in skillet over low heat,

Canadian Rum Cake   **Halibut Paysanne**

stirring constantly, until brown.

RÔTI D'AGNEAU (Roast Leg of Lamb)
1 leg of lamb (4 to 5 pounds)
1 garlic clove, slivered
2 tablespoons butter
1 onion, chopped
½ cup diced celery
5 carrots, sliced
Parsley
Salt and pepper
¾ cup dry white wine

Wash lamb and pat dry. Make several cuts through surface of meat and insert slivers of garlic. Coat lamb with butter. Sear on all sides over high heat. Add vegetables, season, and put in preheated moderate oven (350°F.) for 2½ to 3 hours, or until meat thermometer registers 175°F. for medium. For well done, roast for 3½ to 4 hours, or to 182°F. on meat thermometer. Baste frequently. Just before serving, remove meat, and add wine to pan drippings to make gravy. Serve very hot. Makes 6 to 8 servings.

PAIN DE VEAU
(Veal Loaf)
2 tablespoons butter
1 onion, minced
2 pounds veal, ground
½ pound salt pork, ground
1 teaspoon salt
½ teaspoon pepper
1 tablespoon chopped parsley
1 tablespoon fresh lemon juice
½ cup dry bread crumbs
2 tablespoons tomato sauce
¼ cup milk
1 egg
Bacon fat from 2 slices of bacon

Heat butter and sauté onion until golden brown. Combine onion with remaining ingredients except bacon fat, and blend well. Pack mixture into a loaf pan (9 x 5 x 3 inches). Brush top with bacon fat. Bake in preheated moderate oven (350°F.) for about 1 hour. This loaf may be eaten cold or served hot with gravy or tomato sauce. Makes 4 to 6 servings.

YUKON MOOSE OR CARIBOU STEW
2 pounds moose or caribou
    or stewing beef, cubed
3 tablespoons fresh lemon juice
1 teaspoon salt
1 teaspoon chili powder
⅓ cup all-purpose flour
2 tablespoons shortening
Hot water
½ cup chopped parsley

Sprinkle meat with lemon juice. Season with salt and chili powder. Dredge with flour. Heat shortening and brown meat in it on all sides. Add hot water to cover. Simmer, covered, over low heat for about 2 hours, or until meat is tender. Remove cover 15 minutes before serving and cook down gravy to desired consistency. Add parsley. Serve with boiled potatoes, noodles, or rice. Makes 4 to 6 servings.

RAPPIE PIE
1 stewing chicken (about 5 pounds)
2 large onions, peeled
6 large potatoes
Salt and pepper
2 tablespoons butter or margarine

Wash cleaned chicken and pat dry. Place in a deep pot with 1 onion and boiling salted water to cover. Simmer, covered, for 1½ to 2 hours, or until chicken is tender. Remove skin and bone from chicken and cut meat into slices. Boil stock down to make about 1½ cups. Peel potatoes and grate them. Place potatoes on a double thickness of cheesecloth and squeeze out all the liquid. Chop the second onion coarsely. In shallow baking dish place layers of grated potato and chicken, sprinkling each with salt, pepper, and chopped onion, ending with a layer of potato. Pour in the reduced stock. Dot with butter. Bake in preheated moderate oven (350°F.) for about 1½ hours, or until potatoes are crisply brown on top. Makes 6 servings.

STUFFED BREASTS OF GROUSE
Bone the breasts of the bird with a sharp knife. Using your favorite stuffing, put boned breasts together in pairs, sandwich fashion. Wrap together with bacon strips; fasten with toothpicks or small skewers. Bake in preheated moderate oven (350°F.) for 45 minutes, basting frequently with orange juice. Serve with white dill sauce. (Add ⅓ cup minced dillweed to 2 cups medium white sauce.) Allow 1 bird for each serving.

ROAST SNOW GOOSE
1 goose (8 to 10 pounds)
3 to 4 cups cooked wild rice
Salt and pepper
All-purpose flour
½ teaspoon each of crumbled
    dried tarragon and thyme
3 to 4 strips of salt pork
½ cup dry red wine
½ cup beef bouillon
2 tablespoons melted butter

Wipe goose with a damp cloth. Stuff with rice and close opening. Rub goose with salt, pepper, flour, tarragon, and thyme. Place on a rack in a roasting pan. Lay pork slices over breast. Roast in preheated hot oven (400°F.) for 10 minutes. Reduce heat to slow (325°F.) and continue to roast for 1½ hours, or until tender (this will depend on the age of the goose). Baste several times with wine mixed with bouillon and butter. Makes 6 to 8 servings.

POTATO CAKES
½ cup all-purpose flour
1 teaspoon baking powder
1 teaspoon salt
2 cups mashed potatoes
2 tablespoons cream or undiluted
    evaporated milk
1 egg, beaten

1 tablespoon grated onion
¼ cup melted margarine

Sift together flour, baking powder, and salt. Beat mashed potatoes with cream, egg, and onion. Combine both mixtures and add melted margarine. Knead lightly; dough should be soft enough to roll. If too stiff, add a little milk, 1 teaspoon at a time; if too soft, a little flour, 1 teaspoon at a time. On lightly floured board roll out dough to ½-inch thickness. Cut into rounds with glass or cookie cutter. Bake on hot griddle for 5 minutes on each side. Makes 4 servings.

FRESH PEAR PIE
Pastry for 2-crust 9-inch pie, unbaked
4 to 5 pears
⅔ cup sugar
⅛ teaspoon salt
¼ teaspoon each of ground mace
    and ginger
1½ tablespoons quick-cooking tapioca
3 tablespoons fresh orange juice
1 teaspoon fresh lemon juice
1 tablespoon butter

Line 9-inch pie pan with pastry. Slice peeled and cored pears into pastry, heaping pears somewhat in center of pie. Combine sugar, salt, mace, ginger, and tapioca. Sprinkle over pears. Add orange and lemon juice. Dot with butter. Cover with top crust, vent, flute rim. Bake in preheated oven (425°F.) for 40 to 50 minutes, or until pears are tender. Makes 6 to 8 servings.

APPLE SLICE
2 cups sifted all-purpose flour
2 teaspoons baking powder
¼ teaspoon salt
½ cup shortening
¾ cup sugar
1 egg
1 teaspoon vanilla extract
3 to 4 medium apples
¼ cup firmly packed brown sugar
¼ teaspoon ground nutmeg
Granulated sugar

Sift flour, measure, and sift together with baking powder and salt. Cream shortening; add sugar gradually, mixing until well blended. Add egg; beat well. Add vanilla. Add dry ingredients to creamed mixture. Blend together. Mixture will be dry and crumbly. Put half the cake mixture in 8-inch square cake pan, spread evenly, and lightly pat down. Peel cooking apples and slice *very thin*. (A vegetable peeler will slice about the right thickness.) Place sliced apples over the cake mixture about 1-inch deep. Combine brown sugar and nutmeg; sprinkle over apples. Cover with remaining cake mixture; lightly pat down. Bake in preheated moderate oven (350°F.) for 40 minutes, or until done. Remove from oven; sprinkle about 2 tablespoons granulated sugar over top of slice. When cool, cut into squares. May be served alone or with ice cream. Makes 6 servings.

RHUBARB FOOL

6 cups cut-up rhubarb
½ teaspoon salt
¼ cup water (about)
1½ cups sugar
  Heavy cream, whipped
½ teaspoon vanilla extract

Cook rhubarb with salt and just enough water to prevent scorching. Drain off excess liquid. Strain through food mill or whirl in blender. Stir in sugar to taste. Measure rhubarb and add equal amounts of whipped cream. Add vanilla; blend. Chill before serving. Makes 6 servings.

CANADIAN RUM CAKE

1 pound dates, pitted
1 pound walnuts, shelled
¾ cup butter
1½ cups firmly packed light brown sugar
1 teaspoon baking soda
1 cup boiling water
3 eggs, well beaten
2¼ cups sifted all-purpose flour
¾ teaspoon salt
2 tablespoons rum
  Rum Glaze (optional)

Chop dates and walnuts. Cream butter and sugar until well blended. Add dates and nuts. Mix soda with water and pour over first mixture. Add eggs. Stir in flour and salt, beating until smooth. Add rum and blend well. Turn into greased pan (13 x 9 x 2 inches) and bake in preheated slow oven (300°F.) for 1½ hours. Cool in pan on wire rack for 10 minutes, then remove from pan. May be frosted with Rum Glaze, if desired. Makes 10 to 12 servings.

Rum Glaze

Mix ¾ cup confectioners' sugar with 2 teaspoons sugar and 1 tablespoon rum. Frost cake while it is still warm.

CANAPÉ—The literal translation for the French word *canapé* is "couch." As a culinary term, it is used for small pieces of bread, toast, crackers, or pastry, topped with a bit of tasty food. In other words, the topping sits on the bread or other base as if it were sitting on a couch.

Canapés can be plain pieces of bread spread with something as simple as a savory butter, or they can be ornate little shapes piled high with a filling. They can be either hot or cold, but they must be open-faced. They are served whenever a tidbit is needed: at cocktail parties, at coffee or teatime, or for midnight snacks. Ideally, canapés intrigue the appetite and the eye; they are not meant to still serious hunger.

CANAPÉ BUTTERS

Cream butter and add other ingredients.

Caraway or Poppy Seed—½ cup butter, ½ cup caraway or poppy seeds, ground.

Caviar—¼ cup butter, 2 tablespoons caviar, ¼ teaspoon grated onion, 1 teaspoon fresh lemon juice.

Caviar-Cream Cheese—Cream ¼ cup butter and 3 ounces cream cheese. Top with caviar and garnish.

Chive—½ cup butter, ¼ cup chopped chives, dash of Worcestershire.

Curry—½ cup butter, 2 finely chopped shallots sautéed in 1 tablespoon butter, 1 to 2 tablespoons curry powder, 1 teaspoon arrowroot, 2 tablespoons heavy cream. Force through a fine sieve.

Green Pepper—¼ cup butter, 2 tablespoons grated green pepper, well drained, a few drops of fresh lemon juice.

Honey—¼ cup butter, ¼ cup honey.

Horseradish—½ cup butter, ¼ cup grated horseradish.

Lemon—¼ cup butter, ½ teaspoon grated lemon rind, 1 tablespoon fresh lemon juice.

Mushroom—½ cup butter, 1 cup finely chopped raw mushrooms, ½ teaspoon salt, dash of pepper. Force through a fine sieve.

Mustard—½ cup butter, ¼ cup prepared mustard.

Olive—¼ cup butter, 2 tablespoons finely chopped green or stuffed olives, few drops of onion juice.

Paprika—¼ cup butter, 2 teaspoons paprika, a few drops of fresh lemon juice.

Pimiento—½ cup butter, ¼ cup mashed pimiento, 2 teaspoons drained pickle relish.

Piquant—½ cup butter, 1 tablespoon capers, 1 tablespoon chives, 2 small sweet gherkins, 1 anchovy fillet, 3 or 4 pickled onions, and a few leaves of fresh tarragon, chopped together. Force through a fine sieve.

Sardine—1 cup butter, 1 cup finely mashed skinless boneless sardines; juice of half or whole lemon. Force through a fine sieve.

Shrimp—1 cup butter, 1 cup minced cooked shrimps, ¼ teaspoon salt, dash of paprika, 1 tablespoon fresh lemon juice.

Tomato—½ cup butter, ¼ teaspoon salt, dash of pepper, chopped pulp of 2 firm tomatoes. Force through a fine sieve.

CANAPÉ SPREADS

Almond-Olive—¼ pound salted almonds, finely chopped, ¼ cup chopped stuffed olives, 2 tablespoons mayonnaise, 1 teaspoon French dressing.

Bologna—1 cup minced bologna, 2 teaspoons minced onion, 2 tablespoons minced celery, mayonnaise to bind.

Celery-Pickle—½ cup minced celery, ¼ cup chopped sweet pickle, ¼ cup chopped pimiento, 3 tablespoons mayonnaise.

Cheese-Deviled Ham—¾ cup grated Cheddar cheese, ⅓ cup deviled ham, ½ teaspoon Worcestershire, ¼ cup heavy cream.

Cheese-Pickle—1 cup grated Cheddar cheese, ¼ cup chopped sweet pickle, mayonnaise to moisten.

Chicken Liver-Bacon—1 cup mashed cooked chicken livers, 2 tablespoons minced cooked bacon, 4 drops of hot pepper sauce, 1 tablespoon fresh lemon juice.

Chicken Liver-Shrimp—½ cup ground cooked chicken livers, ½ cup ground cooked shrimps, 2 tablespoons minced onion, ¼ cup minced green pepper, chili sauce to bind.

Chicken-Pineapple—¾ cup minced cooked chicken, ⅓ cup crushed pineapple, 3 tablespoons mayonnaise.

Cottage Cheese, Celery, and Olive—½ cup cottage cheese, ⅓ cup minced celery, 8 minced green olives, ⅓ cup minced green onion, and salt, pepper, paprika to taste.

Crabmeat-Horseradish—1 cup of minced cooked crabmeat, 2 tablespoons cream, 1 tablespoon prepared horseradish.

Cream Cheese-Olive—3 ounces cream cheese, ½ cup minced stuffed olives, ¼ cup mayonnaise, 1 tablespoon prepared mustard, 1 teaspoon minced onion.

Cream Cheese-Roquefort—3 ounces cream cheese, 1½ ounces Roquefort cheese, ½ cup heavy cream, ⅛ teaspoon salt. Blend. Fold in ¼ cup heavy cream, whipped.

Deviled Ham-Egg—¾ cup deviled ham, 1 chopped hard-cooked egg, 1 tablespoon mayonnaise, 1 tablespoon chili sauce.

Dried Beef, Cheese, and Celery—¾ cup ground dried beef, ¼ cup grated cheese, ¼ cup minced celery, mayonnaise to bind.

Egg-Caviar—8 hard-cooked eggs, pressed through ricer, ¼ cup soft butter, 2 tablespoons caviar, salt and pepper to taste. Spread on slices of cooked celery root.

CANAPÉ

Egg-Nut—4 hard-cooked eggs, minced, ¼ cup ground walnuts, almonds, or filberts, 3 minced sweet cucumber pickles or ¼ cup pickle relish, 2 tablespoons mayonnaise.

Egg-Pickle—3 hard-cooked eggs, mashed, 6 sweet pickles, minced, 1 tablespoon peanut butter, prepared mustard, pickle juice to moisten.

Egg-Watercress—4 hard-cooked eggs, mashed, few sprigs chopped watercress, mayonnaise to moisten.

Ham-Chutney—½ cup minced cooked ham, ½ cup minced chutney.

Liverwurst—1 cup mashed liverwurst, 2 tablespoons mayonnaise, 1 tablespoon fresh lemon juice, ¼ teaspoon pepper.

Lobster—1 cup minced lobster, 1 tablespoon fresh lemon juice, ⅛ teaspoon pepper, ¼ teaspoon salt, 1 tablespoon mayonnaise, 1 tablespoon French dressing.

Pimiento Cheese-Bacon—½ pound pimiento cheese, 2 tablespoons chopped sweet pickle, 4 slices of broiled bacon, minced.

Salmon—1 cup flaked salmon, ¼ cup mayonnaise, 3 tablespoons chopped sweet pickle, salt and pepper to taste.

Sardine-Beet—1 cup mashed sardines, 3 tablespoons mayonnaise, ¼ cup chili sauce, ⅓ cup chopped pickled beets.

Spicy Ham—1 cup minced cooked ham, ¼ teaspoon ground cloves, ¼ teaspoon ground mace, dash of salt, ¼ cup heavy cream.

Tuna—½ cup mashed tuna, 2 tablespoons mayonnaise, 1 tablespoon fresh lemon juice, 2 tablespoons chopped stuffed olives, dash of Worcestershire.

MELBA TOAST

Cut bread into ⅛-inch slices and then into desired shapes for canapés. Put on cake racks. Pile cake racks one on top of the other with one empty rack on top. Put stack in a very slow oven (250° F.) and leave in oven until bread is dry and delicately browned.

To prevent toast from becoming soggy when using moist toppings, dip each piece of toast into a little raw egg white. Put in a warm oven for a few minutes.

PUFF PASTE

1 pound sweet butter
4 cups unsifted all-purpose flour
1 teaspoon salt
1 tablespoon fresh lemon juice
1¼ cups cold water (about)

Shape the butter into a brick about 3 x 5 x ¾ inches.
Roll butter in 3 tablespoons of the flour, coating all sides. Wrap in wax paper and chill.
Put remaining flour in a large bowl. Make a well in the center. Add salt and lemon juice. Gradually begin to add water, only enough to make a rather firm, slightly sticky dough.
Knead dough thoroughly on floured board for 20 minutes. Pound it on the table at intervals to achieve the right consistency. It should be very elastic and smooth. Form it into a ball; place on well-floured cloth.
With a rolling pin make the ball of dough into the shape of a four-leaf clover. Roll ends out, leaving the center thick. Well rolled, the dough will have a thick cushion in the center and 4 thinner "petals."
Put brick of butter in center of four-leaf clover. Fold petals over dough by stretching them over butter and sealing all edges so that butter is completely enclosed. Wrap in wax paper and chill for 20 minutes.
On a well-floured cloth gently roll out block of dough as evenly as possible into a rectangle slightly less than ⅓ inch thick and about 3 times as long as it is wide. Do not roll over ends in the length, but when dough is long enough, roll it lightly in the width, flattening ends to same thickness as the rest of the dough. Fold dough into thirds, making 3 layers, and chill for 20 minutes. Turn folded sides toward you and roll out dough; fold again into thirds. (Rolling, folding, and turning is called a "turn.") It is necessary to make a total of 6 turns, after which the dough is ready for use. The dough should be chilled between each turn and again after cutting.

Cheese Allumettes

Cut rolled Puff Paste into strips 1 x 3 inches. Cover with thin strips of Swiss cheese and bake in preheated hot oven (425°F.) until well browned.

Bouchées

Roll Puff Paste to ¼-inch thickness. Cut with a round scalloped cutter of the size desired. Cut small rounds from the centers of half the pieces. Brush rings and whole rounds with water and press gently together. The tiny centers can be baked and used for canapé bases or for cheese puffs if sprinkled with grated Parmesan or Swiss cheese. Put rounds on a cookie sheet and bake in preheated extremely hot oven (500°F.) for 5 minutes. Reduce heat to 450°F. and bake until browned, reducing heat 50° every 5 minutes down to moderate (350°F.). Cool; fill with any creamed or curried meat, fish, or poultry. (Ingredients should be chopped fine.) Finely chopped sautéed chicken livers with onion also make a good filling for Bouchées.

BARQUETTES

Roll a flaky pastry made with butter or margarine to ⅛-inch thickness on floured board. Line tiny boat-shape barquette or round tart pans with pastry. Fill centers with rice to prevent overbrowning. Bake in preheated hot oven (425°F.) until lightly browned. Discard rice.

If barquette pans are hard to find, roll out pastry thinly on top of heavy-duty aluminum foil. Cut foil and pastry with scissors into ovals 3 x 2 inches. Moisten ends of oval pastry with water and pinch ends together using foil to shape pastry. Leave foil on pastry. Bake as above. Remove foil.

Clam Barquettes

24 baked Barquettes or tiny tart shells
1 can (10½ ounces) minced clams, drained
1 tablespoon instant minced onion
¼ cup minced green pepper
1 egg
½ cup heavy cream
2 tablespoons minced celery and leaves
½ cup fine dry bread crumbs
1 tablespoon butter, melted
Dash of cayenne
¾ teaspoon salt
¼ teaspoon pepper

Fill Barquettes with remaining ingredients mixed together. Put under broiler until golden brown. Serve at once. Makes 2 dozen.

BRIOCHE FOR CANAPÉS

1 teaspoon (about ½ package) active dry yeast or ½ cake compressed yeast
2 tablespoons water*
⅓ cup milk, scalded and cooled to lukewarm
⅓ cup soft butter or margarine
1 egg
2 egg yolks
1 tablespoon sugar
½ teaspoon salt
2¼ cups sifted all-purpose flour

*Use very warm water (105°F. to 115°F.) for dry yeast; use lukewarm (80°F. to 90°F.) for compressed. Sprinkle yeast or crumble cake into water in large bowl. Let stand for a few minutes, then stir until dissolved. Add next 6 ingredients and 1¼ cups flour. Beat for 10 minutes by hand or for 3 minutes at medium speed of electric mixer. Add 1 cup flour and beat well. Let rise at room temperature for 3 hours. Punch down, cover, and chill overnight, or for at least 3 hours. Shape into a loaf and put in greased loaf pan (9 x 5 x 3 inches). Let rise until light. Bake in preheated moderate oven (350°F.) for about 10 minutes.

Note: This bread is baked in a loaf pan so that it can easily be sliced for canapés.

Brioche Canapés

Cut loaf of Brioche into ¼-inch slices. Cut into small rounds with a canapé cutter or biscuit cutter. Spread half of rounds with one of Canapé Butters, page 279, and top with a second slice of Brioche. Roll the edges first in mayonnaise and then in minced parsley.

Onion Brioche Canapés

Cut loaf of Brioche into ¼-inch slices. Cut into small rounds with a canapé cutter or biscuit cutter. Spread rounds with mayonnaise. On half of slices put a very thin slice of raw onion, just the size of the round, and salt it well. Put another slice of Brioche on top. Roll the edges first in mayonnaise and then in minced parsley.

CANAPÉ PIE

Use a round loaf of white, rye, or pumpernickel bread and cut into thin slices. Spread slices with soft butter. Starting in the center, spread with separate rings of canapé spreads. Use spreads that contrast in colors and blend well in flavor. Separate each ring with a ring of seasoned cream cheese, applying cheese with a pastry tube, if possible. Cut the pie into small wedges and arrange around a pile of assorted olives.

EGG-TOMATO CANAPÉS

8 bread rounds
   Mayonnaise
   Sliced tomatoes
   Sliced hard-cooked eggs
   Salt
4 pimiento-stuffed olives, sliced

Toast bread rounds on one side and spread untoasted side with mayonnaise. Add thin slices of tomato, then slices of egg. Sprinkle lightly with salt and garnish with a slice or two of olive. Makes 8 canapés.

BACON ROLLS

½ pound sliced bacon
24 thin slices of very fresh white bread
   Butter
½ cup grated Parmesan cheese
¼ cup minced parsley
   Paprika and cayenne

Cook bacon until crisp. Drain well on absorbent paper and crumble. Remove crusts from bread and spread with butter. Down middle of each slice, put a line of crumbled bacon and sprinkle with cheese and parsley, then with paprika and a dash of cayenne. Roll each slice up tightly and fasten with a toothpick. Broil until brown. Makes 24.

LORENZO À LA FILIPINI

2 tablespoons butter
1 tablespoon minced onion
2 tablespoons flour
½ cup chicken broth
1 cup flaked crabmeat
   Dash of cayenne
   Salt and pepper
1 tablespoon milk
2½ tablespoons each of grated
   Parmesan and Swiss cheese
6 slices of toast, crusts removed

Melt 1 tablespoon butter and cook onion in it until transparent but not brown. Stir in 1 tablespoon flour. Gradually stir in broth. Cook over low heat, stirring constantly, until smooth. Add crabmeat and simmer gently for a few minutes. Season to taste with cayenne, salt, and pepper. Melt remaining butter, stir in remaining flour, and mix until smooth. Gradually stir in milk and cheeses. Cook, stirring constantly, until cheeses are melted and blended. Cool, and form into 6 little balls. Spread crab mixture on toast and top each slice with a cheese ball. Place in preheated very hot oven (450°F.) for 5 minutes. Cut each slice into halves. Makes 12.

CANDIED FRUIT—To candy fruit is to preserve it in sugar (usually in sugar syrup) so that it keeps its original shape and color. Candied fruit is also called *glacé* fruit.

The usual procedure in candying fruit is to boil it in a number of sugar syrups of varying degrees of thickness. The last boiling is in a glazing syrup, which gives the fruit its attractive, smooth, glossy appearance. Then the fruit is dried.

Crystallized fruit, a form of candied fruit, is prepared in the same manner, but without processing the fruit in the final glazing syrup. Thus the sugar crystallizes on exposure to the air.

Candied and crystallized fruit is eaten as a confection, used in baking (as in fruitcake) and in decorating cakes and desserts.

The art is an old one, known to the ancient people of the Middle East, the Greeks, and the Romans. Candied fruits were the forerunners of all candy, and to this day, they are served to the visitor in Morocco, France, Italy, Turkey, and Persia, to name but a few of the countries that produce delicious candied fruit.

Fruit is seldom candied at home, except for the occasional fun of it. Most fruit candied in the United States is of the citrus-peel variety, but candied whole fruits are also made (mostly in California and Florida) and sold in specialty food stores. There, you will also find the candied fruits imported from Italy and France, which are as exquisite to look at as to eat. Of great charm are the French crystallized flowers, such as mimosa, violets, angelica, and rose petals which make beautiful, edible decorations for all cakes and desserts.

Whole candied fruits are available in confectionery stores and in gourmet departments of food stores.

Candied peels, slivered and diced, are sold in bulk, or in jars and packages, in most food stores.

Caloric Value

☐ Citron, lemon and orange peel, candied, 3½ ounces = about 316 calories

QUICK CRYSTALLIZED CITRUS PEEL

1 medium grapefruit
2 oranges
   Water
   Sugar

Select bright fruit with a thick peel. Wash, cut into halves, and remove pulp and membrane inside. Cut peel into ¼-inch strips or into wedges. Place in saucepan and cover with 2 quarts water. Boil for 5 minutes. Drain; repeat process 3 times to remove bitter flavor. Do not boil more than 5 minutes each time, or fruit will be overcooked. Drain peel and lay on kitchen towels. Press gently to remove excess moisture. Combine 2 cups sugar and 1 cup water. Boil until sugar is dissolved. Add drained peel and cook over low heat for 10 minutes. Cover and let stand overnight. Then cook over low heat until most of the syrup is absorbed. Watch for scorching. Lift peel from syrup and roll in granulated sugar. Place on rack to cool. Roll again in sugar. Store in container with a loose lid. Peel will keep for 2 to 3 weeks.

CANDIED VIOLETS OR ROSES

1 cup hot water
2 cups sugar
4 cups violets or 2 cups small rosebuds

The flowers, very fresh and firm, should be washed, drained, and stemmed.

Combine water and sugar. Stir until sugar is thoroughly dissolved. Add flowers. Simmer over medium heat until syrup reaches the soft-ball stage (234°F. on a candy thermometer). Stir flowers gently with a wooden spoon. Remove from heat and continue stirring until syrup begins to crystallize and reaches the consistency of coarse meal. Drain over colander. Shake off excess sugar. Cool on wax paper. Pack into sterilized jars. Use for decorating fruit salads, cakes, and desserts.

CANDIED NUTS

1 cup sugar
¼ teaspoon each of ground cloves, cinnamon, and ginger
⅛ teaspoon cream of tartar
¼ cup hot water
1½ cups nuts
½ teaspoon vanilla extract

Combine sugar, spices, cream of tartar, and water. Boil until syrup forms a firm ball in cold water (250°F. on candy thermometer). Add nuts and vanilla. Remove from heat. Stir until sugar crystallizes. Drain on several layers of wax paper. Separate nuts and cool. Store in an airtight container in a cool dry place.

CANDY COOKBOOK

**A COLLECTION OF RECIPES
FOR BONBONS AND FUDGE,
CARAMEL AND DIVINITY,
TAFFY AND BRITTLE—
ALL THE OLD-FASHIONED FAVORITES**

CANDY

CANDY—"Sweets to the sweet," said Hamlet, and who can resist? It is a rare person who is born without a sweet tooth. Our word candy comes from the Persian word *qand*, or "candy," and although there is no one ingredient necessary to its making, the end result must be sweet. Egyptians used that age-old sweetener, honey, to which they added figs, dates, nuts, and spices. These early confections were made in various shapes and sometimes colored. The Arabs and Chinese also made a sweet consisting of different fruits, juices, and honey. It was the Arabs who made the biggest contribution to candy-making: the early refining and processing of sugar. They spread the knowledge of sugar cane from Persia to the Mediterranean, although it was not until after the Crusades, in the 14th century, that the acquaintance with sugar became widespread. Venice, that aristocratic lady of the Adriatic, carried on an extensive sea trade, and it was to this port that sugar was brought and made into tasty confections.

From Italy, as well as from the Arab influence in Spain, the use of sugar spread throughout Europe. For a time European candy-making remained in the hands of the apothecaries. Soothing and beneficial properties were ascribed to its consumption. Caraway comfits, sugar-coated caraway seeds, were considered a most pleasurable way of settling the stomach after a large medieval feast. The sugar-coated pill was an early invention: Greek and Roman physicians had once advised smearing the rim of a cup holding a bitter draught with honey. Now medicine could be made palatable by the coating of sugar.

Sugar and Candy in America

Columbus brought sugar to the New World, specifically San Domingo, on his second voyage in 1493. By 1511, growing sugar cane was an established practice in Cuba, and from there it spread to most of the West Indian islands and to Central and South America. Sugar was one of the important early imports into the Colonies. Again it was the druggist who had charge of candy-making. Candy drops containing peppermint, hoarhound, and wintergreen were healing as well as tasty. At home, children depended on molasses, honey, maple, or jam to satisfy their sweet tooth. The nearest thing to candy was a type of "sugar candy" made by boiling sugar in water and letting it crystallize. The first real candy was made in the form of stick candy. Later additions were molasses taffy and the sugar plum (not a plum at all but a plum-shape bonbon).

By 1845 the candy trade in this country had not grown to any appreciable extent. In Europe, too, candy-making as an industry moved slowly. The introduction of machinery, around 1840, gave impetus to the trade throughout Europe. Although, on a nutritional level, there seems no earthly reason to justify the pleasure of eating candy, it does supply quick energy for physical exercise. Admiral Richard E. Byrd took two and a half tons of candy to the South Pole on one of his expeditions.

Today, candy-making is an important industry in the United States. But most good cooks enjoy turning out their own occasional batch of fudge to please the youngsters, or to recapture the nostalgia of olden days, when the fragrance of homemade candy brought old and young to the kitchen.

In general, candies fall into two classes: creamy or crystalline, and amorphous or noncrystalline.

Creamy or Crystalline

Creamy candies include fondant, fudge, penuche, divinity, and seafoam. When making creamy candies, the chief concern is to control the mixture so that the sugar crystals in the finished candy are so small they cannot be seen or felt when eaten. The texture must be smooth and creamy, never gritty or sugary.

Caloric Values

- [ ] Fondant, 3½ ounces = 364 calories
- [ ] Fudge, vanilla, 3½ ounces = 398 calories
- [ ] Fudge, vanilla, with nuts, 3½ ounces = 424 calories
- [ ] Fudge, chocolate, 3½ ounces = 400 calories
- [ ] Fudge, chocolate, with nuts, 3½ ounces = 426 calories

Amorphous or Noncrystalline

Chewy or hard candies such as caramels, butterscotch, taffy, lollipops, nougat, brittles, gumdrops, and marshmallows become a solid mass as the candy hardens. (Gumdrops require ingredients which are not readily available in grocery stores.)

- [ ] Caramels, plain or chocolate, 3½ ounces = 399 calories
- [ ] Butterscotch candy, 3½ ounces = 397 calories
- [ ] Nougat, chocolate coated, 3½ ounces = 416 calories
- [ ] Brittle, peanut, 3½ ounces = 421 calories
- [ ] Marshmallows, 3½ ounces = 319 calories
- [ ] Gumdrops, 3½ ounces = 347 calories

Suggestions for Candy Makers—Follow recipes carefully. Use a candy thermometer if possible. Always make sure the thermometer bulb is in the boiling mixture but does not touch bottom of the pan. Read the thermometer with your eye in a direct line with the upper level of the mercury. During cooking wash down the sides of the pan with a wet pastry brush to make sure all sugar dissolves. For all candy except fondant, grease pans or slabs that are to be used. For fondant, moisten the slab with cold water. Grease hands before pulling taffy. Use a heavy saucepan for candy-making. Many mixtures with milk or cream, or those cooked to a higher temperature, will burn easily. Watch candy carefully, especially during the last few minutes of cooking. Temperatures rise quickly at the end. For best results, don't double or make substitutions in the ingredients. Finally, allow plenty of time when making most candies. Many, such as caramels, take long cooking and stirring.

If you do not have a candy thermometer, see the chart on Candy-Making Tests, page 284, for tests you can use to determine the approximate temperature of the sugar syrup.

Fondant—This is the foundation for most mints, bonbons, and the creamy centers for chocolates. Many short-cut recipes have been devised but anyone who really enjoys candy-making should try a real fondant at least once. The chief ingredients are sugar and water, plus corn syrup or an acid such as cream of tartar to aid in keeping sugar crystals small, so that the candy will be smooth. After cooking, the candy is beaten, then kneaded. It needs a ripening period of 12 to 24 hours to make it easier to handle.

Fudge—A creamy, smooth confection which is the pride and joy of all youngsters in their first candy-making adventure. In fudge, milk and some agent such as corn syrup are used to help keep the texture smooth. The candy is also beaten after a cooling period. An important point to watch is the temperature before beating. If stirring or beating is started too soon, the candy will be less smooth. Once beating is started, it should not be interrupted. In the beating process, the candy will go through interesting changes in appearance. At first it will be shiny and quite thin. As beating continues, the shininess will begin to disappear and by the end of the beating period, it will be lusterless and, of course, thick.

There are many varieties of fudge: chocolate, cocoa, or peanut butter, plain, or with nuts, fruits, or spices added.

The same general method is used for making Penuche and Pralines.

Divinity and Seafoam—Fluffy, porous candy is made by boiling sugar, water, and corn syrup to the firm or hard-ball stage, then slowly beating this syrup into egg whites, and beating constantly until the mixture is very stiff. The candy is then dropped by spoon onto wax paper, cut when firm, or sometimes kneaded.

Caramel—It is characterized by its chewy consistency. This is achieved by the high fat content of butter and/or cream and corn syrup, or molasses. Candies containing milk or cream must be stirred constantly while cooking but, in many cases, not at all after removing from heat. They are poured to desired thickness, cooled, and cut into pieces with scissors or knife.

Butterscotch—A butter-flavored caramel which can be poured into a pan and cut into squares. If cooked a little longer, it can be dropped by a spoon onto wax paper and used as a hard candy.

Taffy—A syrup cooked without stirring until it reaches the hard-ball or soft-crack stage; then the mixture is allowed to cool until it can be pulled with the hands. Here, as with fudge, the temperature of the candy is important.

Nougat—Chewy candy made by adding syrup to stiffly beaten egg whites, then stirring in nuts, usually chopped almonds. Commercially made nougats are poured onto and covered with wafer paper, then pressed to form smooth surfaces. Since wafer paper is not always readily available to homemakers, a light dusting of cornstarch may be substituted. Nougats should stand for several hours before cutting.

Brittle—There are two ways of making this hard candy. One is to caramelize sugar in a skillet over low heat until melted and golden brown, then add nuts. A second way is to cook syrup in a saucepan to the hard-crack stage, then add butter and soda to make a tender, more porous brittle. In either case nuts are added when cooking is completed. Mixture is poured immediately so that the candy is 1/8 to 1/4 inch thick; sometimes it is pulled even thinner as it begins to harden. When hard, it is cracked into pieces.

Marshmallows—These are very simple to make because there is no cooking involved. However, the mixture must be beaten for 15 minutes and a good electric mixer is necessary. It is almost impossible to beat the mixture with a rotary beater.

Storage—Keep different types of candy separately. Brittles soften if stored with

CANDY-MAKING TESTS

TEMPERATURE-DEGREES F.- of syrup at sea level (indicating concentration desired)	STAGE	DESCRIPTION OF TEST
230 to 234	Thread	Syrup spins a 2-inch thread when dropped from fork or spoon.
234 to 240	Soft ball	Syrup, when dropped into very cold water, forms a soft ball which flattens on removal from water.
244 to 248	Firm ball	Syrup, when dropped into very cold water, forms a firm ball which does not flatten on removal from water.
250 to 266	Hard ball	Syrup, when dropped into very cold water, forms a hard ball which holds its shape, yet is plastic.
270 to 290	Soft crack	Syrup, when dropped into very cold water, separates into threads which are hard but not brittle.
300 to 310	Hard crack	Syrup, when dropped into very cold water, separates into threads which are hard and brittle.

creamy candies. Airtight storage in a cool place is best. Some candies may be frozen, but avoid freezing those made with fruits and nuts.

FONDANT

3 cups sugar
1 1/3 cups water
1/4 teaspoon salt
1/3 cup light corn syrup

Mix all ingredients in large saucepan. Bring to boil, stirring. Cover; boil for 3 minutes. Remove cover and cook until a small amount of mixture forms a soft ball when dropped into cold water (238°F. on candy thermometer). Wash down sides of pan several times with a fork covered with cheesecloth and dipped into water, using an up-and-down motion. Pour out onto ungreased platter. Cool to lukewarm (110°F.). Beat with fondant paddle or spatula until mixture turns cloudy. Gather into a ball and knead with lightly buttered hands until smooth and creamy. Put away in crock or glass jar and allow to "ripen" for 2 to 3 days before using. Makes about 2 1/4 pounds.

Fondant Patties

Melt small amount of Fondant (about 1 cup) at a time over hot water. Keep water in bottom of double boiler just below boiling point. Stir melted fondant enough to blend. Add coloring, if desired, and a few drops of flavoring oil such as peppermint, wintergreen, or spearmint. Drop patties from tip of teaspoon onto wax paper. As soon as firm, loosen and lift. Decorate if desired.

Bonbons

Using two thirds of Fondant planned for any one flavor of bonbon, work in desired flavoring and coloring, a little at a time. Shape into 3/4-inch balls for centers. Bits of nuts, candied or dried fruits, or coconut can be added to these centers. Let stand on wax paper, covered, overnight. Next day, melt remaining third of the fondant set aside for this batch in top part of metal double boiler over boiling water. Add flavoring and coloring to match fondant centers. Remove from heat. Set pan in cold water for a moment and then put over hot, not boiling, water to keep fondant warm and soft. With dipping fork, or other fork, dip bonbon centers, one at a time, into melted fondant to cover. Stir after each bonbon is dipped to keep crust from forming on top. If this fondant becomes too thick, reheat or add a few drops of hot water. Tip bonbon over onto wax-paper-covered tray. Decorative circles can be made by holding dipping fork on top of bonbon for a moment. Decorate at once with bits of nuts, candied fruits, silver shot, or colored sugar, as desired. Leftover dipping fondant can be dropped onto wax paper to make patties. Store, covered, in cool dry place.

UNCOOKED FONDANT
⅓ cup soft butter or margarine
⅓ cup light corn syrup
½ teaspoon salt
1 teaspoon vanilla extract
3½ cups (1 pound) sifted
confectioners' sugar

Blend all ingredients but sugar; mix in sugar; knead until blended. Makes about 1⅓ pounds.

Candied-Fruit Squares
Substitute rum extract for the vanilla in Uncooked Fondant recipe. Add ½ cup finely chopped candied fruit (cherries, pineapple, orange and lemon peels). Roll ½ inch thick; cut into squares.

Peanut Squares
Add ¾ cup chopped unsalted peanuts to Uncooked Fondant recipe. Roll about ½ inch thick. Cut into squares.

Mocha Logs
Add 2 teaspoons instant coffee to Uncooked Fondant recipe. Shape into rolls ½ x 2 inches. Roll in chocolate sprinkles.

OLD-TIME CHOCOLATE FUDGE
3 or 4 ounces (3 or 4 squares)
unsweetened chocolate
1¼ cups milk
3 cups sugar
¼ teaspoon salt
1 tablespoon light corn syrup
3 tablespoons butter or margarine
1½ teaspoons vanilla extract
1 cup chopped nuts

Combine chocolate and milk in large heavy skillet. Cook over low heat, stirring, until smooth and blended. Stir in sugar, salt, and corn syrup; continue cooking without stirring until 236°F. registers on candy thermometer, or until a small amount of mixture when dropped into very cold water forms a soft ball. Remove from heat; add butter, vanilla, and nuts. Cool, without stirring, until lukewarm (110°F.). Beat vigorously until mixture thickens and loses its gloss. Pour quickly into a buttered 8-inch square pan. Cut into squares and remove from pan while warm. Makes about 2 pounds.

OPERA CREAMS
2 cups sugar

2 tablespoons light corn syrup
1 cup light cream
⅛ teaspoon salt
1 teaspoon vanilla extract
½ cup broken nuts

Mix all ingredients except last 2 in saucepan. Bring to boil and cook, without stirring, until 236°F. registers on candy thermometer, or until a small amount of mixture dropped into cold water forms a soft ball. Remove from heat and let stand until lukewarm (110°F.). Add vanilla and nuts; beat until mixture is thick and loses its gloss. Drop by dessertspoon onto wax paper and let stand until firm. Makes about 20 creams.

Opera Fudge
Make Opera Creams and pour candy into buttered 8-inch square pan. When firm, cut into squares.

OLD-TIME PENUCHE
4½ cups (2 pounds) firmly packed
light brown sugar
1 cup evaporated milk, undiluted
½ cup butter or margarine
¼ teaspoon salt
1 teaspoon vanilla extract
2 cups chopped walnuts

In large saucepan mix sugar, milk, butter, and salt. Cook, stirring, until sugar is dissolved. Continue cooking until 238°F. registers on candy thermometer, or until a small amount of mixture dropped into cold water forms a soft ball. Remove from heat and let stand until lukewarm (110°F.). Add vanilla and walnuts. Beat until mixture is thick and loses its gloss. Pour into buttered 9-inch square pan. When firm, cut into squares. Makes about 3 pounds.

PECAN PRALINES
1 cup granulated sugar
2 cups firmly packed light brown sugar
¼ cup light corn syrup
⅛ teaspoon salt
1¼ cups milk
1 teaspoon vanilla extract
1½ cups unbroken pecan halves

Combine sugars, corn syrup, salt, and milk in saucepan. Bring to boil and cook, without stirring, until 236°F. registers on candy thermometer, or until a little of mixture dropped into cold water forms a soft ball. Remove from heat and let stand until lukewarm (110°F.). Add vanilla and pecans and beat with spoon until mixture begins to thicken and loses its gloss. Drop from tablespoon onto wax paper and spread to form patties about 4 inches in diameter. Let stand until firm. Then wrap individually in moistureproof paper. Store in airtight container. Makes 12 pralines.

Vanilla Pralines
Use 3 cups granulated sugar in place of white and light brown sugars in Pecan Praline recipe.

DIVINITY
½ cup light corn syrup
2½ cups sugar
¼ teaspoon salt
½ cup water
2 egg whites
1 teaspoon vanilla extract
1 cup coarsely chopped nuts

In saucepan mix corn syrup, sugar, salt, and water. Cook, stirring, until sugar is dissolved. Continue cooking, without stirring, until 248°F. registers on candy thermometer, or until a small amount of mixture dropped into cold water forms a firm ball. Beat egg whites until stiff but not dry. Pour about half of syrup slowly over whites, beating constantly. Cook remainder until 272°F. registers on candy thermometer, or until a small amount of mixture dropped into cold water forms hard but not brittle threads, the soft-crack stage. Add slowly to first mixture and beat until mixture holds its shape. Add vanilla and nuts and drop by dessert-spoonfuls onto wax paper, or spread in buttered 9-inch square pan. When firm, cut into squares. Makes about 1½ pounds.

Seafoam
Follow Divinity recipe, substituting light brown sugar for granulated sugar.

Chocolate Divinity
Follow Divinity recipe, using 6-ounce package semisweet chocolate pieces and 1 cup nut halves. Beat until mixture begins to hold its shape; then add vanilla, chocolate, and nuts. Beat until well blended.

Holiday Divinity
Follow Divinity recipe, adding ¼ cup each of chopped candied cherries and pineapple with the nuts.

Ginger Divinity
Follow Divinity recipe, using 6 tablespoons water and 2 tablespoons preserved-ginger syrup for the liquid. Add ½ cup finely diced ginger with the nuts.

VANILLA CARAMELS
2 cups sugar
2 cups warm light cream
1 cup corn syrup
½ teaspoon salt
⅓ cup butter or margarine
1 teaspoon vanilla extract
½ cup broken nuts

Mix sugar, 1 cup of the cream, the corn syrup, and salt in large saucepan. Cook, stirring, for about 10 minutes. Add remaining cream very slowly so that mixture does not stop boiling. Cook for 5 minutes longer. Stir in butter, 1 teaspoon at a time. Cook slowly, stirring, until 248°F. registers on candy thermometer, or until a small amount of mixture dropped into cold water forms a firm ball. Remove from heat; add vanilla and nuts and mix gently. Pour into buttered 8-inch square pan, and cool. Turn out on

Mints

Butterscotch

Opera Creams

Penuche

Pecan Roll

Rum Balls

Popcorn Balls

Molasses Taffy

Pralines

FRAGRANT, TEMPTING, DELICIOUS CANDY.

Truffles

Divinity

Chocolate Fudge

Raisin-Peanut Clusters

Toffee

Candied Peel

Nougat

Peanut Brittle

Caramels

WHO CAN RESIST IT?

board, mark off ¾-inch squares, and cut. Wrap in wax paper. Makes about 2 pounds.

Chocolate Caramels
Follow recipe above, adding 3 or 4 ounces (3 or 4 squares) unsweetened chocolate to mixture before cooking.

POPCORN BALLS
1 cup molasses
1 cup corn syrup
1 teaspoon cider vinegar
3 tablespoons butter
½ teaspoon salt
2 quarts freshly popped corn

In saucepan combine molasses, syrup, and vinegar. Cook until 266°F. registers on candy thermometer, or until a small amount of mixture dropped into cold water forms a hard ball. Stir in butter and salt and pour slowly over popped corn, stirring so that each kernel is coated. Butter hands slightly and shape into 3-inch balls. Cool; wrap balls individually in wax paper or plastic wrapping. Makes 6 balls.

PULLED MINTS
3 cups granulated sugar
1 cup water
2 tablespoons light corn syrup
¼ teaspoon salt
10 drops oil of peppermint or spearmint
1 cup sifted confectioners' sugar
½ cup cornstarch

Combine granulated sugar, water, corn syrup, and salt in saucepan. Put over heat and stir until sugar is dissolved. Bring to boil; cover and boil for 2 minutes. Uncover and continue cooking, without stirring, until 265°F. registers on candy thermometer, or until a little of mixture dropped into cold water forms a very hard ball. Remove from heat and pour out onto large platter. Cool until comfortable to handle (mixture should still be quite warm). Add oil of peppermint. Then pull with fingers until light-colored and glossy. Stretch into long rope about ½ inch in diameter. Cut into 1-inch pieces and put at once into mixture of confectioners' sugar and cornstarch. Let stand in warm place overnight to allow mints to mellow. Then shake in strainer to remove excess sugar mixture. Store in airtight container.
Note: Red or green vegetable coloring may be added with the oil of peppermint or spearmint. If more than one color is desired, make recipe twice, or make half of recipe twice, as all of candy must be pulled at one time.

BUTTERSCOTCH CANDY
2 cups sugar
⅔ cup dark corn syrup
¼ cup water
¼ cup light cream
¼ cup butter or margarine

Combine all ingredients except butter in saucepan and bring to boil, stirring.

Cook, stirring often, until 260°F. registers on candy thermometer, or until a small amount of mixture dropped into very cold water forms a hard ball. Add butter and cook, stirring, until 280°F. registers on candy thermometer, or until a small amount of mixture dropped into very cold water separates into threads which are hard but not brittle, or the soft-crack stage. Pour into buttered 8-inch square pan. When almost set, cut into squares. When cold, break apart. Makes about 1¼ pounds.

ALMOND NOUGAT
1½ cups light corn syrup
2 cups sugar
¼ teaspoon salt
¼ cup water
2 egg whites
½ teaspoon almond extract
Red or green food coloring
¼ cup soft butter or margarine
1 cup chopped toasted almonds
¼ cup chopped candied cherries

Mix first four ingredients in heavy saucepan. Cook, stirring, until sugar is dissolved. Cook, without stirring, until 250°F. registers on candy thermometer, or until a small amount of mixture dropped into cold water forms a hard ball. Beat egg whites until stiff but not dry in large bowl of electric mixer. Gradually beat in about one fourth (not more) of the syrup and continue beating until mixture holds its shape. Cook remaining syrup until 300°F. registers on candy thermometer, or until a small amount of mixture dropped into cold water separates into hard and brittle threads. Gradually beat into first mixture and continue beating until mixture begins to hold its shape. Add flavoring and food coloring to tint a delicate shade. Beat in butter; continue beating until very thick and satiny. Stir in nuts and cherries. Press into a buttered 8-inch square pan and smooth top. Let stand until firm. Turn out of pan and cut into pieces 1 x 1½ inches. Wrap each piece individually in wax paper. For best flavor, store for several days in a cool place before serving. Makes about 2 pounds.

PEANUT BRITTLE
2 cups granulated sugar
1 cup firmly packed light brown sugar
½ cup light corn syrup
½ cup water
Pinch of salt
¼ cup butter or margarine
⅛ teaspoon baking soda
1½ cups peanuts

Combine sugars, corn syrup, and water in saucepan. Cook, stirring, until sugar is dissolved. Cook, without stirring, to 300°F. on candy thermometer, or until a little of mixture dropped into cold water becomes very brittle. Remove from heat; add salt, butter, and soda and stir just to mix. Add nuts and turn into

shallow greased pan. Let stand for a minute or so and then pull quite thin. When cold, break up. Makes about 1½ pounds.

OLD-FASHIONED MOLASSES TAFFY
½ cup butter or margarine
2 cups sugar
1 cup molasses
1½ cups water
¼ cup light corn syrup

Combine all ingredients in large saucepan and cook over high heat, stirring, until sugar is dissolved. Cook rapidly until mixture begins to thicken. Lower heat slightly and cook until 260°F. registers on candy thermometer, or until a little of mixture dropped into cold water forms a hard ball. Pour onto greased platter. When cool enough to handle, butter hands lightly and pull candy until light in color and too hard to pull further. Stretch out into long rope ½ inch in diameter; cut with scissors into 1-inch pieces. Wrap in wax paper. Makes about 1½ pounds.

TOFFEE
1⅔ cups sugar
⅔ cup dark corn syrup
⅓ cup light cream
¼ cup butter or margarine
½ teaspoon vanilla extract
⅓ cup chopped nuts

Combine sugar, syrup, and cream in heavy saucepan; cook over medium heat, stirring constantly, until sugar is dissolved. Add butter. Turn heat low and cook, stirring occasionally, until 260°F. registers on candy thermometer, or until a small amount of mixture dropped into cold water forms a hard ball. Remove from heat and stir in vanilla and nuts; stir for 2 minutes longer. Pour into buttered 8-inch square pan. When almost set, mark into squares with knife. When cold, cut or break into squares as marked. Makes about 1⅓ pounds.

MARSHMALLOWS
1 envelope unflavored gelatin
⅓ cup cold water
Sugar
⅔ cup light corn syrup
½ teaspoon vanilla extract
Cornstarch

Soften gelatin in cold water and dissolve over hot water or low heat. Add ½ cup sugar, and stir until dissolved. Put in large mixer bowl with the corn syrup and vanilla. Beat at high speed for 15 minutes, or until mixture is very thick and of marshmallow consistency. Cover bottom of 9 x 9 x 2-inch pan with equal parts of sugar and cornstarch. Pour in mixture, and smooth top. Let stand in cool place for 1 hour, or until set. Loosen from pan, and turn out on board sprinkled with mixture of equal parts cornstarch and sugar. Cut in squares with knife wet with cold water. Roll in cornstarch and sugar. Makes 1 pound.

Coconut Marshmallows

In above recipe, do not cover pan with cornstarch-sugar mixture. Instead, butter pan, and sprinkle with part of 2 cups flaked coconut, toasted. Pour in mixture, and sprinkle with toasted coconut. When firm, cut, and roll in remaining coconut.

CANDIED GRAPEFRUIT OR ORANGE PEEL
    Peels of 2 large or 3 medium grapefruits
      or 3 large oranges
    Water
    3 cups sugar

Cover peel with cold water. Bring to boil and cook until tender, pouring off water and adding fresh cold water several times. Drain. With spoon remove white inner portion of peel. With scissors or sharp knife cut peel into thin strips. Make syrup by heating 2 cups sugar with 1 cup water. Add peel; cook over low heat until peel has a clear, candied appearance. Remove peel, 2 or 3 pieces at a time, allowing excess syrup to drain back into saucepan. Roll strips separately in remaining 1 cup sugar until well coated. Place on rack to cool. Store in tightly covered container in cool dry place. Keeps for at least a month. Makes about 1 pound.
Note: For candied grapefruit peel, add a few drops red or green food coloring before adding peel.

TWO-TONE TRUFFLES
    1½ cups finely chopped filberts
    1½ cups sifted confectioners' sugar
    1 egg white
    2 tablespoons rum
    1½ cups semisweet chocolate pieces
    ¾ cup sweetened condensed milk,
      undiluted
    1 tablespoon butter

Mix well filberts, sugar, egg white, and rum. Spread in buttered wax-paper-lined 8-inch square pan. Melt chocolate in top part of double boiler over hot water. Stir in milk and butter and cook until thickened, about 5 minutes. Pour into pan over nut mixture. When firm, cut into small squares. Makes about 2 pounds.

RAISIN-PEANUT CLUSTERS
    1 cup (6-ounce package) semisweet
      chocolate pieces
    1 can (14 ounces) sweetened
      condensed milk, undiluted
      Dash of salt
    1 cup seedless raisins
    1 cup shelled roasted peanuts

Melt chocolate in top part of double boiler over hot water. Add milk and salt and cook for 10 minutes, or until thickened, stirring constantly. Add raisins and peanuts. Drop from tablespoon onto wax paper. Refrigerate until firm. Makes about 20 clusters.

PECAN ROLL
    1 jar (7½ ounces) marshmallow creme
    3½ cups (1 pound) confectioners' sugar

    1 teaspoon vanilla extract
    ¼ teaspoon almond extract
    1 pound bought caramels
    2½ pounds pecans, coarsely chopped
      (about 10 cups)

Combine first 4 ingredients, kneading in the last of the sugar gradually. Shape into 8 rolls, 1 inch in diameter. Wrap in wax paper and put in freezer or refrigerator frozen-food compartment overnight, or until candy is very hard. Remove paper from caramels. Melt caramels in top part of a metal double boiler over boiling water. Remove from heat but keep over hot water. Dip marshmallow rolls first into caramel to cover, then roll in nuts, pressing nuts firmly into caramel with hands. Cool. Store, covered, in a cool dry place. Makes about 5 pounds.

Pecan-Roll Slices

Shape marshmallow mixture (first 4 ingredients in recipe above) into 1 or 2 large rolls. Dip into caramel and roll in nuts. Cool. When thoroughly dry, cut into ½-inch slices with a sharp thin knife.

RUM BALLS
    1 cup crushed vanilla wafers
    1 cup confectioners' sugar
    1½ cups chopped pecans
    2 tablespoons cocoa
    2 tablespoons light corn syrup
    ¼ cup dark rum
    ¼ cup fine granulated sugar

Combine fine crumbs, confectioners' sugar, 1 cup pecans, and cocoa. Add corn syrup and rum, and mix well. Shape into 1-inch balls. Roll half in granulated sugar and remainder in ½ cup nuts. Makes 2 dozen.

APRICOT-APPLE DROPS
Mix together until smooth 1 cup nonfat dry milk solids, ½ cup confectioners' sugar, ½ cup junior apricot-applesauce, and a little grated lemon rind. Drop from a teaspoon onto wax paper. Let stand for about 1 hour.

CANNING—Canning is a process of food preservation in which all organisms which might cause food spoilage are killed by heat. Canning can be done in a number of ways and the method selected must be suited to the kind of food to be canned. The food, once rendered completely sterile, is kept in sterilized, hermetically sealed containers.

The development of canning in the 19th century was a major breakthrough in the world of food. Before then, foods had been preserved by drying, pickling, and salting, methods which change their appearance, flavor, and nutritive values. Most foods, if not so preserved, had to be eaten quickly and in the same locality in which they were produced. Canned foods, on the other hand, can be produced under economical circumstances, taking advantage of crops and the places they grow; they can be stored and transported with ease; they can be used as is or quickly heated; and their appearance and nutritive values are scarcely changed.

Today, the most often home-canned foods are tomatoes, pickles, relishes, corn, and peaches. And many people can a few jars of an old favorite, or a special food.

CANNING EQUIPMENT

Canning equipment can be expensive and it requires a certain amount of storage space. Before starting on a canning program, the prospective home canner should face her own private moment of truth, and ask herself if the initial outlay for the canning equipment will be justified by its subsequent use. If you are going to do a great deal of canning, it is better to invest in the largest canner available. If space is limited and you cannot store the two types of canners discussed below, select a steam pressure canner for both types of canning.

Canners

Boiling Water Bath Canners—They can be bought, made from aluminum with a tight-fitting lid, in about 20-quart capacity. Or they can be made at home, if a large metal or enamelware kettle with tight cover is available. A canner must be fitted with a rack to keep jars or tins from touching the bottom. The rack may be metal or wood, and should have partitions to keep the jars from touching one another or falling against the side of the canner. It must be deep enough so that water can boil well over the tops of the jars or tins, preferably 2 to 4 inches above tops. A clean wash boiler or lard can may also be used.

When canning only 3 to 4 small jars, a large kettle with a lid may be used with a cake cooling rack on the bottom.
Steam Pressure Canners—These are made

from heavy cast aluminum with a gasket-sealed lid, in about 16- to 20-quart capacity. They are equipped with racks. Some have a pressure gauge, others a weighted gauge and a safety valve petcock or vent. This is a part of the pressure canner which, when open, provides a vent for the escape of air and steam. When closed it holds the steam inside, allowing pressure to build up so foods may be heated at 240°F. The petcock may be in one unit with the safety valve, or each may be a separate part. The safety valve is so adjusted that, if the pressure in the cooker is allowed to rise too high, steam is automatically released through the valve. These vents should be kept clean by drawing a string or narrow strip of cloth through them. Do this at the beginning of and often during the canning season. All steam pressure canners need careful inspection and cleaning before and during each canning season. When canning foods usually processed in a Boiling Water Bath Canner (acid foods), just set the cover of your Steam Pressure Canner in place without fastening it and leave the safety petcock open to prevent pressure from building up.

Canning Containers—Two types are used, glass jars and bottles, and tin cans. Glass jars are the most readily available. Tin cans require a can sealer. They are only practical in large-scale canning, such as 300 cans or more. Bottles can be used for canning some juices.

Glass Jars—There are several types and the one you select is largely a matter of personal preference. However, if you will be pressure canning, make sure the jars you choose will stand up to a heat of 240°F. or more. Jars come in ½-pint, pint, quart, and ½-gallon sizes. The lids vary but, generally speaking, metal lids are the easiest to use and the least fragile. Any kind of lid is good so long as it is airtight. To test, fill the jar with water. Cap properly and turn upside down. If there are no leaks the jar is safe. Keep jars and lids scrupulously clean. Since different types of jars and lids require specific methods of handling and cleaning, follow the manufacturer's directions.

Rubber Rings—Have clean new rings of the right size for jars. Unused leftover rubber rings may deteriorate from one canning season to the next. Test them, and new rings too, by bending them in small pleats. If they crack, throw them away. Or stretch them slightly. If they don't return to their original shape, they are not good. To use, wash and rinse, then keep wet until needed. When putting in place on the jar, stretch ring just enough to place it flat on the sealing shoulder. If a wire-bail type jar is being filled, the lip of the rubber ring must be

on the side of the jar opposite the wire side. After filling jar, wipe off rubber ring and jar rim with a clean, damp cloth. When the lid is put on, it should rest on the rubber. Then seal jar. When opening jars with rubbers, it is best to pull out rubber part way, rather than pry up top (if glass) and chance nicking the jar or top.

Bottles—Some juices such as tomato juice, apple juice, citrus juices, etc., may be canned in bottles. There are caps and sealers available for this purpose.

Caps—Cork-lined bottle caps. These must be put on with a Bottle Capper.

Tin Cans—Three types are available:

C—enamel for corn, hominy

R—enamel, sanitary or standard enamel, for beets, red berries, red or black cherries, plums, pumpkin, rhubarb, winter squash

Plain—for all other fruits and vegetables and for meats

Four sizes are available:

No. 1 cans hold about 1¼ cups
No. 2 cans hold about 2¼ cups
No. 2½ cans hold about 3¼ cups
No. 3 cans hold about 4 cups

Some tin cans may be re-used. See manufacturer's directions.

Before using check to see that cans, lids, and gaskets are perfect. Discard badly bent, dented, or rusted cans and lids with damaged gaskets. Keep cans in paper packing until ready to use. Wash cans just before using, drain upside down. Do not wash lids; this may damage gaskets. If lids are dusty or dirty, rinse with clean water or wipe with damp cloth. Check the sealer and make sure it is properly adjusted. To test, put a little water into a can, seal it, then submerge can in boiling water for a few seconds. If air bubbles rise from can, the seam is not tight. Adjust sealer, following manufacturer's directions.

Other Canning Equipment—This includes:

Sharp knives and parers for quick and neat work

Cutting board and slicing knives

Chopping bowl and chopping knife

Fruit or vegetable press or food mill

Measuring devices: 1-cup, quart, and 4-quart measures, measuring spoons

Jar filler and funnel, for large hot foods and for juices

Ladles and large stirring spoons: wood and metal, long and short handles

Household scales, helpful to check weights of food or sugar

Timer

Strawberry huller

Spatula for removing air bubbles

Large kettles with covers

Wire basket or cheesecloth

Bowls

Vegetable brushes

Jar tongs, a must if Boiling Water Bath Canner does not have lifting rack

Scissors

Shallow pans or trays for sorting, transporting

Colander

Potholders

GENERAL CANNING DIRECTIONS

Foods

Fruits and Vegetables—Use only firm, fresh, unbruised and fully ripe fruits and vegetables. They must be mature enough to be full flavored, yet firm enough to hold their shape during processing. Sort according to size for even cooking. Scrub and wash fruits and vegetables thoroughly, in small quantities at one time, under running water or in several changes of water. Don't let them soak or they will lose their flavor and nutrition.

Meat—Beef, veal, mutton, lamb, pork, and rabbit may be successfully canned at home. So can various kinds of poultry, chicken, duck, goose, guinea hen, squab, turkey. Meat of large game animals like beef and small game animals like poultry may be canned. Wash poultry and game, but do not wash meats. Wipe them with a clean damp cloth.

Preparation—Get out all your equipment before starting to can. Make sure it is absolutely clean and in perfect working order. Read instructions carefully for use of equipment and canning. Make sure that your jars, lids, canner, and rack are absolutely clean.

Sterilization—In canning, the heat treatment used must be sufficient to destroy all enzymes and microorganisms present in the food. When the directions for method, heat, and time of processing are followed, the foods will be sterile and will remain so in their sealed containers until container is opened.

Consequently, the question often asked is, "Must jars and lids be sterilized before canning?" The answer, nowadays, is "no" because when proper canning methods are used, the jars are sterilized along with the food. Both jars and tins should be scrupulously clean and, to prevent breakage, glass jars should be kept in hot water until filled.

Blanching—The most important function of blanching in canning is to stop the action of some undesirable enzymes. Blanching also shrinks the food and drives out air so that the food can be packed more closely and it is used to loosen skins on tomatoes or peaches to make them easier to peel.

To blanch foods, place them in a wire basket in quantities of about 1 quart at one time. Immerse them in boiling water for 5 minutes, counting from the time the water begins to boil again after the

NONACID FOODS

PRESSURE CANNER METHOD   (10 POUNDS PRESSURE)

PRODUCT	PREPARATION	HOT PACK	COLD PACK
ASPARAGUS 2½ to 2¼ lbs. = 1 qt.	Wash; trim off scales and tough ends. Wash again. Cut into 1-inch pieces. To can whole spears in glass jars: Select young slender spears. Cut stalks of equal lengths to stand upright in jars. Tie in bunches of 20 to 30 stalks. Stand bunches upright in boiling water reaching to tips. Boil for 3 minutes, then turn bunches on sides and boil for ½ minute longer. Remove string and pack in jars with tips up. Add salt. Cover with boiling liquid leaving ½ inch of space at top. Adjust lids. Process in pressure canner pints for only 20 minutes.	Cover pieces with boiling water; boil for 2 to 3 minutes. Pack loosely to top. Add salt. Cover with boiling hot liquid or boiling water. Leave ½ inch of space at top. Adjust lids. Process in pressure canner. Pints 25 minutes Quarts 30 minutes	Pack tightly to ½ inch from top. Add salt. Cover with boiling water leaving ½ inch of space. Adjust lids. Process in pressure canner. Pints 30 minutes Quarts 35 minutes
CORN (in husks) 3 to 6 lbs. = 1 qt. kernel style	Can only young, tender, *newly harvested* corn. Cut off ends of each ear, then husk (silk is easier to remove this way). Trim off any spots. Wash only if necessary. **Cream Style:** Cut off only about top half of kernels, then with back of knife or a metal spoon, scrape rest of kernels from cob. **Whole Kernel Style:** Cut off whole kernels only; do not scrape cob.	Add 1 pint boiling water to each quart of corn. Heat to boiling. Pack hot corn to 1 inch from top of jars. Add salt. Adjust jar lids. Process in pressure canner. Pints 85 minutes To each quart of kernels, add 1 pint boiling water. Heat to boiling. Pack hot corn to 1 inch from top; cover with boiling liquid to 1 inch from top. Add salt. Adjust lids. Process in pressure canner. Pints 55 minutes Quarts 85 minutes	Pack corn to 1 inch from top. Do not shake or press down. Add ½ teaspoon salt to each jar. Fill to top with boiling water. Adjust lids. Process in pressure canner. Pints 95 minutes Pack kernels to 1 inch from top; do not shake or press down. Add salt. Fill to top with boiling water. Adjust lids. Process in pressure canner. Pints 60 minutes Quarts 90 minutes
MEAT AND LARGE GAME	Fresh, clean meat: wipe with a damp cloth, cube meat, and remove bones.	Cook meat in enough boiling water to cover. Cook until meat is medium done and no pink color remains. Pack meat tightly into jars, leaving 1 inch of space. Cover meat with broth. Adjust lids. Process in pressure canner. Pints 75 minutes Quarts 90 minutes	Pack cubes of raw meat in jars leaving 1 inch of space. Do not add liquid. Add salt. Set jars in a large kettle filled with warm water covering all but 2 inches of the jars. Cover and boil slowly for 75 minutes. Ready to process when interior of meat reaches 170°F. Adjust lids on jars. Process in pressure canner. Pints 75 minutes Quarts 90 minutes
POULTRY AND SMALL GAME	Wash and dry thoroughly. Cut meat into meaty pieces, bony pieces, and giblets. Cook bony pieces for broth. Trim fat and excess skin.	**WITH BONE** Trim large bones and remove breast bone. Cover with hot broth and simmer until medium done. Pack pieces tightly in jar, placing skin next to glass. Add salt. Leave 1 inch of space. Add hot broth. Adjust lids. Process in pressure canner. Pints 75 minutes Quarts 90 minutes **WITHOUT BONE** Follow directions above, remove bones but do not remove skin. Process as above.	**WITH BONE** Pack raw meat into clean jar. Set jars in kettle with water 2 inches below top of jars. Cover and boil slowly for 75 minutes. Remove jars, adjust lids. Process in pressure canner. Pints 65 minutes Quarts 75 minutes **WITHOUT BONE** Follow directions above, remove bones but do not remove skin. Process as above.

ACID FOODS
BOILING WATER BATH

PRODUCT	PREPARATION	HOT PACK	COLD PACK
APPLES, slices 1½ to 3 lbs. = 1 qt. 1 bu. = 16 to 20 qt.	Wash, pare, and core. Slice or cut into small pieces. If needed, put in water solution to prevent darkening after peeling. (See Peaches.) Precook: drain and boil in syrup or water for 5 minutes. Use ascorbic acid, ½ teaspoon for each quart of fruit.	HOT PACK ONLY Pack hot fruit in jars to ½ inch from top. Cover with hot syrup. Adjust lids. Process. Pints 10 minutes Quarts 20 minutes	NO COLD PACK
APPLESAUCE	Make applesauce, sweetened or unsweetened. Heat to simmering, stirring to keep from sticking to pan.	Pack hot into jars to ¼ inch from top. Adjust lids. Process. Pints 10 minutes Quarts 10 minutes	NO COLD PACK
BERRIES (except strawberries which do not can well) 1½ to 3 lbs. (1- to 2-qt. boxes) = 1 qt. 24-qt. crate = 12 to 18 qt.	Wash berries. Lift from washing water and drain well. Cap and stem as needed. **For cold pack:** Prepare syrup. **For hot pack:** Measure berries. Add ½ cup sugar for each quart berries. Put in pan, cover, and bring to boil. Shake pan to keep berries from sticking.	Use firm berries. Pack hot into jars to ½ inch from top. Adjust lids. Process. Pints 10 minutes Quarts 15 minutes	For soft berries. Fill jars to ½ inch from top. Shake berries down when filling for a full pack. Cover fruit with boiling syrup; leave ½ inch of space at top. Process. Pints 10 minutes Quarts 15 minutes
PEACHES 1 lb., about 4 medium 2 to 3 lbs. fill about 1 qt. 1 bu. fills 16 to 25 qts.	Wash peaches and strip off skins. If they are hard to remove, dip fruit into boiling water, then into cold water. Cut into halves or slice; remove pit. To prevent darkening, drop into mixture of 1 gallon water, 2 tablespoons each of salt and vinegar. Drain. Use ascorbic acid, ½ teaspoon for each quart of fruit.	Heat peaches in syrup! If fruit is very ripe and juicy, sugar alone may be used. Pack in jars as raw peaches; cover with syrup; adjust lids. Process. Pints 20 minutes Quarts 25 minutes	Pack in jars to ½ inch from top. Cover fruit with boiling syrup, leaving ½ inch of space at top. Adjust jar lids. Process. Pints 25 minutes Quarts 30 minutes **Brandied peaches:** Use a heavy syrup; add 1 to 2 tablespoons brandy to each pint jar just before pouring in boiling syrup.
PEARS 1 lb., about 3 medium 2 to 3 lbs. fill 1 qt. 1 bu. fills 18 to 27 qts.	Wash pears. Pare, cut into halves, and core. Use a ball cutter for coring to make even round centers. Use ascorbic acid, ½ teaspoon for each quart of fruit.	**Either Raw or Hot Pack** For a change: Add a little mint extract and green color to syrup. Stir until combined. Then add pears. Cook for 10 minutes. **Proceed as Directed for Peaches** For variety: Put a maraschino cherry in each pear cavity before packing.	
PICKLED BEETS	Cut off beet tops leaving 1 inch of stems. Leave root intact. Wash, cover with boiling water, and cook until tender. Remove skins and slice. Make syrup: 2 cups vinegar, 2 cups sugar; heat to boiling.	Pack hot beets in jars to ½ inch from top. Add ½ teaspoon salt to pints, 1 teaspoon to quarts. Cover with boiling syrup; leave ½ inch of space at top. Adjust jar lids. Process. Pints 30 minutes Quarts 30 minutes	NO COLD PACK
PLUMS (greengage, fresh prunes, etc.) 1 lb., about 12 medium 2 to 2½ lbs. fill 1 qt. 1 bu. fills 22 to 25 qts.	Wash plums. For whole, prick skins with sharp fork. Freestone may be halved and pitted.	Heat fruit to boiling in syrup. If fruit is extra juicy, sugar alone may be used. Process. Pints 20 minutes Quarts 25 minutes	Pack jars to ½ inch from top. Cover fruit with boiling syrup; leave ½ inch of space at top. Adjust lids. Process. Pints 25 minutes Quarts 30 minutes

PRODUCT	PREPARATION	HOT PACK	COLD PACK
TOMATOES 1 lb., about 4 medium 2½ to 3½ lbs. fill 1 qt. 1 bu., about 20 qts.	Select only perfect, ripe tomatoes. To loosen skins, put in wire basket, dip into boiling water for about ½ minute. Put immediately into cold water. Cut out stem ends and slip off skins. Leave whole or cut into halves or quarters.	Quarter peeled tomatoes. Bring to boil; stir to keep from sticking. Pack boiling hot to ½ inch from top. Add ½ teaspoon salt to pints, 1 teaspoon to quarts. Adjust lids. Process. Pints 10 minutes Quarts 10 minutes	Pack in jars to ½ inch from top, pressing down gently to cause some juice to run and fill spaces. Do not add water. Add ½ teaspoon salt to pints, 1 teaspoon to quarts. Adjust lids. Process. Pints 35 minutes Quarts 45 minutes
TOMATO MIXTURE or other relishes	Wash and chop coarsely 6 sweet peppers, 1 quart onions, 1 quart celery. Add 1 quart water and cook for 20 minutes. Add 4 quarts peeled and cut-up red tomatoes, 3 tablespoons salt, 2 tablespoons sugar. Bring to boil.	Pack hot into jars, filling to ½ inch from top. Process. Pints 35 minutes Quarts 45 minutes	NO COLD PACK

Salt amount (unless otherwise specified):
Glass Jars
½ teaspoon for pints
1 teaspoon for quarts

foods have been immersed. Take wire basket out and dip foods 2 to 3 times up and down in cold water to cool quickly.

Salt, Sugar, and Other Preservatives—Foods are usually canned using salt and water, or sugar and water, or vinegar as preservatives. Foods may be canned safely without salt if necessary for diets or preferred.

Salt—Any regular table salt may be used for canning and it is also used for flavor.

Sugar—To help canned fruit hold shape, color, and flavor, sugar is used.

For very juicy fruit, packed hot, sugar may be added without liquid. Add about ½ cup sugar to each quart of raw, prepared fruit. Heat to simmering (185°F. to 210°F.) in a kettle on top of the stove over low heat. Pack the fruit in the juice that cooks out.

Light corn syrup or mild-flavored honey may replace as much as half the sugar called for in canning fruit. Do not use brown sugar, or molasses, sorghum or other strong-flavored syrups; their flavors overpower the fruit flavor and they may darken the fruit.

Sugar Syrup—Most directions call for canning most fruit with a sweetening in the form of a sugar syrup. To make sugar syrup: Mix sugar with water or with juice extracted from some of the fruit. Use thin, medium, or heavy syrup to suit the sweetness of the fruit and your taste. The proportions are:

	SUGAR	WATER OR JUICE	YIELD
Thin	2 cups	4 cups	5 cups
Medium	3 cups	4 cups	5½ cups
Heavy	4¾ cups	4 cups	6½ cups

Boil sugar and water or fruit juice together for 5 minutes. Skim if necessary.

Three quarters to one cup sugar syrup is needed for each quart of fruit.

Sweeteners Other Than Sugar—Use a sodium-cyclamate base type, in tablet or liquid form. Ask for canning directions. In general, the methods are the same as for canning fruit in water.

Fruit may be canned without sweetening, in its own juice, in extracted juice, or in water. Sugar is not needed to prevent spoilage and the processing is the same for unsweetened fruit as for sweetened.

With most sodium-cyclamate base sweeteners, 1 tablet sodium equals 1 teaspoon sugar; ⅛ teaspoon liquid noncaloric sweetener equals 1 teaspoon sugar. Consult package or box for conversion into sugar.

Salt-Vinegar Solution—To prevent darkening of fruits when they are peeled, drop pieces of peeled fruit into a salt-vinegar water solution (2 tablespoons salt and 2 tablespoons vinegar added to 1 gallon cold water). Let stand for 10 to 15 minutes, then rinse well under running water.

Ascorbic Acid—This is used to keep fruits from darkening in the jars. To every quart of fruit add ½ teaspoon ascorbic acid when syrup is added. An ascorbic-acid mixture may be used following the instructions on the package. Pure ascorbic acid is also called citric acid and may be bought in drugstores. Ascorbic-acid compounds for home-canning (and freezing) are available in grocery stores.

Canning Methods—The two most common methods used in home-canning are the *cold* or *raw pack,* and the *hot pack.* The word "pack" refers to the way in which food is put into containers.

Cold or Raw Pack—The food is placed raw or blanched into the jar or tin without heat or cooking. When this method is used, the food is packed tightly into the containers because it will shrink during processing. Fruits are prepared and cut into desired sizes, packed in tightly, and covered with boiling hot syrup, juice, or water. Tomatoes, however, are pressed down in the containers so they form, and are covered by, their own juice; no other liquid is added. Vegetables are packed tightly and covered with boiling water. Meats and poultry are also packed in this way, with hot broth or water used for liquid.

Hot Pack—The food is cooked and packed hot into jars or tins. Hot food should be packed fairly loosely, and it should be at or near boiling temperature when packed. Fruits are heated in syrup, water steam, or in extracted juice before packing. Some juicy fruits and tomatoes may be preheated without added liquid and packed in the juice that cooks out. Vegetables are heated in water or steam, then packed hot into containers, and the boiling liquid or boiling water poured over them. The cooking liquid is recommended for flavor and because it may contain the minerals and vitamins dissolved out of the food. However, boiling water should be used when the cooking liquid is dark, gritty, or strong-flavored, or when there isn't enough.

Whatever the pack may be, fruits and vegetables should be packed to within ½ inch of the top. Sugar syrup should be filled to within ½ inch of the top.

Lima beans, dried beans, peas, corn, and meat should be packed to within 1 inch of the top and filled with boiling water to within ½ inch of the top.

Release all air bubbles trapped in the food by running a long thin knife down the side of the jar and moving contents to release air.

Boiling Water Bath—This is the name of the procedure used in canning acid foods. Foods are packed, by the cold or hot pack method, in containers of glass or tin, sealed partially or completely, then heated in a hot water bath for a given period of time until the contents reach a temperature of at least 170°F. To can by this method, see Step-by-Step Canning Directions for Tomatoes or Fruits, page 295.

Steam-Pressure Canning—This is the name of the procedure recommended for the canning of low- or nonacid foods. These include most vegetables and all meat, poultry, and fish. Food is packed by cold or hot pack, in glass jars or tin cans, and put in canner with 2 to 3 inches of boiling water. Canner is covered and locked. Over full heat and with the vent open, the steam is allowed to escape for 10 minutes. Then the vent is closed, the heat adjusted to hold even temperature, and the food processed according to the time given in chart. See Step-by-Step Canning Directions for Vegetables, Meats, Poultry, and Game, page 295.

Open Kettle and Oven Canning—These two methods, once popular, are no longer recommended because the temperatures achieved are not high enough to guarantee the destruction of all spoilage organisms and because spoilage bacteria may also be introduced when the food is transferred from kettle to jar.

Labels—After glass jars are wiped clean and before storing, it is advisable to label with the date and, if more than one lot was canned the same day, the lot number. Tins should also be labeled for content.

Storing Home-Canned Foods—They keep a long time but not indefinitely. Once the jars have been tested to make sure that they are properly sealed, they should be stored in a cool, dry place at a temperature below 70°F., but well above freezing.

If the sterilization was not quite complete, warmer temperatures will encourage the growth of bacteria and possible spoilage. Warmth and light also may change the color and flavor of the food. Dampness may cause the jar closings to deteriorate.

Check stored jars and cans at regular intervals for spoilage. We cannot stress proper canning methods and storage strongly enough. If they are not followed, botulism, a serious and often deadly food poisoning, may result.

■ **Warning**—Do not use any jars or cans that bulge at the can ends, jar lids, or rings, or that leak. After opening, check for off-odors, spurting liquid or gas bubbles, and pronounced color or texture changes.

It is possible for canned vegetables to contain the poison-causing botulism without showing signs of spoilage. There is no danger of botulism if pressure canner was used where recommended and if the canner was in perfect order and if every canning step was done correctly. But unless this was done and you were absolutely sure of gauge and canning method, boil home-canned vegetables before tasting. To do this: Bring vegetables to a rolling boil, then cover and boil for at least 10 minutes. Boil spinach and corn 20 minutes. If the food looks spoiled, foams, or has an off-odor during heating, destroy it. *Burn spoiled vegetables or dispose of the food so that it will not be eaten by humans or animals.*

Spoilage—Spoilage in foods can be caused by enzymes and microorganisms. Enzymes are substances which are produced in the living tissues of plants and their activities often continue after harvesting. Unless controlled they can be responsible for chemical changes affecting the flavor and color of food, and are especially noticeable in the cut surfaces of some fruits. The enzymes can be destroyed by boiling water or steam (the processing of canned foods) or controlled by the addition of a citric acid (such as vinegar or lemon juice) or ascorbic acid.

The second group of spoilage agents are microorganisms and these include the bacteria, molds, and yeasts. They are, as the name indicates, tiny in size. In canning, methods must be used to destroy these completely.

Bacteria are always present in the air, water, and soil. In order to avoid food spoilage caused by bacteria fermentation and putrefaction, keep the food and canning equipment scrupulously clean. Since many bacteria will survive in spite of this, they must be destroyed by heat in the processing of canned foods. The organism which causes botulism is one of these bacteria.

Molds are microorganisms which reproduce by spores that are widely distributed in the air. When they lodge on food, spoilage soon occurs. They can be destroyed by heating the food to 150°F. to 180°F. In canned foods molds are easily detected for they can be seen. If a light mold occurs on the surface of a canned food such as a fruit, juice, or tomato product, it may be removed and the rest of the product used. However, a fuzzy gray or white growth plus frothy appearance and bad odor means the food is unwholesome.

Yeasts are most troublesome and cause spoilage in sweet foods, sweetened canned fruits, jellies, and jams. They literally live on sugar and are tolerant to acids, hence must be destroyed by heat when canning or preserving. They multiply by budding, but perpetuate through spores with thick walls. Thus they can remain dormant without food or correct temperatures until these are supplied them, and then they will multiply rapidly.

Recanning—Many times people wish to know whether canned or frozen fruits purchased in large containers may be canned in smaller cans. It is possible in terms of safety, so long as the original directions for canning the fresh food are followed. However, it will be of much lower quality than if canned fresh.

Altitude—Processing times recommended and given in the charts which follow on pages 293 to 294 are only for foods prepared and packed at altitudes of 1,000 feet above sea level or less. So, those living and working at higher altitudes must increase the cooking (processing) time. (Recall the old law of physics that water boils at 212°F. at sea level. At an altitude of 2,000 feet this goes down to 208°F. and at 5,000 feet water boils at only 203°F.)

Thus at altitudes of 1,000 feet or more, food must be processed in a Boiling Water Bath for a longer time. If your altitude is over 1,000 feet, increase processing time given in charts according to table below:

Altitude	If Time Given Is 20 Minutes or Less, INCREASE	If Time Given Is More Than 20 Minutes, INCREASE
1,000 ft.	1 min.	2 mins.
2,000 "	2 mins.	4 "
3,000 "	3 "	6 "
4,000 "	4 "	8 "
5,000 "	5 "	10 "
6,000 "	6 "	12 "
7,000 "	7 "	14 "
8,000 "	8 "	16 "
9,000 "	9 "	18 "
10,000 "	10 "	20 "

STEP-BY-STEP CANNING DIRECTIONS

Acid foods include tomatoes, pickled vegetables and fruits, and these are processed by the Boiling Water Bath method. Nonacid foods include all vegetables (except tomatoes), meats, poultry, and game, and these must be processed by the Steam Pressure method.

Process food according to directions which follow and charts on pages 291, 292 and 293. After processing, open the canner, turning the lid away from the face to prevent steam burns.

To remove the hot jars use the rack, if it has handles. If it does not, use tongs. Place the hot jars on several thicknesses of towel or on a rack to prevent sudden cooling. Close lids by screwing cap tight or pushing the wire seal down. Leave it alone if the jar is a self-sealing type. Above all, do not open the jar after processing as this will contaminate the food. Tin cans can be cooled more quickly in cold running water.

After jars or tins are cooled, test the seal by turning upside down.

Label and store properly in cool dry

place and check occasionally for signs of spoilage.

TOMATOES AND PICKLED VEGETABLES: COLD OR RAW PACK GLASS JARS

Boiling Water Bath (212°F.) Method

1. Select firm, ripe tomatoes. Examine for spots and cracks; use only the best. Wash just enough for one canner load if you are working alone. (Same general directions apply to fruits.)

2. Put tomatoes in a wire basket or large clean cloth; lower into a kettle of rapidly boiling water. Cover kettle. After about ½ minute, remove and dip into cold water about 1 minute. Drain. (If skins are difficult to remove from fruits such as peaches, use same method. Test ease of removing skins and adjust time in boiling water.)

3. Cut out stem ends of tomatoes and slip off skins. (Peaches are usually cut in halves, pits removed, then halves dropped into a cold-water solution containing 1 tablespoon each of salt and vinegar for each 2 quarts of water, or use ascorbic-acid mixture according to directions, about 3 tablespoons for each 2 quarts water.) Put clean jars and lids in water to heat. Then, when ready to pack, they will be hot.

4. Work rapidly at this point. Cut tomatoes in halves or quarters or leave whole. Put hot jar on heatproof surface or in a shallow pan filled with hot water. Pack tomatoes into hot jars, pressing down gently until spaces fill with juice, or fill with hot tomato juice. Fill jars to ½ inch from top. (Peach halves are packed in jar, overlapping, cavity side down, then a boiling syrup poured in, leaving about ½ inch at top of jar.)

5. Add ½ teaspoon salt to each pint, 1 teaspoon salt to each quart. Run a knife or rubber bottle scraper down inside between tomatoes and jar to release air bubbles. Wipe jar rim with clean, damp cloth. Put lids with sealing compound on jar, or put on washed rubber rings. Screw on bands or tops, or put glass top in place. Seal jars as instructed, see Canning Containers, page 290. (For fruit, omit salt. Add about ¾ cup to 1 cup sugar syrup for each quart of fruit. Rest of instruction is the same.)

6. Place filled sealed jars on rack in canner containing hot, but not boiling, water. Make sure jars are spaced out and do not touch. Pour in boiling water if needed, enough to cover tops of jars by 1 to 2 inches. Do not pour water directly on jars.

7. Put cover on canner. Bring water to a boil, then begin to time. At sea level, process pint jars of tomatoes 35 minutes,

quart jars 45 minutes. Keep heat regulated so water boils gently but steadily.

8. When time is up, remove jars from hot water immediately. Complete seal on those which require it; do not adjust jars with metal lids with sealing compound. To cool, place jars on a wooden surface or on towels or newspapers, spaced out and away from drafts. Do not cover.

FRUITS: HOT PACK GLASS JARS

Boiling Water Bath (212°F.) Method

1. Follow first 5 steps given for Tomatoes, Cold Pack.

2. Prepare syrup. See Sugar Syrup, page 293. Heat to boiling. Put in fruit, draining any which may have been put in a solution to prevent darkening. Heat fruit through, but do not cook until soft.

3. Pack fruit loosely in hot jars. Peaches, pears, and other fruits with pits removed should be packed in overlapping layers, cavity side down. Leave ½ inch of space at top of jar. (Put on rubber ring if this type of jar is used.)

4. Cover fruit with boiling syrup, leaving the required amount of headspace at top of jar. It will take about ¾ to 1 cup syrup for each quart.

5. Run bottle scraper or similar nonmetal utensil between fruit and jar to release air bubbles. Add more syrup if needed. Wipe top and threads of jar, adjust lids and tops. Seal as required.

6. Follow steps 7 and 8 for Tomatoes, processing for length of time given in direction chart, page 292.

VEGETABLES, MEATS, POULTRY, AND GAME: COLD OR RAW PACK OR HOT PACK

Steam-Pressure Canner (240°F.) Method

1. Read manufacturer's directions for use of the canner and follow *specific* directions given there. The following are *general* directions for the steam-pressure canner.

2. Get the canner ready; check the gauge, petcock, and other points needed. Have all canning containers ready.

3. Prepare vegetables according to directions given on chart, page 291.

4. For *cold or raw pack* have boiling water ready. Pack prepared vegetables in hot jars, add salt, and fill jars as directed with boiling water. For *hot pack* prepare and precook according to chart. Pack in jars, add salt, and fill jars, as directed, with boiling liquid or water. Seal or otherwise prepare for processing glass or tin cans.

5. Have 2 or 3 inches of water boiling in the bottom of canner (more may be required if the weight-type gauge is used). The total amount of water required will depend on size and shape of canner.

6. Put rack in bottom of canner, arrange filled glass jars (or tin cans) on it so

they will not touch each other or the sides, and thus allow steam to flow around and between them. If a second layer is to be put in, put rack in place and stagger the jars or tins.

7. Put on cover and fasten securely so no steam can escape except through vent (petcock or weighted gauge opening).

8. Put on heat and watch until steam pours steadily from vent. Let it escape for 10 minutes to force the air out of cooker and allow gauge to register correctly. Then close petcock or put on weighted gauge. Let pressure rise to 10 pounds: the temperature will then be 240°F. at sea level. Immediately start counting processing time. Watch heat and regulate to keep pressure constant; do not lower pressure by opening petcock. Keep drafts from blowing on canner.

For additional information on home-canning of foods, write manufacturers of canning equipment or consult special canning books, or contact the extension services of the Agriculture Department of your state and of your state university, or contact your county agent. "Home Canning of Fruit and Vegetables" and "Home Canning of Meats" are two worthwhile publications. They can be obtained by writing to the Office of Information, U.S. Department of Agriculture, Washington, D. C. 20402

CANTALOUPE—This is a variety of the muskmelon, with a sweet and fragrant taste. The cantaloupe was named for a castle in Italy. Like all melons, it originated in Asia, and was well known to the ancient Romans and other Mediterranean peoples.

Availability—May to December, peak crop in the late summer. Crop comes from Arizona, California, Texas, and Mexico.

Frozen cantaloupe is available as melon balls, mixed with honeydew. Serve these partially thawed. If allowed to thaw completely, they become mushy.

Purchasing Guide—According to variety, the flesh of a cantaloupe may be salmon, pink, or green-colored. The salmon-col-

CAPERS

ored are the most prevalent.

Sweetness, fine texture, and pungent aroma are the characteristics of a good cantaloupe, and are found only in the well-matured melons. It is difficult to distinguish a ripe melon; however, there are two clues worth observing. The outside or netting should be well raised, coarse, and grayish. The stem-end scar, where the melon was attached to vine, should be slightly sunken, smooth, and well-calloused. When only half the scar is slightly sunken and the other half is rough, the melon was picked at "half slip," or before it matured on the vine. The melon should have a fruity fragrance, with no soft spots in the skin.

Storage—If melon is ripe, keep in refrigerator. Other melons should be kept at room temperature until ripening is completed.

☐ Refrigerator shelf: 4 to 8 days
☐ Refrigerator frozen-food compartment, prepared for freezing: 1 month
☐ Freezer, prepared for freezing: 9 months

Nutritive Food Values—Cantaloupe is an excellent source of vitamin A and vitamin C.

☐ ½ melon, 5 inches in diameter = 37 calories

Basic Preparation—Cut into halves or wedges, remove seeds, and serve with slices of lime or lemon. Serve halves filled with other fruits or ice cream. Cut crosswise into 1-inch slices, remove rind, place on plates, and fill centers as above. Cut into wedges or chunks and combine with other fruits, fruit cups, or salads. The flesh may be pickled or made into preserves.

☐ **To Freeze**—Use ripe firm melon. Cut into halves. Scoop out seeds. Peel. Cut into cubes or balls and pack in sugar syrup (2 cups sugar to 1 quart water). Use syrup to cover melon, allowing 1-inch headspace.

FRESH CANTALOUPE AND PINEAPPLE COMPOTE

Combine ¼ cup sugar, ½ cup water, and ¼ cup fresh lemon juice. Bring to boiling point. Remove from heat and cool for 15 minutes. Add ¼ cup fresh orange juice, 2 cups diced fresh cantaloupe, and 1 cup fresh pineapple wedges. Chill. Serve in sherbet glasses garnished with a sprig of fresh mint. Makes 6 servings.

MELON DELIGHT

1 medium cantaloupe
2 ripe peaches
⅓ cup sugar
2 tablespoons fresh lemon juice
½ teaspoon salt
2 tablespoons rosewater
  Crushed ice

Cut melon into halves. With a melon-ball cutter, scoop out melon. Place balls in a bowl. Add melon juice which collects while melon is being scooped. Peel peaches, pit, and slice thinly. Add to melon balls. Add sugar, lemon juice, and salt. Place in refrigerator and let chill for several hours. One half hour before serving, add rosewater and replace in refrigerator. When ready to serve, place mixture in sherbet glasses and top with very finely crushed ice. Makes 5 or 6 servings.

FRESH CANTALOUPE AND PROSCIUTTO APPETIZERS

Wrap bite-size wedges of fresh cantaloupe in thin slices of prosciutto. Serve on toothpicks with cocktails.

FRESH CANTALOUPE AND GRAPE CUP

Combine 1½ cups diced fresh cantaloupe, 1½ cups green seedless grapes, 3 tablespoons fresh lemon juice, and 2 tablespoons sugar in a mixing bowl. Toss lightly and chill. Serve as a dessert, garnished with fresh mint and cantaloupe balls. Makes 5 or 6 servings.

FRESH CANTALOUPE AND SHRIMP LUNCHEON SALAD

Cut 3 cantaloupes into halves. Remove seeds. Fill with a mixture of 2 cups cold cooked deveined shrimps, 1 cup chopped celery, 1 tablespoon fresh lemon juice, ½ teaspoon salt, ⅛ teaspoon pepper, and ¼ cup mayonnaise. Toss lightly. Serve as a main-dish supper or luncheon salad. Makes 6 servings.

MELON ICE-CREAM SAUCE

Cut ripe cantaloupe into halves. Scoop out seeds. Peel. Sieve cantaloupe or whirl pieces of cantaloupe in a blender. When puréed, add fresh lemon or lime juice and sugar to taste. Chill, and serve over vanilla ice cream.

CAPERS—They are the unopened flowers of the caper bush, a shrub native to the Mediterranean but grown now in the southern part of the United States and cultivated in greenhouses in the North. During the flowering season, the buds are picked before the petals can expand and preserved in vinegar and salt. Those labeled "nonpareil" are the most expensive because they are the smallest, tenderest buds. Capers add liveliness to white and other sauces, to salads and creamed dishes and, as condiments, to appetizers, meats, and seafood.

Availability—Bottled; may be in vinegar and salt solution or in salt only.

Storage—Keep covered in cool, dry place or in refrigerator.

Basic Preparation—Drain capers. Leave whole or chop finely.

EGG AND CAPER SAUCE

¼ cup butter or margarine
3 tablespoons all-purpose flour
½ teaspoon Worcestershire
1 teaspoon prepared mustard
1½ cups milk
3 hard-cooked eggs, diced
1 tablespoon capers

Melt butter in a saucepan. Blend in flour and seasonings. Add milk and cook until thickened, stirring constantly. Add eggs and capers. Makes about 2 cups.

TUNA IN CAPER SAUCE

1 cup diced celery
2 tablespoons butter
2 tablespoons all-purpose flour
¾ teaspoon salt
⅛ teaspoon pepper
1½ cups milk
1 can (about 7 ounces) tuna, drained and flaked
2 tablespoons capers
  Chopped parsley
  Hot cooked rice or noodles

Cook celery in small amount of boiling salted water for 5 minutes; drain. Melt butter; blend in flour, salt, and pepper. Gradually add milk, stirring constantly; cook until thickened. Add tuna, celery, and capers; heat thoroughly. Put in serving dish and sprinkle with parsley. Serve on rice. Makes 4 servings.

CAPON—Capons are male chickens which have been castrated at six to eight weeks of age to produce birds with more tender flesh and a generous fat covering. They are sold at seven to ten months of age. Even though more expensive than roasting chicken, capons are a good buy for a large group of people. Capons can be roasted or braised. Roast capons for twenty-two to thirty minutes per pound.

MIDDLE-EAST ROAST STUFFED CAPON

1 capon (about 6 to 7 pounds)
  Salt and pepper
⅓ cup melted butter or margarine
1 large onion, chopped
1½ cups cooked white or brown rice
½ cup chopped blanched almonds
½ cup yellow raisins
⅓ cup chopped dried apricots
1 small sweet apple, cored and diced
1 teaspoon salt
½ teaspoon crumbled dried thyme
¼ teaspoon white pepper
  Spice Mixture

Wash capon and pat dry. Sprinkle inside and out with salt and pepper. Melt butter. Sauté onion in butter until golden brown. Combine sautéed onions and but-

297

ter with next nine ingredients. Use mixture to stuff body and neck cavities of capon. Sew openings. Place capon on a rack in a shallow roasting pan. Roast in preheated moderate oven (325°F.) for 1½ hours. Sprinkle capon with Spice Mixture and roast for 1½ hours longer, basting capon with pan drippings. Makes 6 servings.

Spice Mixture

Combine ¼ teaspoon each of ground cinnamon, nutmeg, allspice, salt, and white pepper. Blend well; sprinkle on capon.

CAPSICUM—Red pepper is another name for this pod-bearing plant which is native to tropical America and one of the most important spices.

The capsicum family is a very large one, and its fruits vary in size, shape, color, and pungency. The family includes such varieties as sweet or bell peppers, chilies, paprika, and pimientos.

Capsicum is not related to black or white pepper, which is a berry that grows on a tropical vine.

Capsicum peppers have been used in the New World since pre-Inca days: green, ripe, or dried, whole or ground. The Spaniards brought the seeds of the capsicum pod back to Europe, and by 1600 it had reached the eastern tropics.

To this day red pepper is widely used, either crushed or ground, to give zest to foods that are often heavy and starchy. The pods are available whole (to be crushed and seeded before using) or commercially packed in crushed or ground form. The spice may be labeled "pepperoni rosso," "pizza pepper" or "cayenne red pepper."

Used with discretion, capsicum adds a great deal of zest to sauces, egg and cheese dishes, vegetables, and all foods that are bland, as well as to Italian and Mexican dishes.

PEPPY PORK SAUSAGE

1 pound ground lean pork
1 pound ground pork fat
2 tablespoons water
2 teaspoons salt
1 tablespoon ground sage
½ teaspoon ground thyme
½ teaspoon crushed red pepper
¼ teaspoon ground black pepper
Dash of garlic powder

Mix lean pork and pork fat. Add water and seasonings. Mix; put through a meat grinder or food chopper, using the fine blade. Let stand in refrigerator overnight for flavors to blend. Shape into patties. Brown on both sides in a hot skillet. Makes 6 servings.

CARAMEL, CARAMELIZE— The word "caramel" has two meanings. It describes a candy with a chewy consistency and it is also a culinary term that refers to burnt sugar by itself or thinned with water. In the latter sense it is used by cooks to add color, flavor, and style to various foods, from stews and gravies to desserts. To caramelize a mold is to coat it with sugar in the caramel stage.

The more sugar is caramelized, the less its sweetening power. To caramelize sugar, melt 1 cup granulated sugar in a mold or heavy skillet and cook over medium heat to 338°F. Use a candy thermometer to check heat. Cook, stirring constantly, until sugar forms a golden-brown syrup. Remove from heat immediately. Use this type of syrup to coat molds for custards and ice cream and as a glaze over caramelized custards and small cream puffs. When caramelizing a mold, rotate the sugar in it in all directions to coat the inside of the mold evenly.

To make a thick syrup, add ¼ cup very hot water slowly to hot sugar syrup. Stir constantly and heat for another 8 to 10 minutes over very low heat. Store in container for later use. If the syrup hardens in the container, place the container in hot water until the syrup melts. If a thinner syrup is desired, add more water.

To obtain a *croquant,* or "brown nougat," add 1 tablespoon water to the sugar when it is straw-colored. Cook, stirring, for 8 to 10 minutes. Cool; when hardened, crack, then roll into small pieces. Use for sprinkling over cakes, into puddings, and as flavorings in many other desserts to add a stylish touch.

To burn sugar for coloring: heat 1 cup granulated sugar over low heat until black and smoky. Add, drop by drop, 1 cup boiling water. Stir over low heat until completely dissolved. Use for coloring gravies. Can be stored indefinitely.

CARAMEL SYRUP

Put 1 cup sugar in a heavy skillet over low heat; stir constantly until it has melted to a brown liquid. When it bubbles over the entire surface, remove from heat; very slowly add 1 cup boiling water, stirring constantly. Pour into containers, and cool. Cover and store at room temperature. The syrup is now ready for use in the following recipes. Makes 1½ cups.

CARAMEL CAKE

½ cup shortening
1¼ cups sugar
¼ cup Caramel Syrup
2 cups sifted all-purpose flour
2 teaspoons baking powder
½ teaspoon salt
⅔ cup milk
2 eggs

Cream shortening; add 1 cup sugar gradually, beating until light and fluffy. Beat in syrup. Sift flour, baking powder, and salt, and add to creamed mixture alternately with milk. Beat for 3 minutes. Beat eggs until foamy; add remaining sugar and beat until there is a fine spongy foam. Stir into cake batter until blended. Bake in 2 greased and wax-paper-lined 8-inch layer-cake pans in preheated moderate oven (375°F.) for about 20 minutes.

CARAMEL TORTE

3 eggs, separated
½ cup sugar
¼ cup Caramel Syrup
6 tablespoons all-purpose flour
½ teaspoon baking powder
½ teaspoon salt
¼ teaspoon cream of tartar
⅓ cup chopped almonds
Whipped cream

Beat egg yolks until thick. Beat in ¼ cup sugar and syrup. Sift flour, baking powder, and salt, and stir in. Beat egg whites until foamy; add cream of tartar. Beat until whites begin to hold their shape. Gradually add remaining sugar and beat until stiff but not dry. Fold into first mixture. Add almonds. Pour into ungreased 9-inch layer-cake pan and bake in preheated moderate oven (350°F.) for about 25 minutes. Remove from pan and let cool; top with whipped cream.

Note: This torte will shrink somewhat as it cools.

CARAMEL SQUARES

¼ cup butter or margarine
1 cup sugar
2 eggs
1 cup sifted all-purpose flour
¼ teaspoon salt
1 teaspoon baking powder
¼ cup Caramel Syrup
¼ cup chopped nuts

Cream butter and sugar until light and fluffy. Add eggs and beat well. Sift together dry ingredients and add to creamed mixture alternately with syrup, beginning and ending with dry ingredients. Add nuts. Pour into greased and floured pan (9 x 9 x 2 inches) and bake in preheated slow oven (300°F.) for about 20 minutes. Cut into squares and let cool in pan.

CARAMEL FROSTING

⅓ cup Caramel Syrup
3 cups sugar
⅛ teaspoon salt
½ cup light or dark corn syrup
1 cup heavy cream or undiluted evaporated milk
2 tablespoons butter or margarine

Put caramel syrup, sugar, salt, corn syrup, and cream in saucepan. Bring to a boil and cook, stirring, until 235°F. registers on a candy thermometer, or until a small amount of syrup dropped into very cold water forms a soft ball. Let cool to lukewarm (110°F.). Add butter. Beat at low speed with an electric mixer, or by hand, until slightly creamy. At this stage, the frosting has not completely crystallized and has the consistency of thick syrup. *Refrigerate for 6 to 8 hours before using.* Makes about 3 cups.

■ **To use**—Put frosting needed in top part of double boiler over boiling water to soften. Stir constantly and remove as soon as it reaches spreading consistency (should not take more than 2 minutes). **Note:** This frosting may curdle, especially if made with evaporated milk, but it blends together when beaten. Frosting can be stored in a covered container in refrigerator for several weeks.

SWEDISH CARAMEL CUSTARD

1 cup and 3 tablespoons sugar
3 tablespoons boiling water
6 eggs
¼ teaspoon salt
2½ cups milk
1 cup light cream
1 tablespoon vanilla extract
Toasted slivered blanched almonds

Melt 1 cup sugar in skillet over low heat, stirring until lightly browned. Add boiling water and heat, stirring, until syrup forms. Pour into 1½-quart baking dish, turning dish to coat bottom and sides. Break eggs into a large bowl; add 3 tablespoons sugar and the salt; beat until frothy. Add milk, cream, and vanilla and beat until thoroughly mixed. Pour mixture into syrup-coated dish. Set on rack in pan of hot water (water should be about 1 inch below rim of dish). Bake in preheated slow oven (300°F.) for 1½ hours, or until set (knife should come out clean when inserted in middle of custard). Cool on rack; then chill. Unmold in deep serving dish, allowing sauce to run over custard. Garnish with almonds. Makes 8 servings.

CARAWAY (Carum carvi)—This oval-shape brown seed was named after the ancient district of Caria in Asia Minor, demonstrating once more the antiquity of food seasonings. The caraway plant grows to a height of about two feet, with lovely feathery green leaves and yellow-white flowers that resemble Queen Anne's Lace. It is widely cultivated and grows well from Bulgaria to Morocco, Russia to Japan, and in various parts of the United States. Caraway has become one of the commonest field herbs in Maine, brought there by German settlers in the 18th century.

A most ancient herb, caraway was known to the Neolithic Swiss Lake Dwellers. Its medicinal properties were mentioned in the Medical Papyrus of Thebes, dating from 1552 B.C. Greeks and Romans appreciated its culinary values as well. Caraway was cultivated in the 8th century gardens of Charlemagne. This aromatic herb seems never to have lost favor. Cooks of the Middle Ages used the feathery leaves in soups and salads and the seeds in breads and sweetmeats. Tasty, good for the stomach, it also "restoreth hair where it has fallen away." Shakespeare, in the second part of Henry IV, speaks about "a dish of caraways." The Germanic and Slavic peoples, in particular, have always greatly favored the seed.

The uses of caraway are as varied today as they were hundreds of years ago. Fresh young leaves add a delicious flavor to soups, salads, cheeses, vegetables, and meat, especially pork. The roots may be steamed and eaten as a vegetable. Caraway seeds are used to season soups, meats, vegetables, breads such as rye, cakes, and pastries. Oil extracted from the seed provides the distinctive flavor of the liqueur kümmel.

CARAWAY PORK CHOPS

2 teaspoons crushed caraway seeds
1 teaspoon ground sage
½ teaspoon garlic salt
⅛ teaspoon salt
¼ teaspoon pepper
4 large pork chops
　Water
½ cup dry white wine

Combine herbs and seasonings. Rub mixture on both sides of chops and put chops in skillet. Pour water over chops to cover. Cook, covered, over low heat for about 1 hour. When the water has evaporated, chops will begin to brown. Turn several times until browned on all sides. When chops are browned, add wine. Bring to boil and remove from heat. Put chops in heated serving dish; pour sauce over top. Makes 4 servings.

OVEN BEEF GOULASH

2 pounds boneless beef chuck
1 teaspoon salt
¼ teaspoon pepper
1 teaspoon seasoned salt
1 teaspoon paprika
¼ cup all-purpose flour
2 tablespoons fat
2 cups water
1 tablespoon Worcestershire
1 garlic clove, minced
1 teaspoon powdered mustard
1 bay leaf
1 teaspoon caraway seeds
1 tablespoon cider vinegar

Cut beef into 1-inch cubes. Mix next 5 ingredients. Dredge beef with the mixture and brown on all sides in hot fat in skillet. Put beef in 2-quart casserole. Sprinkle with remaining flour, if any. Add remaining ingredients, cover, and bake in preheated moderate oven (350° F.) for 2 hours. Serve with rice or noodles. Makes 6 servings.

CARAWAY COTTAGE OR CREAM CHEESE

1 cup cottage or cream cheese
2 tablespoons light or heavy cream
½ teaspoon salt
1½ teaspoons caraway seeds
⅛ teaspoon instant minced onion
　or onion salt
⅛ teaspoon cayenne

Blend cheese with cream until smooth. Add other ingredients and mix thoroughly. Serve as a salad or spread on dark bread. Makes about 1 cup.

CARAWAY OR SEED CAKE

2 cups sifted cake flour
½ teaspoon salt
½ teaspoon ground mace
1 cup butter
1 cup sugar
3 eggs, separated
2 tablespoons caraway seeds

Sift together flour, salt, and mace. Cream butter until soft. Gradually beat in sugar, about 2 tablespoons at a time. Beat in egg yolks, one at a time, beating well after each addition. Beat egg whites until they stand in stiff peaks. Fold into batter. Add flour, beating only until absorbed in batter. Stir in caraway seeds. Turn into greased and floured loaf pan (9 x 5 x 3 inches). Bake in preheated moderate oven (350°F.) for 45 to 50 minutes, or until cake tests clean. Cool on rack. Serve cut into very thin slices.

CARBONATED—The term is applied to beverages made sparkling, bubbling, or fizzing by charging them under pressure with a gas called carbon dioxide. Soda water is the best known carbonated beverage. The term does not apply when the gas is produced within the beverage itself by the natural process of fermentation.

Carbonated beverages are flavored by syrups, cola, spices, and aromatic roots. Some are heavily sugared, others are made with low-calorie sugar substitutes. All carbonated beverages enjoy enormous popularity with old and young. Flavorful carbonated beverages can be served with ice cream as sodas, with fruit juices in punches, with fruit garnishes, with sherbet, with flavored syrups, or as a mixer for alcoholic beverages.

CARDAMOM (Elettaria cardamomum)

—The plant grows to a height of eight to twelve feet, and the seeds which we use as a flavoring grow in groups within a pod that resembles a capsule. The capsules are sun-dried and marketed whole. The cardamom is a native of India and is used as a seasoning, but the name is also given to the seeds of other species that grow in Asia, Africa, and the Pacific Islands. These are more bitter in taste and serve as a substitute for pepper.

Cardamom is said to be the world's second most precious spice, the costliest one being saffron. An acre of land will yield only about 250 pounds of cardamoms, and their harvesting requires a good deal of hand labor.

Cardamom seeds are brown, and they have an aromatic odor and a warm, spicy taste. They turn up in curries and in such meats as frankfurters and sausages, in pickling-spice blends, and in baked foods. The spice is sold either whole in the form of bleached white pods, or ground.

Cardamoms have been used in the western world for at least 2,000 years. The word is Greek, and Dioscorides, the Greek authority on medicinal herbs (41-68 A.D.), mentions them as the best of a group of aromata.

Cardamom is the spice preferred in Scandinavia where it is used in a most imaginative manner, especially at Christmas time, in spiced cakes, sweet pastries, and cookies as well as in ground meat dishes. In India, it is an age-old practice to chew cardamom seeds like candy. In drug preparations the pleasant flavor of the seed is used to cover up the taste of certain medicines.

Whole cardamom pods must be crushed before using. When they are to be added to such dishes as soups, curries, or stews, the crushed outer shell pieces of the pod need not be removed. They will disintegrate and disappear during the cooking.

When whole cardamom is to be used in baking, it is advisable to pick out the little black seeds from the crushed outer shell and crush these seeds as well. All the crushing can be done either in a mortar and pestle, or by placing either pods or seeds in a paper bag or between two sheets of wax paper and pounding them with the back of a plate, a rolling pin, or a mallet or hammer.

One word of caution: use cardamom with a light hand since a little goes a long way. Also, it should not be stored for too long since it rapidly loses its flavor.

CURRIED LAMB, INDIAN STYLE

    3 tablespoons instant minced onion
    3 tablespoons water
    2 tablespoons shortening or salad oil
    1 tablespoon ground coriander seed
    ¾ teaspoon ground cuminseed
    ½ teaspoon each of ground cardamom, tumeric, and ginger
    ¼ teaspoon instant garlic powder
    ⅛ teaspoon each of ground red and black pepper
    1 cinnamon stick
    1½ pounds boneless lean lamb stew meat
    1¼ cups water
    ¾ teaspoon salt
    ¼ cup tomato puree
    2 tablespoons yogurt

Soak onion in 3 tablespoons water for 5 minutes. Heat shortening in a skillet. Add onions and spices and sauté for 5 minutes, or until onions are limp and transparent. Trim excess fat from the lamb, cut into 1-inch cubes, and add. Cook lamb until lightly browned, about 10 to 15 minutes, over moderate heat. Add water, salt, and tomato purée and blend with mixture. Simmer for 30 to 40 minutes, or until sauce has thickened. Add yogurt just before removing from heat. Serve with hot cooked rice and chutney. Makes 4 servings.

PEAS AND RICE PILAF

    1½ cups long-grain rice
    2 tablespoons butter or margarine
    1 cinnamon stick
    3 cardamom pods, cracked
    4 peppercorns
    4 whole cloves
    3 cups boiling water
    1½ teaspoons salt
    ½ cup frozen peas
    ¼ teaspoon instant minced garlic
    1 tablespoon yogurt

Wash rice and soak for 30 minutes in water to cover. Drain. Melt butter in a saucepan. Add cinnamon. Tie cardamom pods, peppercorns, and cloves in a cloth bag, and add. Sauté spices until butter begins to brown. Add drained rice. Stir and cook until rice is dry and begins to stick to bottom of pan. Add boiling water and salt. Stir only once. Cook, uncovered, in a casserole or ovenproof dish in preheated moderate oven (350°F.) for 25 minutes, or until rice has absorbed all the water. Combine peas, instant minced garlic, and yogurt. Add to rice and toss lightly with a fork. Cover and return to oven, cook for 15 minutes in a very slow oven (250°F.). Serve hot. Makes 6 servings.

QUICK CARDAMOM CAKE

    1 cup sugar
    3 eggs
    1 cup butter or margarine, melted
    3 cups all-purpose flour
    1 teaspoon baking powder
    ½ to ¾ teaspoon ground cardamom
    3 tablespoons sugar
    ½ cup chopped nuts.

Beat sugar into eggs, a little at a time. Beat well after each addition. Add melted butter and beat until batter is light-colored, about 3 minutes with electric blender at medium speed, or 5 minutes by hand. Sift together flour, baking powder, and cardamom. Gradually stir flour mixture into batter. Grease a baking pan (15 x 10 x 1 inch). Spread dough to ½-inch thickness in pan. Sprinkle top with sugar and nuts. Bake in preheated moderate oven (350°F.) for 25 minutes, or until lightly browned. Cool, and cut into squares. Makes about 48 squares.

CARDAMOM SUGAR

It is delicious sprinkled over baked apples and cooked or fresh-fruit compotes. Combine ⅛ to ¼ teaspoon ground cardamom with ½ cup sugar in jar and shake well to blend. Or whirl together in electric blender ¼ teaspoon ground cardamom and ½ cup sugar.

CARDOON

—This thistlelike, silvery-green, prickly plant is closely related to the artichoke but it looks more like an outsize stalk of celery since its average length is four to five feet. Cardoons are grown for the leafy midribs of the plant, which are fleshy and tender. The flavor is delicate and resembles that of the artichoke and the oyster plant.

Cardoons are a favorite French and Italian winter vegetable. In America, they are grown in California, mostly for Italian markets. They are well worth eating and easy to prepare. However they are to be served, they must be boiled first.

Basic Preparation—Remove tough outer stalks and wilted stalks. Strip tender inner stalks free of leaves. Cut them into three-inch pieces and remove stringy parts. Trim heart and cut into pieces. Drop at once into acidulated cold water (water with lemon juice or vinegar) to keep pieces from turning dark. Cook in boiling salted water over moderate heat until tender. Drain. Serve with melted butter and a little lemon juice or with a white sauce, a tomato sauce, or with hollandaise.

They can also be sautéed in olive oil, or dipped into egg yolk and bread crumbs and fried in deep fat.

Caribbean Stews

by Shirley Sarvis

Concentrate on a Caribbean stew and you have the air of festivity innate in a foreign menu. You have the excitement of a new taste. You have the drama and color of tropical foods. You have almost the total menu in one dish.

Just a stew can stage all this because the stews of the Caribbean are exceptional and exotic. They are, for good reason. For the cuisine on each island is a culinary compilation of native dishes with the foods of whatever peoples crossed that island in the course of colonizing history: perhaps Dutch, Portuguese, British, French, Danish, Spanish, African, Indian, Chinese. The resulting stews are understandably unusual, combining strangely pleasing mixtures of fruits, meats, vegetables, and spices.

We have selected four such stews, each from a different Caribbean isle, as the focal point for a Caribbean Stew Party, a late supper, or informal dinner.

Choose any one for your party. Each is well suited to party giving, particularly when the hostess is the cook. Each stew is a hearty one-dish meal. You add only rice or bread, sometimes salad, to complete the major part of the meal. Dessert is concise and simple and served with dark-roast coffee, cream, and sugar. If you wish, serve rum cocktails before the meal and a favorite appropriate wine or beer with it; however Caribbeans would most likely have only before-dinner rum cocktails and offer water with the meal.

Each stew can be prepared almost entirely ahead of time and is adaptable to large or small groups. You can multiply or divide the following recipes to suit your needs. Each recipe is authentic in origin, but available ingredients replace Caribbean specialties which are difficult to purchase in the United States.

You can easily set the scene and atmosphere for your Caribbean party with brightly colored table linens and table decorations of vivid flowers and tropical fruits; bananas, pineapples, papaya, oranges, limes, grapefruit, mangoes, coconuts. For background music, play recordings of steel bands or calypso or Latin meringues.

◆◆◆ CHICKEN SANCOCHO ◆◆◆
(From the Dominican Republic)

Sancocho, often considered the national dish of the Dominican Republic, is presented in many forms. This Chicken *Sancocho* calls for chicken as the basic meat while other versions might use pork or beef. When served, each person has a wide soup-bowl serving, including a portion of chicken, ham, each vegetable, and plenty of broth, accompanied with an avocado and tomato salad on one side and an individual casserole of white rice on another. Part of the ritual of eating the stew is cutting the avocado into bites and dipping it into the stew broth.

CHICKEN SANCOCHO
AVOCADO-TOMATO SALAD
STEAMED WHITE RICE
GUAVA PASTE OR JAM
CHEESE
SESAME-TOPPED CRACKERS

CHICKEN SANCOCHO

For simplest party preparation, we suggest that several hours before the party, you assemble the stew, cook it for the first 30 minutes, and prepare the vegetables. In time for serving, add vegetables and finish cooking.

1 large onion, finely chopped
¼ cup butter or margarine
1 large fresh tomato, peeled, seeded, and chopped
2 frying chickens (about 3 pounds each), cut into pieces
Salt and pepper
½ pound lean boneless smoked ham, cut into ¾-inch cubes
2 cups water
2 garlic cloves, minced or mashed
1 bay leaf
¾ teaspoon crumbled dried oregano
½ teaspoon monosodium glutamate
2 medium-size white potatoes, peeled and cut into ½-inch crosswise slices
About ⅔ pound winter squash, peeled and cut into ¾-inch slices
3 medium-size carrots, peeled and cut into pieces about 4 inches long, ½ inch thick
About 1 teaspoon salt
About ½ teaspoon pepper
3 tablespoons chopped fresh parsley

In a large kettle sauté onion in butter until limp. Add tomato. Sprinkle chicken pieces with salt and generously with pepper. Place in kettle. Add ham, water, garlic, bay leaf, oregano, and monosodium glutamate. Stir gently. Cover and simmer for 30 minutes. Add potatoes, squash, and carrots; cover and simmer for 30 minutes more, or until chicken and vegetables are tender. Taste broth and add salt and pepper to taste. Add parsley and simmer for 5 minutes more. Serve in heated wide soup bowls, arranging in each bowl a portion of chicken, ham, potato, squash, and carrot. Makes 6 servings.

AVOCADO-TOMATO SALAD

Line chilled salad plates with crisp salad greens. Arrange on each plate 2 or 3 thick slices of tomato and thick lengthwise slices of avocado. Sprinkle with salt, coarsely ground black pepper, and fresh lemon juice. Garnish with a thin lemon wedge.

STEAMED WHITE RICE

Steam long-grain white rice. Season with butter. Serve in individual heated casseroles or rice bowls. Garnish each with a strip of red pimiento.

GUAVA AND CHEESE DESSERT

Arrange on each dessert plate several sesame-topped crackers, a generous slice of guava paste (available in Puerto Rican, Spanish, and Mexican food stores and in some specialty food shops), and several slices of mellow natural light-colored cheese (California's Monterey Jack or Teleme are similar to the local cheese of the Dominican Republic, or use Muenster, Edam, or cream cheese). Serve with cheese. or fruit knives. If guava paste is not available, you could assemble the cheese-and-crackers before serving, topping each cracker with a slice or spreading of cheese and a deep layer of chilled guava jelly.

◆◆◆ STEW SHRIMP ◆◆◆
(From Trinidad)

Out of perhaps the most cosmopolitan of all the cities of the Caribbean comes this fresh-tasting, delicate stew. Almost paradoxically, it is a simple dish, honoring the indigenous and utterly fresh foods of the island rather than any of the exotic foods from far-off parts of the world imported to the busy Port of Spain.

As the name indicates, the shrimps delicately "stew" with butter to a pungent juiciness. You serve them with brown rice cooked just-tender, so the grains are completely separate.

STEW SHRIMP
GINGER BROWN RICE
WATERCRESS SALAD BOWL
FRENCH BREAD AND BUTTER
(OPTIONAL)
BROWN-SUGARED ROASTED
FRESH COCONUT BITES

STEW SHRIMP

2 pounds large raw shrimps, shelled and deveined
3 tablespoons fresh lime juice
1 large sweet onion, very thinly sliced
2 medium-size tomatoes, peeled, seeded,.and diced
1 large garlic clove, minced or mashed
1 tablespoon finely snipped chives
½ teaspoon each of salt and crumbled dried thyme
Dried crushed red pepper to taste (begin with ¼ teaspoon)
⅛ teaspoon ground black pepper
¼ cup butter or salad oil
½ teaspoon each of monosodium glutamate and curry powder

Sprinkle shrimps with lime juice and toss to mix. Add onion, tomatoes, garlic, chives, salt, thyme, red pepper, and black pepper. Toss gently to mix well. Allow to marinate for 30 minutes at room temperature, or for 1 to 3 hours covered and chilled. Just in time for serving, melt butter in a large frying pan. Stir in monosodium glutamate and curry. Add shrimps with marinating mixture. Cover and cook over medium heat just until shrimps turn pink and onion is slightly wilted, about 8 minutes; turn shrimps and stir gently once or twice. Serve immediately over Ginger Brown Rice. Makes 6 servings.

GINGER BROWN RICE

Cook long-grain brown rice just until tender, using chicken stock for the liquid, and seasoning with 1½ teaspoons grated fresh gingerroot or 1 teaspoon ground ginger and ¼ teaspoon pepper for each cup of uncooked rice.

WATERCRESS SALAD BOWL

Break tender crisp salad greens into salad bowl. Add a generous proportion of crisp sprigs of watercress and thin tomato wedges. Toss lightly with a mellow French dressing made simply of oil, vinegar, fresh lime juice, salt, pepper, dry mustard, and a pinch of sugar.

BROWN-SUGARED ROASTED FRESH COCONUT BITES

Cut the meat, with brown skin, from a fresh ripe coconut into bite-size triangles. Place, white side up, on baking sheet. Broil, about 3 inches from heat, just until edges turn light brown. Dot with butter. Sprinkle with raw sugar or brown sugar. Return to broiler just until butter and sugar melt. Arrange about 6 coconut triangles in a ring on each dessert plate. Eat with fingers.

♦♦♦ BANANA STOBA ♦♦♦
(From Curaçao)

In native form, this stew would be built upon the broth and flavors of smoke-cured pigs' feet or pigs' tails; the "bananas" would be both bananalike (but starchy) plantains and the sweet eating bananas we know. *Funchi*, a cornmeal-mushlike dish seemingly ever-present in local Curaçaoan cuisine, would be the accompaniment.

For a party here, we make the stew with meaty ham hocks, long simmered to tenderness and served to resemble individual little plump hams—one or two to a person. We use ripe but firm bananas, and *funchi* becomes crispy cubes of cheesed cornmeal floating in the stew broth as croutons.

BANANA STOBA
CHEESE-CORNMEAL CROUTONS
GREEN-PEPPER STRIPS
GINGERED FRESH PINEAPPLE

BANANA STOBA

Purchase meaty ham hocks for this stew, and ask your meatman to saw each into two or three serving pieces. You can make the stew as far ahead of time on the day of your party, or the day before, as you wish. Just be sure to add the vegetables only in time to cook to tenderness.

About 4 pounds smoked ham hock, cut into serving pieces
About 2 quarts cold water
1 whole onion, peeled
5 whole cloves
¼ teaspoon each of dried thyme and pepper
3 medium-size white potatoes, peeled and quartered
3 medium-size sweet potatoes or yams, peeled and cut into 1-inch crosswise slices
Salt (optional)
4 ripe but firm bananas, peeled and cut into 2-inch lengths
⅓ cup sliced green onions

Wash ham hock pieces and place in large kettle. Pour over ham enough cold water to cover. Stud onion with cloves and add to kettle along with thyme and pepper. Cover. Heat until boiling; reduce heat; simmer for about 1¼ hours. (At this point you could cool stew, chill, remove fat on top; reheat and add vegetables to cook before the party.) Add potatoes and simmer for 40 minutes more, or until vegetables are tender; skim off any excess fat on top of broth. Taste broth; add salt if needed. Add banana pieces and green onions and simmer for 5 minutes more, or until heated through. Serve immediately with a portion of all stew ingredients in each large shallow soup or stew bowl, or serve ham hock on a plate alongside the bowl of broth and vegetables. Pass Cheese-Cornmeal Croutons for each person to add to soup broth. Makes 6 generous servings.

CHEESE-CORNMEAL CROUTONS

You can make and mold the cornmeal mush, preparatory to making it into croutons, a day ahead. Brown the cubed cornmeal in butter before the party. Reheat in the oven in time to serve.

Combine in a saucepan ⅔ cup each of cold water and white or yellow cornmeal and ¾ teaspoon salt. Stir in 2 cups boiling water. Cook, stirring, until mixture thickens and boils. Reduce heat, cover, and cook over low heat for 10 minutes; stir frequently. Turn into a buttered loaf pan (about 5 x 9 inches). Chill until firm. Cut into 1-inch cubes. Coat each cube with flour. Sauté in butter until brown and crisp on all sides. Before serving, heap into heatproof serving bowl, sprinkle generously with shredded natural cheese (Edam, Gouda, or mild Cheddar). Place in oven or under broiler to heat and melt cheese. Makes croutons for 6 generous stew servings.

GREEN-PEPPER STRIPS

Pass a relish plate of cold and crisp green-pepper strips garnished with whole cherry tomatoes.

GINGERED FRESH PINEAPPLE

Generously sprinkle chunks or thin slices of fresh pineapple with chopped candied or preserved gingerroot. Chill for 1 hour or more. Serve chunks in stemmed sherbet glasses or overlapping thin slices on chilled dessert plates.

♦♦♦ CUCUMBER LAMB ♦♦♦
(From Aruba)

This second island in the Antillean chain consistently offers *funchi* with its stew, too. But we find the character of cornmeal more appealing in toasted golden corn bread, served as toast points beneath the stew and as bread accompaniment.

This is a meaty stew; lamb cubes richly flavored in juices of sautéed onion, celery, garlic, and sweet and hot peppers. To "cool" the spicy hotness of the stew, you blend in shredded fresh cucumbers just before serving. Garnish the stew generously with overlapping paper-thin cucumber slices and a fat tomato wedge alongside so the garnish makes the salad. Serve guava jelly both as a stew condiment and a spread for toasted corn bread; its fruit sweetness also serves to counter the hotness of the stew.

ARUBA CUCUMBER LAMB
CUCUMBER GARNISH
TOMATO WEDGES
CRISP GOLDEN CORN POINTS
GUAVA JELLY
BANANAS IN RUM CUSTARD SAUCE
LACE PRALINE

ARUBA CUCUMBER LAMB

You can make this stew as far ahead as the day before the party, if you wish, and reheat it in time to serve. Because fresh and dried hot chilies vary in their degree of hotness, you must add them according to taste. Begin with a very small amount and taste broth during cooking, adding more hot peppers as needed to make the stew just hot enough to be pleasing.

3 pounds lean boneless lamb shoulder, cut into 1½-inch cubes
Salt and pepper
3 tablespoons salad oil
2 medium onions, thinly sliced
2 celery stalks, finely chopped
1 green pepper, finely chopped
Finely minced fresh hot chilies or crushed dried red pepper to taste
2 garlic cloves, minced or mashed
⅜ teaspoon ground black pepper
About 1½ cups water
2 cucumbers, peeled, seeded, and shredded
1 cucumber, peeled in alternating lengthwise strips and sliced paper-thin
Tomato wedges

Season meat with salt and pepper. In a large kettle brown meat cubes well on all sides in salad oil. Remove meat and set aside. Discard from kettle any oil in

Aruba
Cucumber
Lamb

excess of 3 tablespoons. Add to kettle onions, celery, green pepper, and fresh hot chilies (if you use them); sauté until limp. Return meat to kettle along with crushed dried red pepper (if you use it, begin seasoning by adding ⅜ teaspoon), garlic, black pepper, and water. Cover and simmer for 2 hours, or until meat is very tender. If necessary, add water, a few tablespoons at a time, during cooking. Taste and add salt and more hot chilies or crushed red pepper if necessary. Just before serving, stir in shredded cucumber; heat through. Serve stew over Crisp Golden Corn Points. Garnish each serving with a line of overlapping cucumber slices and a tomato wedge. Makes 6 servings.

CRISP GOLDEN CORN POINTS
Make the corn bread ahead, cool, split, and butter; at serving time, broil-toast it.

Beat 2 eggs in a mixing bowl. Stir in 1 cup milk, ¼ cup melted butter, and 1 cup yellow cornmeal. Sift together into mixing bowl 1 cup all-purpose flour, 2 tablespoons sugar, 4 teaspoons baking powder, and 1 teaspoon salt. Mix just to blend. Pour into buttered baking pan (about 9 x 13 inches). Bake in preheated hot oven (400°F.) for 20 minutes, or until golden on top and browned at edges. Allow to cool. Cut into diamond shapes. Split; spread cut surfaces with butter. Before serving, slip under broiler to toast. Makes corn-bread points to accompany 6 stew servings.

BANANAS IN RUM CUSTARD SAUCE
Make the rum custard sauce far enough ahead so it can chill thoroughly; assemble desserts at serving time.

Beat together thoroughly in top of double boiler 4 egg yolks, 2 cups half-and-half (half milk and half cream), ¼ cup sugar, and ¼ teaspoon salt. Cook over hot water, stirring, until mixture thickens slightly and coats a silver spoon. Strain custard, add 1 tablespoon dark rum and 1 teaspoon vanilla, allow to cool, cover, and chill. At serving time, ladle over 6 thinly sliced bananas in 6 stemmed dessert glasses. Sprinkle generously with Lace Praline. Makes 6 servings.

LACE PRALINE
Thickly butter a chilled baking sheet. Sprinkle with ⅛- to ¼-inch layer of brown sugar rubbed through a strainer. Broil about 6 inches beneath heat until sugar bubbles; watch carefully. Cool until candy hardens slightly. Loosen and ease off sheet with a flexible spatula. Cool thoroughly. Break into large pieces and sprinkle over bananas in sauce.

CARP—*Cyprinus carpio,* to give the scaly freshwater fish its ichthyological name, is a native of Asia that came to this country via Europe during the last century. It is a robust fish that thrives almost anywhere, preferring muddy waters. Carp in the United States reaches a length of two feet and may weigh as much as forty pounds. One of the hardiest and wiliest of fishes, carp is able to withstand extremes of temperature and lives to the ripe old fish age of twenty to forty years, but not to hundreds of years, as legend has it. Unfortunately the presence of carp in a lake or river tends to stir up mud, making the water uninhabitable for other fish.

Carp has been prized in Europe for hundreds of years, acquiring through the years a distinguished literary background. It still is one of the favorite fishes of French, Central European, and Slavic cooking. The monasteries of the Middle Ages all had their carp ponds, and so did the great French and English estates of the 17th and 18th centuries. In Europe's Catholic countries, carp is the traditional fish of the fast days preceding great holidays, such as Christmas and Easter.

The best time for eating carp is from November until April. In the summer they tend to develop a muddy flavor. Skinning the fish and soaking it in mild salt water helps remove this muddiness. The younger, smaller fish (up to seven pounds) are the best eating. They may be fried (if two to three pounds), poached, or baked.

Purchasing Guide—Carp is usually sold whole, weighing 2 to 8 pounds, or in fillets. Look for fish with pink gills, tight shiny scales, a bright skin, and firm flesh.

Storage—Fresh fish is very perishable and should be used within two days of purchase. Wrap cleaned and dressed fish in moisture-proof paper or place in a tightly covered dish and refrigerate immediately.

Nutritive Food Values—Carp is a lean fish. Fish is a good source of protein and contains iron, calcium, and B vitamins.
☐ 3½ ounces, raw = 115 calories

Basic Preparation—Rinse fish quickly in cold salted water. Let stand in ice water for 30 minutes to remove muddy flavor. Fresh carp may be baked, poached, stewed, or fried. Cook fish at low or moderately high temperatures, until it flakes easily with a fork. Handle fish carefully to prevent it from falling apart. If fish is overcooked it will become dry and tough.

CARP CASSEROLE
2 garlic cloves
1 tablespoon butter
1 medium onion, thinly sliced
½ lemon, sliced
2 bay leaves, crumbled
1 tablespoon chopped chives
1 tablespoon chopped parsley
1 3- to 4-pound carp, cut into large pieces
1 teaspoon salt
½ teaspoon pepper
1 pint beer
1 tablespoon butter
1 tablespoon all-purpose flour
⅛ teaspoon ground cloves
Dash of hot pepper sauce

Rub casserole with garlic and grease with butter. Place onion, lemon slices, bay leaves, chives, and parsley on bottom of casserole. Top with carp. Sprinkle fish with salt and pepper. Pour beer over fish. Bring to a quick boil. Simmer, covered, over low heat for 25 to 30 minutes. Remove fish to hot serving platter and keep hot. Strain pan liquid. Knead butter and flour together into balls the size of a pea. Reheat strained pan liquid and drop butter-flour balls into liquid, stirring constantly. Add cloves and hot pepper sauce. Cook, stirring all the time, until sauce is smooth and thickened. Pour over fish. Makes 4 servings.

CARROT—Carrots have been cultivated for over 2,000 years and have a long and honored history. The Greeks and Romans ate them in stews or as a vegetable. Elizabethan England adored them, and not only as food, for when they were first introduced there women adorned their hair with the wispy, fernlike leaves of the carrot. Virginia saw carrots first in 1609, and New England in 1629.

Carrots are not only very healthy fare, but also convenient vegetables since they store well and combine excellently with practically all slow-cooking foods. They are at their best when young, slender, and tender. Tiny, freshly picked baby carrots, eaten either raw or briefly cooked in butter, are a true gourmet's delight.

Availability—All year round. Major crops from California, Texas, Arizona, Florida.

Purchasing Guide—Look for firm, smooth, well-shaped, bright-colored carrots. Harvested slightly before maturity, carrots are washed and sorted for commercial use. Cracked carrots are discarded. Most of the crop is sold bunched, with tops removed, or in film bags holding 1 to 1¼ pounds each. When buying carrots with tops, look for tops that are fresh and green. The fall crop keeps well in cold storage until late spring.

☐ 1 pound, raw = 2½ cups, cooked
☐ 1 pound, raw = 4 cups, shredded, raw

Storage—Remove tops, if intact; rinse carrots, then place in plastic bags or wrap in aluminum foil and store in the refrigerator.

☐ Fresh, refrigerator shelf or vegetable compartment: 1 to 4 weeks
☐ Fresh, refrigerator frozen-food compartment, prepared for freezing: 2 to 3 months
☐ Fresh, freezer, prepared for freezing: 1 year
☐ Canned, kitchen shelf: 1 year
☐ Canned, refrigerator shelf, opened and covered: 4 to 5 days

Nutritive Food Values—Carrots are one of the best sources of vitamin A, which is necessary for good eyesight and good bone formation. Carrots also contain small amounts of other vitamins and minerals.

☐ 3½ ounces, raw = 42 calories

Basic Preparation—Scrub well with a stiff brush. Young carrots need no scraping; they may be cooked in their skins. Mature carrots should be scraped with a vegetable parer. Cut into lengthwise strips, round slices, dice, or leave whole. Cooking time: whole, 20 to 30 minutes; quartered or sliced, 15 to 20 minutes; diced, 10 to 15 minutes; shredded, 5 to 10 minutes.

☐ **To Cook, Whole or in Strips**—Carrots cooked whole or cut into strips lose fewer nutrients in cooking than those that are sliced or diced. Have 1 inch of water boiling in a saucepan. Add carrots and ½ teaspoon salt per cup of water. Cover. Cook until tender; remove cover and continue cooking for a few minutes to reduce liquid. Season; add butter and serve with or without the carrot liquid.

☐ **To Cook, Shredded**—Put 2 to 3 tablespoons of water in a saucepan. Add shredded carrots and cover. Bring quickly to a boil, then lower the heat and cook until tender. Season with salt and pepper; add butter. Serve with or without the carrot liquid.

☐ **To Bake, Whole**—Whole carrots may also be baked with roast meats. Boil carrots first until just tender. Place them in baking pan 30 to 45 minutes before the meat is done. They will be glazed and browned and taste delicious.

☐ **To Freeze**—Choose young tender carrots. Remove tops and scrape. Slice or dice. Blanch in boiling water for 2 minutes. Chill in cold water for 5 minutes. Drain. Pack in containers with ½-inch headspace. Cover.

HOW TO MAKE CARROT CURLS

1. Scrape carrot; then cut off a lengthwise slice that is ¼ to ½ inch thick at the top. This gives a broad flat surface with a generous showing of lighter-colored core.
2. Using a vegetable parer, cut thin strips from the flat surface, starting at the tip end. Strips sometimes curl themselves; if not, curl around finger and fasten with a toothpick.
3. Drop into cold water and refrigerate for several hours, or put in bowl of ice water for an hour; drain before serving. Attractive as a relish or garnish.
Note: The shape of carrots is important for making the curls uniform, so use large fat ones.

VEGETABLE DIP

¼ cup light cream
2 cups creamed cottage cheese
¼ cup minced raw carrots
¼ cup thinly sliced scallions
8 radishes, sliced very thinly
½ teaspoon salt
¼ teaspoon pepper

Combine all ingredients and chill before serving. Makes about 2¾ cups.

VEGETABLE-STUFFED FISH ROLLS

2 medium carrots, shredded
2 parsley sprigs, chopped
2 pimientos, chopped
2 green onions, chopped
2 cups stale white bread cubes
   Melted butter (about ⅓ cup)
   Salt and pepper
2 pounds fillet of sole

Mix together first 5 ingredients, ¼ cup melted butter, and salt and pepper to taste. Spread each fillet with some of mixture.

Roll fillets up from small end and secure with toothpicks. Put in shallow baking dish and brush with melted butter; sprinkle with salt and pepper. Bake in preheated moderate oven (375°F.) for 30 minutes, or until done. Makes 6 servings.

CARROT SOUFFLÉ

3 medium carrots
3 tablespoons butter or margarine
3 tablespoons all-purpose flour
1 cup milk
½ teaspoon salt
4 eggs, separated

Scrape and dice or slice carrots and cook in boiling salted water until just tender. Drain and mash or put through a fine sieve. Measure. You should have 1 generous cup of pulp. Melt butter in a skillet or in top part of a double boiler. Stir in flour, blending thoroughly. Slowly stir in milk, a little at a time. Cook over low heat, stirring constantly, until smooth and thickened. Add salt and let mixture cool slightly. Beat egg yolks until light and lemon-colored; add to cooled mixture. Add carrot pulp and blend. Beat egg whites until stiff but not dry. Fold half of beaten whites into carrot mixture thoroughly. Add remaining whites and fold in gently. Butter a 2-quart soufflé dish and fill with mixture. Bake in preheated moderate oven (375°F.) for 30 to 40 minutes, or until soufflé is puffed and lightly browned. Makes 4 servings.

DILLED CARROT STICKS

2 pounds carrots
   Salted water
1⅓ cups white vinegar
1⅓ cups water
½ teaspoon each of celery seed, caraway seed, and mustard seed
1 cup sugar
1 teaspoon coarse salt
½ teaspoon crushed hot peppers
1½ teaspoons dill seed

Wash and peel carrots and cut into thin sticks. Cook in a little boiling salted water for about 10 minutes, or until almost tender. Drain; pack carrots closely into hot sterilized pint jars. Combine remaining ingredients in a saucepan. Bring to a full rolling boil. After boiling for 2 minutes, pour syrup over carrots to overflowing and seal jars. Serve chilled with salads or sliced cold meat. Makes 4 pints.

BRAISED CARROTS AND CELERY

Wash and scrape 4 carrots; cut into chunks. Cook in a little boiling salted water for about 15 minutes. Drain. Cut celery stalks into 2-inch pieces. Measure 2 cups. Lightly brown carrots, celery, and 1 chopped small onion in 2 tablespoons butter. Add ¾ cup water and season with salt and pepper. Cover and cook until vegetables are tender. Uncover, to evaporate liquid. Sprinkle with chopped parsley. Makes 4 servings.

CREAMED CARROTS

Scrape 6 medium carrots and slice diagonally. Cook in a little boiling salted water until just tender, about 15 minutes. Drain, reserving any liquid for use in making sauce. Melt 2 tablespoons fat in a saucepan; remove from heat and stir in 2 tablespoons all-purpose flour. Mix 3 tablespoons nonfat dry milk with enough carrot liquid and water to make 1 cup milk. Add to saucepan. Return to heat. Cook over low heat, stirring constantly, until thickened. Add carrots and heat a little longer. Makes 4 to 6 servings.

CARROTS PARMESAN

Heat carrot strips. Drain and put in serving dish. Pour melted butter or margarine over them and sprinkle generously with grated Parmesan cheese.

CHEESE-GLAZED CARROTS

6 large carrots
  Salt
¼ cup honey
1 cup shredded American cheese

Peel carrots and cut into halves crosswise. Cook in a little boiling salted water until tender, about 15 minutes. Drain, dip each carrot half into honey. Place in baking dish; sprinkle with cheese. Bake in preheated hot oven (400°F.) for 10 minutes; or broil until cheese melts. Makes 6 servings.

ZANAHORIAS NATAS
(Braised Carrots)

Scrape 10 young carrots and cut into julienne strips. Braise slowly in 1 tablespoon butter until tender. Add ¼ teaspoon salt. Top with sour cream and chopped chives. Stir and serve. Serves 6.

GINGER CARROTS

6 medium carrots, scraped and
  cut into ½-inch slices
2 teaspoons fresh lemon juice
¾ teaspoon salt
½ teaspoon ground ginger
  Dash of pepper
2 tablespoons butter

Put carrots in buttered 1-quart casserole. Mix lemon juice and seasonings; pour over carrots and dot with butter. Cover and bake in preheated hot oven (400°F.) for 1 hour, or until carrots are tender. Makes 4 servings.

PANNED CARROTS AND ONIONS

¼ cup bacon fat or margarine
6 medium carrots, scraped and shredded
1 large onion, chopped
  Salt and pepper

Heat fat in skillet. Add carrots and onion; sprinkle with salt and pepper. Cover and cook over low heat, stirring occasionally, for 10 minutes, or until carrots are just tender. Makes 4 servings.

Oranged Carrots

Prepare as above. Use margarine or butter. Cut carrots into slices. Sprinkle with salt and pepper. Cover and cook as above for 15 minutes. Just before serving, add 2 navel oranges cut into sections, and 1 tablespoon brown sugar.

CARROTS WITH CELERY SEED

6 medium-size carrots
1 teaspoon butter
4 large lettuce leaves
½ teaspoon salt
½ teaspoon crumbled dried thyme
½ teaspoon celery seed
3 tablespoons dairy sour cream
  Salt and pepper

Wash and scrape carrots. Slice diagonally. Use butter to grease a small skillet. Line skillet with 2 lettuce leaves. Add carrots and salt. Top with remaining lettuce leaves. Cover pan and cook until the carrots are tender. Remove lettuce and add thyme and celery seed. Stir in sour cream and salt and pepper to taste. Reheat slightly and serve hot. Makes 4 to 6 servings.

CARROTS AND GLAZED APPLES

1 large onion, sliced
¼ cup butter or margarine
6 medium carrots, peeled
2½ cups (one 1-pound, 4-ounce can)
  apple slices, drained
¼ cup sugar
¼ teaspoon salt
¼ teaspoon ground sage
⅛ teaspoon ground nutmeg

Cook onion in butter for 5 minutes. Cut carrots crosswise into 4 pieces each. Add to onion mixture with remaining ingredients. Cover and cook over low heat for 1 hour, stirring occasionally. Serve with pork or other meats. Makes 6 servings.

CARROTS AND ASPARAGUS

Cook 2 cups sliced carrots until almost tender. Add 1 package (10 ounces) frozen cut asparagus; sprinkle with salt and pepper and cook until tender. Drain. Pour a little melted butter over vegetables and sprinkle with chopped parsley. Makes 4 to 6 servings.

CARROT-COCONUT SALAD

1 cup flaked coconut
1½ cups shredded raw carrots
¼ cup seedless raisins
2 tablespoons fresh lemon juice
1 cup (one 11-ounce can) mandarin
  oranges, drained
⅓ cup mayonnaise
  Salt to taste
  Salad greens

Mix all ingredients except greens. Chill and serve on greens. Makes 4 to 6 servings.

CARROT SLAW

Combine 2 cups shredded cabbage with 1 cup shredded carrot and a little chopped parsley. Toss with dressing made of ⅔ cup buttermilk, 1 tablespoon prepared horseradish, and salt and pepper to taste. Makes 4 to 6 servings.

CARROT AND RAISIN SALAD

Combine 2 cups shredded carrots with ½ cup seedless raisins. Moisten with mayonnaise or French dressing. Serve on lettuce. Makes 6 servings.

CARROT AND ONION TEA SANDWICHES

Grate raw carrots fine. Add a small amount of scraped onion and mayonnaise to moisten. Season to taste. Spread on small triangles or squares of buttered bread.

CARROT AND PEANUT-BUTTER SANDWICHES

Grate raw carrots fine to make ½ cup. Stir into 1 cup crunchy-style peanut butter. Use immediately. Spread on white or whole-wheat bread.

CARROT AND CORN PUDDING

2 tablespoons butter
2 tablespoons all-purpose flour
1 teaspoon each of salt and sugar
¼ teaspoon each of pepper and paprika
1 cup milk
1 tablespoon instant minced onion
1½ cups cooked or canned whole-kernel
  corn
1½ cups finely ground raw carrots
½ green pepper, ground
2 eggs, beaten

Melt butter in a saucepan over low heat. Blend in flour and seasonings. Gradually stir in milk; cook over low heat, stirring constantly, until thickened. Add remaining ingredients and mix well. Put in buttered 1½-quart casserole and bake in preheated moderate oven (350°F.) for about 45 minutes. Or divide among individual casseroles and bake for 30 minutes. Makes 6 servings.

STEAMED CARROT-WALNUT PUDDING

½ cup butter or margarine
1 cup sugar
3 eggs, separated
½ teaspoon ground cinnamon
½ teaspoon salt
1 cup soft stale bread crumbs
1 cup fine dry bread crumbs
½ cup raisins
1 cup coarsely chopped walnuts
2 cups mashed cooked carrots
  (7 medium)
2 teaspoons aromatic bitters
2 tablespoons heavy cream

Cream butter and sugar until light. Add egg yolks and remaining ingredients and beat until smooth. Fold in stiffly beaten egg whites. Put into two greased 3-cup molds or two 1-pound coffee cans. Cover tightly with mold lid or two thicknesses of foil. Put on rack in kettle. Add water, keeping water level well below top of molds. Cover kettle tightly. Bring water to boil and steam over medium or low heat for 1½ hours. Keep water boiling and check occasionally to see if more is needed. Cool, wrap, and freeze to keep. Reheat for 1½ hours to serve. Makes 12 servings.

Dilled Carrot Sticks ▼   Carrot and Raisin Salad ▲   Cheese-Glazed Carrots ▼

Note: Serve with whipped cream or hard sauce.

STEAMED CARROT PUDDING

1 cup coarse dried bread crumbs
1 cup firmly packed light brown sugar
½ cup all-purpose flour
1 teaspoon each of baking powder and baking soda
¾ teaspoon salt
1 teaspoon ground cinnamon
½ teaspoon each of ground allspice and nutmeg
1 egg
½ cup diced candied orange peel
1 cup golden raisins
1 cup grated scraped raw carrot
1 cup grated peeled raw potato
1 cup chopped peeled tart apple
½ cup butter or margarine

Combine all ingredients in order given; mix well. Pack into greased 1½-quart pudding mold. Cover and steam for 4 hours, or until done. Serve warm, topped with hard sauce and a few strips of candied orange peel, if desired. Makes 8 to 10 servings.

CARROT TORTE

4 eggs, separated
1 cup sugar
1 cup grated raw carrot
Grated rind of 1 lemon
Juice of ½ lemon
½ cup sifted all-purpose flour
1 teaspoon baking powder
¼ teaspoon salt
1 cup heavy cream, whipped

Beat yolks until thick and lemon-colored. Gradually beat in sugar, a few tablespoons at a time. Add carrot, lemon rind, and juice. Sift together dry ingredients and fold into yolk mixture. Beat egg whites until stiff but not dry and fold into first mixture. Pour into two ungreased 8-inch layer-cake pans. Bake in preheated moderate oven (350°F.) for 25 to 30 minutes. Remove from oven and let stand in pan until cold. Remove from pan; spread sweetened whipped cream between layers and on top.

CARROT-ORANGE COOKIES

1 cup shortening
¾ cup sugar
1 egg, unbeaten
1 cup mashed cooked carrots
1 teaspoon vanilla extract
2 cups sifted all-purpose flour
2 teaspoons baking powder
½ teaspoon salt
Orange Frosting

Cream shortening until light and fluffy. Gradually beat in sugar. Add egg, carrots, and vanilla; beat well after each addition. Sift together dry ingredients and combine with carrot mixture. Mix well. Drop batter by tablespoonfuls onto greased cookie sheets. Bake in preheated moderate oven (350°F.) for about 20 minutes. Remove to racks to cool. Frost with Orange Frosting while still warm. Makes about 4 dozen.

Orange Frosting

Combine juice of ½ orange, grated rind of 1 orange, 1 tablespoon butter, and

Zanahorias Natas ▼

about 1 cup sifted confectioners' sugar.

PICKLED CARROTS
1 pound carrots
1½ cups white vinegar
½ cup water
1 cup sugar
3 tablespoons mixed pickling spice

Wash and scrape carrots and cut into thin sticks. Cook carrots in a little boiling salted water for 10 minutes, or until almost tender. Drain. Combine remaining ingredients in a saucepan and simmer for 10 minutes; strain. Add carrot sticks; bring to a boil. After boiling for 2 minutes, pack carrots into hot sterilized jars. Pour syrup over carrots; seal. Makes about 2 pints.

CARROT-ALMOND CONSERVE
2 pounds carrots
4 cups water
2 lemons
4 cups sugar
½ teaspoon salt
1⅓ cups slivered blanched almonds

Wash and trim carrots and force through food chopper, using medium blade. Put in kettle with water and cook, covered, for 10 minutes, or until almost tender. Do not drain. Force lemons through food chopper and add to first mixture. Add sugar and salt; cook rapidly for 25 minutes, or until thick, stirring occasionally. Add almonds and pour into 8 hot sterilized ½-pint jars. Seal at once. Makes 8 jars.

CARVE—In culinary terms the word is used to describe the process of cutting meat, game, and poultry to serve at the table.

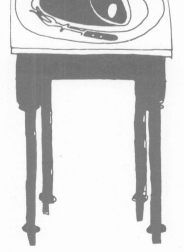

The Art of CARVING
by James A. Beard

Carving (in French *"decoupage"*) is the cutting or slicing of meat, fowl, and fish for the purposes of serving, presumably with a basic knowledge of anatomy and dexterity with the carving knife. This process, which is both a science and an art, has been an important part of food traditions around the world for centuries. From ancient times the Chinese habit of eating with chopsticks necessitated the cutting of food into neat strips and dice, and thus Chinese chefs and stewards became superb carvers, in both the sculptural and gastronomic sense —a skill which has been transmitted through generations. Cutting, in fact, is the first great lesson taught for cooking in Chinese or Japanese style. A visit to a *sushi* bar in Tokyo or New York or to a first-rate Chinese restaurant demonstrates the purveyor to be a master in the technique of beautiful cutting and carving, as well as arrangement.

In Elizabethan times the mistress of the household was elevated from social insignificance to a position of prestige when she was seated "above the salt" at table. Here, she carved for her lord and his guests, making certain that those at the exalted end of the table were elegantly plied with delicate slices of meat and fish. Later in history, noblemen were trained to carve at court, an accomplishment which added to one's honor. Later still, Louis Napoleon was renowned as an exceptional carver. In 1808, Grimod de la Reyniere, who was a fairly prolific writer on matters pertaining to good living, came forth with a small book of less than 120 pages on the fine art of dissecting meats, game, and fish at table, a treatise which had enormous influence on carving practices of the nineteenth century.

As late as Edwardian times, carving was an important part of family dining— normally a duty assigned to the head of the household, although I remember a neighboring family in my youth whose paterfamilias could not wield the carving knife deftly enough to suit his wife. As a result, all roasts had to be carved perfectly in the kitchen and reassembled before being brought to table. Papa only pretended to carve.

This story is in sharp contrast to the famous *Docteur* Becart in France who created a school of carving in which the bird or joint was impaled on a fork over a beautifully shaped bowl or shell and carved in midair, as it were, while the juices flowed into the container below—a marvelously surgical and showmanlike feat. Some few of Becart's followers are still practicing his art, and one encounters them in restaurants and hotels occasionally. They are worth one's attention.

Today, good carving is rarely found. A recent informal survey of top restaurants in New York brought to light only six chefs who could be called masters of carving. And home carvers, good or bad, have nearly disappeared. It was not too long ago that mothers and fathers taught their children how to carve, along with basic table manners. Nowadays few people will risk carving in public. They prefer to operate out of sight, in the kitchen. A pity, too, for such refinements were a delightful part of dining.

TOOLS

Apart from technique, two things are important to good carving. First, the proper tools; and second, the proper surface on which to carve.

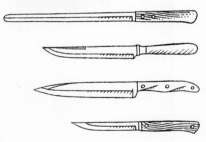

Knives: Good knives are a carver's joy and necessity. Most serious carvers guard their best knives jealously, never allowing others to use them. And wise they are. Those who do not understand the art of *decoupage* and the handling of good steel can ruin a blade in a flash. I have a fine collection of knives gathered from around the world, and I use them all at one time or another. There are some I prefer for general use. I like, for example, a long, rounded slicing knife for beef, hams, and large roasts. I have this style in several lengths: 9½, 11, 12, and 14 inches from tip to tip. These are of fine, supple steel which holds an edge well and produces thin, even slices when properly used. I also favor an 8-inch knife with a fairly narrow blade for running between flesh and bone, say, of a standing rib roast. Another knife which I find useful is a serrated German knife with a 12-inch blade about 1-inch wide. This will produce thin slices and is a boon to any carver who is uncertain of his prowess.

Wood is generally considered the best surface on which to carve, being the kindest to one's knives, although there is disagreement about whether the wood should be hard or soft. Naturally the latter is easier on steel but is less durable. Porcelain, it goes without saying, is not as suitable as wood, and metal is a brutal surface on which to expose your finest edge.

Forks: A carving fork holds the roast firm while you carve. It is also an axis on which you turn a roast. It should be fairly large with a comfortable grip. You may use it or a smaller fork for serving.

Poultry Shears: A sturdy scissors made to cut through the bones of fowl. Very useful for game, ducks, and squab.

KEEPING KNIVES SHARP

One should have a good steel and a carborundum. Good carvers take pride in keeping their knives clean and well edged. *Sharpen* your knives in this manner. Hold knife sharpener (steel) in your left hand. Place the lower edge of the knife (near handle) at the top of the steel's tip. Sharpener and blade should be at a 20° angle. With a diagonal motion, swing the knife across the sharpener at the 20° angle until the tip of the

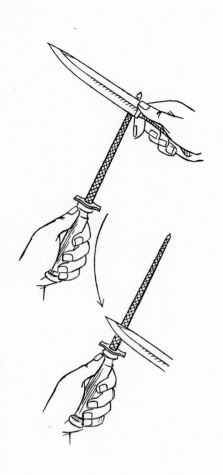

knife touches the bottom of the sharpener. Swing back to the first position at the opposite side of the sharpener. Repeat procedure; 12 strokes should be sufficient. They should be light. Only the edge of the knife should touch the sharpener. If the blade touches it, the blade will be scratched. Professional sharpeners are available. It is wise to leave your knives occasionally with them. If you do not know one, consult your butcher.

HOW TO CARE FOR CARVING KNIVES

Do *not* crowd your knives in a drawer. They will become blunted or nicked by rubbing against hard surfaces. Keep them well separated from each other in special drawer compartments with slots for the blades. *Better still,* keep them in a portable or stationary knife rack. When buying such a rack, make sure that it suits your own knife collection. Magnetic racks are not advised for good knives; they tend to damage the edges. Wooden slotted racks are preferable.

Do *not* crowd your knives into a receptacle when cleaning them or they will become blunted. Do not immerse them totally in water, since water will weaken the bond between blade and handle.

Clean your knives by wiping them with a damp or wet sponge or cloth after each use and drying them promptly. If your knives stain, clean them with steel wool, and coarse salt mixed with a little vinegar. Or the British standby: rotten stone or English Tripoli.

In the following paragraphs, the techniques of carving are described in detail. I should be happy to see a revival of the showy art of carving birds and roasts at table. Certainly few things add such legitimate theatricality to the pleasures of good eating.

HOW TO CARVE BEEF

Standing Rib Roast—Stand meat upright on a platter or board on its widest end. Secure roast with fork between two ribs. With a sharp knife, cut between ribs and meat so that slices will flow. From the outside in, carve individual slices of the thickness you prefer. Thin slices are called English cut, thick ones American cut.

Standing Rib Roast

Rolled Rib Roast—Place the larger side of the meat on the platter so that it will rest firmly. Secure with fork held in left hand. Since rolled rib roasts are held together with string, remove string, but only one piece at a time, or the roast will fall apart. Cut slices straight across the meat, from right to left. Thickness depends on personal preference. Be cer-

tain knife is *very* sharp. Not a cut to carve with ease!

Rolled Rib Roast

Roast Sirloin—Cut a piece of meat from the larger end of the roast. Use the tip of your knife or a small knife to remove the meat from the bone. Carve into thin slices from the fat side down.

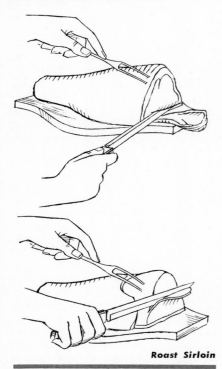

Flank Steak

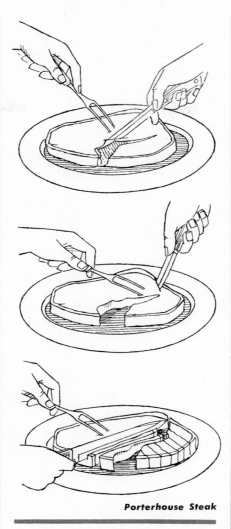

Roast Sirloin

Beef Fillet or Boneless Tenderloin—Cut straight across the meat into slices of desired thickness, from ¾ inch to 1 inch.

Porterhouse Steak

HOW TO CARVE PORK

Pork Loin Roast—To make carving easier, have your butcher saw across the ribs close to the backbone. During cooking, the backbone will loosen so that it can be cut off before the actual carving. Stand the roast, rib ends up, on a platter, with the rib side toward the carver. Cut between the ribs into individual chops. If a thinner portion is desired, cut thinner rib chops with a thin slice between rib bones, or remove the loin section entirely by cutting close to the bone. Carve the resulting fillet in thin slices.

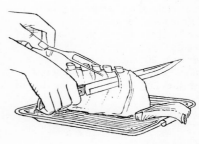

Beef Fillet or Boneless Tenderloin

Pork Loin Roast

Porterhouse Steak—Cut around the bone with a small sharp knife. Reserve bone. Cut off tail of the steak. Slice the fillet (tenderloin) section on the diagonal with a sharp small-bladed knife. Carve the larger loin section in the same way. Serve each person a piece of fillet and a piece of the loin.

Sirloin Steak—Use the same principle employed with the porterhouse. Remove the bone and then cut the steak into diagonal slices about one inch in width.

Flank Steak—Due to the coarser grain of this meat, the meat must be broiled rare and sliced very thin. Flank steak is sometimes used for London broil, which is properly carved in long narrow strips. A long knife with a thin, flexible blade is necessary. Holding the meat firmly on a carving board with a two-pronged fork, start carving at the small end of the flank steak. The knife blade should be at an angle almost parallel to the board. Keeping this same angle for each slice, cut meat with the grain, and very thin.

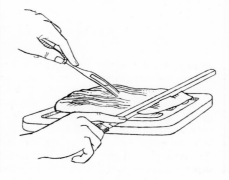

Whole Ham—The carving technique is essentially the same for a smoked, cured, or fresh roasted ham. Place ham, fat side up, on a board with the shank end at the carver's left. A slice or two may be first taken from the bottom to form a flat base. Turn ham onto flat base. Hold firmly with heavy fork or with hand. At the shank end, cut a small wedge, then begin slicing straight down toward the leg bone. Carve thin, delicate slices, preferably, that may be pushed back with knife blade toward the shank end as they are cut. Or, carve in the French manner. Place ham on platter and cut a small wedge at the shank end. Carve ham in thin slices at about a 30° angle across the top. This gives preferred slices. Ham may be turned and carved on the reverse side. When a sufficient number have been cut, run the knife underneath them at right angles to the slices, releasing them from the bone.

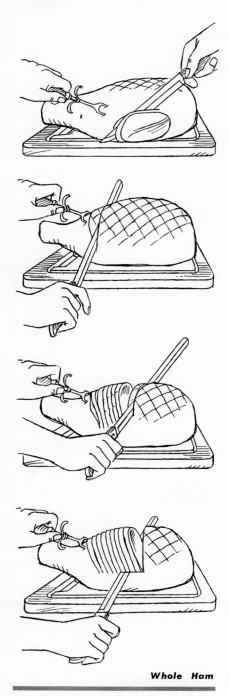

Whole Ham

slices across the top at a 30° angle, turning from time to time from right to left in easy turns. This gives more attractive slices.

Leg of Lamb

Rack of Lamb—In carving a rack of rib chops, the meat is placed on the platter with the Frenched (scraped) bone tips pointing away from the carver. The chops are separated individually by carving between the ribs, starting the first cut at the top where the chops are joined.

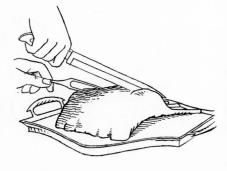

HOW TO CARVE LAMB AND VEAL

Leg of Lamb—If a whole leg of lamb is to be carved, it is best to remove the tail and pelvic bone after the meat is cooked, in the kitchen. The meat is then placed on a platter, bone side down, with the shank pointed to the left of the carver. Beginning at the shank end, the slices are cut thin and at right angles to the bone. The slices may be freed by running the knife parallel to the leg bone as in the carving of a whole ham.

The preferred French fashion is to hold leg bone in hand or in forceps designed for that purpose and slice in thin

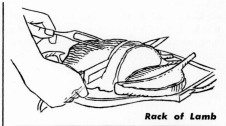

Rack of Lamb

Crown Roast of Lamb or Pork—A double rack tied in the form of a crown is very easy to carve. Cut between the ribs, allowing two ribs and a portion of the center dressing or vegetable per person.

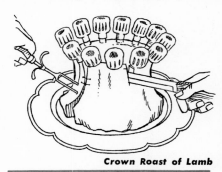

Crown Roast of Lamb

Saddle of Lamb—Place the saddle, bone side down, on a carving board. Remove the layer of fat from the top by cutting parallel to the meat. Slice thin, even lengthwise slices, carving down toward the bone with knife parallel to the spine.

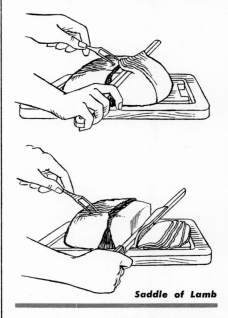

Saddle of Lamb

Saddle of Veal—A saddle of veal may be carved using the same technique as for the saddle of lamb, or it may be cut into scallops or fillets. For a smaller roast, buy half a saddle (a rack or loin of veal) and carve this into individual chops like a rack of lamb. To carve a scallop or fillet, first make a slice all the way down on one side of the spine. Then cutting down toward the rib bones, at a slight diagonal, carve ½-inch fillets. This time the knife is perpendicular to the spine. The fillet is released by cutting around the bone at the bottom.

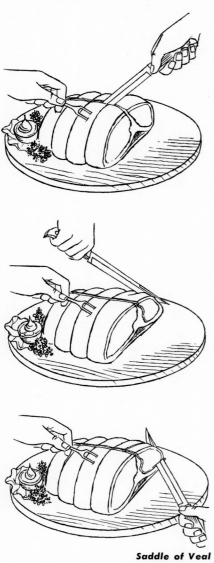

Saddle of Veal

HOW TO CARVE TURKEY

The turkey comes to the table on its back and placed with the legs at the carver's right. With the tip of the knife, remove the entire leg and thigh from the bird at the joint, being careful to cut the skin between the leg and the body so that it will not tear. The thigh may be separated from the drumstick on a separate plate or platter. The drumstick is sliced downward and the thigh section sliced to provide servings of dark meat. You may have to use a fork to give leverage to the bird as you cut the wing joint. Next, remove the wing. Again with the tip of

the knife, find the joint and sever the wing. Carve on an angle down the breast in thin slices. Still on an angle, carve alternately from the front and back ends of the breast. Repeat process on other side.

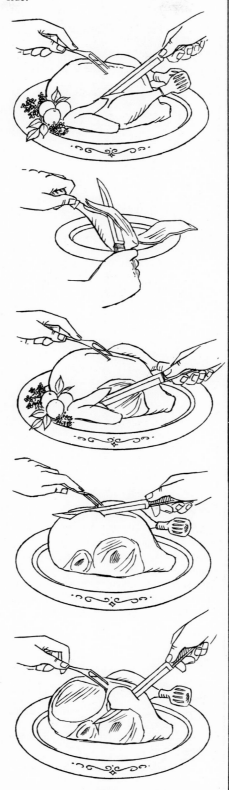

HOW TO CARVE CHICKEN

A chicken is carved in the same manner as a turkey. If desired, the breast and wing section may be removed in one piece (sometimes called a supreme). In such case, the legs and thighs are removed first. Cut the breast meat in one piece as close to the bone as possible and then continue cutting through the wing until the wing is removed as well.

HOW TO CARVE DUCK AND GOOSE

The position of the bird on the table is the same as for a turkey or a chicken. Due to the greater portion of meat on the breast, some carvers prefer slicing the breast meat before removing the legs and wings. The leg meat is cut completely around, in any case, to loosen it from the breast. A section at the neck end of the goose may be removed, by cutting straight across, to facilitate carving of the breast meat. A long-bladed, flexible slicer is needed. A duck is more often carved in quarters or halves either with a sharp knife or with carving shears.

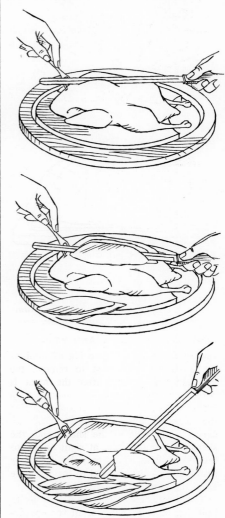

CASABA—Like many melons, the casaba was first cultivated in Persia thousands of years ago. It is a large winter melon, globular in shape with a pointed stem end and a rough furrowed rind. When ripe, the flesh is creamy white, soft and juicy, but almost without fragrance. It has a distinctive, mild cucumberlike flavor. The rind is yellow and although wrinkled, it is not netted.

Availability—Casaba melons are most abundant in September, October, and November. Crop comes from California.

Purchasing Guide—Look for melons with a yellow rind and a softening at the blossom end, which are signs of ripeness. Avoid melons with dark, sunken areas, which are an indication of decay.

Storage—Ripe melons should be kept in the refrigerator. If melon is not fully ripened, keep it at room temperature.
☐ Refrigerator shelf, whole and ripe: 1 week
☐ Refrigerator shelf, cut and tightly wrapped: 2 to 4 days

Caloric Value
☐ 3½ ounces = 27 calories

Basic Preparation—Cut chilled melon into wedges. Remove seeds. Serve casaba melon with a sprinkling of salt or with wedges of lemon or lime.

CASABA SALAD WITH SOUR CREAM
3 cups diced casaba
½ teaspoon salt
⅛ teaspoon pepper
3 tablespoons mayonnaise
¼ cup dairy sour cream
½ teaspoon fresh lemon juice
½ teaspoon paprika
Salad greens

Mix all ingredients except greens. Chill. Serve on greens with a sprinkling of paprika, if desired. Makes 4 servings.

CASHEW—This sweet, plump, white kidney-shape nut is the edible seed of a tropical evergreen tree, native to tropical America and found widely in India and equatorial Africa. Most of the cashews sold in the United States are imported from India. They are a popular ingredient in any salted-nut dish and are also used in some main dishes, especially curries and casseroles, and in salads, desserts, and candies.

Availability and Purchasing Guide—Most cashew nuts are roasted and salted. They are sold in bulk by the pound, whole and in pieces, in specialty food stores. They are available in food stores in vacuum-packed cans and in jars, dry-roasted (without oil) in various sizes. Unsalted cashews are available in gourmet sections of food stores.
☐ 1 pound = 3 to 3½ cups

Storage—Keep nuts in a film bag or a tightly closed container in the refrigerator. They may be frozen in freezer containers.
☐ Refrigerator shelf: 6 months
☐ Freezer compartment, prepared for freezing: 1 year

Nutritive Food Values—Cashews contain some protein, iron, and various B vitamins. They are high in fat content.
☐ 3½ ounces = 561 calories

Basic Preparation

☐ **To Chop**—Use a long, straight knife and wooden board or a chopping bowl and chopper. If a blender is used, place ½ cup nuts at a time in blender container, cover and whirl for 30 seconds at high speed.

☐ **To Grind**—Use a nut grinder, except for butters and pastes; for these you should use a meat grinder or blender.

TUNA-CASHEW CASSEROLE
¾ cup elbow macaroni, cooked and drained
1 cup dairy sour cream
¼ teaspoon ground oregano

2 cans (7 ounces each) tuna, drained
½ cup sliced ripe olives
1 can (4 ounces) sliced mushrooms, drained
¼ cup chopped green pepper
½ cup chopped unsalted cashew nuts
1½ teaspoons seasoned salt
¼ teaspoon white pepper
1 cup shredded sharp Cheddar cheese

Combine all ingredients except cheese and mix well. Put in shallow 1½-quart baking dish. Sprinkle with cheese. Bake in preheated moderate oven (350°F.) for about 25 minutes. Makes 4 to 6 servings.

CHICKEN AND RICE SALAD WITH CASHEWS
3 cups cooked rice
2 cups coarsely diced cooked chicken
½ cup diced celery
2 green onions, chopped
1 tablespoon fresh lemon juice
½ cup chopped salted cashew nuts
¾ cup salad dressing or mayonnaise
Salt and pepper
Salad greens

Combine rice, chicken, celery, onions, lemon juice, and nuts. Add salad dressing and mix lightly. Season to taste with salt and pepper. Chill, and serve on salad greens. Makes 4 servings.

CASHEW-RICE STUFFING
1 cup butter or margarine
½ cup minced onion
1 teaspoon each of ground thyme, sage, and marjoram
1½ teaspoons salt
¾ teaspoon pepper
⅓ cup chopped parsley
¾ cup chopped celery and leaves
6 cups cooked rice
½ cup salted cashew nuts

Melt butter in skillet and add all ingredients except rice and nuts. Cook for 5 minutes. Combine with rice and nuts. Makes about 6 cups.

COFFEE-NUT MACAROONS
2 egg whites
1⅓ cups sugar
2 tablespoons instant coffee
⅔ cup chopped salted cashews
1 teaspoon vanilla extract

Beat egg whites until they begin to hold their shape. Mix sugar and coffee; gradually beat into egg whites, beating constantly until stiff but not dry. Fold in nuts and vanilla. Drop by teaspoonfuls onto well-greased cookie sheets. Bake in preheated slow oven (325°F.) for about 15 minutes. Makes 4 dozen.

CASHEW BRITTLE
Melt 1 cup sugar in heavy skillet over low heat, stirring constantly until sugar is completely melted and golden brown. Remove from heat, add 1 cup salted whole cashew nuts, and pour into buttered pan to make a thin sheet. When nearly cold, mark off squares, or allow to cool and break into irregular pieces. Makes ½ pound.

Casserole cooking, that neat, compact way of preparing and serving food, is the answer to a busy homemaker's prayer because so much of the work can be done at her convenience

Casserole Cook Book

CASSEROLE

CASSEROLE—The word casserole has two meanings:

1. A deep cooking vessel of French origin, designed to retain heat and to be used for long, slow cooking. A casserole container is usually round, with a tight-fitting lid and with handles. Casseroles can be made from any kind of metal, tempered glass, terra-cotta, or fireproof porcelain. Many of them are handsome enough to be used as serving dishes. The classic French and Italian casseroles are made from brown earthenware. They are excellent for cooking, but they cannot be used over direct heat. More practical, and equally successful, are enameled cast-iron casseroles which can be used both in the oven and over direct heat. They come in attractive colors, are manufactured in this country, and are also imported from France, Holland, Denmark, and Belgium.

2. Casserole also means a cooked dish in which a number of raw and/or cooked ingredients are simmered together in the oven or on top of the stove. In the United States, the term has become synonymous with one-dish meals. Casserole cookery is extremely convenient since such dishes need little watching and are easy to serve. Casseroles will wait for guests, but not for an indefinite period of time, since the food, as all food, will then be overcooked or dried out.

Hints for Casserole Cookery

■ Do not overcook food.

■ A covered casserole will keep moisture in the cooking liquid, and the sauce will be thinner. An uncovered one will have the opposite effect. Thus, if the sauce in your casserole is too thin, cook the mixture for a while without the casserole lid.

■ If more liquid has to be added to a casserole while it is cooking, heat the liquid first, even if it is only water. Never add cold to hot.

■ A cooked casserole should be cooled to room temperature before being refrigerated.

To Freeze Casseroles

■ Freeze as soon as possible after cooling thoroughly.

■ Wrap tightly, allowing 1-inch headspace. Pack food tightly to remove air spaces.

■ Do not store longer than 2 to 6 months.

■ Thaw in the refrigerator overnight before reheating; then bake for only 30 minutes. Or, if not thawed, bake, covered, in a preheated moderate oven (350°F.) for 1 to 1½ hours. Times are approximate and depend on type and size of casserole.

BEEF CASSEROLES

HAMBURGER-VEGETABLE CASSEROLE

2 pounds beef chuck, ground
1 egg
  Salt and pepper
1 tablespoon instant minced onion
½ teaspoon Worcestershire
⅓ cup fine dry bread crumbs
½ cup water
3 tablespoons fat
½ teaspoon ground marjoram
2 cans (10¾ ounces each) beef gravy
8 carrots
8 small white onions
8 medium potatoes
2 fresh mushrooms, sliced
1 tablespoon butter
  Chopped parsley

Combine meat, egg, 1½ teaspoons salt, ¼ teaspoon pepper, and next 4 ingredients. Shape into 12 large balls and brown on all sides in hot fat. Place meatballs in a large casserole. To drippings add marjoram and gravy. Scrape carrots, peel onions and potatoes, and cook in a small amount of boiling salted water for about 15 minutes. Add to casserole. Bring gravy to boil and pour over top. Cover and bake in preheated moderate oven (350°F.) for 1 hour. Brown mushrooms in butter. Garnish casserole with the mushrooms and parsley before serving. Makes 4 to 6 servings.

MEAT LOAF-VEGETABLE CASSEROLE

2 medium potatoes, sliced
1 package (10 ounces) frozen baby Lima beans
1 onion, sliced
1 teaspoon salt
1½ pounds beef chuck, ground
1 cup soft bread crumbs
1 can (8 ounces) tomato sauce
2 tablespoons water
1 teaspoon prepared mustard
1½ teaspoons seasoned salt
1 tablespoon instant minced onion
¼ teaspoon pepper

Put vegetables in 2-quart casserole and sprinkle with salt. Mix remaining ingredients and spread on vegetables. Bake, uncovered, in preheated moderate oven (350°F.) for about 1 hour. Makes 4 to 6 servings.

LASAGNA

8 ounces lasagna noodles
2 tablespoons salt
1 tablespoon olive oil
1 pound ricotta cheese
8 ounces Mozzarella cheese, sliced
  Tomato-Meat Sauce
½ cup grated Parmesan cheese

Cook noodles in boiling salted water for 25 minutes, or until tender, stirring frequently. Drain; add oil. Arrange noodles and remaining ingredients in shallow 2½-quart baking dish. Make 3 layers each of cooked noodles, ricotta, Mozzarella, Tomato-Meat Sauce, and grated cheese. Bake, uncovered, in preheated slow oven (325°F.) for about 45 min-

utes. Makes 6 servings.

Note: Wide noodles can be substituted for lasagna, cottage cheese for ricotta, and Muenster for Mozzarella, if these Italian products are not available.

Tomato-Meat Sauce

1 medium onion, minced
2 garlic cloves, minced
¼ cup olive oil
1 pound beef, ground
3½ cups (one 1-pound, 12-ounce can) tomatoes
1 can (6 ounces) tomato paste
2 teaspoons salt
¼ teaspoon cayenne
1 teaspoon sugar
  Pinch of basil
1 bay leaf
2 cups water

Sauté onion and garlic in oil until lightly browned. Add beef and brown. Add remaining ingredients. Stir well and simmer, uncovered, for 1½ hours.

END-OF-THE-MONTH CASSEROLE

½ cup chopped green pepper
½ cup sliced onion
3 tablespoons shortening
2 cups ground leftover steak
¼ cup chopped parsley
3½ cups (one 1-pound, 12-ounce can) tomatoes
1 teaspoon Worcestershire
2 cups cooked rice
1 cup cooked kidney beans or other beans
1 teaspoon chili powder
1 teaspoon salt
½ teaspoon pepper
⅛ teaspoon crumbled dried thyme

Sauté green pepper and onion in hot shortening until soft but not brown. Add ground steak and cook, stirring frequently, until brown. Add all other ingredients and toss lightly. Put in greased 2-quart baking dish. Bake, covered, in preheated moderate oven (350°F.) for about 30 minutes. Makes 4 to 6 servings.

CRUSTY BEEF, CHEESE, AND NOODLE CASSEROLE

2 tablespoons vegetable oil
1 onion, chopped
2 pounds ground beef
4 cans (10¼ ounces each) meatless mushroom sauce (for spaghetti)
1 teaspoon salt
1 pound fine noodles, cooked and drained
1 pound sharp Cheddar cheese, grated or shredded
  Seasoning salt

Heat oil; add onion and cook until golden. Add meat and cook until meat loses its red color, stirring. Add mushroom sauce and salt; heat. Arrange in casserole half of noodles, half of sauce and half of cheese; sprinkle with seasoning salt. Make another layer of noodles; add sauce and top with cheese. Bake in preheated moderate oven (325°F.) for 1 hour; top should be nicely browned. Makes 8 to 10 generous servings.

VEAL CASSEROLE

VEAL AND PORK RAGOÛT

- 1½ pounds boneless stewing veal
- 1½ pounds boneless pork shoulder
  All-purpose flour
- 3 tablespoons butter or margarine
- 1 onion, chopped
- 1 cup hot water
- ½ cup dry red wine
- 1 tablespoon salt
- ½ teaspoon pepper
- 2 parsley sprigs
- ½ bay leaf
- 1 garlic clove, minced
  Veal bone, if desired
- 4 to 6 small potatoes, peeled and quartered
- ½ pound mushrooms, halved
  About 2 cups (one 1-pound can) onions, drained
  About 2 cups (one 1-pound can) tiny carrots, drained
- ½ cup frozen peas

Cut meat into 1½-inch cubes. Dredge with flour and brown on all sides in butter. Add onion and brown a few minutes longer. Add next 8 ingredients. Bake covered, in preheated moderate oven (350°F.) for 1½ hours. Remove bone, and add potatoes, mushrooms, and enough water to almost cover. Return to oven; cook for 40 minutes. Add onions, carrots, and peas; cook for 20 minutes. Makes 6 to 8 servings.

PORK CASSEROLES

PORK CHOPS À L'AUVERGNE

- 1 head white or green cabbage
  Salt and pepper
- 1 cup heavy cream
- 4 loin pork chops
- ¼ cup butter
- ½ teaspoon crumbled dried sage
- ½ cup dry white wine
- ¼ cup freshly grated Parmesan cheese

Wash, quarter, core, and shred cabbage. Put in saucepan and sprinkle with salt and pepper. Add cream, bring to boil, and simmer for 5 to 10 minutes. Trim excess fat from chops and panfry in 2 tablespoons butter until golden brown. Cover and cook slowly until very tender. Remove chops. Add sage and wine to skillet. Scrape skillet to remove all browned bits. Add to cabbage and season to taste. Put a layer of cabbage in shallow casserole. Cover with chops. Add remaining cabbage and pour skillet liquid over top. Sprinkle with cheese and dot with remaining butter. Bake in preheated moderate oven (350°F.) for about 45 minutes. Makes 4 servings.

HAM, CHEESE, AND POTATO CASSEROLE

- 2 cups diced cooked ham
- 2 cups diced process cheese
- 1 can (4 ounces) pimientos, drained
- 6 medium potatoes, cooked, peeled, and diced
- 1½ cups medium white sauce

Put ham, cheese, and pimientos through food chopper, using medium blade. Spread mixture in greased baking dish (12 x 7 x 2 inches). Cover with diced potatoes and pour white sauce over top. Bake, uncovered, in preheated moderate oven (350°F.) for 40 minutes. Makes 6 to 8 servings.

Veal and Pork Ragoût

HAM TAMALE PIE

1 large onion, chopped
¼ cup chopped green pepper
1 garlic clove, minced
¼ cup butter or margarine
½ cup plus 1 tablespoon all-purpose flour
2 teaspoons chili powder
2 cups diced cooked ham
1 can (12 ounces) whole-kernel corn, drained
2¼ cups tomato juice
¼ cup seedless raisins
1 tablespoon sugar
1 egg
½ cup yellow cornmeal
1 teaspoon paprika
1 teaspoon baking powder
½ cup milk

Sauté onion, green pepper, and garlic in 2 tablespoons butter for 5 minutes. Blend in 1 tablespoon flour and chili powder. Add next 4 ingredients and heat. Pour into large shallow casserole. Cream remaining butter with sugar. Beat in egg. Add ½ cup flour, cornmeal, and remaining ingredients. Mix well and spoon around edge of casserole to form a border. Bake, uncovered, in preheated moderate oven (375°F.) for about 30 minutes. Makes 6 servings.

LAMB CASSEROLES

LAMB AND VEGETABLE CASSEROLE

2 pounds lean lamb, cut into 1-inch cubes
¼ cup olive oil
2 onions, chopped
4 cups (two 1-pound cans) tomatoes
½ cup chopped parsley
Salt and pepper
2 packages (9 ounces each) frozen cut green beans or 2 packages (10 ounces each) okra or peas

Brown lamb on all sides in hot oil. Add onions and cook until soft, stirring frequently. Add tomatoes, parsley, salt, and pepper. Bake, covered, in preheated moderate oven (350°F.) for 1 hour. Add vegetable and bake, covered, for 20 minutes longer. Makes 6 servings.

SAVORY LAMB CASSEROLE

1½ pounds lean lamb, cubed
3 tablespoons all-purpose flour
1½ teaspoons salt
⅛ teaspoon pepper
¼ cup butter or margarine
1 onion, chopped
½ green pepper, chopped
1 cup diced celery
Few parsley sprigs, chopped
1 teaspoon paprika
Pinch of rosemary
1 cup hot water
1 package (10 ounces) frozen peas, thawed
1 can (1 pound) tiny potatoes, drained

Dredge lamb with flour seasoned with salt and pepper. Brown on all sides in hot butter in skillet. Put in 2-quart casserole. Add next 4 ingredients to butter remaining in skillet and sauté for 5 minutes. Add to lamb. Sprinkle with pa-

prika and rosemary. Add hot water; cover and bake in preheated moderate oven (375°F.) for 1¼ hours. Add peas and potatoes and bake, uncovered, for 30 minutes longer. Makes 6 servings.

LAMB AND ONION CASSEROLE

2½ pounds lean lamb, cubed
2 tablespoons butter or margarine
2½ pounds (8 large) onions, peeled
½ cup dry white wine
1 tablespoon tomato paste
Few parsley sprigs, minced
Salt and pepper

Brown lamb in hot butter in skillet. Put in 2½-quart casserole. Chop enough of the onions to make ½ cup; brown lightly in same skillet. Add to meat. Combine wine, tomato paste, parsley, salt and pepper, and remaining onions, sliced very thin; mix well. Pour over meat, cover, and bake in preheated moderate oven (350°F.) about 1½ hours. Serves 6 to 8.

FRANKFURTER AND SAUSAGE CASSEROLES

SAVORY BEAN CASSEROLE

1 pound dried pea beans, washed and drained
6 cups water
1 bay leaf
2 garlic cloves
2 teaspoons salt
1 can (4 ounces) pimientos, drained and chopped
1 large green pepper, minced
1 bunch green onions, minced
½ cup cooking or olive oil
1 garlic clove, mashed
¼ cup wine vinegar
Salt and pepper
1 pound frankfurters
¼ cup minced parsley

Cover beans with water. Bring to boil and boil for 2 minutes. Cover and let stand for 1 hour. Add bay leaf, garlic cloves, and salt; simmer until tender; drain. Combine pimientos, green pepper, onions, oil, mashed garlic, and vinegar and mix with drained beans. Season to taste with salt and pepper. Put in 2½-quart casserole. Top with frankfurters and bake, covered, in preheated hot oven (400°F.) for about 15 minutes. Sprinkle with minced parsley. Makes 8 servings.

SAUSAGE AND SPLIT-PEA CASSEROLE

1 pound split peas, washed and drained
5 cups water
1 teaspoon salt
1 pound pork sausage meat
2 tablespoons minced onion
½ teaspoon seasoned salt
¼ teaspoon pepper
½ teaspoon Worcestershire
1 cup grated Cheddar cheese

Cover peas with water; add salt and bring to a boil. Reduce heat and simmer for 35 minutes, or until peas are just tender. Drain, reserving ½ cup of the liquid. Brown sausage meat, breaking up

with fork. Mix peas lightly with sausage and fat, pea liquid, and remaining ingredients except cheese. Put in shallow baking dish. Sprinkle with cheese. Bake, uncovered, in preheated hot oven (400° F.) about 30 minutes. Serves 6 to 8.

POULTRY CASSEROLES

CHICKEN AND OYSTER CASSEROLE

1 large fryer (about 3 pounds), cut up
¼ cup all-purpose flour
1¼ teaspoons salt
¼ teaspoon white pepper
2 tablespoons shortening
½ cup boiling water
½ cup heavy cream
18 oysters
2 tablespoons toasted slivered blanched almonds

Reserve back, wings, and neck of chicken for later use. Wash remaining pieces and dry. Dredge with flour mixed with ½ teaspoon salt and ⅛ teaspoon pepper. Brown on all sides in hot fat. Remove to 2 -quart casserole. Add boiling water, cover, and bake in preheated moderate oven (350°F.) for 1 hour, or until tender. Add cream, remaining salt and pepper, and the oysters. Cover and bake for 10 minutes longer. Sprinkle with almonds and serve at once with hot baking-powder biscuits, if desired. Serves 4.

CHICKEN AND MUSHROOMS IN SOUR-CREAM SAUCE

1 fryer (about 3 pounds), cut up
¼ cup milk
⅓ cup all-purpose flour
6 tablespoons butter or margarine
Salt and pepper
½ pound fresh mushrooms, sliced
2 cups dairy sour cream
Paprika

Dip chicken pieces into milk, then roll in flour. Brown on all sides in hot butter in skillet. Put in 3-quart casserole and sprinkle with salt and pepper. Brown mushrooms lightly in butter remaining in skillet. Place on top of chicken, and season. Cover and bake in preheated moderate oven (350°F.) for 45 minutes to 1 hour, or until chicken is tender. Add sour cream seasoned with ½ teaspoon salt. Cover and bake for 10 minutes longer, or until cream is just heated. Sprinkle with paprika. Makes 4 servings.

DUCK AND SWEET-POTATO CASSEROLE

2 large ducks, quartered
Salt and pepper
8 partially cooked sweet potatoes, halved
½ cup chicken bouillon
1½ cups fresh orange juice
Grated rind of 1 orange
1 can (8 ounces) mandarin oranges, juice reserved
1 tablespoon cornstarch
Curaçao

Sprinkle duck with salt and pepper, and bake in shallow pan in preheated hot oven (400°F.) for 1 hour. Drain off fat.

Put duck in a large casserole and add sweet potatoes. Combine bouillon, orange juice and rind, and juice drained from mandarin oranges. Bring to boil and thicken with cornstarch mixed with a little cold water. Cook until clear; add a little Curaçao. Pour over duck and potatoes. Cover and bake for about 45 minutes, or until tender. Baste several times with sauce in pan. At serving time, top with mandarin oranges. Serves 8.

FISH CASSEROLES

FISH FILLETS, FLORENTINE

Cook and drain 2 packages (10 ounces each) frozen chopped spinach. Put in shallow casserole. Place 1 pound whitefish fillets in boiling salted water in skillet. Simmer for 5 to 10 minutes. Remove fish and place on spinach. Dilute 1 can frozen shrimp soup with ¼ cup milk. Pour over fish. Bake, covered, in preheated hot oven (400°F.) for 15 to 20 minutes. Makes 4 servings.

CRABMEAT PILAF

- ¾ cup raw rice
- 1 onion, chopped
- 2 tablespoons butter
- 2 cups (one 1-pound can) tomatoes
- ⅔ cup diced celery
- ¼ teaspoon white pepper
- ½ teaspoon each of salt and seasoned salt
- ½ bay leaf, crumbled
- ½ teaspoon sugar
- ¼ cup shredded Cheddar cheese
- 1 can (6½ ounces) crabmeat, drained and flaked

Cook rice according to package directions. Brown onion lightly in butter. Add remaining ingredients except crabmeat. Heat, stirring, until cheese is melted. Add rice and crabmeat; put in shallow casserole; cover. Bake in preheated slow oven (325°F.) for 25 minutes. Serves 4.

Lobster Pilaf

Prepare Crabmeat Pilaf, substituting 1 can (6½ ounces) lobster, drained and flaked, or 1½ cups diced cooked lobster meat for crabmeat. Proceed as directed for Crabmeat Pilaf.

LOBSTER-NOODLE CASSEROLE

- 10 rock lobster tails, frozen (4 ounces each), cooked as directed on package
- ½ cup butter or margarine
- ¼ cup all-purpose flour
- 2½ teaspoons salt
- 1½ teaspoons paprika
- ½ teaspoon white pepper
- 1 teaspoon instant minced onion
- 1 teaspoon aromatic bitters
- 4 cups milk
- 1 cup light cream
- ½ cup dry sherry
- 1 package (12 ounces) broad noodles, cooked
  Buttered bread crumbs
- ¼ cup capers, drained

Remove shells from cooked lobster tails, keeping meat in one piece. Cut 5 lobster tails into bite-size chunks. Melt ¼ cup butter in saucepan, stir in flour, salt, paprika, pepper, onion, and bitters. Gradually stir in milk and cream; cook over

Lobster-Noodle Casserole

CASSEROLE

low heat until thickened, stirring constantly. Add sherry and lobster chunks to sauce. Combine noodles and sauce in 3-quart casserole. Top with buttered crumbs and bake, uncovered, in preheated moderate oven (375°F.) for about 30 minutes, until hot and bubbly. Cut remaining 5 lobster tails into halves lengthwise. Place on top of noodle mixture and brush with ¼ cup melted butter and capers. Return to oven for about 10 minutes longer. Makes 8 to 10 servings.

FESTIVE TUNA CASSEROLE

1 can cream-of-mushroom soup
2 cups (one 1-pound can) peas, undrained
1 can (4 ounces) pimientos, sliced
1 small onion, minced
1 tablespoon Worcestershire
2 cans (7 ounces each) tuna, drained and flaked
1 cup grated process American cheese
1 can (4 ounces) potato sticks

Combine undiluted soup, peas with liquid, and next 3 ingredients. Fold in tuna and cheese. Put in 1½-quart casserole. Arrange potato sticks around edge. Bake, uncovered, in preheated moderate oven (375°F.) for 25 minutes. Makes 6 servings.

MEATLESS CASSEROLES

COTTAGE EGGS WITH RICE

⅔ cup raw rice
6 hard-cooked eggs
½ cup garden-salad cottage cheese
2 tablespoons mayonnaise
   Salt and pepper
¼ cup butter or margarine
¼ cup all-purpose flour
1 teaspoon instant minced onion
2 cups milk
   Paprika

Cook and drain rice and put in shallow baking dish. Slice eggs lengthwise and remove yolks. Mash yolks with cottage cheese and mayonnaise. Season to taste with salt and pepper. Fill whites with the mixture and arrange on rice. Melt butter in a saucepan and blend in flour. Add onion and gradually stir in milk. Cook over low heat, stirring constantly, until thickened. Season to taste. Pour sauce over eggs and sprinkle with paprika. Bake, uncovered, in preheated moderate oven (350°F.) for 20 minutes, or until heated. Makes 4 servings.

ONION BAKE WITH MUSHROOM-CHEESE SAUCE

6 tablespoons butter or margarine
¼ cup all-purpose flour
½ teaspoon salt
¼ teaspoon paprika
¼ teaspoon celery salt
1½ cups milk
1 pimiento, minced
2 cups thinly sliced onion rings
3 eggs, beaten
⅔ cup soft bread crumbs
   Mushroom-Cheese Sauce

Melt butter in a saucepan; blend in flour

Crusty Beef, Cheese, and Noodle Casserole

and seasonings. Gradually stir in milk. Cook, stirring constantly, over low heat until thickened. Add remaining ingredients except Mushroom-Cheese Sauce and mix well. Pour into greased 1½-quart casserole. Set in pan of hot water and bake in preheated moderate oven (350°F.) for 45 minutes, or until firm. Serve with Mushroom-Cheese Sauce.

Mushroom-Cheese Sauce
¼ pound mushrooms, sliced
1 teaspoon butter
1 egg, beaten
1 cup milk
¾ teaspoon dry mustard
¼ teaspoon paprika
½ pound process American cheese, cubed

Sauté mushrooms in hot butter until lightly browned. In top part of double boiler combine egg, milk, mustard, and paprika. Heat over boiling water. Stir in cheese and blend until cheese is melted and sauce thickened. Add mushrooms and reheat. Makes 6 servings.

EGGPLANT PARMIGIANA
1 large eggplant (about 2 pounds)
¾ cup olive oil
1½ cups canned tomato sauce
¼ cup grated Parmesan cheese
½ pound Mozzarella cheese, sliced thin

Peel eggplant and cut into ¼-inch slices. Fry on both sides in oil in skillet until brown. Drain well on absorbent paper. Put layer of eggplant slices in shallow baking dish; cover with some tomato sauce, a little of the Parmesan cheese, and a few slices of Mozzarella. Repeat layers until all ingredients are used, ending with Mozzarella. Bake, uncovered, in preheated hot oven (400°F.) for 15 minutes, or until mixture is thoroughly heated. Makes 4 to 6 servings.

SWEET-POTATO PUFF
¼ cup butter or margarine, melted
4 cups mashed cooked sweet potato
½ teaspoon salt
⅛ teaspoon white pepper
1½ tablespoons sugar
2 eggs, separated
Ground cinnamon

Combine all ingredients except last 2. Beat egg whites until stiff. Then beat egg yolks until thick. Fold yolks into potato mixture; then fold in whites. Put in greased shallow casserole. Sprinkle with cinnamon. Bake, uncovered, in preheated moderate oven (375°F.) for about 30 minutes. Makes 6 servings.

OMELET SOUFFLÉ
3 tablespoons butter or margarine
3 tablespoons all-purpose flour
¾ teaspoon salt
⅛ teaspoon pepper
1 cup milk
6 eggs, separated

Melt butter in saucepan and blend in flour, salt, and pepper. Gradually stir in milk and cook over low heat, stirring constantly, until thickened. Beat egg whites until stiff. Beat yolks until thick and lemon-colored. Stir white sauce into yolks, then fold in whites. Pour into 3-quart casserole and set in pan of hot water. Bake in preheated moderate oven (350°F.) for 35 minutes, or until tip of knife inserted in center comes out clean. Serve at once. Makes 6 servings.

Cheese Soufflé
Prepare Omelet Soufflé; add ¼ teaspoon dry mustard and dash of cayenne with salt and pepper. Add 1 cup diced sharp Cheddar cheese to hot sauce; stir until melted. Proceed as directed.

Asparagus Soufflé
Prepare Omelet Soufflé; fold 1 cup well-drained finely cut cooked asparagus into mixture with egg whites. Add 1 tablespoon instant minced onion and 1 chopped pimiento with the asparagus. Bake as directed.

My Favorite Spring Casseroles
by Nika Hazelton

In the spring, I get cabin fever. Because "spring, the sweet spring, is the year's pleasant king. Then blooms each thing, then maids dance in a ring, Cold doth not sting, the pretty birds do sing," affects me as it affects all other creatures: we want out.

Thus, for spring, I have prepared a special list of casseroles. The mind may feast on nature's beauties, but the body demands substance, giddy as it is with all that fresh spring air and sun. And this is where the casserole comes in.

What other dish has such virtues? A casserole can be made early in the morning or in the dark of night, so that not a precious moment of sunlight is wasted by staying indoors. A casserole can be whatever you want it to be: fanciful and diverting for sophisticated company, substantial for hungry children, and thrifty when the household money runs low.

A casserole gives leeway to individual creation, for there is no end to the little personal touches that can be applied to any recipe. A casserole does not tire, because no two casseroles are ever the same. And finally, because even a spring-struck housewife still has a conscience about her family, a casserole gives good, balanced nutrition and, just as important, is appetizing.

Here are my favorites, geared to various occasions. Some of the casseroles are grand for spring entertaining, when the nights are soft and scented. Others build muscle and bone. But they all have one thing in common: You can make them at your convenience and bake them as you rush indoors, flushed and wind-blown.

GREEN-NOODLE, BEEF, AND CHEESE CASSEROLE
½ pound green noodles, cooked
½ pound dried beef
2 cups grated Swiss cheese
2 cups well-seasoned medium white sauce
½ cup soft bread crumbs
2 tablespoons butter
4 slices of packaged Swiss cheese, cut into strips

Put half of noodles in buttered 1½-quart casserole. Top with half of beef and grated cheese. Repeat with remaining noodles, beef, and cheese. Pour white sauce (made with ¼ cup butter, ¼ cup flour, 2 cups milk, and seasonings) over mixture. Sauté bread crumbs in hot butter until lightly browned. Sprinkle over casserole. Arrange cheese strips in crisscross pattern. Bake, uncovered, in preheated hot oven (400°F.) for 20 minutes. Makes 6 servings.

LEFTOVER-BEEF CASSEROLE
3 medium onions, chopped
6 tablespoons butter or margarine
1 tablespoon all-purpose flour
1 tablespoon cider vinegar
2 cups hot beef bouillon
1 tablespoon tomato paste
Salt and pepper to taste
2 tablespoons chopped parsley
4 cups sliced cold cooked beef
½ cup soft bread crumbs

Sauté onions in 2 tablespoons butter until soft but not brown. Stir in flour. Moisten with vinegar. Gradually stir in hot bouillon and tomato paste and cook over low heat until thick and smooth, stirring constantly. Add salt, pepper, and parsley. Pour half of sauce into buttered baking dish. Top with beef slices and cover with remaining sauce. Sprinkle with bread crumbs and dot with remaining butter. Bake, uncovered, in preheated hot oven (425°F.) for 15 to 20 minutes, or until well heated. Makes 4 servings.

VEAL MARENGO
2 tablespoons cooking oil
2 tablespoons butter
1½ pounds veal shoulder, cut into 1-inch cubes
1 large onion, chopped
4 large tomatoes, peeled, seeded, and chopped
2 tablespoons all-purpose flour
1 cup dry white wine

1 cup hot chicken consomme
Salt and pepper
1 cup sliced drained canned or fresh
mushrooms
Triangles of buttered toast

Heat oil and butter in heavy skillet. Add veal and onion and sauté until brown. Add tomatoes and cook for 2 minutes. Stir in flour, blending thoroughly. Add wine and chicken consommé, stirring constantly. Season with salt and pepper. Add mushrooms. Turn mixture into 2-quart casserole and cover tightly. Bake in preheated moderate oven (350°F.) for 1 hour, or until veal is tender. Serve with toast. Makes 4 to 6 servings.

ITALIAN LAMB CASSEROLE
1 onion, sliced
1 garlic clove, minced
2 tablespoons cooking oil
2 cups diced cooked lamb
2 teaspoons salt
½ teaspoon crumbled dried basil
2⅓ cups (one 1-pound, 13-ounce can)
Italian-style tomatoes
½ teaspoon pepper
2 cups elbow macaroni, cooked
½ pound Mozzarella cheese, sliced

Sauté onion and garlic in hot oil until soft. Add lamb and brown. Combine lamb and next 5 ingredients. Turn into 2-quart casserole. Top with cheese. Bake, uncovered, in preheated moderate oven (350°F.) for 30 minutes. Makes 4 servings.

CHICKEN OR TURKEY MORNAY ON BROCCOLI
1 package (10 ounces) frozen broccoli
spears
¼ cup butter or margarine
¼ cup all-purpose flour
1 cup poultry broth
½ cup heavy cream
½ cup dry white wine
Salt and pepper
⅛ teaspoon Worcestershire
2 cups chopped cooked poultry
⅓ cup grated Parmesan cheese

Cook broccoli until barely tender. Drain; arrange in buttered 1½-quart size casserole. In separate saucepan melt butter and stir in flour. Add broth and cream. Cook until sauce is thick and smooth, stirring constantly. Stir in wine, salt and pepper to taste, and Worcestershire. Top broccoli with poultry. Cover with sauce and sprinkle with cheese. Bake, uncovered, in preheated hot oven (425°F.) for 15 minutes. Makes 4 servings.

SHRIMP CASSEROLE
½ pound mushrooms, sliced
2 tablespoons butter
1 medium onion, minced
2 large tomatoes, peeled, seeded, and
chopped
2 tablespoons all-purpose flour
½ cup light cream
⅓ cup sherry
1 teaspoon Worcestershire
½ teaspoon hot pepper sauce
2 teaspoons salt
⅛ teaspoon white pepper
3 pounds shrimps, cooked, peeled,

and deveined
½ cup buttered soft bread crumbs

Sauté mushrooms in butter until tender. Add onion and tomatoes and cook for 10 minutes. Stir in flour. Gradually stir in cream. Stir in sherry and seasonings. Add shrimps. Transfer to buttered 2-quart casserole. Top with bread crumbs. Bake, uncovered, in preheated moderate oven (350°F.) for 20 minutes, or until top is browned. Makes 6 to 8 servings.

SALMON CASSEROLE
1 can (1 pound) salmon, drained, boned,
and flaked
2 cups fresh bread crumbs
⅓ cup pimiento-stuffed olives, sliced
1 cup grated Cheddar cheese
½ cup chopped parsley
1 cup milk
3 eggs
1 small onion, minced
Salt and pepper
¼ cup fresh lemon juice
Creamy mushroom sauce

In a large bowl combine salmon, bread crumbs, olives, cheese, and parsley. Beat together milk, eggs, onion, salt, and pepper. Add to salmon mixture. Stir in lemon juice. Turn into greased 1½-quart casserole. Place casserole in a flat baking dish containing hot water 1 inch deep. Bake, uncovered, in preheated moderate oven (350°F.) for 1 hour, or until custard is set and tests clean. Serve with a creamy mushroom sauce. Serves 6.

GLORIFIED CHEESE STRATA
6 slices of white bread
6 tablespoons butter or margarine
1 garlic clove, crushed
6 eggs
½ cup heavy cream
1 cup white wine
½ pound Swiss cheese, grated
1 cup chicken bouillon
¼ teaspoon dry mustard
1 teaspoon paprika

Trim crusts from bread. Cream butter and garlic and spread on one side of bread slices. Arrange bread, buttered side down, in buttered 1½-quart casserole. Beat eggs and cream together until foamy. Stir in wine, cheese, bouillon, mustard, and paprika. Pour sauce over bread. Bake, uncovered, in preheated moderate oven (350°F.) for 25 minutes. Serves 6.

CASSOULET—This is a noble, garlicky bean stew with sausages and meats which comes to us from southwestern France. In the course of time it has risen from a humble, back-of-the-stove, catch-all casserole to one of the glories of French household cooking. The name is from the *cassole d'Issel,* an earthenware utensil

in which a *cassoulet* should be cooked. The ingredients must include a goodly amount of white beans, and they can include fresh pork, lamb, roast duck, various sausages, bacon, smoked ham, and *confit d'oie,* or preserved goose, which is imported from France and can be found in specialty food stores. A *cassoulet* must be cooked slowly, to blend the flavors.

There are a good many versions of the *cassoulet,* which is a national French favorite. The recipes vary depending on the locality and on what the cook has at hand.

Cassoulet has become a favorite French dish in America. Those who have never tasted it should expect a robust casserole, to be eaten with a green salad, washed down with red wine, and followed by fresh fruit.

CASSOULET
4 cups dried pea beans,
washed and drained
2 quarts water
1 tablespoon salt
2 garlic cloves, mashed
2 carrots, quartered
2 onions, each studded with 2 whole
cloves
Bouquet garni
(parsley, celery,
bay leaf, and thyme
tied in cheesecloth)
¼ cup salt pork, diced
2 tablespoons duck or goose drippings,
or cooking oil
1½ pounds lean boneless pork, cubed
1 pound boneless lamb, cubed
2 Bermuda onions, chopped
1 cup chopped shallots or green onions
1 cup celery, thinly sliced
1 cup tomato sauce or juice
1 cup dry white wine
1 garlic or Polish sausage, sliced
1 roast duck or goose, removed from
bones and cut into bite-size pieces
or 1 can confit d'oie

Combine beans, water, and salt in large kettle. Let stand overnight, or boil for 2 minutes and let soak for 1 hour. Add garlic, carrots, onions, *bouquet garni,* and salt pork. Bring to a boil. Simmer, covered, for 1 hour, skimming surface as needed. Heat drippings in skillet. Add pork and lamb and brown on all sides. Add to bean mixture. In the same skillet, cook chopped onions, shallots, and celery until soft. Add tomato sauce and wine and simmer for 5 minutes. Add to beans together with garlic sausage. Simmer, covered, over low heat for 1 hour, or until beans and meats are tender. If necessary, add a little water to prevent scorching. Skim off excess fat. Discard *bouquet garni.* Transfer mixture to large casserole. Add pieces of duck. Bake, covered, in preheated moderate oven (350° F.) for 35 to 45 minutes. Stir 2 or 3 times. Check occasionally for moisture; if necessary, add a little water. Adjust seasoning. Makes 8 to 10 servings.

Cassoulet

100 Menus
to help you plan more varied meals for your family with the recipes in this volume

Recipes for all starred dishes found in this volume.

BREAKFAST

Grapefruit Sections
with Cranberry Sauce
Cold Corn Cereal   Cream
Grilled Canadian Bacon
and Cheddar Sandwiches
Butter Braid*
Coffee

Orange Sections with
Blueberries
Oatmeal
Crisp Bacon
Sally Lunn*   Butter
Coffee

Fruit Juice
Buttermilk Pancakes* with
Strawberries
Grilled Ham Slices
Coffee

Broiled Grapefruit Half
Frizzled Ham
Fried Eggs
Cheese Biscuits*
Jam   Coffee   Milk

Melon Wedges
Western Sandwiches
Streusel Coffeecake*
Coffee

Grapefruit Sections
Creamed Dried Beef
and Eggs
Toasted White Batter Bread*
Butter
Coffee

Fresh Raspberries
Sautéed Chicken Livers
Fried Eggs
Double-Corn Muffins*
Butter   Jam
Coffee   Milk

Bananas
Oatmeal   Cream
Apricot Muffins*
Butter
Coffee   Milk

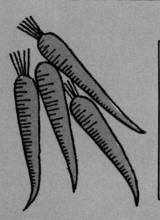

Orange-Pineapple Cup
Country-Style Buckwheat
Groats* with Cream
Fried Eggs
Blueberry Muffins*
Coffee

Mixed Fruit Juice
Cold Cereal
Scrambled Eggs
Fruit Buns*
Coffee   Milk

Sliced Peaches
with Raspberries
Quick Hash Patties*
Poached Eggs
Coconut Bread*
Milk
Coffee

Stewed Dried Fruit
Cooked Cereal
Shirred Eggs
Bacon Muffins* Butter
Coffee   Milk

Grapefruit Juice
Poached Eggs on Sandwich
Almond Popovers*
Coffee   Milk

Stewed Apricots
Scrambled Eggs
Crisp Bacon
Turban Coffeecake*
Coffee

LUNCHEONS AND SUPPERS

Fresh Grapefruit and
Orange Sections
Cold Cereal
Crisp Bacon
Bran Muffins*
Coffee

Fresh Strawberries
Cold Cereal
Soft-Cooked Eggs
Toast   Butter
Buttermilk Doughnuts*
Coffee

Orange Juice
Canadian Bacon and
Eggs
Cranberry Muffins*
Butter
Coffee

Chilled Tangerine Juice
Blueberry Waffles*
Baked Chicken Livers
Warm Maple Syrup
Coffee   Milk

Bean and Bacon Soup
Crisp Relishes
Hot Pumpernickel* Slices
Blancmange*

Peanut Butter and Bacon
Sandwiches
Carrot Sticks
Romaine
Blackberry Roly-Poly*

Oxtail Soup*
Liver and Bacon
Sandwiches
Coleslaw
Spiced Jellied
Blackberries*

Sautéed Bologna Slices
Baked Beans
Sliced Tomatoes
Raw Relishes
Bread Sticks
Raspberry Rhubarb Compote*

Marinated Shrimp
Buttered Toast
Green-Bean Salad
Orange Nut Bread*
Cream Cheese

Cheese and Tomato
Sandwiches
Hot Potato Salad with
Bacon
Raw Relishes
Lemon Iced Tea
Caramel Squares*

Beef Bouillon*
Seafood Salad
Radishes, Green Onions
Whole Wheat Bread,
Toasted   Butter
Fruit Cup

Raised Blini*
Sour Cream   Caviar
Smoked Salmon
Spinach
Baked Bananas

Roast-Beef and Blue-
Cheese Sandwiches
Lettuce and Tomato Salad
Fresh Blueberry Pie*

Shrimp Curry
Fluffy Rice
Chutney
Garlic Bread*
Raspberry Bombe*

Hamburger Steak* with
Curry Butter*
Shredded Lettuce Salad
Toasted Sandwich Rolls
Blueberry Pandowdy*

Hash Lyonnaise*
Seeded Breadsticks
Cucumbers and Radishes
Coconut Blancmange*

Frankfurter and
Macaroni Salad
Hot Rolls
Tomato-Cucumber Salad
Bananas in
Rum Custard Sauce*

Clam Chowder
Carrot, Celery, and
Cucumber Sticks
Onion Bread*
Carrot-Orange Cookies*

Chilled Seafood Bisque*
Chef's Salad
Banana-Nut Bread and
Cream-Cheese
Sandwiches
Melon Delight*

Welsh Rabbit
Tossed Green Salad
Blueberry Buckle*
Cream

Baked Beans with Ham
Carrot Coleslaw
Potato Rolls*
Buttermilk Meringue Pie*

Chicken Salad
Watercress
Olives
Raisin Bread with
Jelly
Almond Cookies*

Beef Patties Parmigiana*
Lettuce and Pimiento
Salad
Blueberry Ice Cream

Grilled Frankfurters
Shredded Lettuce Salad
Corn Bread
Blueberry Cottage-Cheese
Cake*

Bean, Egg, and Salami
Salad
Golden Glory Knots*
Blueberry-Lemon Dessert

Fish Bouillon*
Cheese Soufflé*
Broccoli Salad
Breadsticks
Bananas with Cream

Deviled Roast Beef Slices*
Bean and Cheese Salad
Pepper Rings and
Carrot Curls*
Cottage Pudding, Lemon
Sauce

Chicken Divan*
Caesar Salad
Cheese Straws
Fresh Blueberry Fluff*

Lasagna* with Meatballs
Lettuce and Black-Olive Salad
Green-Onion Bread
Lemon Ice
Assorted Cookies

Beef Stew with Herb Dumplings
Cucumber and Carrot Sticks
Caramel Torte*

Vegetable Soup
Cheese Blintzes*
Tossed Green Salad
Fruited Gelatin

Chesapeake Oyster Bisque*
Crisp Crackers
Cheese Sandwiches
Celery and Cucumber Sticks
Poires Cuites*

Sausage Links
Cheese Pancakes*
Warm Maple Syrup
Carrot Slaw
Orange Sherbet
Old-Fashioned
Sugar Cookies

Chef's Salad
Finnish Coffee Braid*
Minted Ice Tea
Banana Split

Bacon and Eggs
Carrot and Raisin Salad*
Short-Cut Muffins
Stewed Rhubarb
Cookies

Barbecued Pork Sandwiches
Coleslaw
Bran Bread*, Warmed
Apple Slice*

Menus

Frizzled Ham
Glorified Cheese Strata*
Radishes   Celery
Schnecken*

Quick Mushroom Broth*
Roast Beef Sandwiches
(open-face with gravy)
Romaine Salad
Fruit Cocktail

Minestrone
Green-Onion Bread
Swedish Caramel Custard*
Coffee Nut Macaroons*

Lamb Stew
Lettuce, Russian Dressing
Herb Breadsticks*
Apricot Delight

DINNERS

Corned Beef Sandwiches
Coleslaw
Fresh Cantaloupe and
Pineapple Compote*

Jellied Bouillon*
Sandwiches of Sliced Ham
on Cheese Bread, Toasted
Cucumbers in Sour Cream
Lemon Pudding

Ukranian Borsch*
Cottage Cheese Salad
Blueberry-Orange Bread*
Broiled Grapefruit with Honey

Ham, Cheese, and
Potato Casserole*
Melba Toast*
Watercress
Purple Plums

Roasted Beef Tenderloin*
Pan Gravy
Yorkshire Pudding
Green Beans and Mushrooms
Baked Potato
Lettuce and Tomato Salad
Gingered Fresh Pineapple*

Curried Turkey with Rice
Shredded Coconut
Chopped Green Pepper
Slivered Egg White
Sieved Egg Yolks
Chutney
Blackberry Whip*
Nut Butter Cookies*

Yankee Pot Roast*
Duchess Potatoes
Green-Bean Salad
Popovers*
Banana-Cream Pie

Cassoulet*
Asparagus Salad
Pineapple Coffeecake*

Barbecued Chicken
Mashed Potatoes
Broiled Tomatoes
Crisp Vegetable Relishes
Georgia Raised Biscuits*
Assorted Fresh Fruit

Broiled Filet Mignon
with Herb Butter*
O'Brien Potatoes
Marinated Tomatoes and
Cucumbers
Cabbage in Cream*
Blueberry Tarts*

Porc à la Flamande*
Whipped Potatoes
Romaine-Tomato Salad
Baked Alaska

Veal Chops in Foil
Roast Corn
Baked Potatoes with
Sour Cream
Tossed Mixed Salad
Pinwheel Onion Rolls*
Strawberry Dream Torte*

Bouillabaisse*
Hot Buttered Potatoes
Endive Salad
Fruit Cup

Sauerbraten*
Potato Dumplings
Beets and Greens*
Pan Rolls*
Tossed Green Salad
Fresh Peach Kuchen

Boneless Bluefish*
Wax Beans with Pimiento
Whipped Potatoes
Watercress and
Mandarin-Orange Salad
Baking-Powder Biscuits*
Fresh Pear Pie*

Beans and Frankfurters
Spinach Salad
Beaten Biscuits*
Banana Split

Danish Buttermilk Soup*
Baked Spicy Corned Beef*
Baked Potatoes
Marinated Broccoli
Limpa Bread*
Coffee Ice Cream

London Broil* with
Savory Butter*
Baked Potato
Green Peas
Marinated Tomatoes
Onion Bread*
Blueberry Parfait*
Petits Fours

Pot Roast of Beef, Burgundy*
Baked Noodles
Spinach
Seeded Butterhorns
Corn Relish
Peach Shortcake

Tomato Bouillon*
Panbroiled Round Steak*
Oven-Browned Potatoes
Green Beans and Whole Onions
Cucumber Salad
Parkerhouse Rolls*
Ice-Cream Filled
Brazil-Nut Pie Shell*

Baked Macaroni and Cheese
Scandinavian Pickled Beets*
Dark Rye Bread*
Blueberry Lattice Pie*

Corned Beef Baked in Sherry*
Brussels Sprouts in
Browned Butter*
Parsley Carrots
Crisp Relishes
Potato Bread*
Lemon Meringue Pie

Baked Beef Loaf
Baked Potatoes
Broccoli with Sour Cream*
Squash Rolls*
Blueberry Deep-Dish Pies*

Old-Fashioned Beef Stew*
Head Lettuce Salad
French Bread* Butter
Blueberry Turnovers*

Fried Brook Trout*
Stewed Green Beans
with Tomatoes
Crisp Relishes
Rye Bread
Blueberry-Peach Meringue*

Barbecued Lamb Breast
Browned Potatoes
Green Peas
Carrot Coleslaw
Oatmeal Batter Bread*
Blueberry Flummery*

Braised Short Ribs of
Beef, Jardinière*
Green Beans
Sliced Tomatoes
Bacon Batter Bread*
Biscuit Tortoni*

Beef Loaf with Wine*
Lyonnaise Potatoes
Lima Beans
Broccoli Salad
Italian Coffee Bombe*

Köttbullar*
Mashed Potatoes
Spinach
Beet Salad
Brownies*

Tomato Juice Cocktail
Corn Chips
Hamburger Steak* with Sour
Cream Horseradish
Baked Potato
Tossed Green Salad
Oatmeal Bread*
Banana-Strawberry Shortcake

Creamed Dried Beef
on Boiled Potatoes*
Broccoli
Cheese-Filled Rolls*
Head Lettuce Salad
Blueberry Shortcake*

Beef Goulash
Almond Noodles
Spinach
Sliced Tomatoes
Butterhorns*
Blueberry Betty*

Brisket of Beef in
Horseradish Sauce*
Boiled Potatoes
Succotash
Tomato and Watercress Salad
Buttermilk Spoon Bread*
Chocolate Blancmange*

Baked Bluefish Cutlets*
Carrots Parmesan*
Crisp Relishes
Corn Sticks*
Rhubarb Fool*

Fried Clams
Tartare Sauce
Glazed Beets*
Marinated Broccoli Salad
Crisp Golden Corn Points*
Blueberries

Baked Virginia Ham
Candied Yams
Broccoli-and-Cheese Custard*
Spiced Apple Rings
with Watercress
Lemon Snow, Custard Sauce

Chicken Bouillon*
Individual Beef Loaves*
Buttered Noodles
Green Beans
Radishes and Olives
Sennebec Hill Bread*
Gingerbread

Lamb and Onion Casserole*
Lettuce and Radish Salad
Cheese and Caraway French
Bread
Steamed Blueberry Pudding*

Beef Pot Roast
Parsley Potatoes
Boiled Corn
French-Fried Onions
Head Lettuce Salad
Rich Muffins*
Pain d'Amandes*

Barbecued Spareribs
Green Beans
Chinese-Cabbage Salad
Herb Breadsticks*
Pineapple Blancmange*

Roast Leg of Lamb
Whipped Potatoes
Bibb Lettuce Salad
Mint Jelly
Hot Casserole Bread*
Colonial Ginger Poundcake*

Broiled Chicken
Steamed Rice with Minced
Vegetables
Broccoli Piquant*
Sesame Whole-Wheat Bread
Bibb Lettuce
Chiffonade Dressing
Baked Alaska

Roast Pork Loin
Browned Potatoes
Buttered Asparagus
Mixed Green Salad
Corn Sticks*
Blueberry Parfait*
Spongecake

Roast Turkey with
Brazil-Nut Bread Stuffing
Green Peas
Jellied Cranberry Salad
White Bread*
Ice Cream, Butterscotch
Sauce

Roast Turkey with
Giblet Gravy
Candied Yams
Brussels Sprouts and
Chestnuts*
Cranberry Relish
Cloverleaf Rolls*
Pumpkin Pie

Fruit Cup
Rib Roast of Beef*
Glazed Carrots
Baked Potato
Tomato and Watercress
Salad
Butterscotch Pecan Rolls*
Ice Cream

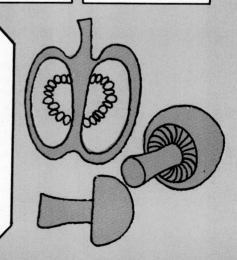

*Recipes for all starred dishes found in this volume.

GENERAL INFORMATION

The Ingredients and Measurements Used in Recipes

All recipes in this book have been tested in the Woman's Day Kitchens with standard American measuring cups (8 ounces = 16 tablespoons), measuring spoons (1 tablespoon = 3 teaspoons), and other standard kitchen equipment. All measurements are level. Liquids are measured in standard 8-ounce glass measuring cups, at eye level.

All sugar is granulated white sugar unless otherwise specified.

All flours, cake and all-purpose, are sifted before measuring unless otherwise specified. No self-rising flour is used.

All baking powder is double-acting baking powder.

All brown sugar is firmly packed when measured.

All confectioners' sugar is sifted before measuring.

All pepper is ground black pepper unless otherwise specified.

Fats and shortening are measured at room temperature, packed firmly into measuring cup and leveled with a straight knife. They are scraped out with a rubber spatula.

Salted butter or margarine, packed in ¼-pound sticks, is used unless otherwise specified. 1 stick = ½ cup = 8 tablespoons = ¼ pound.

1 tall can evaporated milk (14½ ounces) contains 1⅔ cups undiluted evaporated milk. Sweetened condensed milk is an entirely different product, and cannot be used interchangeably with evaporated milk.

⅓ to ½ teaspoon dried herbs can be substituted for each tablespoon fresh herbs. Crumble herbs before using to release flavor.

Before starting to cook or to bake, read the recipes carefully. Assemble all ingredients and equipment. Follow recipe exactly. Do not increase or decrease recipe unless you are a skilled enough cook to recognize what adjustments must be made as to ingredients, pan sizes, and/or cooking time.

Cooking Temperatures and Times

Cooking temperatures and times are approximate for meat. They depend not only on the weight and kind of meat, but also on its shape, temperature, and its bone and fat contents. A meat thermometer was used in testing.

Cooking times for meats are as recommended by the National Live Stock and Meat Board, 36 Wabash Avenue, Chicago, Illinois 60603.

Oven Temperatures

TEMPERATURES (Degree F.)	TERM
250 to 275	VERY SLOW
300 to 325	SLOW
350 to 375	MODERATE
400 to 425	HOT
450 to 475	VERY HOT
500 to 525	EXTREMELY HOT

Important—Preheat oven for 10 to 15 minutes before placing food in it. Many a cake has been spoiled by being placed in a barely heated oven. Baking times are based on the assumption that the oven is already at the stated temperature.

Check the oven temperature control frequently, especially if baking times vary from those given in recipes. (This can be done with a portable oven thermometer.) If a control is consistently off, call your public utility. They should be able to reset the oven temperature control.

Caloric Values

The caloric values, where mentioned, for each food are based on 100 grams, about 3½ ounces edible portion, as mentioned in Composition of Foods, Agriculture Handbook No. 8, Agricultural Service of the United States Department of Agriculture, Washington, D. C., revised December 1963.

COMPLETE RECIPE INDEX—VOLUME 2—658 Recipes